THE BIGGEST, BESTEST BOOK OF SUDOKU

THE BIGGEST, BESTEST BOOK OF SUDOKU

OVER 1,000 HANDCRAFTED PUZZLES

FROM THE EDITORS AT NIKOLI PUBLISHING, THE ORIGINAL SUDOKU MASTERS WHO INVENTED THE GAME

WORKMAN PUBLISHING

New York

Workman
Workman Publishing
Hachette Book Group, Inc.
1290 Avenue of the Americas
New York, NY 10104
workman.com

Workman is an imprint of Workman Publishing, a division of Hachette Book Group, Inc. The Workman name and logo are registered trademarks of Hachette Book Group, Inc.

Design by Galen Smith

The publisher is not responsible for websites (or their content) that are not owned by the publisher.

Workman books may be purchased in bulk for business, educational, or promotional use. For information, please contact your local bookseller or the Hachette Book Group Special Markets Department at special.markets@hbgusa.com.

Library of Congress Cataloging-in-Publication Data is available.

ISBN: 978-1-5235-2429-7

First Edition May 2024

Printed in China on responsibly sourced paper.

10 9 8 7 6 5 4 3 2 1

Contents

Introduction

What Is Sudoku?

1	2	3	4	5	6	7	8	9
4	5	6						
7	8	9						
2								
5								
8								
3								
6								
9								

A deceptively simple exercise in logic, Sudoku is a grid-based number game. Each puzzle is made up of 81 squares (called cells), which form 9 columns, 9 rows, and 9 boxes—each of which is a 3 x 3 square that is set off by a bold line.

The History of Sudoku

The editors of Nikoli, the leading puzzle company in Japan, discovered a puzzle called Number Place in an American magazine in the 1970s and then introduced it to Japanese readers in 1984. (That puzzle was a variation on Latin Squares, developed in the eighteenth century by the Swiss mathematician Leonhard Euler, who himself had been inspired by an older puzzle called Magic Squares, which in turn can be traced to Lo Shu, an ancient Chinese puzzle.) At first the editors called the puzzle "Suuji wa dokushin ni kagiru," which means "it is best for the number to be single." That title was not only too long but also confusing, so they abbreviated it to "Sudoku"—*su* meaning number, *doku* meaning single. The name "Sudoku" is trademarked by Nikoli in Japan, so other companies are restricted to calling their puzzles "Number Place."

Sudoku did not catch on at first, but then, in 1986, the editors introduced two new rules. First, they determined that all the numbers must be arranged in a symmetrical pattern, and second, that no more than thirty numbers can be revealed at the start of any puzzle. The result was magical, and Sudoku became a huge hit. The game soon spread from Japan to other countries, but most of these newer puzzles are generated by computer and lack the simple beauty of the Nikoli puzzles. But more on that later.

The Rules of Sudoku

Very simple to learn, Sudoku involves no math and no calculations, yet provides a surprisingly wide variety of logic situations. Here are the basics:

1. Place a number (1 through 9) in each blank cell.
2. Each row, column, and 3 x 3 box must contain the numbers 1 through 9 without repeating any numbers.

Remembering the Basics

The level of difficulty depends on how many numbers are initially revealed, which also affects the technique you should use in approaching each puzzle. But the logic is always based on the narrowing of possibilities.

BASIC PATTERN 1

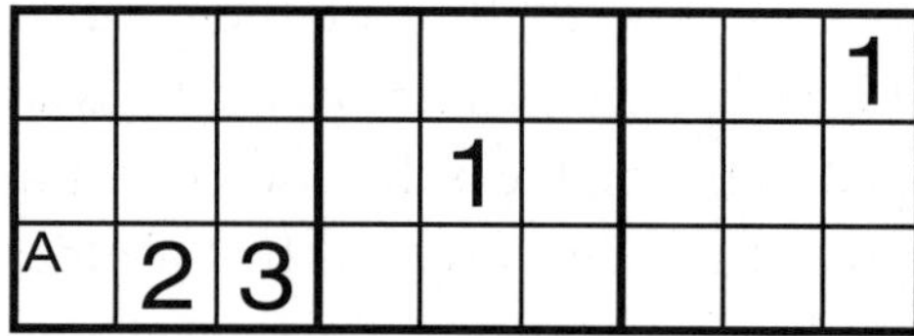

Start at the box on the left. The top two rows cannot contain the number 1 because of the 1s in the middle and right boxes. Therefore, the only place for a 1 in the first box is cell A.

BASIC PATTERN 2

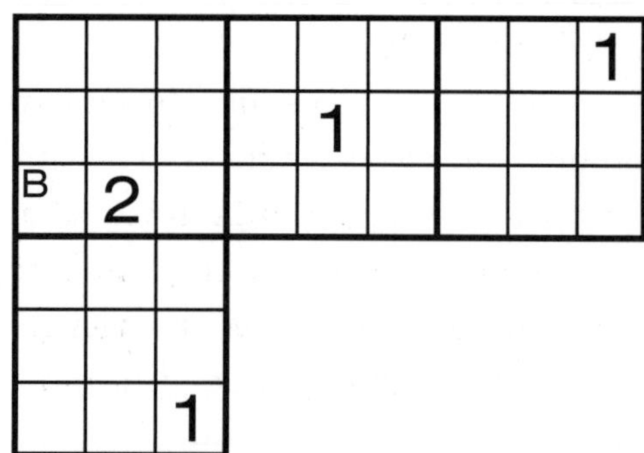

Basic Pattern 2 is similar to Pattern 1. In the upper left box, the top two rows cannot contain the number 1. The cell to the right of the number 2 cannot contain the number 1 either because of the 1 in column three in the box below. Therefore, a 1 must be placed in cell B.

BASIC PATTERN 3

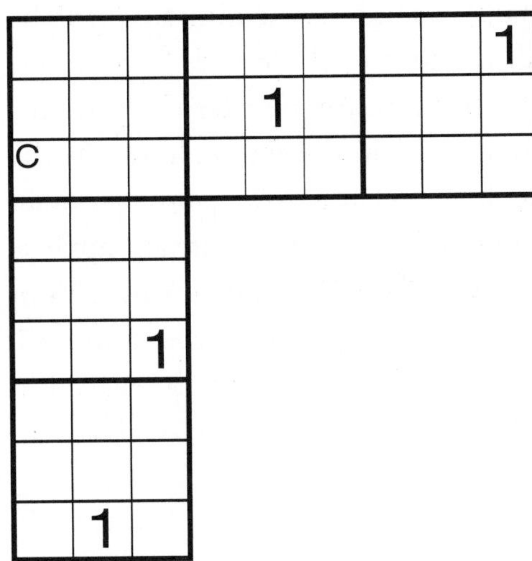

After learning Basic Patterns 1 and 2, it is easy to determine that the number 1 must be placed in cell C since it is the only cell in the upper left box that will not cause a duplication of 1s in either rows one and two or columns three and four.

BASIC PATTERN 4

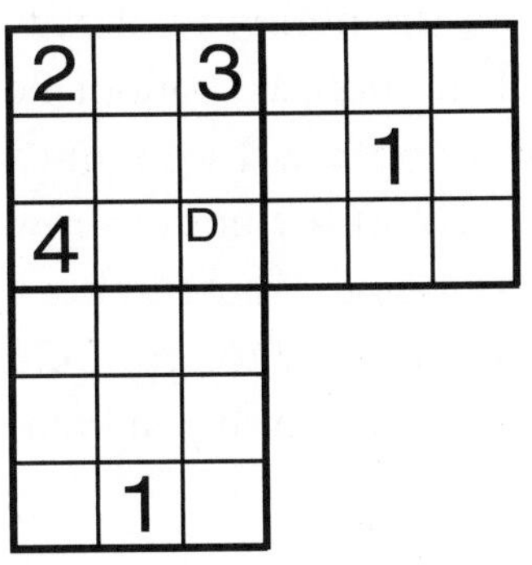

In this pattern, the middle row in the upper left box cannot contain the number 1 because of the 1 in the box on the right. And the middle column can't contain the number 1 because of the 1 in the box below. A 1 must be placed in cell D.

BASIC PATTERN 5

E	2	3	4	5	6	7	8	9

This pattern is an extremely easy one. On the top row, E is the only cell remaining in which one can place the number 1.

ADVANCED PATTERN 1

In the upper left box, the number 1 will be placed in either of the F cells because the 1 in the bottom box negates the possibility of placing 1 in the first column. In the second box, the top row cannot contain the number 1 because a 1 already appears in the top row (in the far right box). Also, the middle row cannot contain a 1 because either of the F cells will contain the number 1. Therefore, in the second box, the number 1 can only be placed in cell G.

ADVANCED PATTERN 2

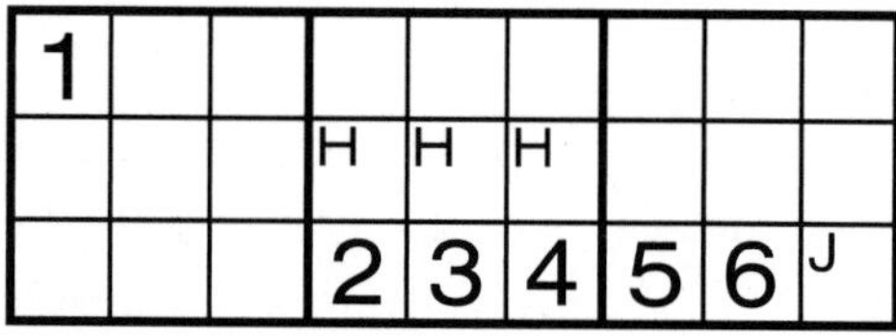

To determine where the number 1 should go in the far right box, first look at the far left box. Because of the number 1 already in the top row of the box, a 1 cannot be placed in the entire top row. In the middle box, with the cells in the bottom row already filled with the numbers 2, 3, and 4, there is no other place for the number 1 than in one of the H cells in the middle row. Therefore, with a 1 in the top row, and the necessity of a 1 in one of the H cells, the only remaining option in the far right box is to place the number 1 in cell J.

ADVANCED PATTERN 3

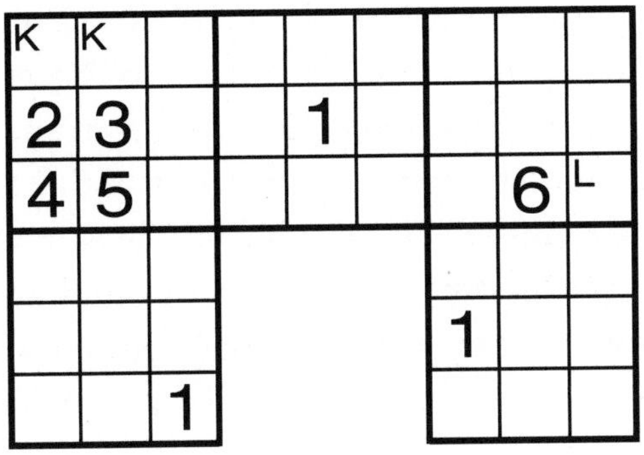

K	K							
2	3			1				
4	5						6	L
						1		
		1						

In the upper left box, the number 1 should be placed in either of the K cells. (Now no other cells in the top row may contain the number 1.) In the upper right box, the top and middle rows cannot contain a 1; its far left column cannot contain a 1 because of the cell that contains a 1 in the box below. Therefore, the number 1 must be placed in cell L.

ADVANCED PATTERN 4

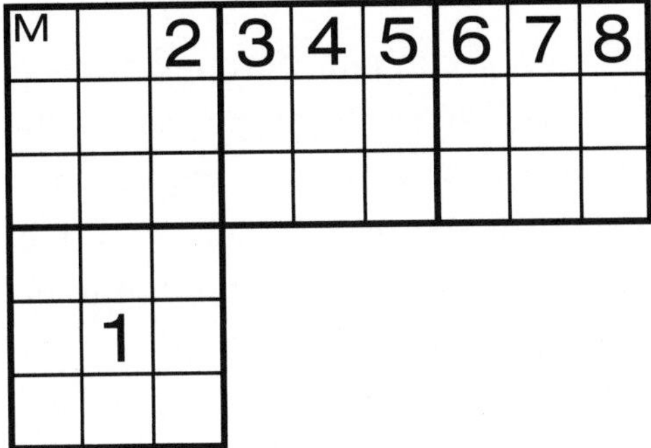

Numbers 1 and 9 are missing from the top row. Because of the 1 already in the lower left box, cell M must contain the number 1 and the cell to its right will contain the number 9.

ADVANCED PATTERN 5

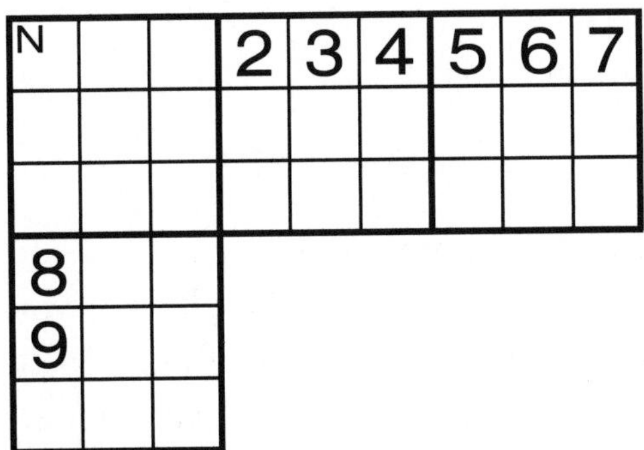

Numbers 1, 8, and 9 are missing from the top row. Cell N cannot contain either an 8 or a 9 because they already appear in the left column in the lower left box. Therefore, the number 1 must be placed in cell N.

MASTER PATTERN 1

			2	3				1
Q	4	P						
	P	5	1					
2								
3								

In the upper left box, the numbers 2 and 3 will be placed in each of the two P cells because the appearance of 2 and 3 in the left column in the lower left box and the top row in the middle box negates any other possibility. The number 1 cannot be placed in the top or bottom rows in the upper left box because of the 1s that appear in the top and bottom rows in the middle and far right boxes. Therefore, in the upper left box, the number 1 must be placed in cell Q.

MASTER PATTERN 2

R					5	6	7	
	2	3						
	4							
8								
9								

Cell R cannot contain the numbers 2, 3, or 4 because they already appear in the same box. It cannot contain the numbers 5, 6, or 7 because they already appear in the same row. It cannot contain the numbers 8 or 9 because they already appear in the same column. Therefore, cell R must contain the number 1. (Note: This deduction may seem simple, but it's easily missed when solving Sudoku!)

Why Handmade?

By Yoshi Anpuku, president, Nikoli

Many modern Sudoku puzzles are manufactured by computer programs, but I would like to explain why Nikoli continues to make Sudoku by hand. The pleasure you feel when you've completed a puzzle is special; however, the process of using logic to input each number is even more satisfying. One of the things that makes Sudoku fun is using different approaches to solve puzzles. A good puzzle works hand in hand with the solver to create a fun, positive experience. The problem with computer-generated Sudoku puzzles is that a computer doesn't think about helping the solver. To explain what I mean, let's take a look at a puzzle made with a computer program.

		4			9			8
	3			5			1	
7			4			2		
3			8			1		
	5						9	
		6			1			2
		8			3			1
	2			4			5	
6			1			7		

2	6	4	3	1	9	5	7	8
8	3	9	2	5	7	4	1	6
7	1	5	4	8	6	2	3	9
3	7	2	8	9	4	1	6	5
4	5	1	6	3	2	8	9	7
9	8	6	5	7	1	3	4	2
5	4	8	7	6	3	9	2	1
1	2	7	9	4	8	6	5	3
6	9	3	1	2	5	7	8	4

If you're having trouble getting started, don't worry. We'll begin by looking at box one (we number the boxes from left to right, starting with the top row, so box one is the upper left 3 x 3 square). There is no number 6 in this box, but there are 6s in both columns one and three. So, in box one, a 6 can only go in column two—but there are two possible cells, so we can't enter it in yet. Now let's look at the number 1. There are no 1s in box four and box seven, but there are 1s in rows four, six, seven, and nine. In box four, a 1 can only go in row five, and in box seven, a 1 can only go in row eight. Through process of elimination, this means that 1 must go in column two for box one. We now know that the two cells of column two in box one will be occupied by a 1 and a 6. Using this information, you can figure out where to put 8 in box one. That's right—column one, row two. Now that we've determined this 8, all the other 8s can be placed easily. Once you have figured out how to solve this problem, the puzzle presents no other difficulties.

This puzzle isn't hard because of its level of difficulty, but because it lacks a vital ingredient: a sense of communication between the author and the solver. It's frustrating to work on a puzzle when it takes a long time to enter the very first number. Wouldn't you like to have more fun with your puzzles? Handmade Sudoku is filled with logic and the joy of problem solving. These puzzles will make you concentrate but aren't stressful. Their combination of logic and communication creates a story, like a good mystery. In addition, the puzzles are designed with "Zen no Ma" in mind—there is careful symmetry and joy in the blank spaces that allows for a peaceful journey through each Sudoku puzzle we create.

Most mainstream contemporary Sudoku creators make puzzles with the help of computers, but computer programs can never take into consideration the way a solver thinks. The most important part of making Sudoku enjoyable is paving a friendly (though challenging) pathway toward solving each puzzle, and nothing does that better than human hands and a human mind. All good Sudoku creators know this.

Maki Kaji, the "Godfather of Sudoku"

Maki passed away at the age of 69 in 2021. Not only did he leave behind a legacy of Sudoku, but he also proved the power of "we" while founding and building Nikoli, a one-of-a-kind puzzle company.

While Maki wasn't interested in balance sheets, he was devoted to providing playful puzzles and stories to readers. To him, work and play were one and the same. For example, since he loved betting on racehorses, in 1980 he decided on "Nikoli" as the name of the first puzzle magazine in Japan after he spotted an Irish racehorse with that name in the newspaper. Fifteen years later, Maki traveled abroad to thank that retired racehorse, who was in Uruguay at the time.

Maki believed puzzles create a "non-routine space" in our lives. In his words, "a lot of things happen in life. When you solve a puzzle, you are teleported to a different space and forget your troubles. Once you finish solving, you can go back to your life right away. I would like to see more people in the world enjoying that spacious moment." He also said that "by solving a puzzle, you become aware of the importance of giving up. Yes, when you are stuck on something, you need to have the grit of giving up, leave it alone for a little while. You can work on other areas of the puzzle. Then sometimes you see the solution where you thought you were stuck."

According to Maki, the secret of Nikoli is that more than 400 contributors come together to create the puzzles. These authors come from varying backgrounds, from teenage students to housemakers, engineers to civil servants, salaried employees to retirees in their nineties. "That is why the puzzles are so varied," said Maki. "[A]nd with our editors' touch, we have surprising, comedic or breathtaking versions. This is the key element in our handcrafted puzzles."

The Sudoku puzzle to the right is the first Sudoku that Maki made. In its comment section, he said, "I cannot quite figure out the last step to make it hard. Someone, please make one." From the very beginning, he relied on his readers.

勝手なタイトル→数字は独身に限る。

2	9					7	6	
	8			2	4		9	5
7		5			3	2	8	
5			6	9			1	
				3	7	6		
	4				5		3	2
		3	1		6			9
4	6	2					7	1
		9	2	7	8		4	

デル社の雑誌にちらっとみかけたものを、作ってみたら面白かった。手の遊び。

ルール

- タテ9列、ヨコ9列のそれぞれは1〜9までの数字が1コずつ入る
- 3x3のマス9コの中にも1〜9までの数字が1コずつ入る
- そのどれも同じ数字が重複することはない。

むづかしくなる一歩手前のむづかしいところが、まだつかめない。誰か作って。

Puzzles

	4			1		3		2
2					3			
		6	5				1	
		2		6			5	4
5			4		1			8
6	3			7		2		
	2				4	1		
			1					5
1		7		3			6	

PUZZLE / 1 Time:_______

4	9			2				7
1	5		3			6		
		2				9	1	
	1				3			
6				5				2
			7				5	
	7	5				8		
		6			1		7	9
2				9			3	5

PUZZLE / 2 Time:_______

		7			4		1	
		8		5			3	4
1	5					2		
					2			6
	7			3			4	
3			1					
		5					2	3
6	8			4		5		
	2		7			1		

PUZZLE / 3 Time:_______

		2			6		3	
	7				9			4
4			2			8		5
5		6		4			2	
			5		1			
	8			3		1		9
6		7			5			3
2			7				4	
	3		1			6		

PUZZLE / 4 Time:_______

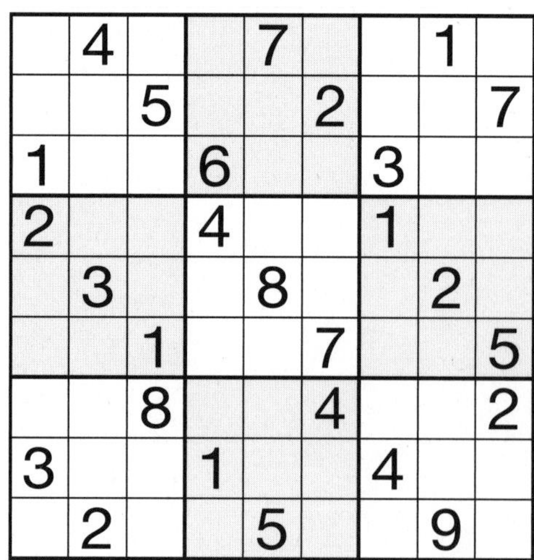

	4			7			1	
		5			2			7
1			6			3		
2			4			1		
	3			8			2	
		1			7			5
		8			4			2
3			1			4		
	2			5			9	

PUZZLE / 5 Time:_______

				1	5			
		3			4	6		
	5	8				4	1	
2	4		8		3			
1				2				6
			1		6		9	3
	6	7				1	8	
		4	2			5		
			3	7				

PUZZLE / 6 Time:_______

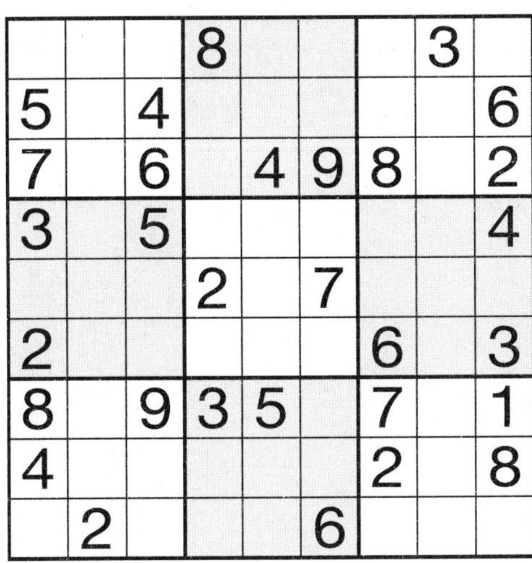

			8				3	
5		4						6
7		6		4	9	8		2
3		5						4
			2		7			
2						6		3
8		9	3	5		7		1
4						2		8
	2				6			

PUZZLE / 7 Time:_______

5	1						4	3
		9	7		8	6		
				1				
		3		6		4		
7			3		4			2
		2		9		1		
				7				
		4	1		3	2		
2	6						5	1

PUZZLE / 8 Time:_______

	4	1			3		6	
8			4			9		2
5			2	7			3	
	7	8	6					9
		3				4		
1					9	5	8	
	8			5	1			7
6		4			7			5
	9		3			8	2	

PUZZLE / 9 Time:_______

5	9				8			
		6		4		2		
			2				6	1
7				9		6		
	4		3		2		5	
		1		7				2
1	3				7			
		7		8		9		
			1				3	4

PUZZLE / 10 Time:_______

	1	4				2	3	
3			8		2			7
8			1		4			5
	2	5		6		8	4	
			2		9			
	3	9		4		1	5	
5			9		6			1
2			5		3			4
	9	8				5	6	

PUZZLE / 11 Time:_______

	3					5		6
7	2			9				
			1		2	3		
	4							3
		7				1		
8							9	
		1	5		8			
				2			6	5
3		4					8	

PUZZLE / 12 Time:_______

1					5			2
	7						4	
			2	6				
7			3		1	6		
		2		9		8		
		1	4		2			3
				5	7			
	6						1	
3			1					5

PUZZLE / 13 Time:_______

	5			8				3
		4	7			2		
6					2		1	
7	4			3		1		
5			1		6			4
		1		2			6	5
	3		5					1
		2			4	7		
1				6			3	

PUZZLE / 14 Time:_______

	1			7			6	
		8			3			2
5			1			7		
		3			4			7
	4			6			8	
1			5			2		
		4			1			3
8			2			1		
	6			5			7	

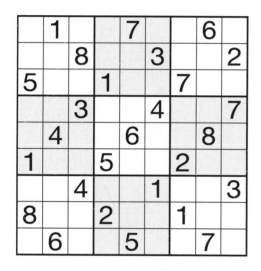

PUZZLE / 15 Time:_______

		2						
	3	9	6			8		
			1			4	5	
					3			4
1								3
2			7					
	4	6			5			
		7			8	1	3	
						2		

PUZZLE / 16 Time:_______

	4				5	6		
5				7			1	
			8					7
	6			1	3			
		4				7		
			6	5			8	
2					8			
	7			2				1
		1	4				6	

PUZZLE / 17 Time:_______

				5	6	1		
8			4				7	2
	2	3						
					4	3	5	
2				1				7
	1	7	3					
						2	4	
3	5				1			6
		4	9	3				

PUZZLE / 18 Time:_______

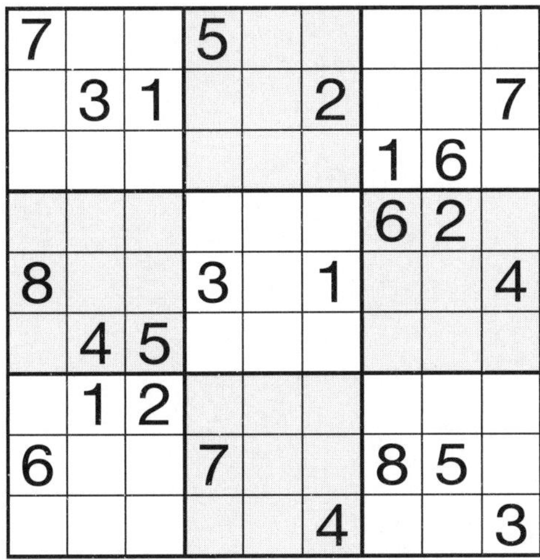

7			5					
	3	1			2			7
						1	6	
						6	2	
8			3		1			4
	4	5						
	1	2						
6			7			8	5	
					4			3

PUZZLE / 19 Time:_______

		2	3			1		
	4			9			6	
6					1			4
		4	2		7			3
	3			8			1	
1			4		5	6		
5			1					2
	2			7			3	
		7			4	5		

PUZZLE / 20 Time:_______

	6						4	
5			1	4			3	2
		1	2			7		
		8			3			6
2				5				1
3			7			5		
		3			6	4		
8	4			2	1			5
	1						2	

PUZZLE / 21 Time:_______

	7						9	
4		5		6		7		3
			7		3			
7		6					3	
			2	8	5			
	5					9		2
			6		4			
2		1		9		4		6
	8						2	

PUZZLE / 22 Time:_______

		1	4		6	2		
6	2			1			4	3
				9				
	3		5		1		2	
		4		3		5		
	1		2		4		6	
				2				
4	7			6			1	5
		9	7		8	6		

PUZZLE / 23 Time:_______

			1		5	8		
		5		8				
	2	3			6	9		5
4			8				9	7
				3				
1	7				2			4
7		9	6			1	5	
				7		2		
		4	3		9			

PUZZLE / 24 Time:_______

1				7				6
		4				2		
	7		3		9		8	
3			7		8			2
		8		4		5		
4			2		1			8
	1		8		4		3	
		3				1		
2				1				7

PUZZLE / 25 Time:_______

4					3	1		7
		5				6	2	
	8	7	2	4			3	5
		1			5			2
		3		1		8		
2			4			5		
1	3			5	7	4	6	
	9	4				7		
5		6	3					8

PUZZLE / 26 Time:_______

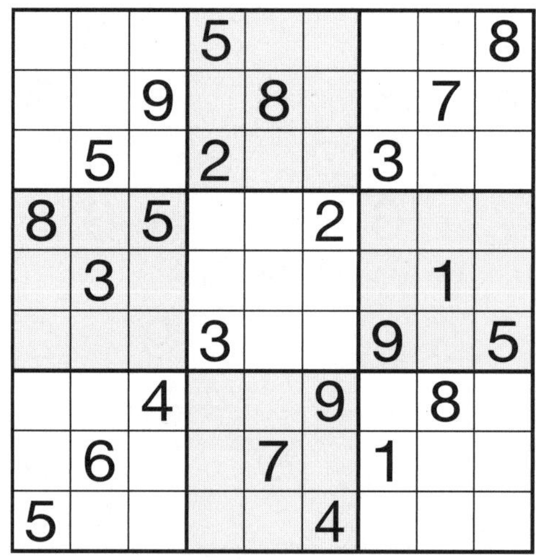

			5					8
		9		8			7	
	5		2			3		
8		5			2			
	3						1	
			3			9		5
		4			9		8	
	6			7		1		
5					4			

PUZZLE / 27 Time:_______

			5	2		1		
	5	2			4		6	
7				3			9	
	9		8		1			7
5		1				9		6
4			2		5		8	
	3			4				9
	1		6			2	3	
		4		1	8			

PUZZLE / 28 Time:_______

7	6				1		3	
4			5				7	8
		8	4	2		6		
	1	6	3		4			7
		2				9		
9			8		2	4	5	
		7		6	3	5		
3	9				8			1
	5		7				8	2

PUZZLE / 29 Time:_______

3				9	8			
		5	7			2		
	9						7	
	6				9			8
2				7				3
4			2				1	
	1						6	
		2			6	3		
			8	3				1

PUZZLE / 30 Time:_______

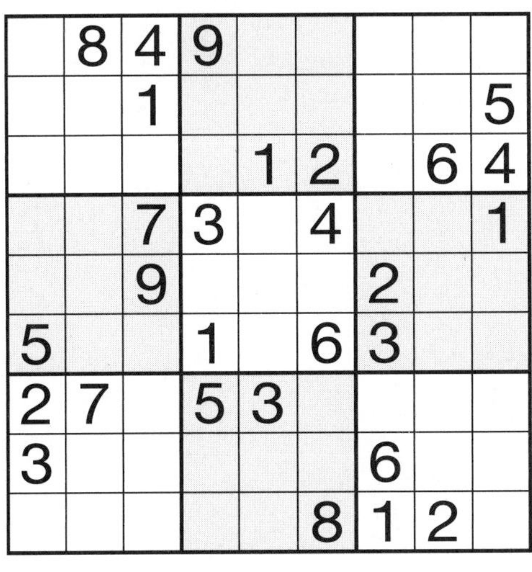

	8	4	9					
		1						5
				1	2		6	4
		7	3		4			1
		9				2		
5			1		6	3		
2	7		5	3				
3						6		
					8	1	2	

PUZZLE / 31 Time:_______

6			5		1			3
1				6				8
	2			9			7	
		8				7		
	9		2		4		5	
		4				2		
	8			2			6	
4				7				5
5			3		9			2

PUZZLE / 32 Time:_______

2			3			1		
	1			5	9			
	3						7	
1			6			3		5
				4				
3		8			7			4
	6						2	
			4	2			1	
		4			1			3

PUZZLE / 33 Time:_______

	6	1			2		5	
4				8				9
			5					6
	5		8			9		
	9			1			2	
		2			7		3	
3					1			
1				6				4
	2		4			3	9	

PUZZLE / 34 Time:_______

			7				5	9
		5		3				2
	3				1			
5			2			8		
	9			5			7	
		2			6			5
			4				6	
6				9		1		
2	1				8			

PUZZLE / 35 Time:_______

	1	2	7	3		4		
6			5			8		
3		7					1	5
4	5				7			
2				1				7
			4				3	2
1	3					7		6
		8			6			4
		5		4	2	1	9	

PUZZLE / 36 Time:_______

			8		4			
		2				9		
	1			3			6	
9			4		8			2
		7		9		3		
5			3		6			8
	8			4			5	
		5				2		
			2		1			

PUZZLE / 37 Time:_______

				7	4	5		
						3		2
	1	4	8					6
			6				1	7
8	6				5			
9					8	7	5	
1		6						
		8	5	4				

PUZZLE / 38 Time:_______

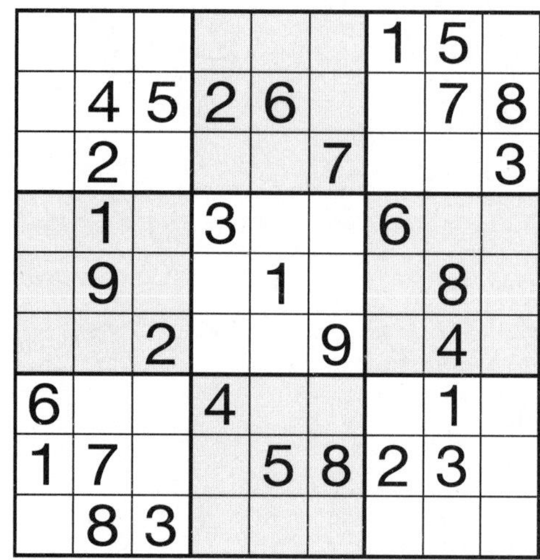

						1	5	
	4	5	2	6			7	8
	2				7			3
	1		3			6		
	9			1			8	
		2			9		4	
6			4				1	
1	7			5	8	2	3	
	8	3						

PUZZLE / 39 Time:_______

1	7						2	
		6	5					
				7	2		1	
	8		4			3		
4				1				7
		9			5		4	
	2		8	4				
					6	1		
	4						3	5

PUZZLE / 40 Time:_______

7	3			1				6
				5		3		2
	8	5	6			4		
				2		8		
4	2		8		9		5	1
		1		4				
		6			4	2	7	
5		2		3				
1				6			4	3

PUZZLE / 41 Time:_______

8	5						7	1
			8		6			
		3		2		8		
	4						5	
2				9				7
	9						6	
		8		7		6		
			5		9			
9	7						3	5

PUZZLE / 42 Time:_______

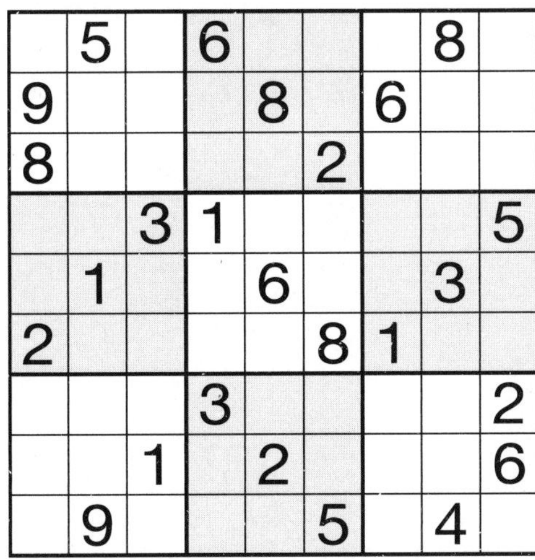

PUZZLE / 43 Time:_______

2	8	3	5					
		1						
	7			1	2	3	4	5
1			7				6	
		6				7		
	5				8			2
4	3	2	1	9			8	
						2		
					4	5	1	9

PUZZLE / 44 Time:_______

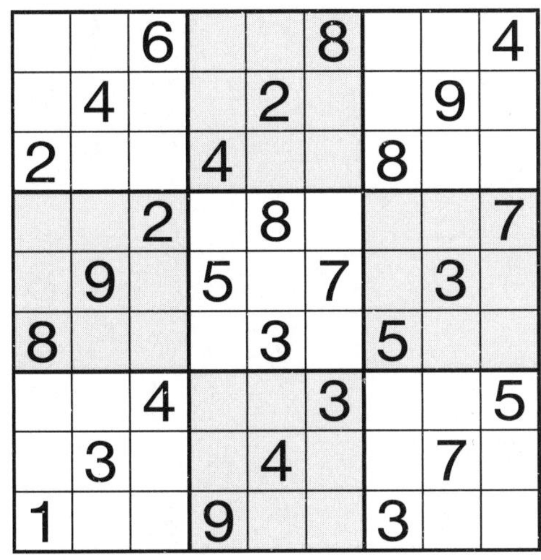

PUZZLE / 45 Time:_______

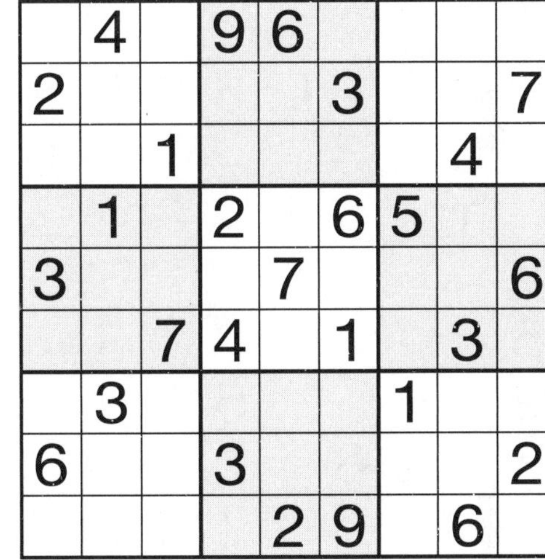

PUZZLE / 46 Time:_______

		7						1
	6				3	5		
5				2			6	
			8		2		7	
		9				2		
	4		1		5			
	8			3				4
		1	4				3	
2						1		

PUZZLE / 47 Time:_______

9			3		2			7
		4		1		8		
	5						4	
1				8				9
		9	1		7	3		
5				6				8
	9						1	
		3		5		9		
2			9		8			5

PUZZLE / 48 Time:_______

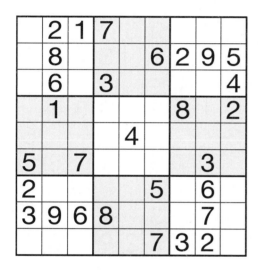

4				6		8		
	1				8		3	
		2	9					1
		1			5		2	
6				9				7
	7		1			6		
2					9	1		
	3		4				5	
		7		2				6

PUZZLE / 49 Time:_______

	2			1			6	
8			7		9			4
		4				2		
	4		5		1		7	
2				6				9
	9		2		7		5	
		5				1		
9			3		2			5
	6			8			4	

PUZZLE / 50 Time:_______

	2	1	7					
	8				6	2	9	5
	6		3					4
	1					8		2
				4				
5		7					3	
2					5		6	
3	9	6	8				7	
					7	3	2	

PUZZLE / 51 Time:_______

		9		2			4	
			1			3		9
8		5					1	
	8			3				
1			9		5			8
				7			3	
	6					4		2
7		2			8			
	3			5		9		

PUZZLE / 52 Time:_______

	3			7			1	
4			8		9			6
				1				
	6		2		7		8	
3		2		8		9		4
	5		6		4		3	
				2				
2			5		3			1
	8			6			9	

PUZZLE / 53 Time:_______

4								2
		9	4			7		
	8		3		2		5	
		3		9		2	8	
			7		5			
	1	8		6		5		
	2		5		6		4	
		5			7	1		
7								5

PUZZLE / 54 Time:_______

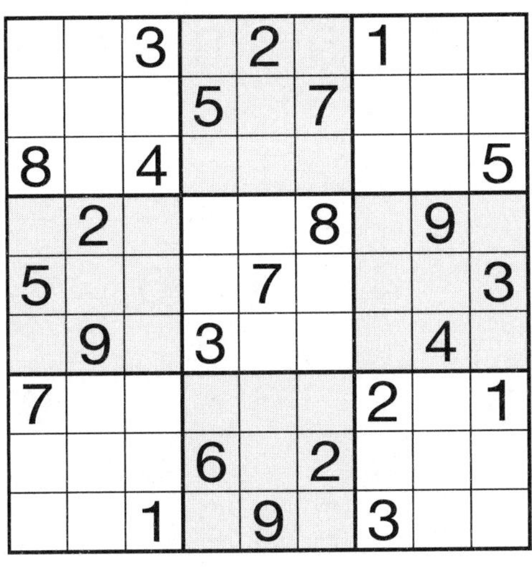

		3		2		1		
			5		7			
8		4						5
	2				8		9	
5				7				3
	9		3				4	
7						2		1
			6		2			
		1		9		3		

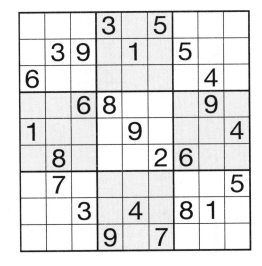

PUZZLE / 55 Time:_______

8				5				7
	6				2		8	
		5	9			3		
		6	1				3	
3				6				8
	5				9	2		
		2			1	5		
	4		2				9	
7				3				2

PUZZLE / 56 Time:_______

						6	1	
				6	7			
		5	9				4	3
5	8				9	7		
				1				
		2	6				3	9
4	9				6	1		
			2	3				
	7	8						

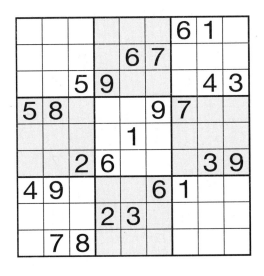

PUZZLE / 57 Time:_______

			3		5			
	3	9		1		5		
6							4	
		6	8				9	
1				9				4
	8				2	6		
	7							5
		3		4		8	1	
			9		7			

PUZZLE / 58 Time:_______

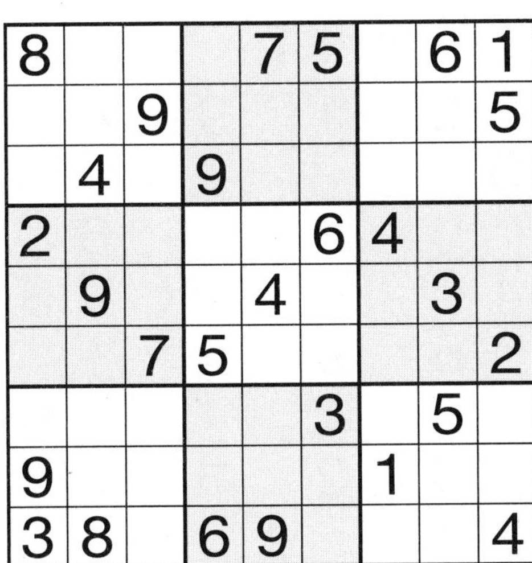

8				7	5		6	1
		9						5
	4		9					
2					6	4		
	9			4			3	
		7	5					2
					3		5	
9						1		
3	8		6	9				4

PUZZLE / 59 Time:_______

					6			7
		9		1		5		
	8		4				9	
		2	7					3
	1			9			4	
5					4	6		
	9				7		8	
		6		4		3		
4			3					

PUZZLE / 60 Time:_______

	5				8		1	
2		6		4		5		
	9		5				7	
7					4			1
				2				
4			1					2
	7				1		9	
		9		5		8		7
	8		9				5	

PUZZLE / 61 Time:________

	2		9		8		5	
		5				4		
7				1				3
			7		4			
		4		9		6		
			1		6			
3				6				9
		6				5		
	4		3		2		6	

PUZZLE / 62 Time:________

7							5	
	6			1	7			3
					4	8		
			6			1	7	
	9			8			2	
	8	4			2			
		5	1					
9			4	7			1	
	4							9

PUZZLE / 63 Time:________

					1			
	7			6		5		
3		2			8		4	
	1		8					4
			4		7			
8					3		7	
	5		1			3		2
		4		5			6	
			3					

PUZZLE / 64 Time:________

		2			4	9		
	5			2			6	
3			6					7
		7						1
	6			3			5	
9						3		
7					3			5
	8			7			4	
		5	4			6		

PUZZLE / 65 Time:________

		2		8				9
	6		1		9		8	
9						5		
	9		3		7		6	
4								3
	5		9		4		1	
		1						6
	4		2		8		7	
2				1		4		

PUZZLE / 66 Time:________

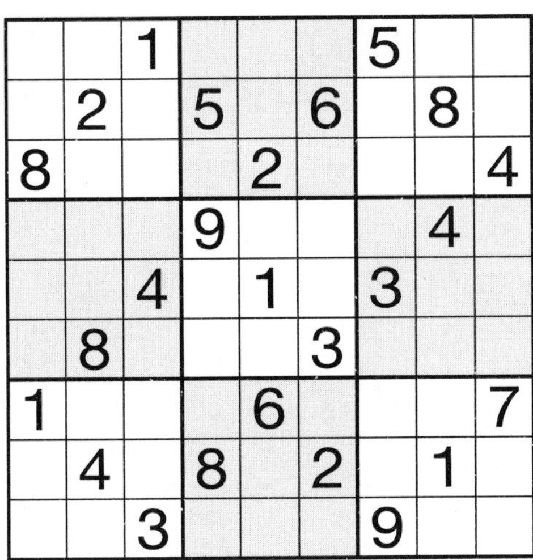

		1				5		
	2		5		6		8	
8				2				4
			9				4	
		4		1		3		
	8				3			
1				6				7
	4		8		2		1	
		3				9		

PUZZLE / 67 Time:_______

				3		4		
	4		6				5	
3					1			
		2		5			4	
1			2		6			5
	7			9		1		
			3					7
	5				9		6	
		8		4				

PUZZLE / 68 Time:_______

		4			5			9
	2					8		
1			6				7	
		6		4		3		
2			1		6			4
		1		2		5		
	9				4			6
		3					8	
5			7			1		

PUZZLE / 69 Time:_______

	9		2					
5				9			6	
	7		8			2		5
					7		2	
		2		5		9		
	1		9					
7		8			3		5	
	6			7				8
					4		1	

PUZZLE / 70 Time:_______

		7			1			
		5	9					
4			2				9	6
	5				7	8	4	
				3				
	9	3	8				2	
3	2				5			9
					8	2		
			4			5		

PUZZLE / 71 Time:_______

	8				6			5
4				7		1		
					1		3	
			2			3		1
	4			1			5	
6		5			3			
	5		8					
		3		5				9
2			3				7	

PUZZLE / 72 Time:_______

	9	6			8			5
4			1			9	7	
						7	2	
2			5		9			3
	1	9						
	7	3			6			8
5			2			1	6	

PUZZLE / 73 Time:_______

		3	6					
	8			9			1	7
2					7	9		
9			1	8				
	2	8				5	4	
				5	2			3
		6	7					8
3	1			6			9	
					5	4		

PUZZLE / 74 Time:_______

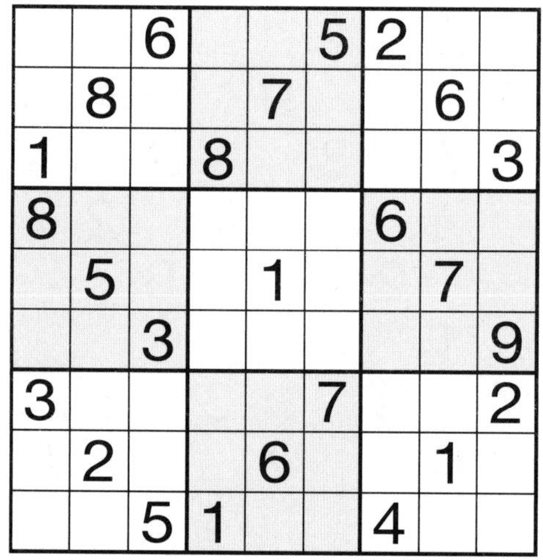

		6			5	2		
	8			7			6	
1			8					3
8						6		
	5			1			7	
		3						9
3					7			2
	2			6			1	
		5	1			4		

PUZZLE / 75 Time:_______

6			7					5
		1		5			6	
	7				3	1		
5					1	9		
	8			9			7	
		3	5					2
		9	1				8	
	6			4		3		
1					7			6

PUZZLE / 76 Time:_______

		5		6				3
	2				1			
1			2			7		
			3				2	9
		7				3		
8	5				2			
		4			6			2
			9				6	
7				1		4		

PUZZLE / 77 Time:_______

	5		1	3				
1					8		6	
6								7
		1			5			2
		7				9		
9			6			5		
2								6
	8		2					9
				9	7		8	

PUZZLE / 78 Time:_______

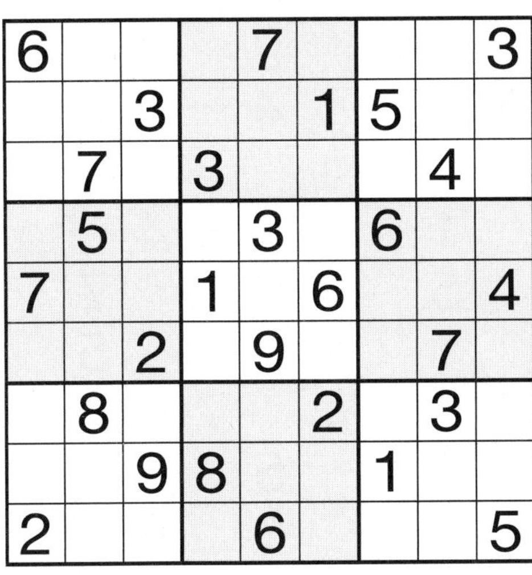

6				7				3
		3			1	5		
	7		3				4	
	5			3		6		
7			1		6			4
		2		9			7	
	8				2		3	
		9	8			1		
2				6				5

PUZZLE / 79 Time:_______

		2			5			6
	9			8		3		
3							5	
	5				6			2
		9		1		6		
2			7				8	
	8							3
		3		9			7	
6			3			1		

PUZZLE / 80 Time:_______

					7		3	8
	1	8		3				9
	5		8					
4					8	1		
	2			4			7	
		7	3					5
					4		5	
5				2		8	6	
9	3		5					

PUZZLE / 81 Time:_______

		8		6		4		
			7		1			
5		4				7		6
	7						1	
2				9				8
	6						4	
4		2				3		5
			5		9			
		3		8		6		

PUZZLE / 82 Time:_______

			6			9		
		9		5			7	
	1		2					6
5		1			3			
	7			2			8	
			4			2		3
1					9		2	
	8			3		5		
		4			5			

PUZZLE / 83 Time:_______

9	7						6	2
6				3				1
		8	9					
		6	2		7			
	3						2	
			3		4	9		
					2	4		
4				8				6
2	9						7	8

PUZZLE / 84 Time:_______

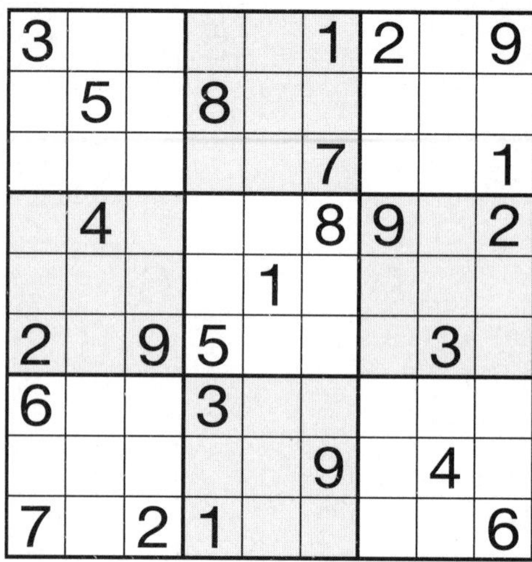

3					1	2		9
	5		8					
					7			1
	4				8	9		2
				1				
2		9	5				3	
6			3					
					9		4	
7		2	1					6

PUZZLE / 85 Time:_______

	6	4		2		7		
3				4			6	
			1					3
	1				3	4		
	5			8			7	
		7	2				5	
1					7			
	4			5				2
		5		3		9	1	

PUZZLE / 86 Time:_______

		3			2			
8			9			5		
	4			5			7	
		6			4			2
	5			7			1	
3			6			8		
	7			1			2	
		4			9			6
			4			3		

PUZZLE / 87 Time:_______

				9	5			
			4			8		
1		8					4	
	1		7		6			9
		3				2		
7			2		1		8	
	3					9		2
		4			8			
			1	5				

PUZZLE / 88 Time:_______

		5	2			9		
	4			8			6	
1					4			7
		7	1					3
	1			4			7	
2					6	8		
8			5					9
	7			6			5	
		9			1	4		

PUZZLE / 89 Time:_______

5	9						2	4
6				4				5
			3		5			
		7		9		5		
	2		6		4		7	
		5		8		4		
			1		9			
2				6				7
4	1						3	6

PUZZLE / 90 Time:_______

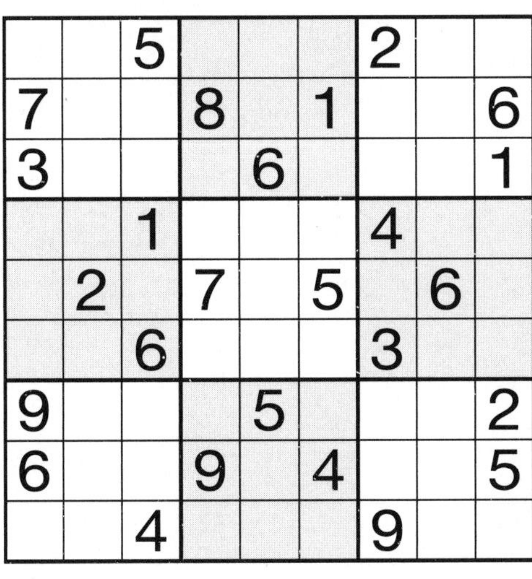

		5				2		
7			8		1			6
3				6				1
		1				4		
	2		7		5		6	
		6				3		
9				5				2
6			9		4			5
		4				9		

PUZZLE / 91 Time:_______

				7	8			
						1	6	
3	9	2						5
	6	7	3					9
				4				
9					2	4	7	
7						2	3	1
	2	1						
			2	5				

PUZZLE / 92 Time:_______

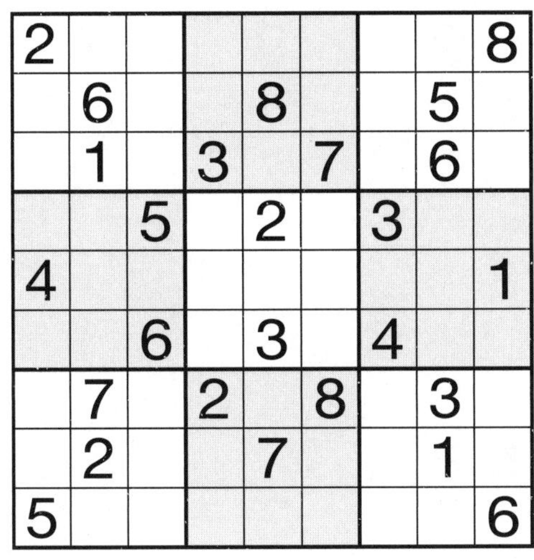

2								8
	6			8			5	
	1		3		7		6	
		5		2		3		
4								1
		6		3		4		
	7		2		8		3	
	2			7			1	
5								6

PUZZLE / 93 Time:_______

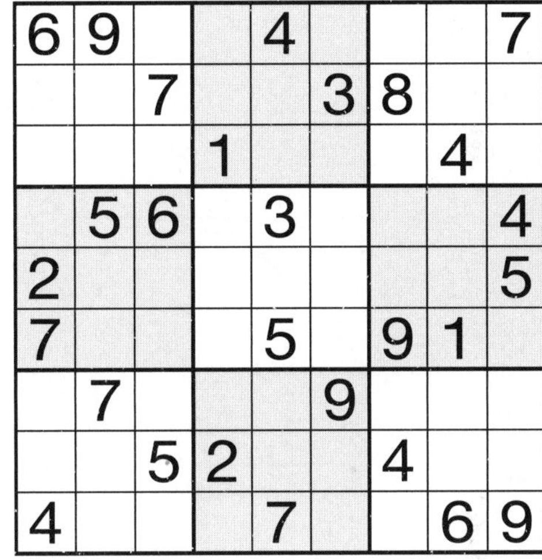

6	9			4				7
		7			3	8		
			1				4	
	5	6		3				4
2								5
7				5		9	1	
	7				9			
		5	2			4		
4				7			6	9

PUZZLE / 94 Time:_______

	3			4			9	
5								7
		9		7		1		
	7		5		9		2	
4				8				9
	6		1		4		5	
		8		6		4		
6								5
	4			5			8	

PUZZLE / 95 Time:_______

4	7			9			3	2
		6				8		
			4	5	1			
3	2						5	6
		1				4		
5	4						7	1
			7	1	6			
		7				3		
2	1			8			9	7

PUZZLE / 96 Time:_______

		6	3					
	9			8		2		
7					1		3	
		8	6					1
	2			9			4	
5					2	7		
	3		8					9
		9		2			8	
					5	3		

PUZZLE / 97 Time:_______

2	3		9					1
	7			2	6			5
					4			
						8	9	
	2						6	
	8	5						
			2					
4			7	1			8	
3					8		2	6

PUZZLE / 98 Time:_______

	4				5		6	
6				2				9
	3		4				7	
		1			9			5
	8			7			4	
4			3			7		
	1				7		9	
3				9				7
	6		5				3	

PUZZLE / 99 Time:_______

	2			9			3	
5	6						9	8
			7		1			
		6				2		
8				1				4
		5				8		
			2		3			
6	9						5	3
	3			7			2	

PUZZLE / 100 Time:_______

		9			4		2	
	2	8	1				6	
3		4		5			7	
		6						
4		5		9		1		7
						6		
	4			6		7		2
	9				8	5	3	
	1		4			8		

PUZZLE / 101 Time:_______

		5		9		4		
			3		4			
	1	4				2	6	
8								3
			9	7	6			
9								1
	6	2				3	9	
			1		9			
		3		8		1		

PUZZLE / 102 Time:_______

4			7		9			1
6				5				2
	9						7	
		7				9		
			3	6	8			
		6				1		
	5						1	
9				7				4
3			6		1			8

PUZZLE / 103 Time:_______

	9				8		2	
1	8			4			9	7
			3					
		9			1			8
	1			3			5	
2			9			4		
					5			
7	2			8			3	4
	6		2				7	

PUZZLE / 104 Time:_______

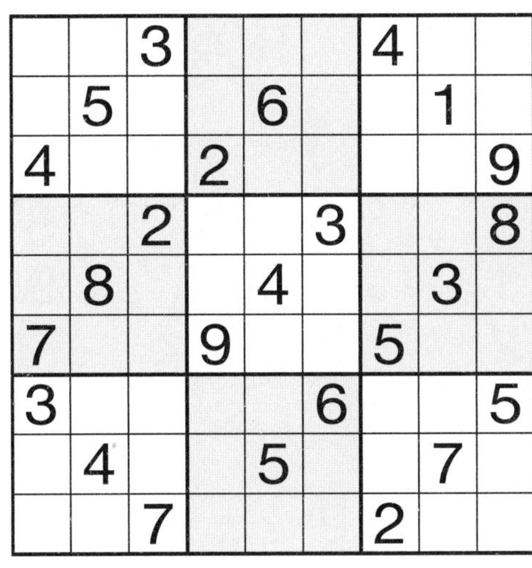

		3				4		
	5			6			1	
4			2					9
		2			3			8
	8			4			3	
7			9			5		
3					6			5
	4			5			7	
		7				2		

PUZZLE / 105 Time:_______

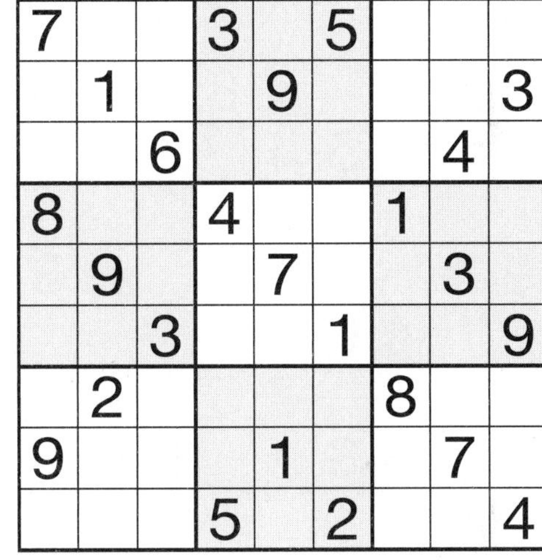

7			3		5			
	1			9				3
		6					4	
8			4			1		
	9			7			3	
		3			1			9
	2					8		
9				1			7	
			5		2			4

PUZZLE / 106 Time:_______

		2		6			4	
		9			4			3
			7					1
3			9				8	
	8			1			3	
	4				5			7
2					6			
4			1			5		
	6			3		8		

PUZZLE / 107 Time:_______

9	8							
			8				5	6
	3			1		9		
	2			3		5		
			6		7			
		3		8			1	
		9		7			6	
3	7				4			
							8	2

PUZZLE / 108 Time:_______

	8				6			
3				7		4	1	
4			5					6
		7					8	
8			9		1			7
	9					5		
2					7			9
	7	5		1				4
			4				6	

PUZZLE / 109 Time:_______

		7	1			4		
	9			6			2	
1					3			8
		4	2		6			7
	5						1	
3			4		5	2		
8			6					9
	1			3			5	
		3			2	8		

PUZZLE / 110 Time:_______

2	7					4	6	
		6			8			3
			5	4				
					1	7		
9	1			5			2	8
		4	6					
				7	5			
6			8			9		
	5	9					7	4

PUZZLE / 111 Time:_______

7				9	4			
	9					1	4	
		1				9	6	
					7			8
1				4				9
2			3					
	8	6				5		
	2	5					7	
			9	2				4

PUZZLE / 112 Time:_______

3				5				9
	8		6		1		2	
		5				8		
	2		1		9		7	
7				8				3
	6		2		7		5	
		6				9		
	7		9		4		3	
9				6				1

PUZZLE / 113 Time:_______

		1			5			9
	6			4		3		
7			6				1	
		6				4	5	
			1		6			
	3	8				1		
	5				4			7
		7		2			4	
6			8			5		

PUZZLE / 114 Time:_______

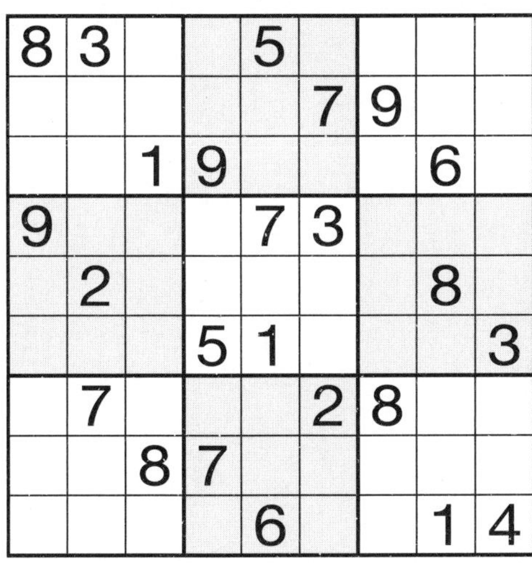

8	3			5				
					7	9		
		1	9				6	
9				7	3			
	2						8	
			5	1				3
	7				2	8		
		8	7					
				6			1	4

PUZZLE / 115 Time:_______

		1			9			
	8			4		9		1
6			1				4	
8					2	1		
	2			5			3	
		3	8					2
	1				6			3
3		6		2			9	
			9			6		

PUZZLE / 116 Time:_______

			9		6			
		6		8		1		
	2						7	
4				7				8
	9		3		1		2	
3				9				1
	1						3	
		8		3		7		
			4		7			

PUZZLE / 117 Time:_______

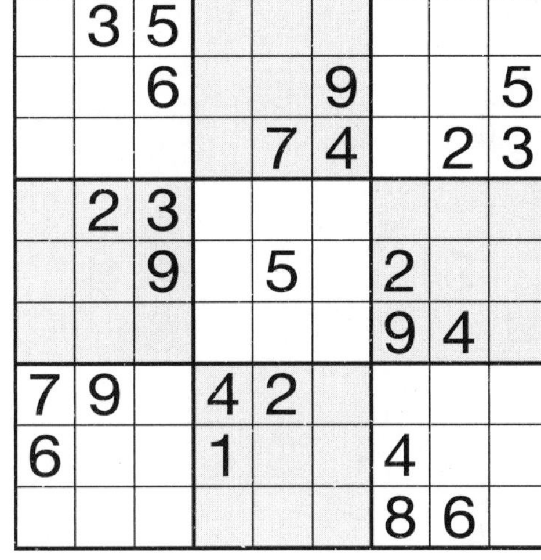

	3	5						
		6			9			5
				7	4		2	3
	2	3						
		9		5		2		
						9	4	
7	9		4	2				
6			1			4		
						8	6	

PUZZLE / 118 Time:_______

2		3				6		
	5			7			3	
7			5			4		9
		4			2			
	9			8			4	
			4			5		
5		1			9			4
	7			3			6	
		6				8		7

PUZZLE / 119 Time:_______

	4		6	7				
	7			1		4	8	
							6	
		6	7					2
9				8				1
8					5	7		
	1							
	8	2		3			1	
				9	1		5	

PUZZLE / 120 Time:_______

	2		8					5
6					2	1		
		5		1			8	
	7			6				4
		9	3		4	5		
1				2			7	
	9			8		2		
		3	2					7
7					1		5	

PUZZLE / 121 Time:_______

	2						4	
			5		6			
	3	9				8	1	
3				2				7
			8		3			
6				1				9
	1	5				3	7	
			7		2			
	8						2	

PUZZLE / 122 Time:_______

8	2				5			7
5				6				
			4			3		
		5			8			2
	9			5			8	
4			3			6		
		4			7			
				9				8
2			5				6	4

PUZZLE / 123 Time:_______

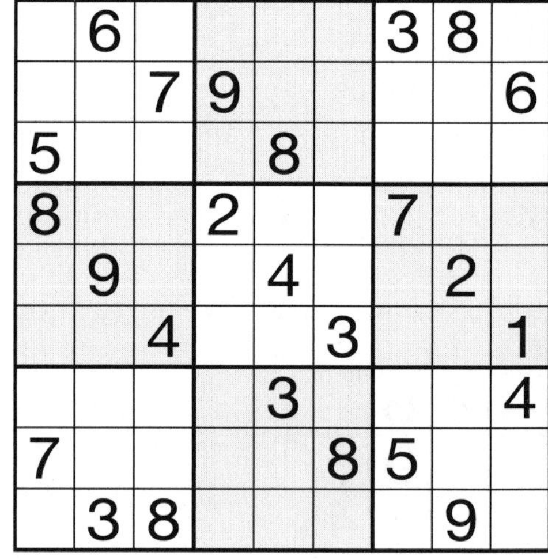

	6					3	8	
		7	9					6
5				8				
8			2			7		
	9			4			2	
		4			3			1
				3				4
7					8	5		
	3	8					9	

PUZZLE / 124 Time:_______

	6			3	8			
9						4		
2						6		7
	4				1			5
		5		7		9		
1			5				3	
3		2						8
		9						4
			1	9			2	

PUZZLE / 125 Time:_______

		6	4					
	7			6	8			
2						6	9	
		1	8					2
	9			3			7	
3					6	1		
	6	2						5
			1	7			2	
					9	8		

PUZZLE / 126 Time:_______

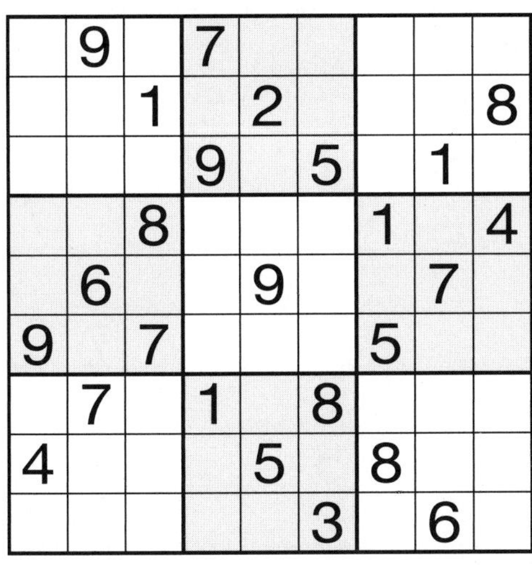

	9		7					
		1		2				8
			9		5		1	
		8				1		4
	6			9			7	
9		7				5		
	7		1		8			
4				5		8		
					3		6	

PUZZLE / 127 Time:________

4				9	2			5
		2	4			3		
	7						8	
8				6			2	
7			5		4			1
	9			3				8
	5						3	
		1			9	8		
2			3	5				4

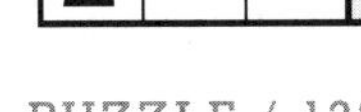

PUZZLE / 128 Time:________

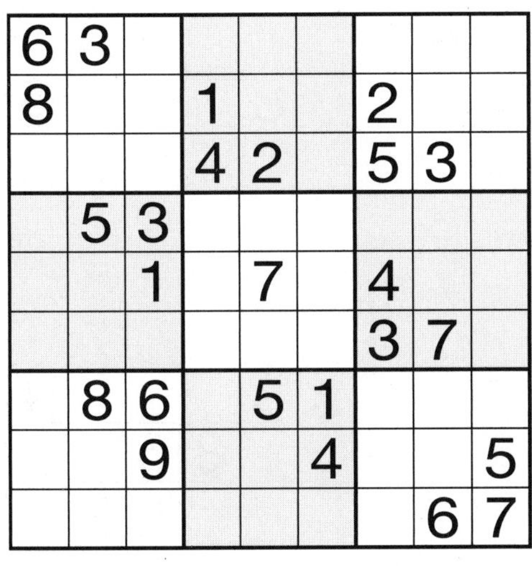

6	3							
8			1			2		
			4	2		5	3	
	5	3						
		1		7		4		
						3	7	
	8	6		5	1			
		9			4			5
							6	7

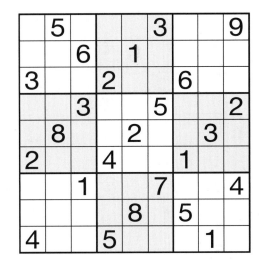

PUZZLE / 129 Time:________

	5				3			9
		6		1				
3			2			6		
		3			5			2
	8			2			3	
2			4			1		
		1			7			4
				8		5		
4			5				1	

PUZZLE / 130 Time:________

				9		3		
		4	7				1	
	6				1			2
	2		9			4		
5				3				6
		7			8		9	
1			8				3	
	3				9	1		
		9		2				

PUZZLE / 131 Time:________

					8		7	
2					3			4
5			1			9		
	7		2			4		
	2			7			9	
		9			6		3	
		3			9			6
1			8					3
	8		7					

PUZZLE / 132 Time:________

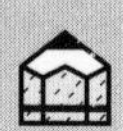

		4		2		7		
	1				3		2	
5			8					9
	5					8		
1				5				7
		2					6	
7					8			6
	8		3				1	
		5		1		3		

PUZZLE / 133 Time:_______

4					6			1
	9				5			2
	8		1			3		
	3					2		
		2		8		1		
		9					7	
		3			1		5	
7			5				1	
8			7					9

PUZZLE / 134 Time:_______

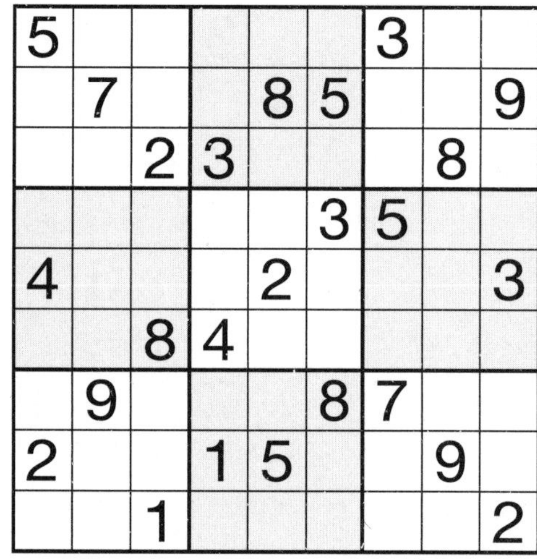

5						3		
	7			8	5			9
		2	3				8	
					3	5		
4				2				3
		8	4					
	9				8	7		
2			1	5			9	
		1						2

PUZZLE / 135 Time:_______

	6	9					3	
2			6	8				9
1					4			
	3					4		
	7			4			5	
		6					7	
			3					2
4				1	6			7
	1					5	9	

PUZZLE / 136 Time:_______

6	9			1				3
		8			3			2
			7	8			4	
	7					3		
3		4				1		7
		5					2	
	3			4	2			
5			1			8		
7				9			3	1

PUZZLE / 137 Time:_______

		6					1	
	1		5			4		6
2		4		9			5	
						9		8
				1				
6		3						
	7			4		1		2
1		5			7		4	
	9					6		

PUZZLE / 138 Time:_______

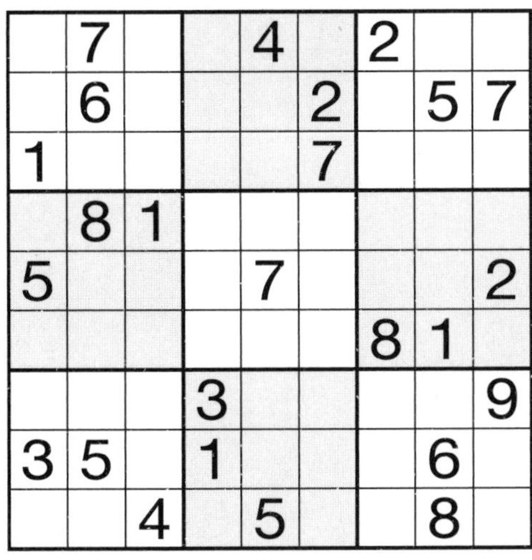

PUZZLE / 139 Time:_______

6							9	
		8		1			2	5
	9	3			7			
			6			7		
	6			3			8	
		4			1			
			5			4	7	
1	8			4		5		
	3							9

PUZZLE / 140 Time:_______

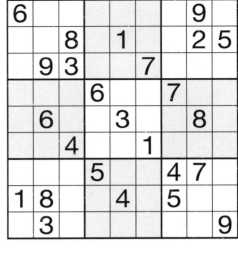

	7						1	
6		5		9		7		2
			8		5			
4			6			3		
	6			3			2	
		3			9			1
			3		7			
9		2		6		8		7
	1						4	

PUZZLE / 141 Time:_______

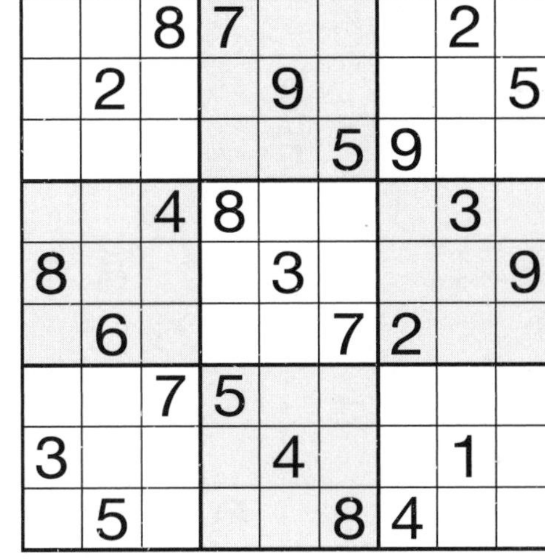

PUZZLE / 142 Time:_______

		9	5				7	
2				4				3
4					3			
			9			6	5	
			2		1			
	3	4			6			
			1					4
1				6				7
	5				9	2		

PUZZLE / 143 Time:_______

		5	3				8	
	3			1				5
4					2		1	
	6		8					
		7				5		
					7		9	
	2		7					6
9				4			2	
	1				9	7		

PUZZLE / 144 Time:_______

					5	9		
		2		6				
	6	8			7			3
			1			3		8
	2			4			1	
9		1			2			
6			8			7	5	
				2		4		
		3	6					

PUZZLE / 145 Time:_______

			4	3		1		
	4	7					9	
8							5	
				5				3
1			9		6			2
5				4				
	5							8
	6					2	4	
		1		6	3			

PUZZLE / 146 Time:_______

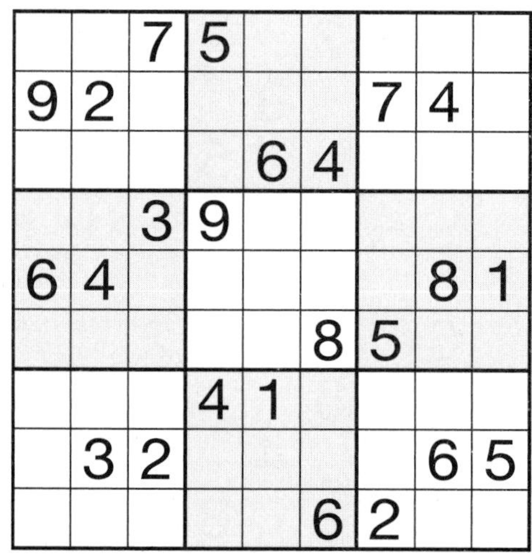

		7	5					
9	2					7	4	
				6	4			
		3	9					
6	4						8	1
					8	5		
			4	1				
	3	2					6	5
					6	2		

PUZZLE / 147 Time:_______

		6						3
8	2				5			
			4	8		6	5	
		3				9		
	9			6			1	
		1				8		
	3	9		1	2			
			5				7	9
5						2		

PUZZLE / 148 Time:_______

			4				9	
3		2		8		6		
	9		7					2
					1			4
	7			9			6	
8			6					
5					8		1	
		1		2		9		7
	2				4			

PUZZLE / 149 Time:_______

		5						8
1			6			4		
	8			4	3			
		4					7	
9		3		6		8		4
	5					6		
			2	8			3	
		7			4			1
2						7		

PUZZLE / 150 Time:_______

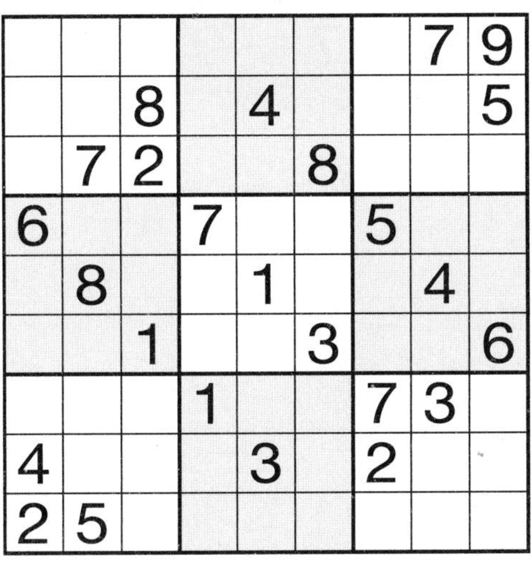

							7	9
		8		4				5
	7	2			8			
6			7			5		
	8			1			4	
		1			3			6
			1			7	3	
4				3		2		
2	5							

PUZZLE / 151 Time:_______

				3			1	
					7	2		
	9	5						
6			2			7	8	
4			7		5			6
	7	8			4			1
						5	4	
		4	5					
	1			6				

PUZZLE / 152 Time:_______

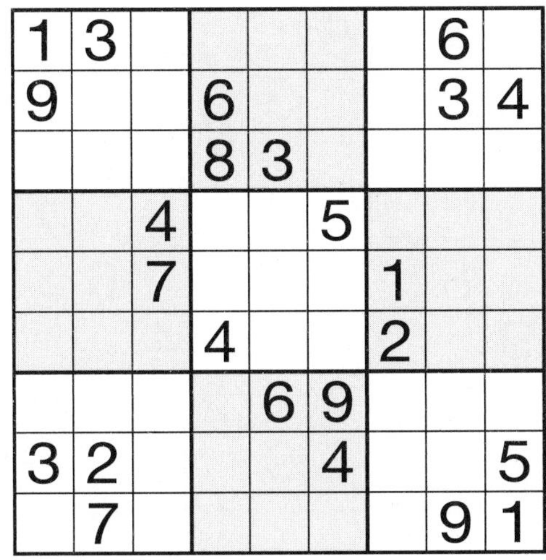

1	3						6	
9			6				3	4
			8	3				
		4			5			
		7				1		
			4			2		
				6	9			
3	2				4			5
	7						9	1

PUZZLE / 153 Time:_______

	9	6					4	
			2	3				9
					7	3		
		4	1				7	3
				2				
2	7				5	8		
		2	5					
7				9	4			
	8					9	6	

PUZZLE / 154 Time:_______

	5			1			2	
7			4					8
					5			
		6		5			4	
5			1		9			3
	2			7		5		
			2					
6					4			9
	9			3			7	

PUZZLE / 155 Time:_______

	4	5				9		
2			7	3			6	
					2		5	
	7				6			4
8			4		3			5
1			2				3	
	8		3					
	2			8	7			9
		9				3	7	

PUZZLE / 156 Time:_______

		7			6			
	3			2		8		
8					7		3	
			8			9		2
	9			7			5	
6		8			1			
	8		4					6
		1		5			9	
			9			3		

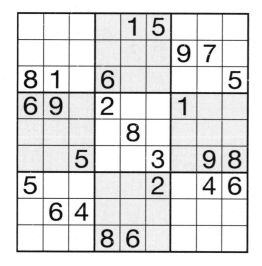

PUZZLE / 157 Time:_______

	6		7		9			
		3				1		6
	2		6				3	
3						4		5
				8				
5		7						1
	5				7		4	
2		9				3		
			4		1		2	

PUZZLE / 158 Time:_______

				1	5			
						9	7	
8	1		6					5
6	9		2			1		
				8				
		5			3		9	8
5					2		4	6
	6	4						
			8	6				

PUZZLE / 159 Time:_______

	4		5			6		
		7		3				1
5					7		9	
		3						7
	8			7			6	
9						4		
	6		4					5
7				9		8		
		5			1		2	

PUZZLE / 160 Time:_______

	5	2					1	
			2	6				3
					5	4		
		6	9				7	
3				4				9
	7				1	2		
		4	1					
7				2	4			
	2					5	6	

PUZZLE / 161 Time:_______

		8						1
	9		8			4		
4				1			3	
		1				9		2
	3			5			6	
5		9				3		
	2			4				8
		5			6		9	
6						2		

PUZZLE / 162 Time:_______

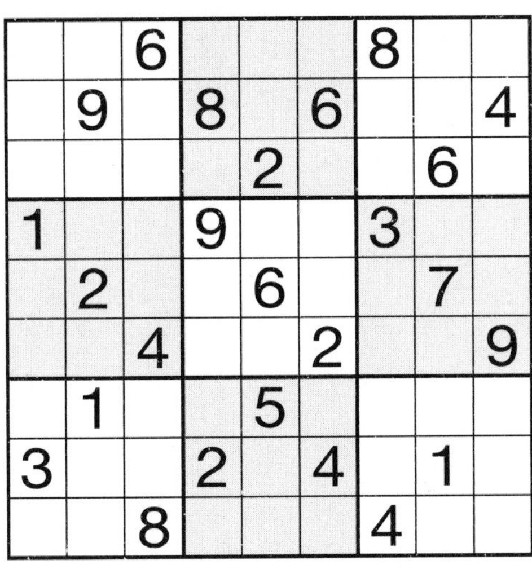

PUZZLE / 163 Time:_______

		3		5				8
6					8	4		
	9		7				2	
	6							5
		2		1		8		
7							3	
	2				7		1	
		5	1					3
9				8		5		

PUZZLE / 164 Time:_______

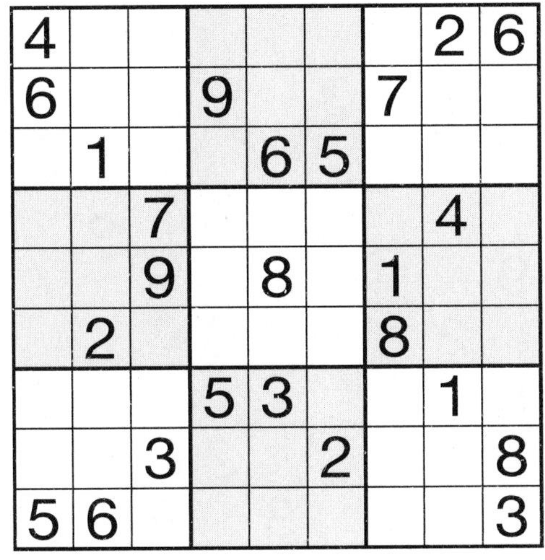

PUZZLE / 165 Time:_______

6		4					5	7
				7				9
8					2			
			3		6	2		
	4			2			1	
		8	1		4			
			7					4
5				1				
4	3					6		5

PUZZLE / 166 Time:_______

		3					4	
			6				1	8
1			4	2				
	2	5			9			
		4				7		
			8			1	3	
				1	8			7
2	4				3			
	5					6		

PUZZLE / 167 Time:_______

						4		7
	1	2			5			
	3			2	4			1
			3			8	7	
		9				6		
	6	8			2			
7			8	3			1	
			5			9	4	
8		1						

PUZZLE / 168 Time:_______

	5						2	
1			2			3		
		9				5		4
		7			9			8
	9			4			5	
3			5			2		
4		3				8		
		2			1			6
	7						4	

PUZZLE / 169 Time:_______

		5			2	7		
	4			7			3	
8			6					5
		9						8
	1			3			7	
4						2		
3					5			4
	6			1			2	
		2	8			1		

PUZZLE / 170 Time:_______

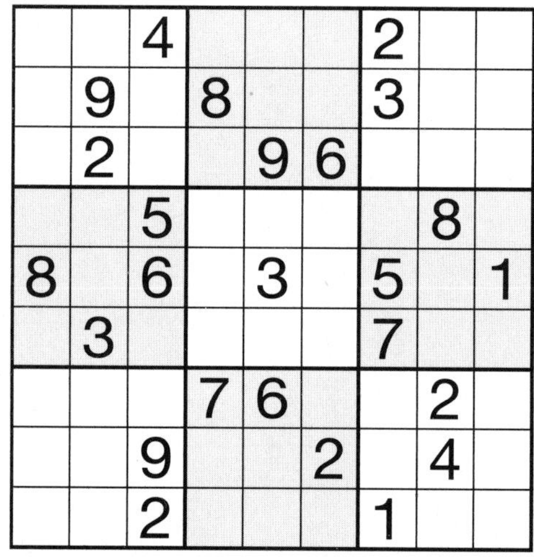

		4				2		
	9		8			3		
	2			9	6			
		5					8	
8		6		3		5		1
	3					7		
			7	6			2	
		9			2		4	
		2				1		

PUZZLE / 171 Time:_______

		3		1		7		
	1		3				5	
4								8
			5		4		8	
9				2				7
	2		7		6			
8								2
	5				2		3	
		1		3		9		

PUZZLE / 172 Time:_______

	4	2					1	
1				2	6			3
						6		
		9	5				2	
	2			8			3	
	5				4	8		
		7						
2			8	6				1
	6					4	7	

PUZZLE / 173 Time:_______

			5		7			
9		4				5		8
	1						4	
		5		6		7		
	2						1	
		3		9		4		
	3						7	
4		1				3		2
			2		5			

PUZZLE / 174 Time:_______

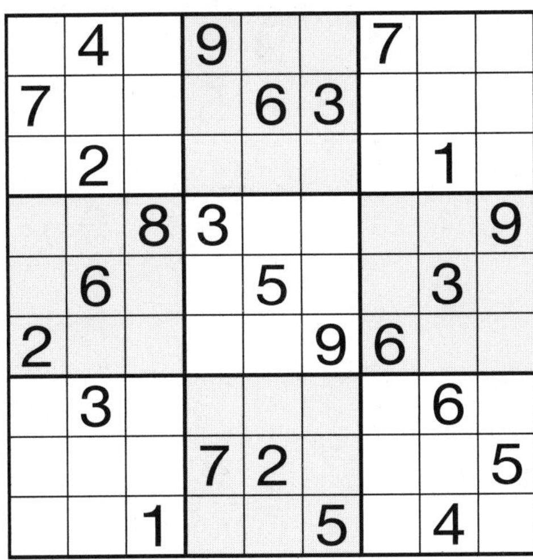

	4		9			7		
7				6	3			
	2						1	
		8	3					9
	6			5			3	
2					9	6		
	3						6	
			7	2				5
		1			5		4	

PUZZLE / 175 Time:_______

			9			2		
1				2	4			8
	3						6	
	6		5			7		
7				4				3
		3			1		2	
	5						8	
2			6	9				4
		9			3			

PUZZLE / 176 Time:_______

	1	8				5	7	
			3		4			
2				7				8
6								3
	8			1			6	
4								5
7				6				2
			9		1			
	9	2				8	3	

PUZZLE / 177 Time:_______

		9				6		
5				6				4
			3		5			
	5		4		1		2	
7				5				6
	9		6		2		7	
			9		7			
8				4				3
		2				8		

PUZZLE / 178 Time:_______

	7	9					4	6
		2			8			9
				9	3			
8	2							
7				5				3
							2	7
			6	8				
4			2			9		
9	6					1	3	

PUZZLE / 179 Time:_______

9			3		6			4
8				9				3
	1						9	
		4		5		7		
5			2		9			1
		6		3		9		
	5						7	
3				2				5
2			5		1			9

PUZZLE / 180 Time:_______

				8		6		
	9				7		4	
2		7				9		
	4		3		6			
1				5				4
			4		1		8	
		5				2		6
	1		2				5	
		8		4				

PUZZLE / 181 Time:_______

		3		9		1		
			6		5			
5		7				3		8
	1						9	
	3			5			8	
	7						2	
9		8				2		6
			7		4			
		1		6		5		

PUZZLE / 182 Time:_______

5							6	3
6			4	9				
		2				4		
			7		8		9	
	5			1			7	
	1		2		6			
		4				2		
				6	4			1
1	9							4

PUZZLE / 183 Time:_______

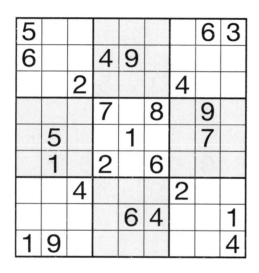

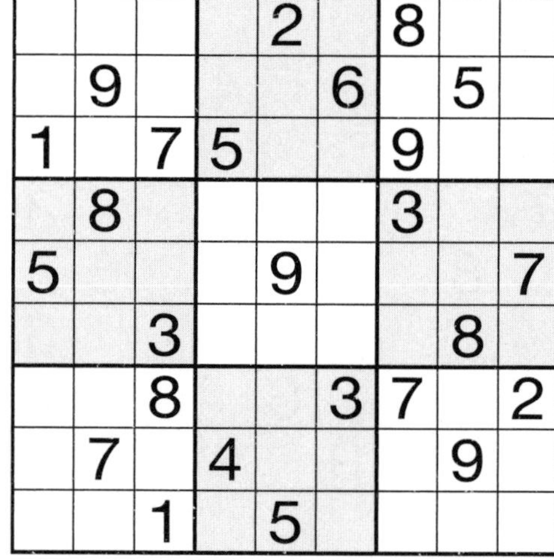

				2		8		
	9				6		5	
1		7	5			9		
	8					3		
5				9				7
		3					8	
		8			3	7		2
	7		4				9	
		1		5				

PUZZLE / 184 Time:_______

			1	8				
	7			9				
1						6	3	
		6	2				1	3
9				4				2
4	2				5	7		
	9	8						7
				1			6	
				5	3			

PUZZLE / 185 Time:_______

		9			2		3	
	3				1			5
8				5				
			3				2	6
		7		1		4		
2	5				7			
				3				1
9			1				6	
	4		9			2		

PUZZLE / 186 Time:_______

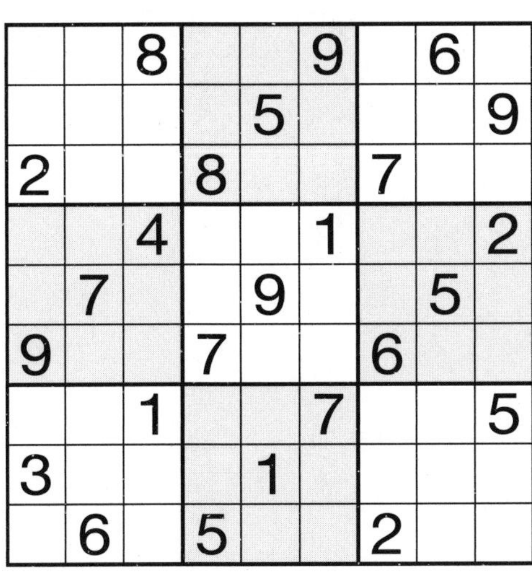

		8			9		6	
				5				9
2			8			7		
		4			1			2
	7			9			5	
9			7			6		
		1			7			5
3				1				
	6		5			2		

PUZZLE / 187 Time:_______

1	9							3
		8						7
			1		6		2	
		4	9		3	5		
				1				
		2	7		8	6		
	2		4		5			
4						3		
6							1	8

PUZZLE / 188 Time:_______

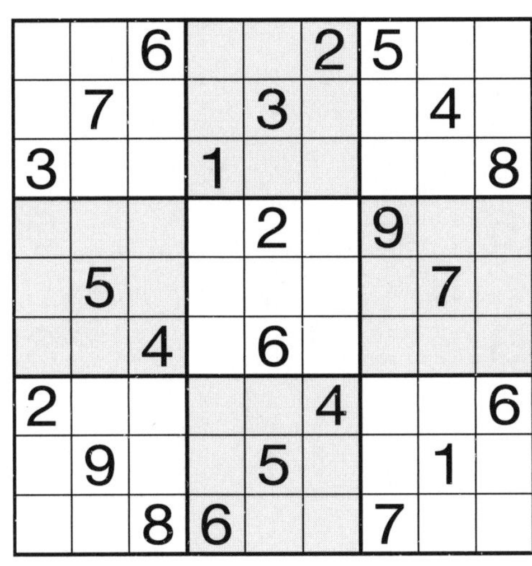

		6			2	5		
	7			3			4	
3			1					8
				2		9		
	5						7	
		4		6				
2					4			6
	9			5			1	
		8	6			7		

PUZZLE / 189 Time:_______

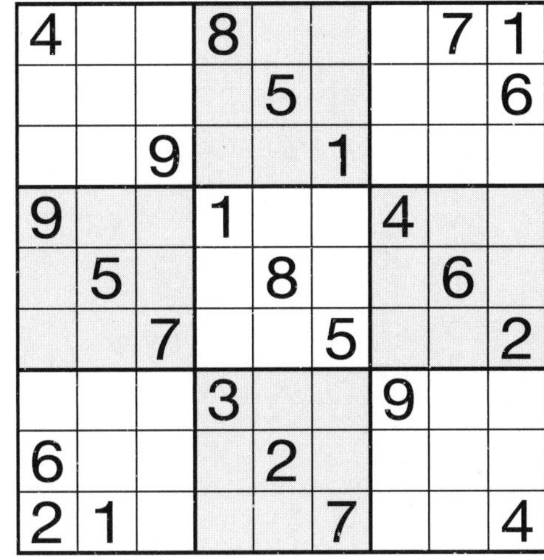

4			8				7	1
				5				6
		9			1			
9			1			4		
	5			8			6	
		7			5			2
			3			9		
6				2				
2	1				7			4

PUZZLE / 190 Time:_______

	7	9		5			2	
4					8			3
				2				6
	6		8		4			
5		3				9		1
			1		5		6	
9				4				
6			9					7
	5			7		8	1	

PUZZLE / 191 Time:_______

	9	5					8	
1				6				5
			1					4
	7			8	4			
		8				2		
			2	5			9	
3					2			
8				4				9
	2					8	7	

PUZZLE / 192 Time:_______

	6		2				4	
5				3				9
		7			9	5		
		1		4				8
	7		8		5		6	
4				9		2		
		8	9			3		
3				6				2
	9				2		8	

PUZZLE / 193 Time:_______

	6		5					9
8				6	3			
					1			
2			9			7	1	
	3			7			5	
	7	8			5			4
			6					
			4	8				7
4					2		3	

PUZZLE / 194 Time:_______

		7			3			
	3		4			1		
	8			6	2			5
		8					4	
		1		3		9		
	2					6		
6			9	4			3	
		2			7		8	
			1			7		

PUZZLE / 195 Time:_______

			5				3	
2				7		9		
	1				9			
6		2	3					9
	8			5			7	
5					8	1		3
			8				1	
		3		1				8
	4				3			

PUZZLE / 196 Time:_______

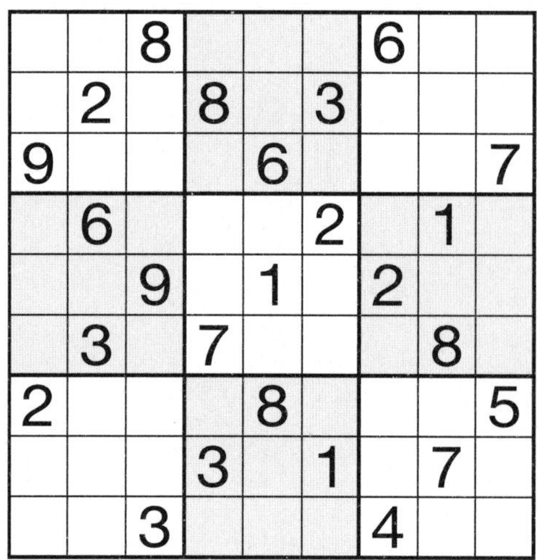

		8				6		
	2		8		3			
9				6				7
	6				2		1	
		9		1		2		
	3		7				8	
2				8				5
			3		1		7	
		3				4		

PUZZLE / 197 Time:_______

			3		5			
		7		1		6		
	5			4			2	
2								3
		1	7		8	4		
9								7
	8			7			9	
		9		3		5		
			8		2			

PUZZLE / 198 Time:_______

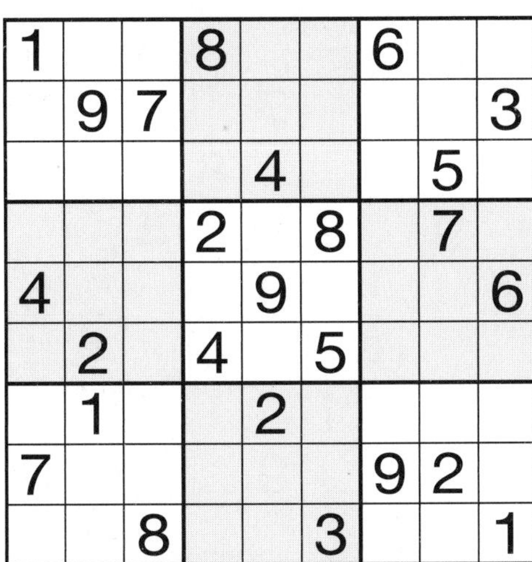

PUZZLE / 199 Time:_______

				9				
	3				4	2		
		6	2				3	7
7				1	5			
	8						4	
			6	4				3
4	5				3	6		
		2	8				9	
				6				

PUZZLE / 200 Time:_______

	7			9			8	
9		3			7			5
			6				3	
	5					2		
7				4				9
		6					5	
	2				5			
6			2			4		3
	1			3			6	

PUZZLE / 201 Time:_______

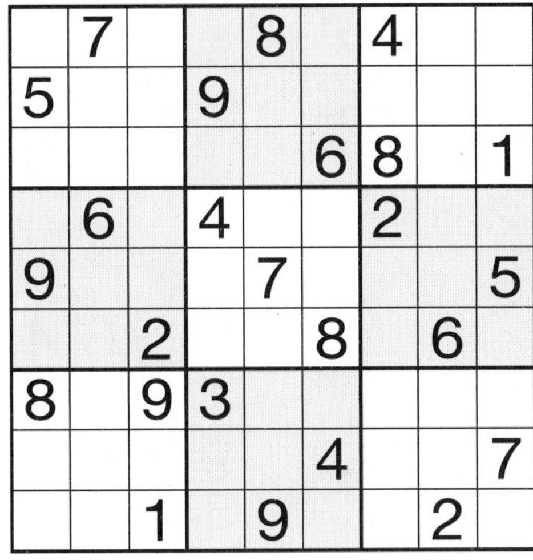

PUZZLE / 202 Time:_______

	2	9						8
8			9	5				
					6	4		
		5	6				7	
7				4				5
	6				2	9		
		6	7					
				1	9			3
1						2	5	

PUZZLE / 203 Time:_______

	6			4	2			
5	8			1				
							1	7
		9	1					2
			6		3			
4					8	7		
1	3							
				5			9	1
			2	8			7	

PUZZLE / 204 Time:_______

							6	9
	8	3	1				5	2
	2		6					
	6	5	2					
					6	4	3	
					1		9	
3	4				9	6	8	
2	1							

PUZZLE / 205 Time:_______

	2					8		
3				7				9
		1			8		5	
	9		2			4		
7				3				5
		6			4		1	
	7		1			5		
5				9				3
		2					4	

PUZZLE / 206 Time:_______

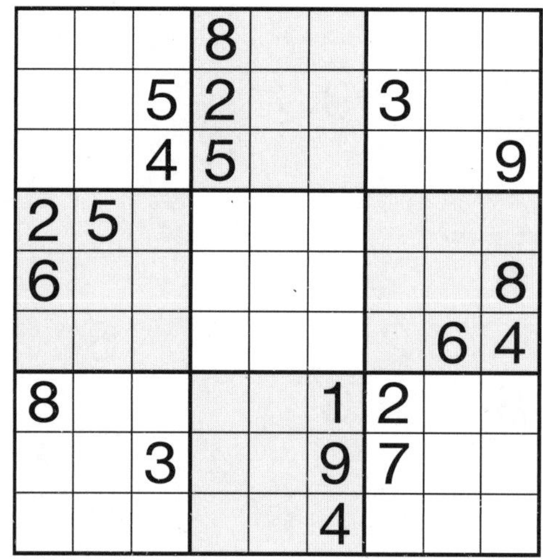

			8					
		5	2			3		
		4	5					9
2	5							
6								8
							6	4
8					1	2		
		3			9	7		
					4			

PUZZLE / 207 Time:_______

		7	9	5				
							8	
3			6			2		
	6							9
	4						5	
8							3	
		6			2			4
	5							
				3	8	7		

PUZZLE / 208 Time:_______

9							7	
	5					3		
		8			2			6
		6		1			5	
		4		9		6		
	2			3		7		
3			8			4		
		1					9	
	6							2

PUZZLE / 209 Time:_______

	8						7	
5			1	2	3			6
						4		
	4	9					5	
			3		2			
	5					3	6	
		6						
1			7	8	9			2
	2						8	

PUZZLE / 210 Time:_______

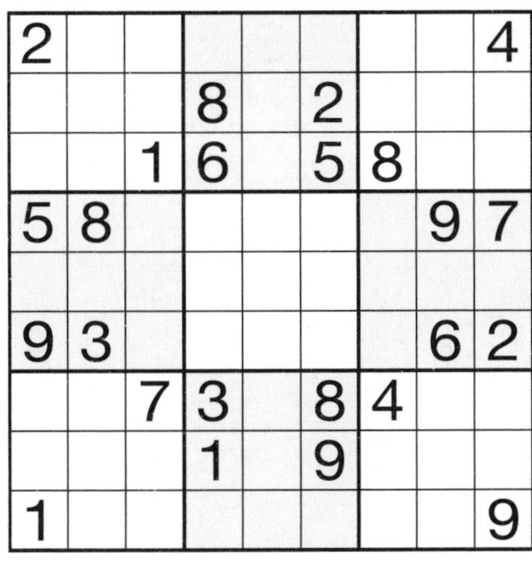

2								4
			8		2			
		1	6		5	8		
5	8						9	7
9	3						6	2
		7	3		8	4		
			1		9			
1								9

PUZZLE / 211 Time:_______

		4	3					
					1	8		
3					2	1		
1		8	4					5
		6	8		3	2		
2					7	9		8
		1	5					6
		7	6					
					9	7		

PUZZLE / 212 Time:_______

2				7				8
5								1
	7		5	3	6		2	
	8	7				6	3	
		9				1		
	5	2				4	7	
	2		4	6	1		9	
9								7
4				8				6

PUZZLE / 213 Time:_______

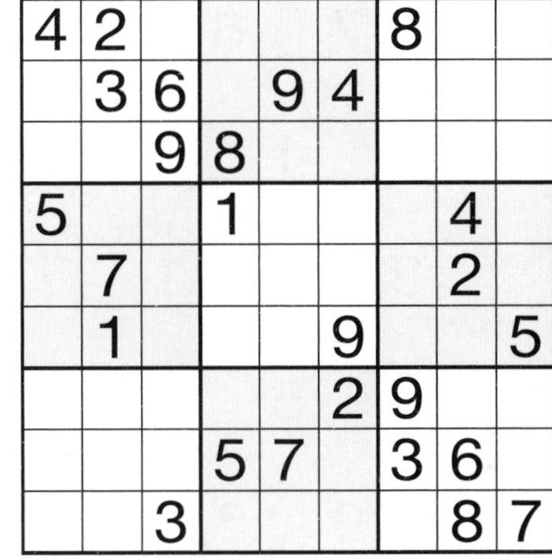

4	2					8		
	3	6		9	4			
		9	8					
5			1				4	
	7						2	
	1				9			5
					2	9		
			5	7		3	6	
		3					8	7

PUZZLE / 214 Time:_______

6								2
	9	1	7					
	5		6	1				
	8	5			6			
		6				7		
			9			4	3	
				3	7		5	
					2	6	9	
7								1

PUZZLE / 215 Time:_______

2								8
	5			2	9		3	
		6				1		
	1		6		5			
	3			8			9	
			1		4		2	
		7				4		
	9		3	5			8	
8								9

PUZZLE / 216 Time:_______

		7					9	
	2				3			5
6				4				
			9		5		7	
		8				1		
	4		6		2			
				7				3
1			5				4	
	9					2		

PUZZLE / 217 Time:_______

3				5				1
		6			7	3		
	5						8	
7							5	
		3		4		9		
	2							4
	1						4	
		8	9			7		
5				3				8

PUZZLE / 218 Time:_______

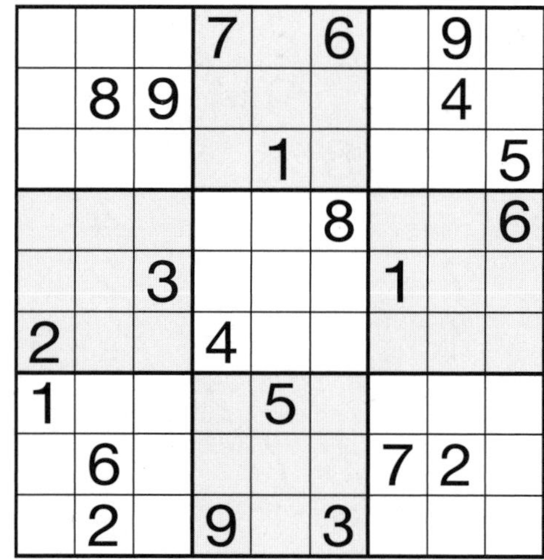

			7		6		9	
	8	9					4	
				1				5
					8			6
		3				1		
2			4					
1				5				
	6					7	2	
	2		9		3			

PUZZLE / 219 Time:_______

	1	2	3	4				
							6	
		5			9		7	
			1				8	
	4						9	
	5				6			
	2		6			7		
	9							
				8	5	3	4	

PUZZLE / 220 Time:_______

				7				
7		8			9			
	3					1		4
	7		1		2			
5								6
			3		4		8	
1		4					9	
			6			2		1
				8				

PUZZLE / 221 Time:_______

				1			9	
				6	8	1	5	
9	7							
		7			1			4
				3				
8			6			3		
							3	9
	2	6	7	4				
	9			5				

PUZZLE / 222 Time:_______

5			6		1			
2							3	1
	8				3		2	
		9	8	4				6
3				5	6	2		
	9		2				8	
1	4							2
			7		9			3

PUZZLE / 223 Time:_______

7	1							
6						2	3	
		8	9			6	7	
		5	2		6			
			8		1	7		
	5	2			4	3		
	3	9						4
							1	8

PUZZLE / 224 Time:_______

4			9	8				7
			5			2		
	1				2			
		1		2			6	4
5			1		3			2
6	7			4		3		
			4				3	
		4			7			
3				5	6			9

PUZZLE / 225 Time:_______

9				8		6		5
		1	2					
	8				9		7	
			3	4				
7		6				3		1
				5	6			
	5		4				2	
					7	8		
3		2		1				4

PUZZLE / 226 Time:_______

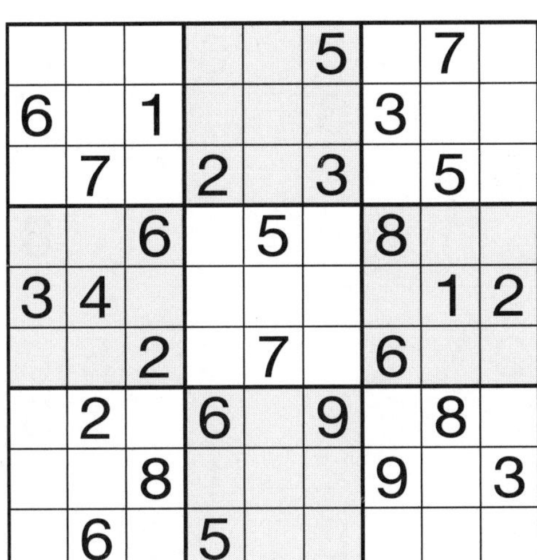

					5		7	
6		1				3		
	7		2		3		5	
		6		5		8		
3	4						1	2
		2		7		6		
	2		6		9		8	
		8				9		3
	6		5					

PUZZLE / 227 Time:_______

	8						2	
		3				7		
4			3		6			8
	1			2			4	
		2				6		
	3			7			1	
1			4		8			3
		6				9		
	5						7	

PUZZLE / 228 Time:_______

	2				5	6		7
8								
		4			3			1
			8			2		6
				9				
1		3			7			
9			2			8		
								3
5		1	6				9	

PUZZLE / 229 Time:_______

1				5			4	3
	2				6			5
		3				7		
			4				1	
5								9
	6				1			
		7				2		
9			2				6	
6	4			9				7

PUZZLE / 230 Time:_______

1	2						5	4
	8	4				3	6	
		6				2		
			7		2			
			3		9			
			1		5			
		2				6		
	6	3				7	4	
4	9						8	1

PUZZLE / 231 Time:_______

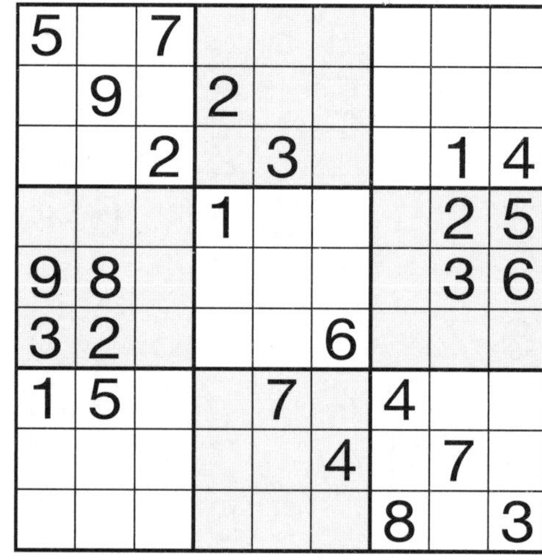

5		7						
	9		2					
		2		3			1	4
			1				2	5
9	8						3	6
3	2				6			
1	5			7		4		
					4		7	
						8		3

PUZZLE / 232 Time:_______

	8		3					
					4		1	
9		5	2			7		3
	4				5			
6				7				8
			1				2	
1		2			9	3		4
	7		8					
					6		5	

PUZZLE / 233 Time:_______

		4			6			5
		7	3					
9	5					8		
	1		4					8
2					8		5	
		6					7	3
					1	9		
3			8			1		

PUZZLE / 234 Time:_______

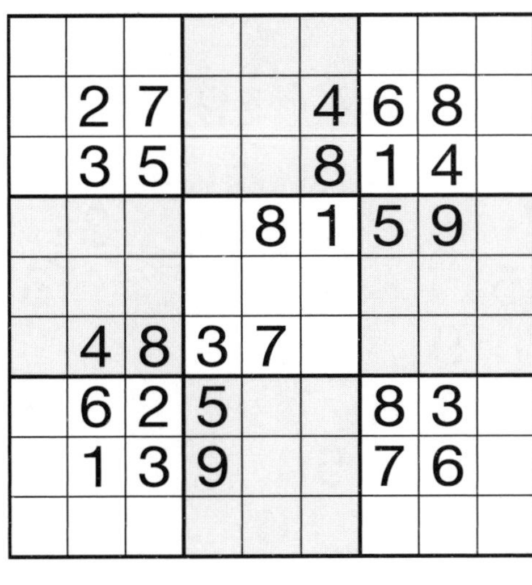

	2	7			4	6	8	
	3	5			8	1	4	
				8	1	5	9	
	4	8	3	7				
	6	2	5			8	3	
	1	3	9			7	6	

PUZZLE / 235 Time:_______

	2						8	
3								6
			8	5	7			
		2	3		9	8		
		8				4		
		9	5		8	2		
			7	6	2			
7								1
	4						9	

PUZZLE / 236 Time:_______

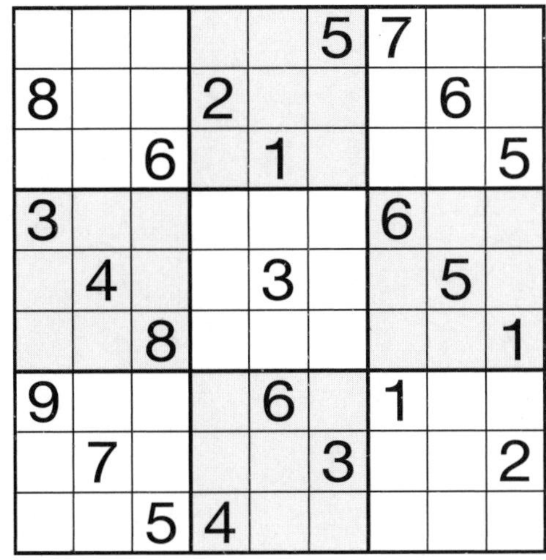

					5	7		
8			2				6	
		6		1				5
3						6		
	4			3			5	
		8						1
9				6		1		
	7				3			2
		5	4					

PUZZLE / 237 Time:_______

	1	6		4				
7			9		2			
8			7			4		
	6	2					5	
1								4
	7					3	9	
		8			1			6
			2		3			9
				6		7	8	

PUZZLE / 238 Time:_______

	6	7	8	9				
4							8	
3					2			
2					3	4		
1								7
		3	9					5
			5					4
	4							3
				7	8	9	1	

PUZZLE / 239 Time:_______

	2		7		3		5	
1		4		9				
	9		2					
3		7						2
	6						9	
2						5		8
					7		4	
				4		1		7
	7		8		6		3	

PUZZLE / 240 Time:_______

7				6				1
		2	3			6		
	3				4			
		6					9	
5				3				7
	4					5		
			9				3	
		4			6	7		
1				8				2

PUZZLE / 241 Time:_______

				1				5
		7			9			
3						2	4	
					8		3	
5								6
	9		2					
	1	6						9
			5			7		
8				4				

PUZZLE / 242 Time:_______

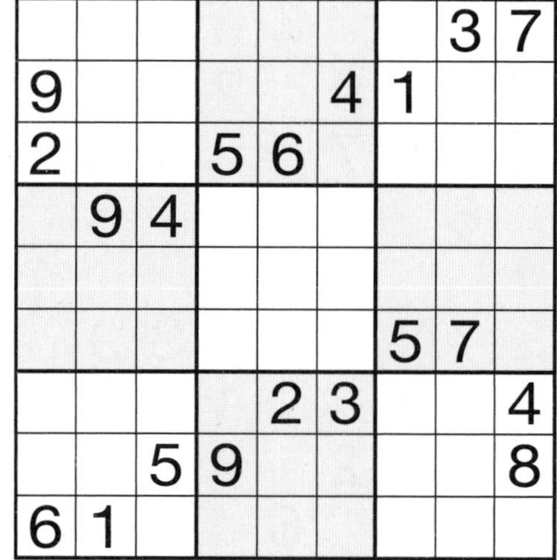

							3	7
9					4	1		
2			5	6				
	9	4						
						5	7	
				2	3			4
		5	9					8
6	1							

PUZZLE / 243 Time:_______

6		9						
	4				2			
				3			8	5
		2	5					4
	3						1	
8					7	6		
7	8			1				
			4				3	
						9		2

PUZZLE / 244 Time:_______

7				4			1	2
3				9				
		1	6			4		
			1		4	8		
5	7						6	1
		3	7		5			
		5			2	9		
				1				4
6	9			5				8

PUZZLE / 245 Time:_______

					3	5	6	
			6			1		9
				7	4	3		
	7						8	3
				9				
5	9						4	
		6	4	5				
9		7			6			
	4	5	8					

PUZZLE / 246 Time:_______

		4	8					
		1	6					
		5	2			1	9	6
						4	2	3
8	9	7						
5	6	3			4	7		
					1	8		
					2	3		

PUZZLE / 247 Time:_______

2			3		5			4
	1						7	
		6				5		
8				6				3
			9		2			
6				5				9
		5				8		
	7						4	
3			6		9			2

PUZZLE / 248 Time:_______

6		3		8				
4		8			7		3	
					2		5	
					6		7	
5								2
	4		2					
	1		9					
	7		1			4		8
				2		6		7

PUZZLE / 249 Time:_______

		5	6	7	8			
	4					9		
3						6		
2					4			
1				5				6
			3					7
		7						1
		4					8	
			1	6	3	7		

PUZZLE / 250 Time:_______

	9						2	
4				1	3			8
			2			1		
	2		5			6		
	5			2			1	
		8			9		5	
		4			7			
6			3	8				7
	3						9	

PUZZLE / 251 Time:_______

			3			8		
2				6				
	5						7	
4			9			7	2	
				1				
	8	7			3			6
	4						1	
				8				2
		8			2			

PUZZLE / 252 Time:_______

		7		4		3		9
		2	8		6			
	9	5	2					
					3	4	6	
			9		4	8		
6		3		5		7		

PUZZLE / 253 Time:_______

5	3		2				6	
8								9
			1		5		2	
1				9		5		
	5						7	
		9		4				2
	7		4		3			
3								4
	9				2		8	3

PUZZLE / 254 Time:_______

			9					
2	9	3			6	4		
4			7		1			9
9	5		1				6	
	3			5			7	
	2				9		5	4
7			4		5			3
		2	6			7	4	8
					2			

PUZZLE / 255 Time:_______

			2	1	5	6		
					3	9		
7	5							
6	1							7
5								6
8							4	3
							2	1
		2	9					
		3	6	5	2			

PUZZLE / 256 Time:_______

	2				1			
9	1			6	2			
		4				5		
			6				3	2
			7		4			
1	6				3			
		5				2		
			8	3			4	6
			9				8	

PUZZLE / 257 Time:_______

		3	9					
7					3	1		
		4	8					5
1					4		2	
	2			6			5	
	4		3					8
9					6	3		
		6	2					9
					9	6		

PUZZLE / 258 Time:_______

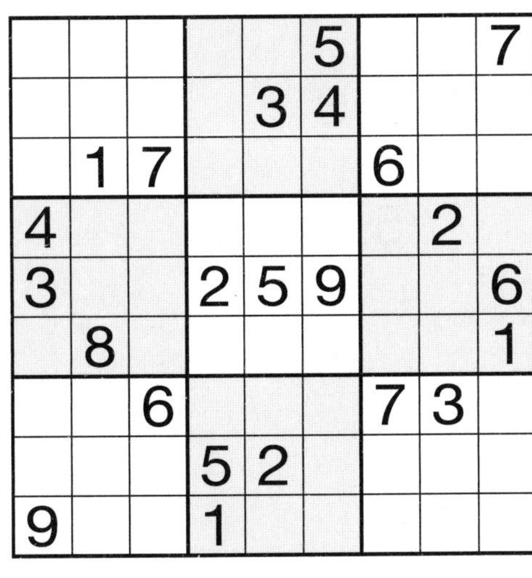

					5			7
				3	4			
	1	7				6		
4							2	
3			2	5	9			6
	8							1
		6				7	3	
			5	2				
9			1					

PUZZLE / 259 Time:_______

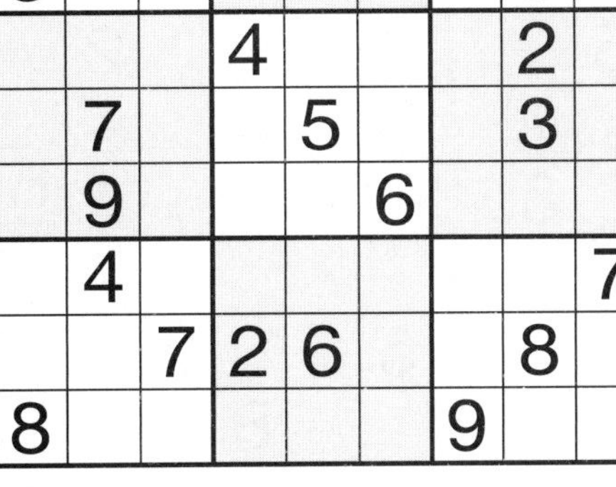

		1						8
	2			7	3	4		
3							9	
			4				2	
	7			5			3	
	9				6			
	4							7
		7	2	6			8	
8						9		

PUZZLE / 260 Time:_______

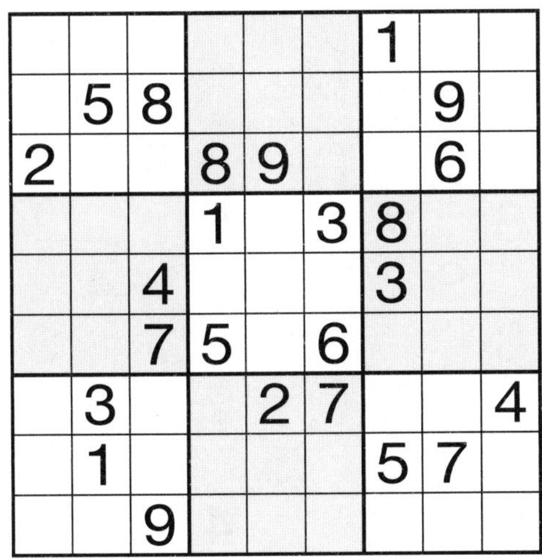

						1		
	5	8					9	
2			8	9			6	
			1		3	8		
		4				3		
		7	5		6			
	3			2	7			4
	1					5	7	
		9						

PUZZLE / 261 Time:_______

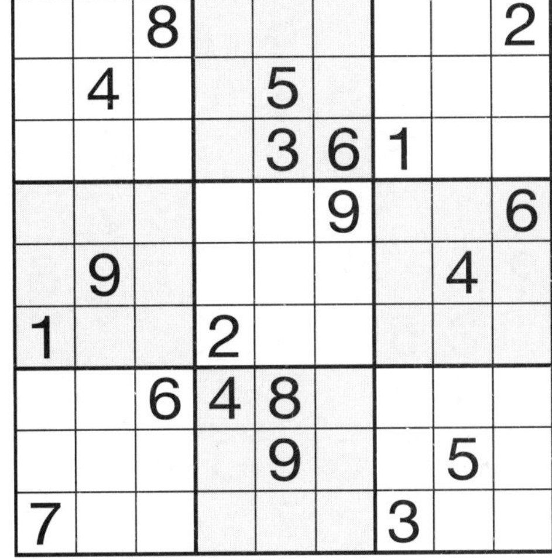

		8						2
	4			5				
				3	6	1		
					9			6
	9						4	
1			2					
		6	4	8				
				9			5	
7						3		

PUZZLE / 262 Time:_______

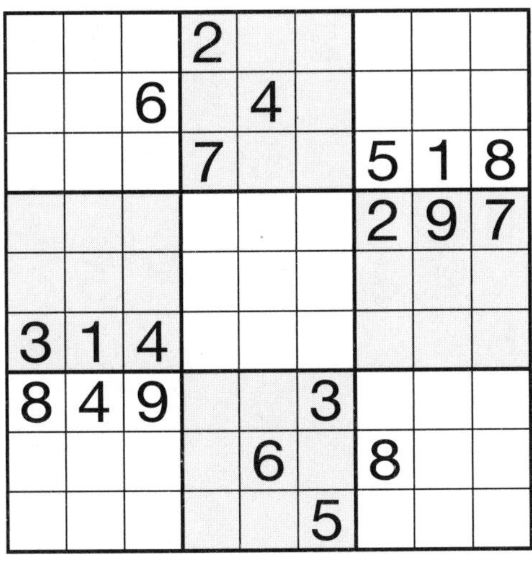

			2					
		6		4				
			7			5	1	8
						2	9	7
3	1	4						
8	4	9			3			
				6		8		
					5			

PUZZLE / 263 Time:_______

		3	5	6				
	2				8	7	4	
	4							
	1		9	2	7		5	
							8	
	8	5	1				9	
				7	6	2		

PUZZLE / 264 Time:_______

			6			4		8
		3			9			
	2					5		1
5							2	
			7		4			
	8							9
9		6					7	
			5			3		
1		4			8			

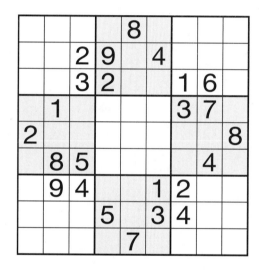

PUZZLE / 265 Time:_______

						5	4	6
	2	7	3	6				
		5	9	4	6			
			7	5	1	8		
				9	4	1	2	
8	3	9						

PUZZLE / 266 Time:_______

				8				
		2	9		4			
		3	2			1	6	
	1					3	7	
2								8
	8	5					4	
	9	4			1	2		
			5		3	4		
				7				

PUZZLE / 267 Time:_______

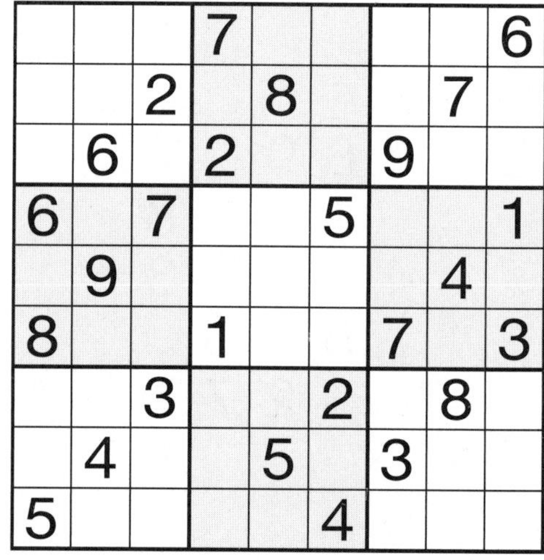

			7					6
		2		8			7	
	6		2			9		
6		7			5			1
	9						4	
8			1			7		3
		3			2		8	
	4			5		3		
5					4			

PUZZLE / 268 Time:_______

				4	1			5
	7					8		
		9	2					3
5								
	1		3		9		2	
								6
4					7	1		
		2					9	
6			8	3				

PUZZLE / 269 Time:_______

	1		2		5		8	
7				1				9
				6				
9								7
	4	3				1	5	
8								4
				9				
4				3				5
	6		8		1		2	

PUZZLE / 270 Time:_______

				4	8	3		
		6						
	5	1	2					9
		9						1
2				8				5
3						7		
7					3	8	5	
						6		
		8	9	2				

PUZZLE / 271 Time:_______

	3	2					4	
5			9			2		8
				6				
2					4			5
		5				1		
8			7					9
				1				
7		9			8			4
	4					6	3	

PUZZLE / 272 Time:_______

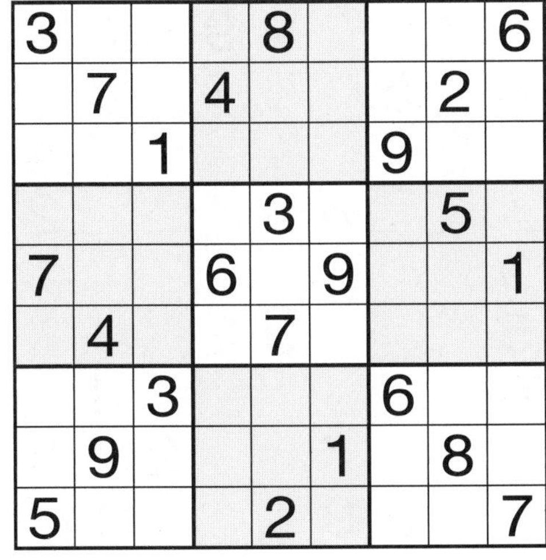

3				8				6
	7		4				2	
		1				9		
				3			5	
7			6		9			1
	4			7				
		3				6		
	9				1		8	
5				2				7

PUZZLE / 273 Time:_______

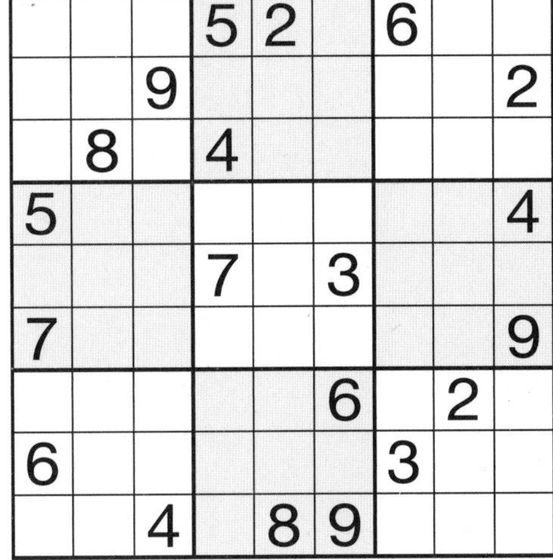

			5	2		6		
		9						2
	8		4					
5								4
			7		3			
7								9
					6		2	
6						3		
		4		8	9			

PUZZLE / 274 Time:_______

1	3						5	
		8				6		
			5		9			2
			6				3	
		3				4		
	2				5			
2			3		6			
		4				7		
	7						8	9

PUZZLE / 275 Time:_______

		5						
		6	7	8			3	1
1	2							4
	3		4					
	4			5			9	
					6		8	
8							7	6
2	1			7	8	9		
						1		

PUZZLE / 276 Time:_______

				2			6	
						5	7	
		2			8		3	
					4	2		
8			6		7			1
		6	3					
	6		5			9		
	5	1						
	7			9				

PUZZLE / 277 Time:_______

		8						
		2	9			5	7	
			6	7			3	2
	3							5
		4				7		
1							6	
5	9			4	1			
	6	7			8	9		
						4		

PUZZLE / 278 Time:_______

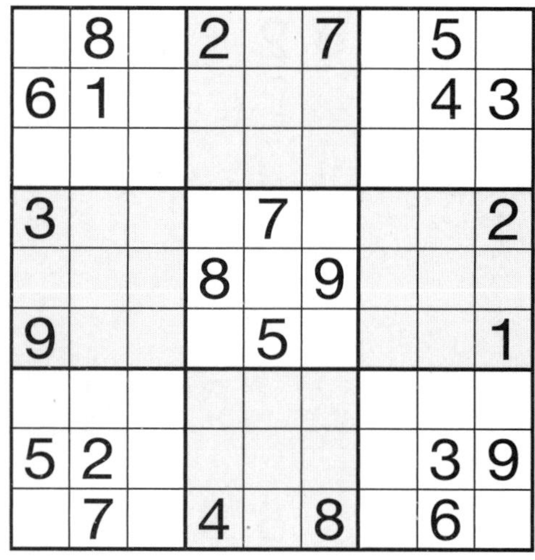

	8		2		7		5	
6	1						4	3
3				7				2
			8		9			
9				5				1
5	2						3	9
	7		4		8		6	

PUZZLE / 279 Time:_______

	3				9	6	8	
4		5			7			
	6							4
			6	8				2
9								1
5				9	3			
8							4	
			7			2		5
	5	2	9				1	

PUZZLE / 280 Time:_______

			8	9			4	
2	8				6			
		1						5
3					4	5		
				2				
		4	5					7
6						7		
			7				3	9
	2			5	1			

PUZZLE / 281 Time:_______

			7			3		
				8			4	1
	1	9			6			
			9			2	3	
	8	4			7			
			8			6	7	
3	5			2				
		1			9			

PUZZLE / 282 Time:_______

3							5	4
6			2					
		5		4		8		
				9			3	
		2	8		6	5		
	4			7				
		3		5		6		
					9			7
2	8							5

PUZZLE / 283 Time:_______

		7	8	4				
9						6		
	6				1			8
5							6	
		6		5		4		
	2							9
4			3				2	
		3						1
				8	2	5		

PUZZLE / 284 Time:_______

	9					5		
4				2			3	
		8	6					2
	7				5	8		
8								6
		6	9				1	
9					3	7		
	2			1				9
		3					8	

PUZZLE / 285 Time:_______

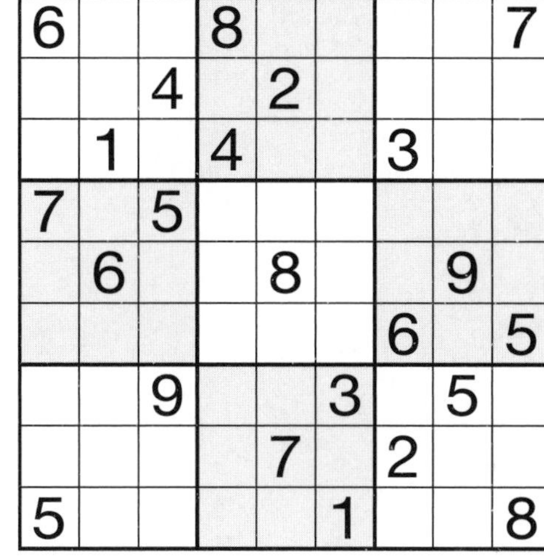

6			8					7
		4		2				
	1		4			3		
7		5						
	6			8			9	
						6		5
		9			3		5	
				7		2		
5					1			8

PUZZLE / 286 Time:_______

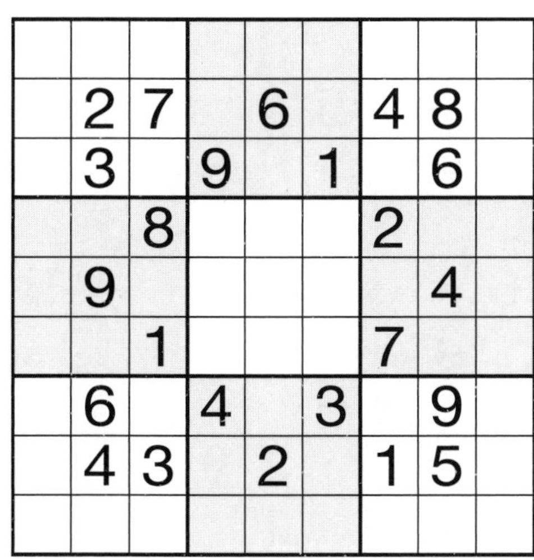

	2	7		6		4	8	
	3		9		1		6	
		8				2		
	9						4	
		1				7		
	6		4		3		9	
	4	3		2		1	5	

PUZZLE / 287 Time:_______

								8
	6	5	1	4			3	
	3					7		
	5				2			
	2			7			8	
			5				4	
		4					2	
	8			5	7	9	6	
9								

PUZZLE / 288 Time:_______

	4				9			
		5					8	
8				3				2
3			2		4			
		1				5		
			8		6			9
2				7				5
	9					4		
			1				6	

PUZZLE / 289 Time:_______

							1	
		1	7			4		2
	7			6			3	
	8			5				
		7	2		8	6		
				3			2	
	1			2			5	
4		2			1	7		
	3							

PUZZLE / 290 Time:_______

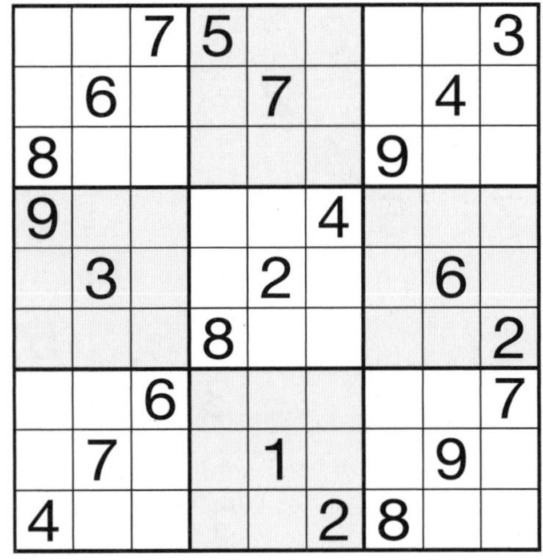

		7	5					3
	6			7			4	
8						9		
9					4			
	3			2			6	
			8					2
		6						7
	7			1			9	
4					2	8		

PUZZLE / 291 Time:_______

	4	8	6					
	3		5				4	2
								7
			8		9		3	4
5	6		7		3			
4								
2	5				6		9	
					2	5	8	

PUZZLE / 292 Time:_______

	1						9	8
		6	4					7
	2			9	5			
		3	7					
	8						5	
					4	6		
			1	7			8	
4					3	9		
5	6						2	

PUZZLE / 293 Time:_______

				6			8	
1			5					6
	9				3	4		
		9					7	
6				2				5
	4					1		
		8	6				4	
2					9			1
	7			1				

PUZZLE / 294 Time:_______

				4		3		
		6		1		2		
1					9			7
	3		8				1	
	4						6	
	5				2		8	
2			7					9
		9		6		8		
		8		5				

PUZZLE / 295 Time:_______

	6				7	5		
							2	
		3	1					9
5			3			9		
	4			2			1	
		9			5			3
7					8	3		
	9							
		1	4				7	

PUZZLE / 296 Time:_______

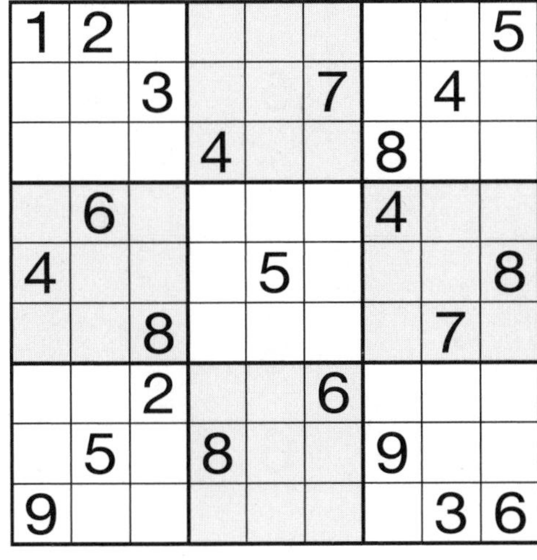

1	2							5
		3			7		4	
			4			8		
	6					4		
4				5				8
		8					7	
		2			6			
	5		8			9		
9							3	6

PUZZLE / 297 Time:_______

8					7			3
			8			9		
	6	4	5			8		
7						6	3	
				5				
	8	9						1
		5			6	1	2	
		7			2			
3			1					7

PUZZLE / 298 Time:_______

		2	8					1
	1			5				
9					6	5		
5							6	
		3		7		9		
	9							7
		6	4					8
				1			3	
8					5	7		

PUZZLE / 299 Time:_______

		1	2		3	4		
	9						3	
	4			5			1	
9					8			6
		8		7		5		
6			9					4
	3			8			5	
	7						4	
		4	1		5	2		

PUZZLE / 300 Time:_______

				1			2	
	2	7			3	4		
5			6					
9			4			1	8	
6								4
	8	3			1			6
					7			8
		4	2			6	5	
	5			9				

PUZZLE / 301 Time:_______

	9	8						
1			6					
5			4					
4			1			6	2	
2			3		9			5
	7	3			4			8
					2			6
					3			7
						5	1	

PUZZLE / 302 Time:_______

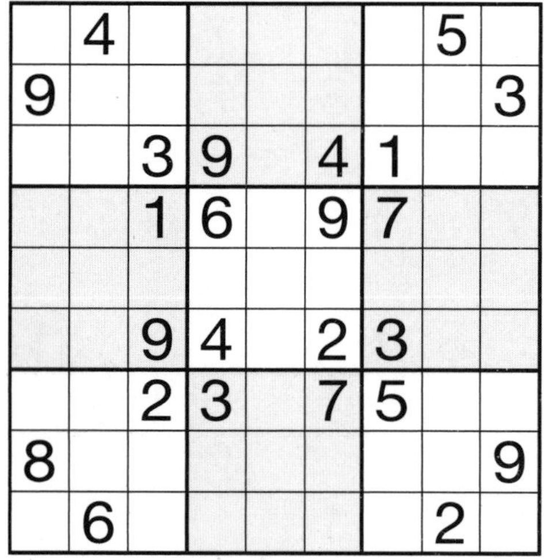

	4						5	
9								3
		3	9		4	1		
		1	6		9	7		
		9	4		2	3		
		2	3		7	5		
8								9
	6						2	

PUZZLE / 303 Time:_______

	4	9					5	
2				5			3	
1		7				6		4
				2			9	
			3		6			
	7			8				
7		4				5		3
	3			6				2
	9					4	7	

PUZZLE / 304 Time:_______

		5	1				3	
								6
6	8				4	9		
2	9					4		
		3					5	9
		1	3				6	5
4								
	6				9	8		

PUZZLE / 305 Time:_______

			2					3
		7				4		
	5			3			1	
2			8		4			
		6		9		8		
			3		2			6
	1			5			6	
		2				7		
4					1			

PUZZLE / 306 Time:_______

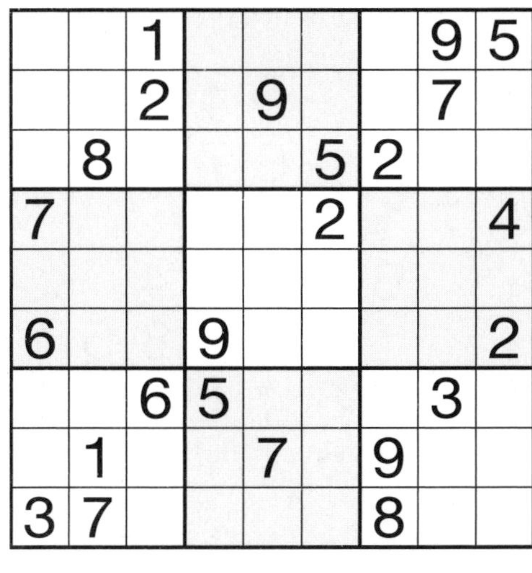

		1					9	5
		2		9			7	
	8				5	2		
7					2			4
6			9					2
		6	5				3	
	1			7		9		
3	7					8		

PUZZLE / 307 Time:_______

8				7			3	
					5	6		
		4			3	2		
				5			7	
1			3		6			8
	2			4				
		6	1			4		
		5	8					
	7			2				3

PUZZLE / 308 Time:_______

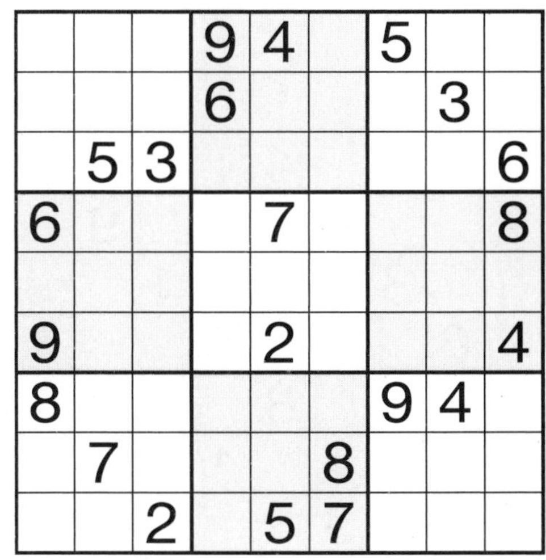

			9	4		5		
			6				3	
	5	3						6
6				7				8
9				2				4
8						9	4	
	7				8			
		2		5	7			

PUZZLE / 309 Time:_______

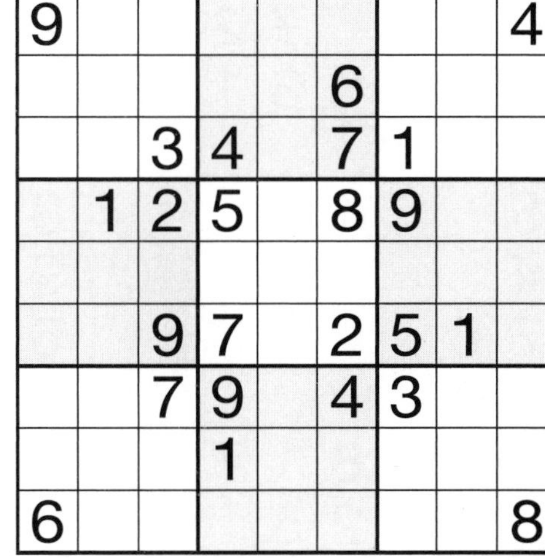

9								4
					6			
		3	4		7	1		
	1	2	5		8	9		
		9	7		2	5	1	
		7	9		4	3		
			1					
6								8

PUZZLE / 310 Time:_______

8	6							
3				2				
			3	8				
		9	4					
	4	5				6	8	
					6	5		
				5	4			
				7				1
							9	3

PUZZLE / 311 Time:_______

			1			8		
	7			2			3	
		4			7			6
2			5			1		
	8						9	
		3			4			8
7			3			2		
	9			1			4	
		5			6			

PUZZLE / 312 Time:_______

1			6			2		
	2			4				
		3			8			4
7						1		
	6			5			2	
		4						8
6			1			7		
				6			8	
		5			4			9

PUZZLE / 313 Time:_______

						2	3	4
9					1			
6				8	7			
	7	1						
		6				4		
						8	5	
			8	4				6
			5					1
8	5	9						

PUZZLE / 314 Time:_______

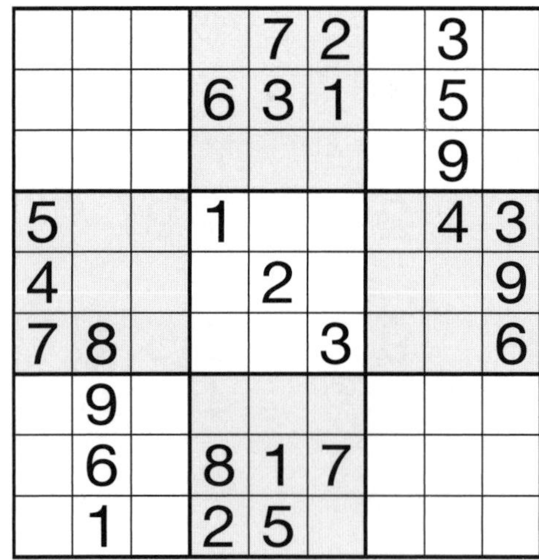

				7	2		3	
			6	3	1		5	
							9	
5			1				4	3
4				2				9
7	8				3			6
	9							
	6		8	1	7			
	1		2	5				

PUZZLE / 315 Time:_______

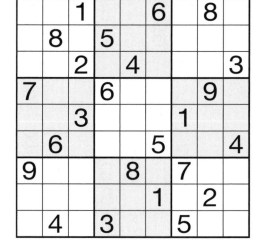

		1			6		8	
	8		5					
		2		4				3
7			6				9	
		3				1		
	6				5			4
9				8		7		
					1		2	
	4		3			5		

PUZZLE / 316 Time:_______

7								9
		8	9				1	
	1		4					
	4		2					
	3	5				9	7	
					6		2	
					7		5	
	9				8	6		
8								4

PUZZLE / 317 Time:_______

	3	8	9				5	
		1	2			4	7	
	9		1		3	8	2	
	1	7	5		6		4	
	5	3			8	6		
	8				7	3	1	

PUZZLE / 318 Time:_______

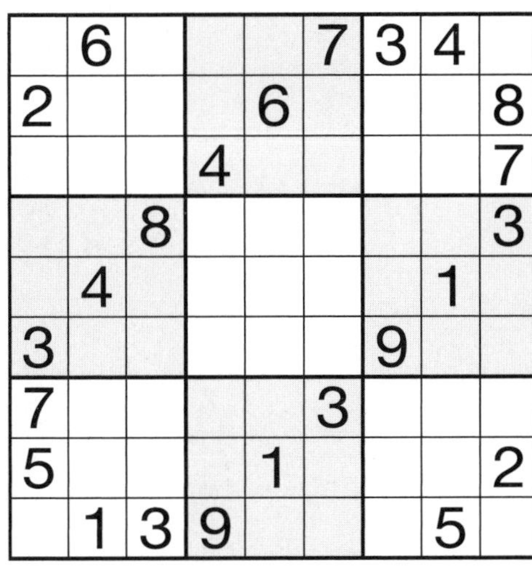

	6				7	3	4	
2				6				8
			4					7
		8						3
	4						1	
3						9		
7					3			
5				1				2
	1	3	9				5	

PUZZLE / 319 Time:_______

3			4	6				
						2	7	
						4	8	
9				1				
4			6		2			1
				8				9
	5	7						
	8	9						
				5	6			2

PUZZLE / 320 Time:_______

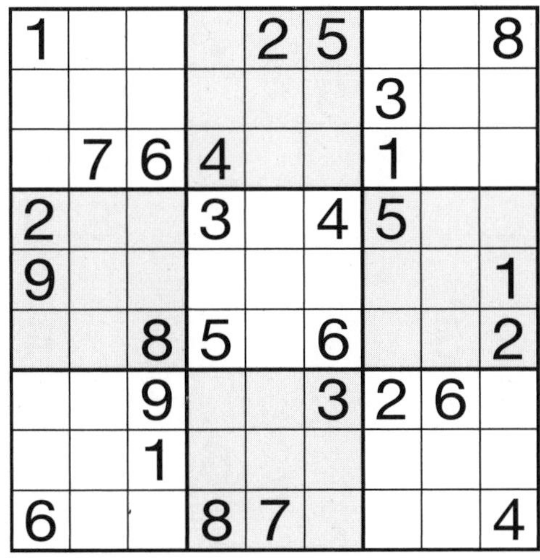

1				2	5			8
						3		
	7	6	4			1		
2			3		4	5		
9								1
		8	5		6			2
		9			3	2	6	
		1						
6			8	7				4

PUZZLE / 321 Time:_______

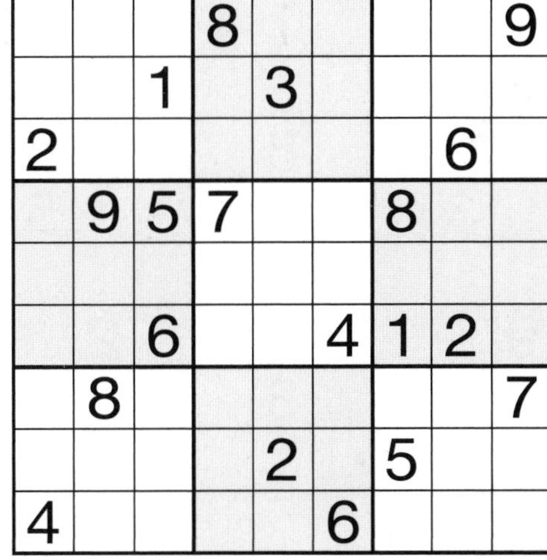

			8					9
		1		3				
2							6	
	9	5	7			8		
		6			4	1	2	
	8							7
				2		5		
4					6			

PUZZLE / 322 Time:_______

	1		2		3		4	
4		5		6		7		9
5								6
			8		9			
9								3
6		4		3		1		2
	2		4		7		8	

PUZZLE / 323 Time:_______

		3					2	6
	8				5			
		4		7				1
					4		7	
1								2
	9		6					
9				1		6		
			3				4	
4	5					9		

PUZZLE / 324 Time:_______

			5				6	
1	9			8			7	
		2		6		3		
								5
	8	7				2	4	
5								
		8		9		6		
	6			2			5	4
	1				3			

PUZZLE / 325 Time:_______

	5	9	3					
		4	1					7
			2				8	4
						4	5	3
7	6	2						
3	2				7			
4					5	8		
					2	6	3	

PUZZLE / 326 Time:_______

		5			1	2		
2							3	
	9			8				4
	3		6					5
				5				
9					7		2	
8				3			9	
	7							6
		6	5			8		

PUZZLE / 327 Time:_______

					7	2		
			9	5				
	1	8					4	5
6					4		8	9
2	5		1					6
9	7					8	3	
				3	6			
		4	2					

PUZZLE / 328 Time:_______

					8	4		
	6			9			1	
		5		7		8		2
			4					3
	3	7				9	4	
9					6			
3		9		8		5		
	7			2			8	
		1	6					

PUZZLE / 329 Time:_______

			8		1			
		9				2		
	4			5			3	
8				7				4
		2	4		3	7		
5				2				6
	3			9			5	
		7				1		
			2		6			

PUZZLE / 330 Time:_______

PUZZLE / 331 Time:_______

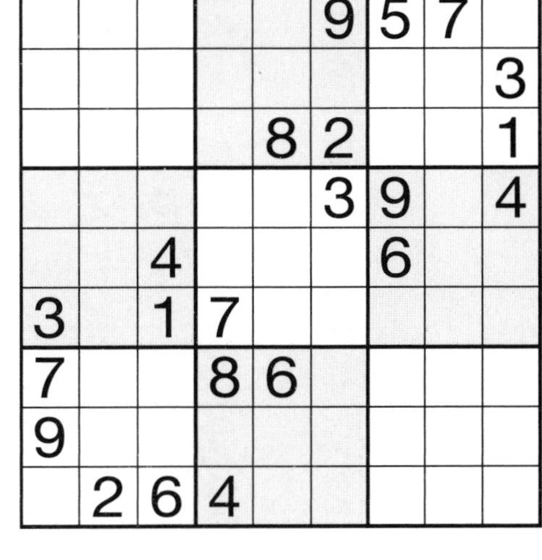

PUZZLE / 332 Time:_______

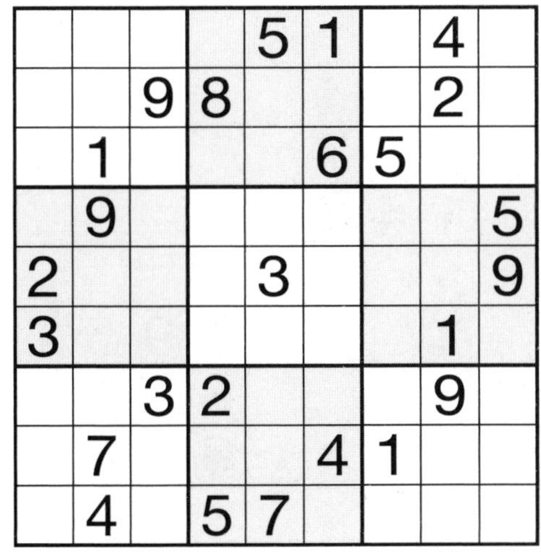

PUZZLE / 333 Time:_______

1				3				
	8		1		2			
4		6				7		
			2		1			5
				6				
3			4		8			
		9				6		1
			5		3		4	
				7				2

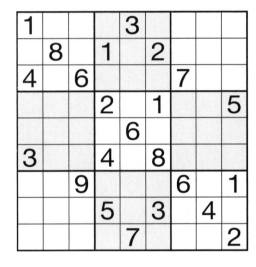

PUZZLE / 334 Time:_______

			7			5	6	
3	2		9					
				5		9		8
2					7		3	
		4				2		
	9		1					5
7		1		8				
					5		8	6
	8	2			1			

PUZZLE / 335 Time:_______

				7	5			
		4				8		
	3		1				6	7
6		5						
	8						1	
						3		4
5	2				6		9	
		9				7		
			3	4				

PUZZLE / 336 Time:_______

MEDIUM PUZZLES

3					2		9	
5			1					
					7	2	4	
					9	5	6	
	1	7	8					
	3	2	4					
					5			1
	6		2					3

PUZZLE / 337 Time:_______

				8		6		
		1	4				9	
	3							7
	6		7		9			
2								4
			1		5		8	
7							5	
	9				2	3		
		8		6				

PUZZLE / 338 Time:_______

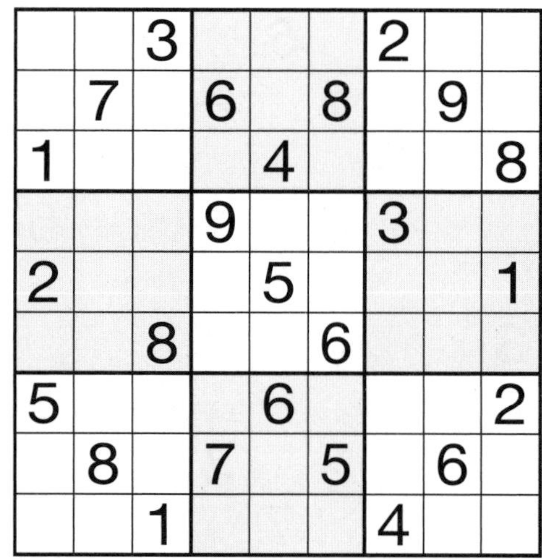

		3				2		
	7		6		8		9	
1				4				8
			9			3		
2				5				1
		8			6			
5				6				2
	8		7		5		6	
		1				4		

PUZZLE / 339 Time:_______

						6	4	
	7	3	4					8
	5		7					3
	1	4	2					
					7	9	5	
9					3		1	
1					8	2	6	
	8	2						

PUZZLE / 340 Time:_______

			3	4				
		8	1			7		
	6					2	8	
8	2							
4				5				8
							3	6
	5	4					9	
		2			9	1		
				2	7			

PUZZLE / 341 Time:_______

	9			6	4	7	8	
			3		7		5	
		6			1	9	4	
	3						1	
	4	8	2			5		
	2		8		5			
	5	1	7	3			6	

PUZZLE / 342 Time:_______

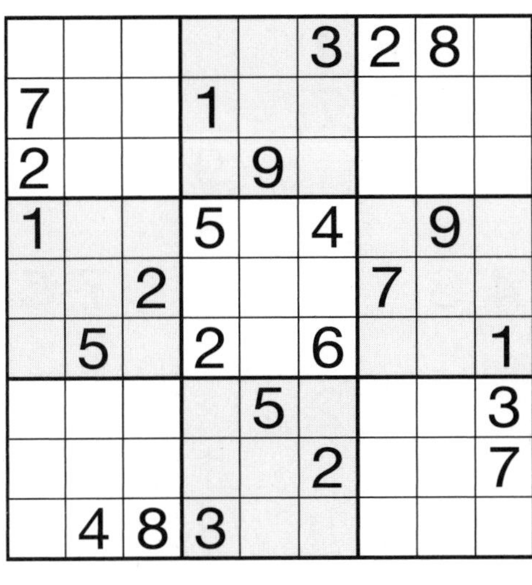

					3	2	8	
7			1					
2				9				
1			5		4		9	
		2				7		
	5		2		6			1
				5				3
					2			7
	4	8	3					

PUZZLE / 343 Time:_______

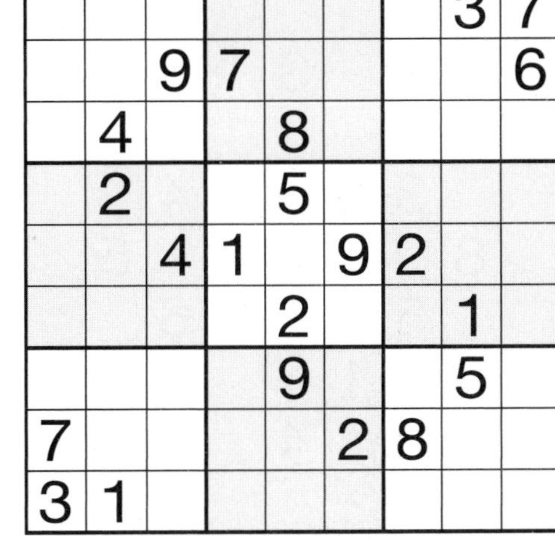

							3	7
		9	7					6
	4			8				
	2			5				
		4	1		9	2		
				2			1	
				9			5	
7					2	8		
3	1							

PUZZLE / 344 Time:_______

					1	8	4	
6	7						1	
4				6				
3			6		2			
		8				6		
			5		3			7
				2				3
	4						8	1
	1	6	9					

PUZZLE / 345 Time:_______

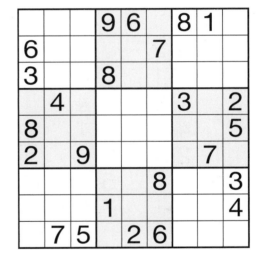

			9	6		8	1	
6					7			
3			8					
	4					3		2
8								5
2		9					7	
					8			3
			1					4
	7	5		2	6			

PUZZLE / 346 Time:_______

8				5				
	6	1	4				9	
						7		3
6			1					
	5	7				2	4	
					3			8
2		5						
	8				7	1	2	
				2				6

PUZZLE / 347 Time:_______

				8	1			
		8	2	6				
	5	3						
	1							5
9	4						6	7
2							9	
						1	4	
				1	2	3		
			7	3				

PUZZLE / 348 Time:_______

8								2
		7		3		5		
	6				1		9	
		3	8			4		
	8			7			5	
		5			2	6		
	9		1				4	
		2		4		7		
1								3

PUZZLE / 349 Time:_______

		6	4					
		5	7					9
					9	1		
	9				8			
4	3						7	5
			5				2	
		1	2					
8					1	6		
					3	8		

PUZZLE / 350 Time:_______

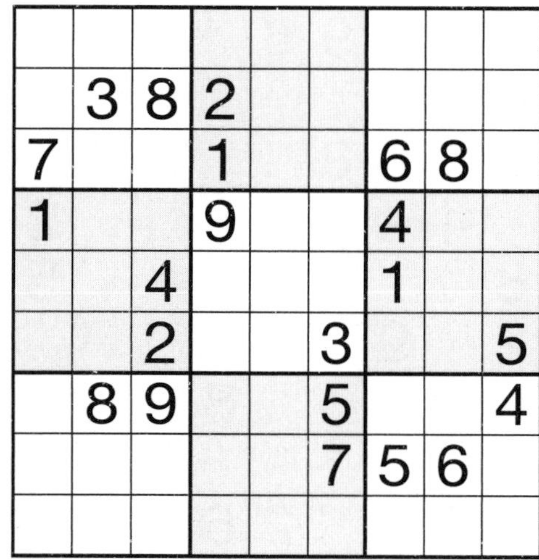

	3	8	2					
7			1			6	8	
1			9			4		
		4				1		
		2			3			5
	8	9			5			4
					7	5	6	

PUZZLE / 351 Time:_______

		7		8			1	4
3			9	1				
		3	7					
	8	4				6	7	
					6	5		
				4	9			2
6	5			3		7		

PUZZLE / 352 Time:_______

6	7						2	8
3								7
			5		9			
		8			7	5		
		3		4		1		
		2	9			6		
			8		1			
5								1
8	9						3	5

PUZZLE / 353 Time:_______

	4			2		8		
6					1			
				7		3		1
	9		6					
5		2				1		8
					3		4	
4		7		5				
			1					9
		1		3			2	

PUZZLE / 354 Time:_______

	7				8			
9		3				7		
	6		4				1	
		8		9				3
			8		1			
1				4		5		
	9				2		8	
		5				4		2
			3				9	

PUZZLE / 355 Time:_______

	5	8						
				6	1			
				5	7		9	2
							8	4
7	8						1	3
2	6							
6	2		3	4				
			5	8				
						5	4	

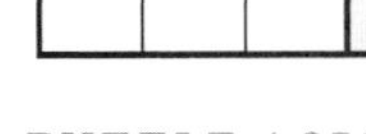

PUZZLE / 356 Time:_______

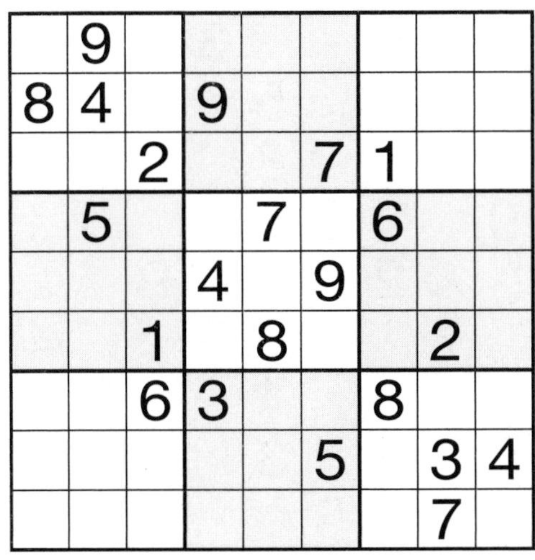

	9							
8	4		9					
		2			7	1		
	5			7		6		
			4		9			
		1		8			2	
		6	3			8		
					5		3	4
							7	

PUZZLE / 357 Time:_______

	2	8						
		7	6					
			4		5	9		
						1	7	
	4			5			8	
	9	3						
		6	1		8			
					2	5		
						3	6	

PUZZLE / 358 Time:_______

								5
					8			3
					3	9		7
			7		5		6	1
5			3		9			4
7	8		4		1			
4		7	5					
9			6					
3								

PUZZLE / 359 Time:_______

	9			3	5	1		7
	4							5
	7							4
			4	9	1			
6							5	
8							2	
3		6	7	2			8	

PUZZLE / 360 Time:_______

3					7	5		
		9	3	2				
	5							6
	2				6			5
		1				8		
8			9				4	
6							1	
				3	2	4		
		7	4					3

PUZZLE / 361 Time:_______

	3			8			7	
5					4	6		
		2	6					1
		8					6	
				7				
	9					5		
2					7	3		
		9	4					5
	4			1			8	

PUZZLE / 362 Time:_______

8				4				
3			6				4	5
		4					9	
		1				6	2	
			1		7			
	7	9				1		
	2					9		
6	5				1			8
				7				3

PUZZLE / 363 Time:_______

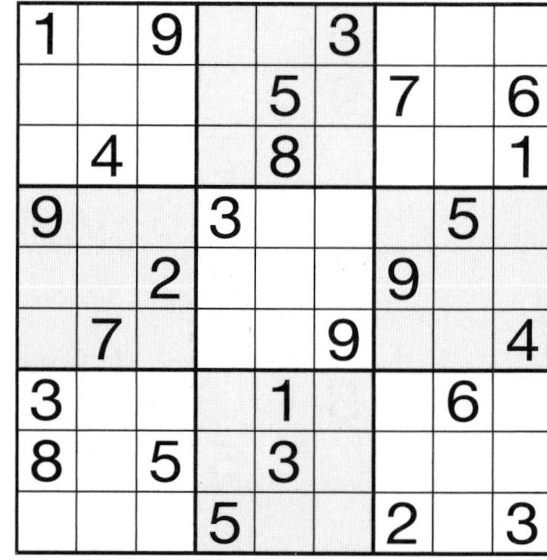

1		9			3			
				5		7		6
	4			8				1
9			3				5	
		2				9		
	7				9			4
3				1			6	
8		5		3				
			5			2		3

PUZZLE / 364 Time:_______

	5	4						1
6			9				2	
2			7			3		
	9	6			1			
				2				
			3			6	7	
		1			2			4
	2				9			5
3						8	9	

PUZZLE / 365 Time:_______

3					4	9		
			7					
			5				6	8
	2	6						
		8				4		
						3	9	
7	8				3			
					9			
		5	6					2

PUZZLE / 366 Time:_______

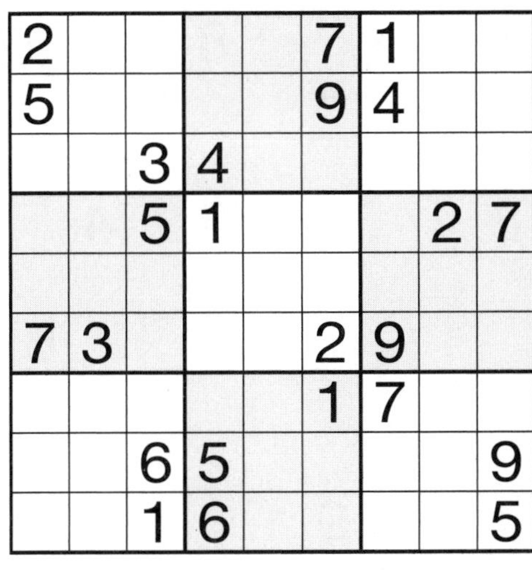

2					7	1		
5					9	4		
		3	4					
		5	1				2	7
7	3				2	9		
					1	7		
		6	5					9
		1	6					5

PUZZLE / 367 Time:_______

		3	5					
			2			9	4	
6							1	
5	4				7			
			9				6	3
	7							2
	9	6			1			
					8	5		

PUZZLE / 368 Time:_______

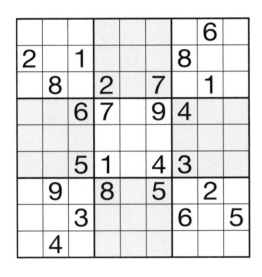

							6	
2		1				8		
	8		2		7		1	
		6	7		9	4		
		5	1		4	3		
	9		8		5		2	
		3				6		5
	4							

PUZZLE / 369 Time:_______

4		8	6					
		7	1					
1	2			3	4			
7	1					6		8
		9				5		
6		4					9	3
			5	2			3	1
					8	7		
					9	8		5

PUZZLE / 370 Time:_______

	4			8		7		
7	9			5			6	
			4					9
		3	7					
1	2						7	6
					1	8		
3					5			
	7			4			1	2
		6		3			8	

PUZZLE / 371 Time:_______

		8					6	
					5			2
4	9			7				
			6		3		8	
		2				1		
	7		4		9			
				8			3	5
1			3					
	6					9		

PUZZLE / 372 Time:_______

9							1	
	3			5				
			2			7	6	
		7	4					
8								9
					7	2		
	4	2			9			
				1			8	
	6							5

PUZZLE / 373 Time:_______

6					8			3
		7	6			2		
	5						7	
8			1		3		4	
				5				
	1		7		9			6
	7						5	
		3			2	9		
4			9					8

PUZZLE / 374 Time:_______

		3	4		6			
	2					7	8	
	1							9
2				4				1
			5		7			
4				6				5
5							4	
	6	7					3	
			8		1	2		

PUZZLE / 375 Time:_______

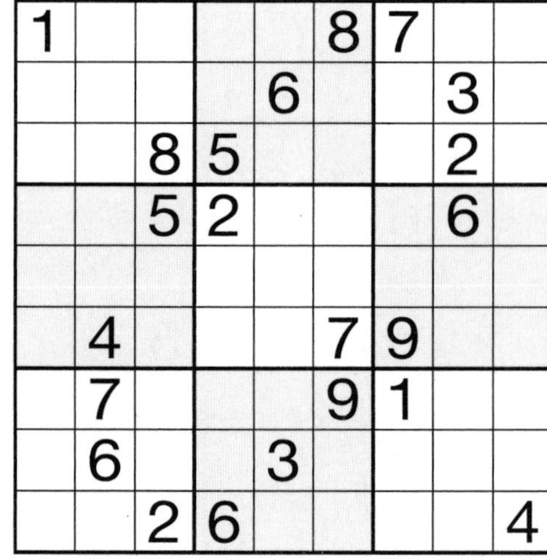

1					8	7		
				6			3	
		8	5				2	
		5	2				6	
	4				7	9		
	7				9	1		
	6			3				
		2	6					4

PUZZLE / 376 Time:_______

6				9				8
	3				2	7	4	
	2							
	6		5					
8								4
					7		2	
							3	
	7	6	3				1	
4				8				9

PUZZLE / 377 Time:_______

		3					5	
	2		4			8		6
1				5			7	
	8		6					
		7		9		5		
					4		6	
	5			3				7
6		4			2		8	
	7					9		

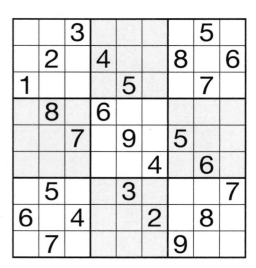

PUZZLE / 378 Time:_______

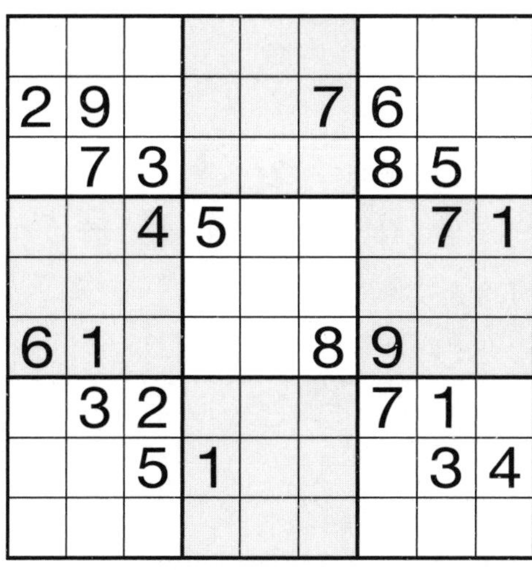

2	9				7	6		
	7	3				8	5	
		4	5				7	1
6	1				8	9		
	3	2				7	1	
		5	1				3	4

PUZZLE / 379 Time:_______

7				6				
	1	9					2	
			3		5			4
			8			7		
	2						8	
		3			1			
8			2		9			
	5					6	1	
				4				3

PUZZLE / 380 Time:_______

		1	3	6				
	6				1			
8						2		
4	7		6			1		
		3		7		8		
		8			9		7	5
		6						7
			8				9	
				1	2	4		

PUZZLE / 381 Time:_______

	1							
	9			1			7	4
		6	5			1		
						6		
	8						9	
		3						
		5			6	3		
2	7			4			8	
							1	

PUZZLE / 382 Time:_______

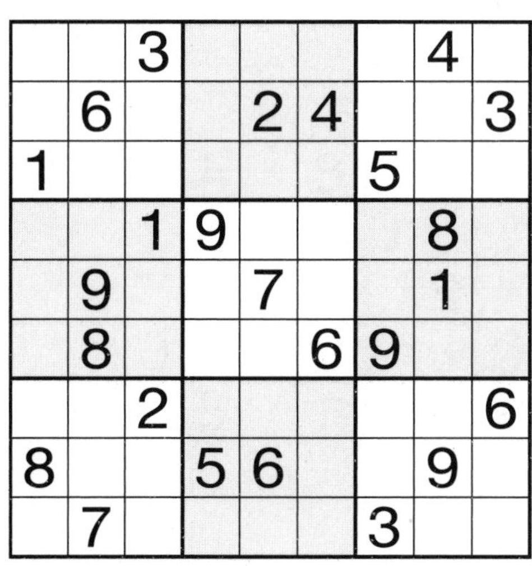

		3					4	
	6			2	4			3
1						5		
		1	9				8	
	9			7			1	
	8				6	9		
		2						6
8			5	6			9	
	7					3		

PUZZLE / 383 Time:_______

			4				2	
		7				9		
	6				5			1
4			2				7	
		1				3		
	9				3			8
2			9				6	
		5				8		
	4				7			

PUZZLE / 384 Time:_______

		8	6	5				2
					3		1	
					2		9	
					4	1	6	
		1				8		
	5	7	9					
	6		8					
	3		1					
9				4	7	5		

PUZZLE / 385 Time:_______

	1							
	4	6						
	2	7		9	3	8	4	
	7	4			1	6	8	
	5	2	8			4	7	
	8	9	5	3		7	6	
						5	3	
							2	

PUZZLE / 386 Time:_______

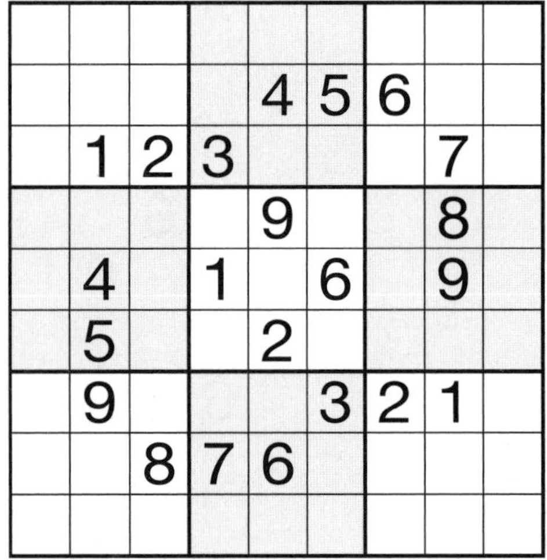

				4	5	6		
	1	2	3				7	
				9			8	
	4		1		6		9	
	5			2				
	9				3	2	1	
		8	7	6				

PUZZLE / 387 Time:_______

		7	3					
		8	5					
9						2	1	
2						4	8	
				2				
	6	1						5
	1	5						3
					6	7		
					4	9		

PUZZLE / 388 Time:_______

		4			9			
	6		1			5		
3				2			4	
	9				8			7
		6				3		
2			5				1	
	4			1				8
		7			6		9	
			3			2		

PUZZLE / 389 Time:_______

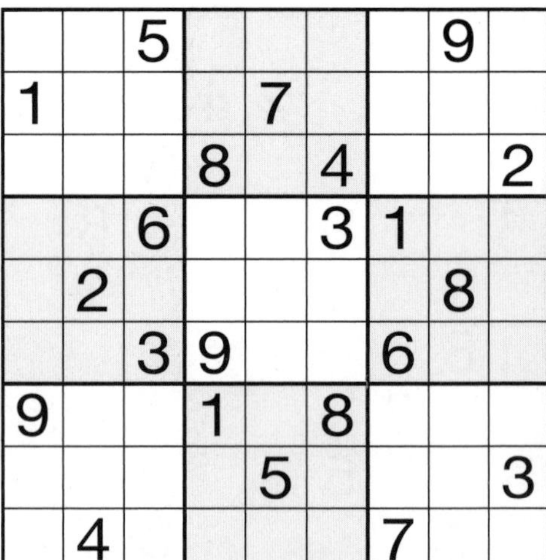

		5					9	
1				7				
			8		4			2
		6			3	1		
	2						8	
		3	9			6		
9			1		8			
				5				3
	4					7		

PUZZLE / 390 Time:_______

	8	4						
2			5			6	1	
	7				3			9
		1		4			7	
	6			3		1		
5			6				2	
	4	8			7			6
						8	9	

PUZZLE / 391 Time:_______

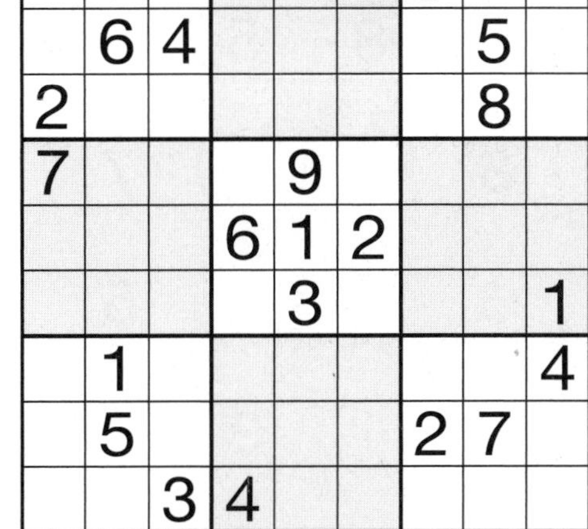

					8	9		
	6	4					5	
2							8	
7				9				
			6	1	2			
				3				1
	1							4
	5					2	7	
		3	4					

PUZZLE / 392 Time:_______

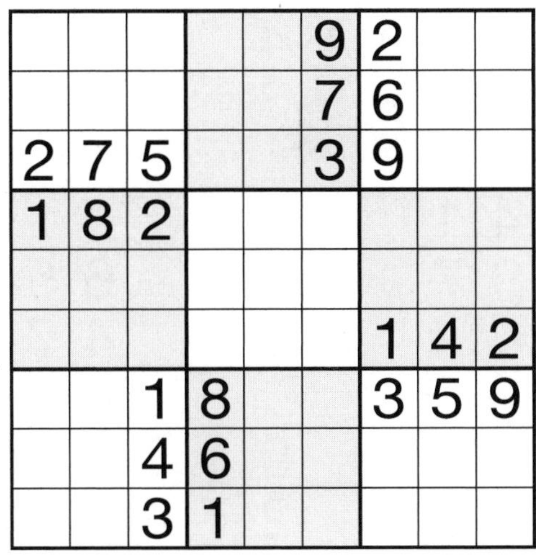

					9	2		
					7	6		
2	7	5			3	9		
1	8	2						
						1	4	2
		1	8			3	5	9
		4	6					
		3	1					

PUZZLE / 393 Time:_______

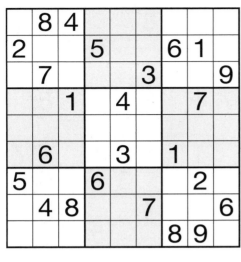

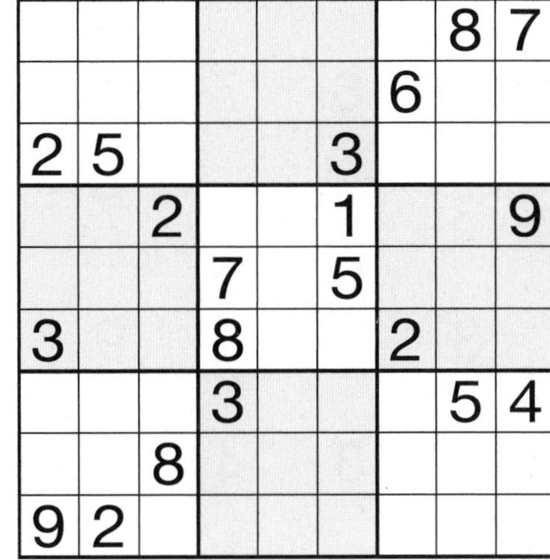

							8	7
						6		
2	5				3			
		2			1			9
			7		5			
3			8			2		
			3				5	4
		8						
9	2							

PUZZLE / 394 Time:_______

			8				2	1
		1		2				3
	4	5			9			
5						7		2
	7						3	
4		6						9
			4			8	5	
9				6		2		
7	8				1			

PUZZLE / 395 Time:_______

		3	4	5	6			
	2					7		
	1					8		
		6	1	4	9			
			3	6	7	2		
		4					3	
		7					8	
			8	1	3	9		

PUZZLE / 396 Time:_______

	2						3	
1			8		5			4
		5				1		
	8			1			7	
			4		2			
	6			3			5	
		4				2		
8			1		3			5
	7						6	

PUZZLE / 397 Time:_______

		9	8					1
	8				6	4		
2				4			3	
7			3		4		5	
		5				9		
	4		5		1			7
	6			3				5
		8	7				2	
1					5	3		

PUZZLE / 398 Time:_______

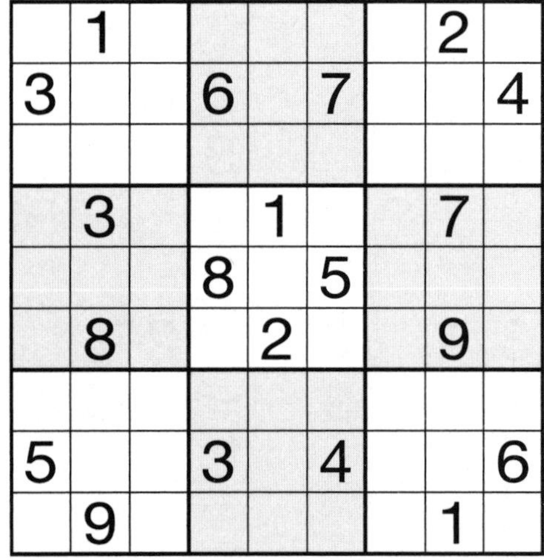

	1						2	
3			6		7			4
	3			1			7	
			8		5			
	8			2			9	
5			3		4			6
	9						1	

PUZZLE / 399 Time:_______

		8	1	4				
		2	9	3				
6	5							
4	1							
9	7						6	5
							4	7
							8	9
				9	1	3		
				2	7	4		

PUZZLE / 400 Time:_______

	4				1	3		9
					3			
	6	7						
		2	5				7	4
6	3				4	8		
						1	5	
			8					
9		4	2				6	

PUZZLE / 401 Time:_______

		3	2					
		8	6					9
		5	8				7	2
	1	9				4	6	
3	7				5	1		
4					1	7		
					4	5		

PUZZLE / 402 Time:_______

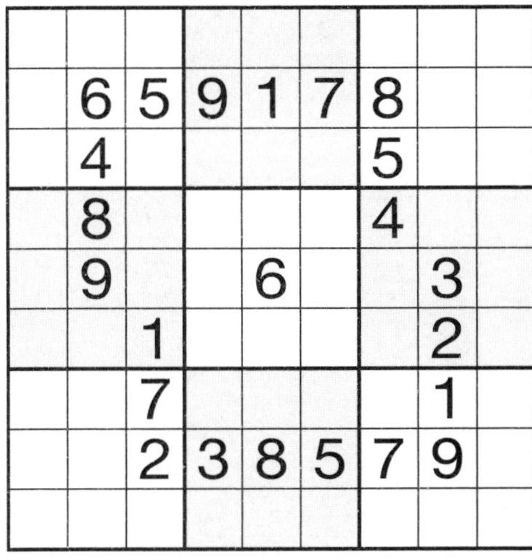

PUZZLE / 403 Time:_______

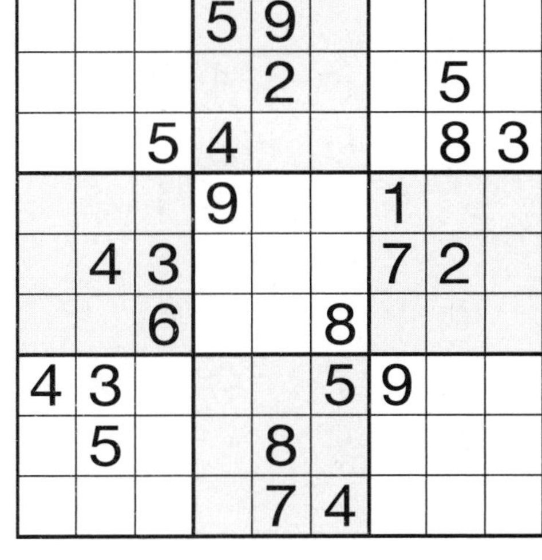

PUZZLE / 404 Time:_______

			6	5	4			
		1			8	9		
	5					7	4	
6							2	7
8	9							6
	4	2					1	
		7	4			3		
			2	9	6			

PUZZLE / 405 Time:_______

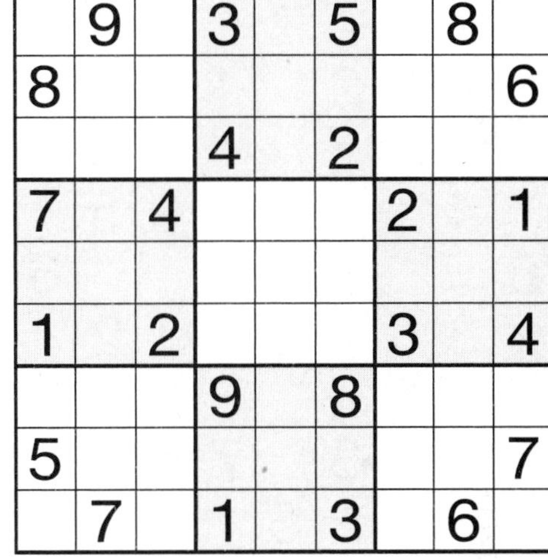

PUZZLE / 406 Time:_______

	8	4	3					
9			1				7	
5			6					
7	6	2						
						3	4	9
					2			5
	3				4			1
					8	9	6	

PUZZLE / 407 Time:_______

			7	8		2		9
	4	5	6					
2	3				9			
1								2
			2				6	5
					3	4	5	
3		8		4	2			

PUZZLE / 408 Time:_______

		6			4	2	1	
	7		6		2		9	
		5			3	1	4	
	9	7	8			5		
	4		7		9		2	
	8	3	5			6		

PUZZLE / 409 Time:_______

5			2					
		4			9			1
								3
						2	8	
		6		4		5		
	3	5						
7								
2			6			7		
					8			9

PUZZLE / 410 Time:_______

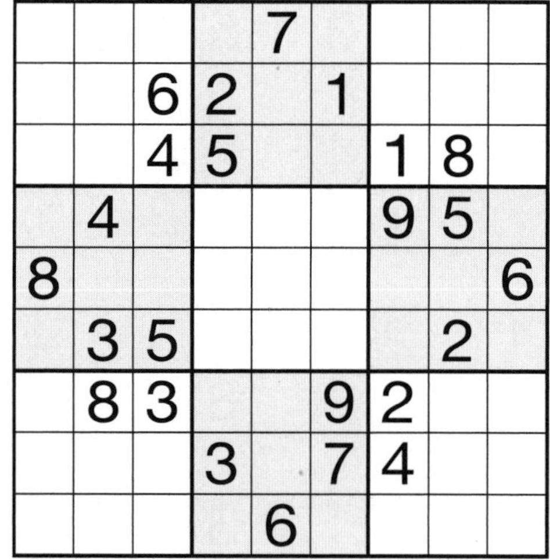

				7				
		6	2		1			
		4	5			1	8	
	4					9	5	
8								6
	3	5					2	
	8	3			9	2		
			3		7	4		
				6				

PUZZLE / 411 Time:_______

		1				3		
	9		7		5		8	
		7		1		2		
			6		4			
		6		8		1		
	4		5		9		6	
		3				8		

PUZZLE / 412 Time:_______

					6	2		
1	7							
					3	5	8	
4	6	3						
						7	1	2
	2	7	1					
							3	4
		8	5					

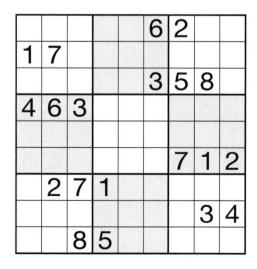

PUZZLE / 413 Time:_______

	7		5		4		1	
4				3				2
						7		
5					8			9
	2						3	
3			6					8
		8						
9				8				6
	5		7		2		8	

PUZZLE / 414 Time:_______

	2	7	6					3
3					9			
8				4		5		
6					2		4	
		2				8		
	4		7					1
		3		1				7
			8					9
9					6	2	8	

PUZZLE / 415 Time:_______

						2		
	8				9		1	
3		9		4		5		
	7			2				
		8	5		1	3		
				6			8	
		5		3		4		6
	9		2				7	
		1						

PUZZLE / 416 Time:_______

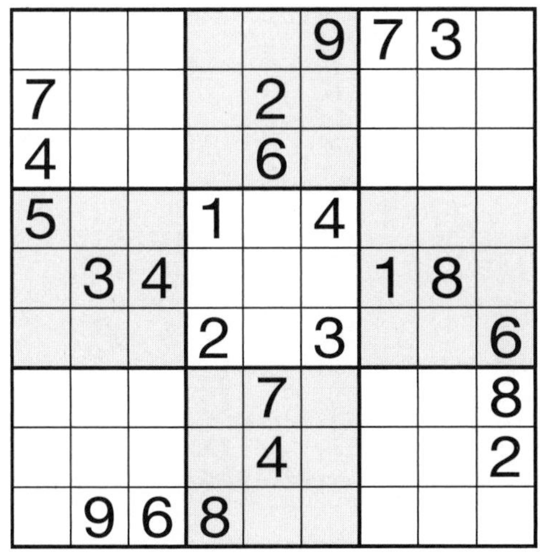

					9	7	3	
7				2				
4				6				
5			1		4			
	3	4				1	8	
			2		3			6
				7				8
				4				2
	9	6	8					

PUZZLE / 417 Time:_______

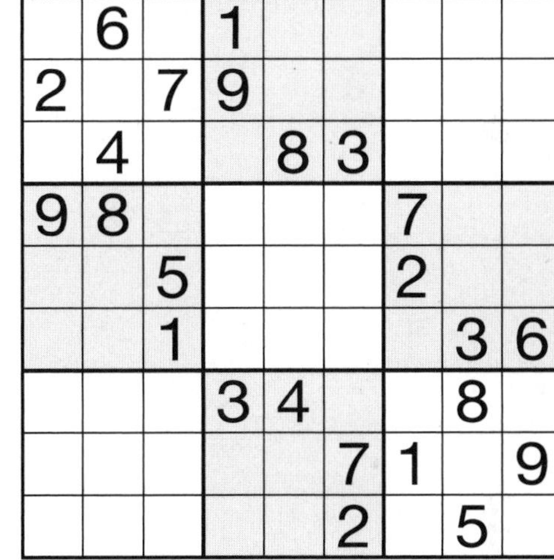

	6		1					
2		7	9					
	4			8	3			
9	8					7		
		5				2		
		1					3	6
			3	4			8	
					7	1		9
					2		5	

PUZZLE / 418 Time:_______

7				5		9		
			8				2	
		5			4	7		3
	6				1	2		
2								4
		1	6				7	
1		4	5			8		
	3				6			
		9		8				5

PUZZLE / 419 Time:_______

		2				6		
	5				7			
1		3		5		7		9
	2		4		6		8	
	6		8		1		3	
5		7		9		2		4
			1				5	
		8				1		

PUZZLE / 420 Time:_______

						6	8	
					3			4
				6	8			2
			6			7	1	
		4				5		
	5	3			2			
4			7	1				
1			4					
	3	9						

PUZZLE / 421 Time:_______

4					5	8	7	
	9			6				3
		2	1					
						3		5
	3						4	
8		9						
					6	1		
7				8			6	
	6	5	2					9

PUZZLE / 422 Time:_______

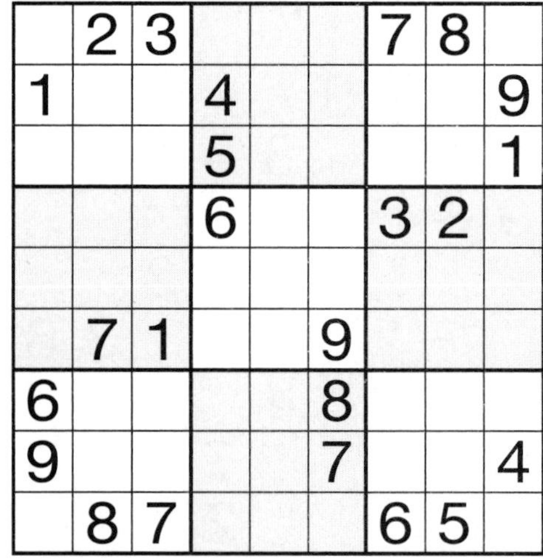

	2	3				7	8	
1			4					9
			5					1
			6			3	2	
	7	1			9			
6					8			
9					7			4
	8	7				6	5	

PUZZLE / 423 Time:_______

							2	
	9	4	5					3
	7		1					
	5	1	7					
					2	6	8	
					6		9	
2					3	8	4	
	1							

PUZZLE / 424 Time:_______

	2		8				3	
			5	4				
4		1				2		
		3	9				6	5
	6						1	
7	8				5	4		
		4				3		2
				7	8			
	1				6		4	

PUZZLE / 425 Time:_______

				2	1			
			3					
		4				7	9	3
	5				6			1
6				7				9
7			8				2	
8	9	3				5		
					3			
			6	1				

PUZZLE / 426 Time:_______

	7						4	
6								3
			2	8	9			
		8		1		9		
		2	4		8	5		
		3		9		4		
			3	6	1			
4								2
	9						7	

PUZZLE / 427 Time:_______

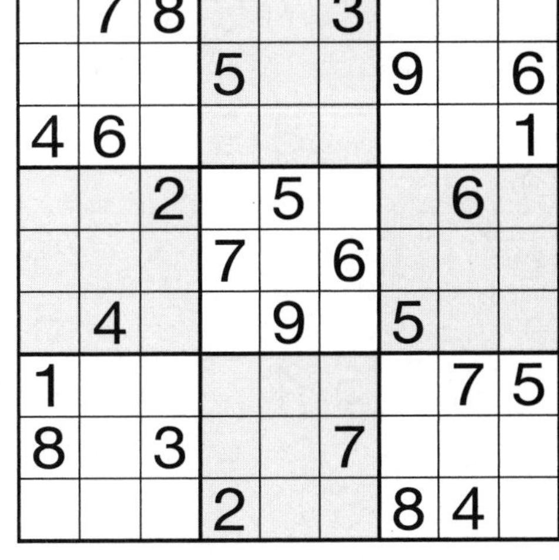

	7	8			3			
			5			9		6
4	6							1
		2		5			6	
			7		6			
	4			9		5		
1							7	5
8		3			7			
			2			8	4	

PUZZLE / 428 Time:_______

				9				
	7	4			6		5	
	8		3			6		
		1	5				7	
2								9
	6				7	8		
		9			4		1	
	5		8			3	6	
				2				

PUZZLE / 429 Time:_______

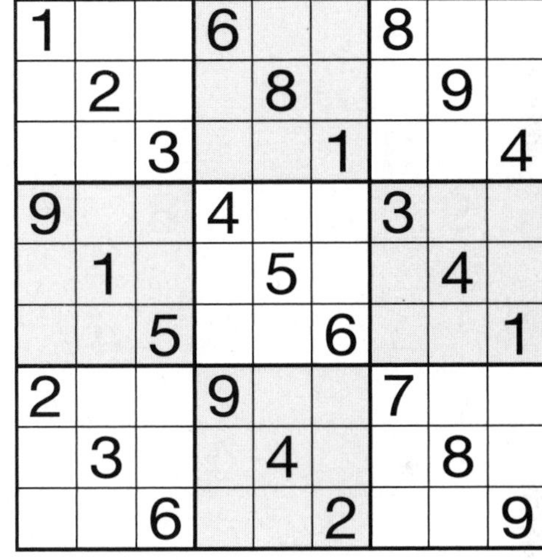

1			6			8		
	2			8			9	
		3			1			4
9			4			3		
	1			5			4	
		5			6			1
2			9			7		
	3			4			8	
		6			2			9

PUZZLE / 430 Time:_______

				4				
9								2
		2	1		7	3		
	3			5			4	
4			2		9			6
	5			8			1	
		6	7		8	9		
7								5
				3				

PUZZLE / 431 Time:_______

3	4				6			
1		5		2			9	
	8		3					
		4						1
	3			5			8	
5						7		
					8		1	
	6			9		5		2
			7				4	8

PUZZLE / 432 Time:_______

			7	3				
	4	3					9	
				8	9		5	
1		8						
6		4				2		5
						9		6
	1		5	4				
	2					1	3	
			6	3				

PUZZLE / 433 Time:_______

				5			1	
	2	7	4					9
	8				9	3		
	5					8		
4				6				1
		8					2	
		1	2				4	
8					3	5	7	
	6			7				

PUZZLE / 434 Time:_______

1					9			
	2		7			4		3
		3					6	
	9		4			8		5
3		1			6		4	
	5					7		
6		2			4		8	
			5					9

PUZZLE / 435 Time:_______

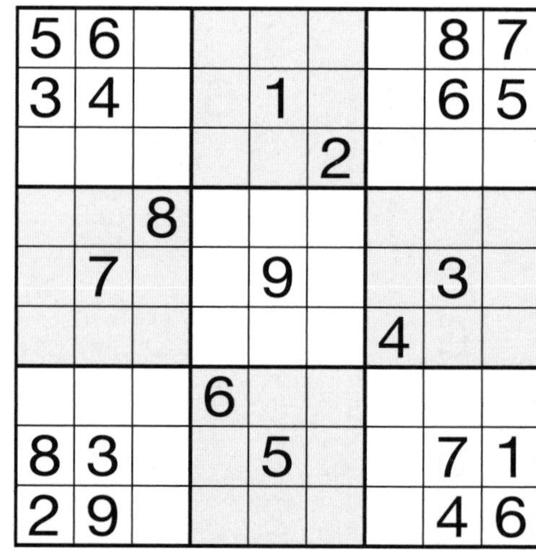

5	6						8	7
3	4			1			6	5
					2			
		8						
	7			9			3	
						4		
			6					
8	3			5			7	1
2	9						4	6

PUZZLE / 436 Time:_______

	2	7	4		3		5	
	6		2			1		
	8	3	9		2		4	
	7		6		4	9	8	
		5			8		1	
	4		7		5	2	9	

PUZZLE / 437 Time:_______

			5	2	3			
	6						8	
		7				9		
5			6		8			2
1								3
7			2		1			6
		9				5		
	3						7	
			4	8	6			

PUZZLE / 438 Time:_______

1	2				7	8		
		3		6				
		4		5				1
8					4		5	
	9						4	
	1		5					3
2				4		6		
				3		7		
		1	2				8	9

PUZZLE / 439 Time:_______

			5					
	4		7			1	6	
	7	9	1			8		
						9	1	2
5	8	7						
		3			5	4	7	
	6	8			1		2	
					6			

PUZZLE / 440 Time:_______

		6				9		
			9				8	
			8	7			4	2
			4				9	
		3				7		
	6				1			
8	7			6	5			
	4				2			
		9				3		

PUZZLE / 441 Time:_______

	1	6				7		
2				8		3		
5							4	6
			6		5			
	9						1	
			3		9			
7	3							8
		4		9				1
		9				5	2	

PUZZLE / 442 Time:_______

	2	3						4
1				6		9		
				5		8		
	5	6			7			
4								5
			3			7	1	
		2		9				
		5		8				3
7						4	8	

PUZZLE / 443 Time:_______

		7	6		3		9	
4				7				2
		1						7
	6		5		9			8
	4						2	
9			4		8		6	
1						2		
5				9				4
	8		3		6	5		

PUZZLE / 444 Time:_______

						9		
			1	8			2	
		4			3			8
	8				9			3
3				4				2
7			8				6	
6			5			7		
	3			7	8			
		5						

PUZZLE / 445 Time:_______

		3	1				6	
	8			9				5
				2				7
			2		4			3
		2				8		
1			9		7			
9				5				
7				3			8	
	6				1	9		

PUZZLE / 446 Time:_______

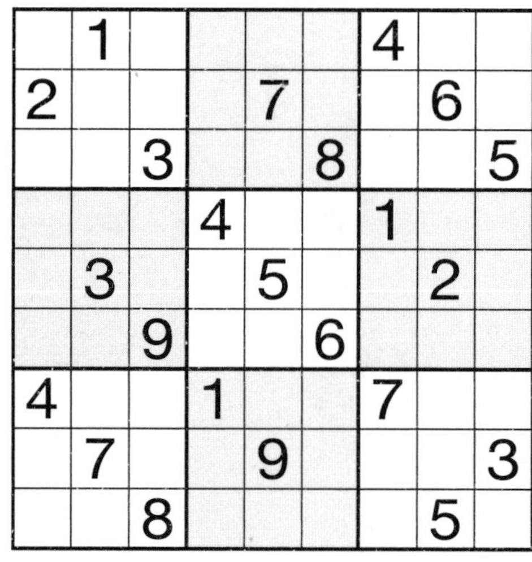

	1					4		
2				7			6	
		3			8			5
			4			1		
	3			5			2	
		9			6			
4			1			7		
	7			9				3
		8					5	

PUZZLE / 447 Time:_______

				9				7
	3				4			
8						5		
		7				2		
	4		5		6		9	
		1				6		
		5						4
			8				3	
6				2				

PUZZLE / 448 Time:_______

		3	6					
	6	2	1					
5	9	8	4					
9	8	7						
						6	7	3
					8	4	9	6
					7	5	1	
					2	7		

PUZZLE / 449 Time:_______

				1				
		6	3		9	5		
	8						2	
	9			3			4	
4			9		2			3
	2			4			7	
	7						3	
		1	6		5	9		
				8				

PUZZLE / 450 Time:_______

		2	3				5	
	1			4				
					5	6		
		3	2				7	
	4			3			8	
	5				1	9		
		6	7					
				8			2	
	8				9	1		

PUZZLE / 451 Time:_______

	4		6		3		1	
2	7			8			6	3
6								8
	1						2	
8								9
7	9			5			3	2
	3		7		1		5	

PUZZLE / 452 Time:_______

	1	6			7	2		
								3
8			1	2				6
6						3		
		8				4		
		7						2
1				6	5			8
4								
		3	7			1	5	

PUZZLE / 453 Time:_______

		4			8	9		
	9			1			8	
7			4					2
		3			9			
		6				1		
			7			3		
6					5			7
	8			6			4	
		1	3			5		

PUZZLE / 454 Time:_______

3				1	6			
	8				5	1		
		9				6	3	
			2				7	5
6	7				4			
	3	2				8		
		4	9				1	
			1	5				3

PUZZLE / 455 Time:_______

					8	4	3	
		1	4		9	5	7	
		2	5					
		3	6					
					4	7		
					5	8		
	7	5	2		6	9		
	4	9	3					

PUZZLE / 456 Time:_______

1	2	3				5	4	
			4					6
			5					1
			6				8	
		7				3		
	8				7			
9					3			
7					1			
	1	4				9	6	2

PUZZLE / 457 Time:_______

		9						1
	6	4						5
				2	3			
8			7					
	3						9	
					5			6
			9	7				
1						8	3	
5						2		

PUZZLE / 458 Time:_______

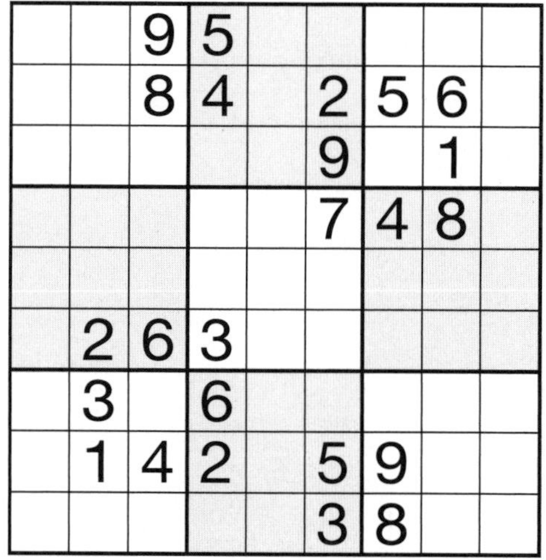

		9	5					
		8	4		2	5	6	
					9		1	
					7	4	8	
	2	6	3					
	3		6					
	1	4	2		5	9		
					3	8		

PUZZLE / 459 Time:_______

	9			6			1	
4								3
			8		7			
		7	6		4	5		
5								1
		8	9		1	2		
			2		5			
3								6
	1			8			7	

PUZZLE / 460 Time:_______

			6			9		
		7			4		5	
	3			8				1
1						5		
	6						4	
		8						2
8				2			7	
	4		3			6		
		2			1			

PUZZLE / 461 Time:_______

				4				1
	4	9	8				2	
	1		5			3		
	3	5						
8				5				6
						5	7	
		7			9		5	
	8				2	4	3	
9				1				

PUZZLE / 462 Time:_______

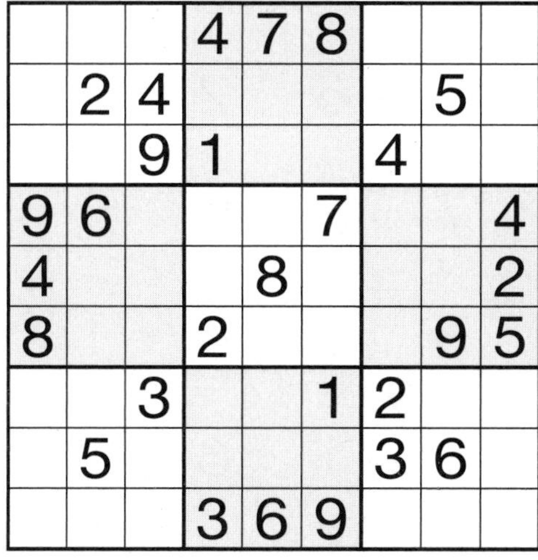

			4	7	8			
	2	4					5	
		9	1			4		
9	6				7			4
4				8				2
8			2				9	5
		3			1	2		
	5					3	6	
			3	6	9			

PUZZLE / 463 Time:_______

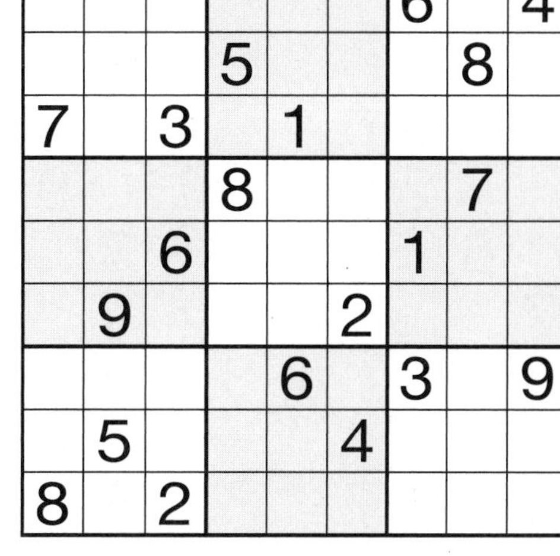

						6		4
			5				8	
7		3		1				
			8				7	
		6				1		
	9				2			
				6		3		9
	5				4			
8		2						

PUZZLE / 464 Time:_______

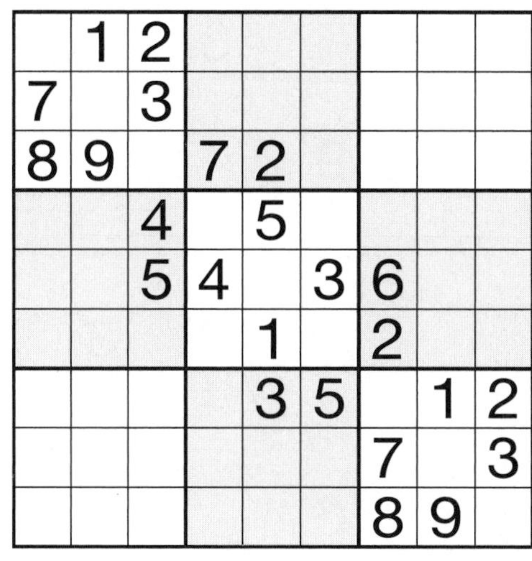

	1	2						
7		3						
8	9		7	2				
		4		5				
		5	4		3	6		
				1		2		
				3	5		1	2
						7		3
						8	9	

PUZZLE / 465 Time:_______

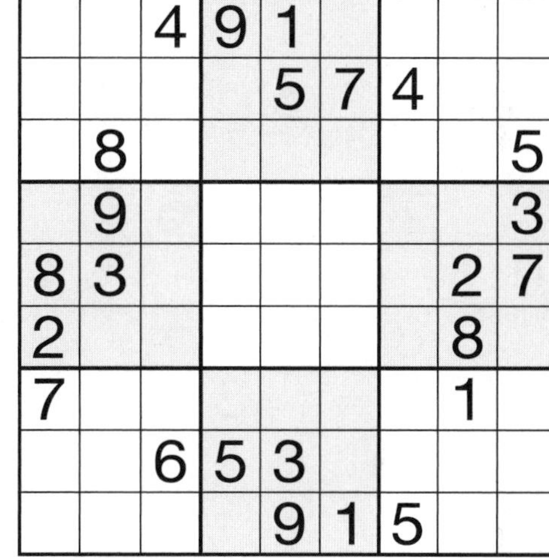

		4	9	1				
				5	7	4		
	8							5
	9							3
8	3						2	7
2							8	
7							1	
		6	5	3				
				9	1	5		

PUZZLE / 466 Time:_______

			5		7			
	1	2				3	4	
	8						1	
9				6				1
			3		8			
7				2				6
	3						9	
	5	6				7	8	
			8		4			

PUZZLE / 467 Time:_______

	1	8	3					
3				1	9			
	7	6	5			2		
							5	
		3		7		8		
	9							
		2			6	3	4	
			7	9				5
					8	6	7	

PUZZLE / 468 Time:_______

					9	7		
		5		3				
	4	8	6					2
		2						9
	6						3	
7						4		
3					8	1	5	
				4		6		
		9	7					

PUZZLE / 469 Time:_______

		9	6		2	8		
	8	1				3	7	
	7		3		9		5	
	3		5		4		1	
	6	7				4	3	
		2	1		6	7		

PUZZLE / 470 Time:_______

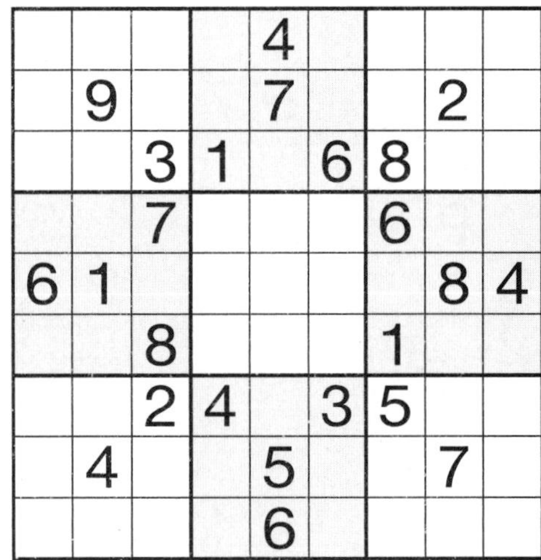

				4				
	9			7			2	
		3	1		6	8		
		7				6		
6	1						8	4
		8				1		
		2	4		3	5		
	4			5			7	
				6				

PUZZLE / 471 Time:_______

					3			1
4							8	
		5	9	7				
	1		8					
		2				7		
					6		3	
				2	4	5		
	8							6
3			6					

PUZZLE / 472 Time:_______

			8					
		7		9	5	3		
	3						6	
		9				7		1
			2		7			
7		3				5		
	6						2	
		2	7	1		9		
					3			

PUZZLE / 473 Time:_______

				1				5
					6		2	
		3		4		9		
			7				8	
5		2				3		6
	1				9			
		5		3		4		
	7		8					
6				5				

PUZZLE / 474 Time:_______

			3		5			
		2				6	7	
	1			4				
9			5		4			1
		6				8		
1			8		7			6
				2			5	
	8	9				4		
			1		3			

PUZZLE / 475 Time:_______

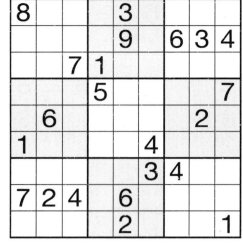

8				3				
				9		6	3	4
		7	1					
			5					7
	6						2	
1					4			
					3	4		
7	2	4		6				
				2				1

PUZZLE / 476 Time:_______

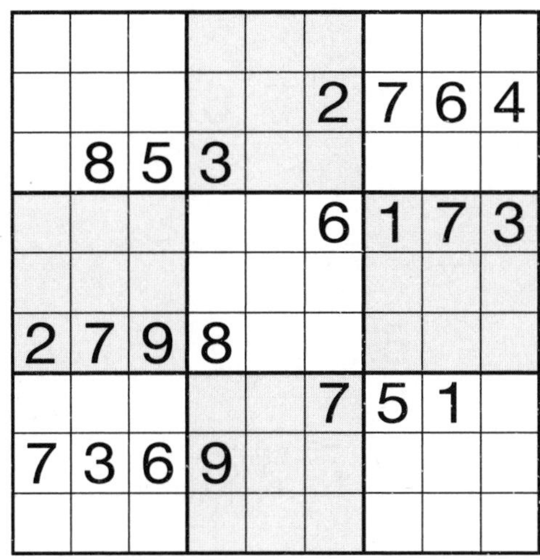

					2	7	6	4
	8	5	3					
					6	1	7	3
2	7	9	8					
					7	5	1	
7	3	6	9					

PUZZLE / 477 Time:_______

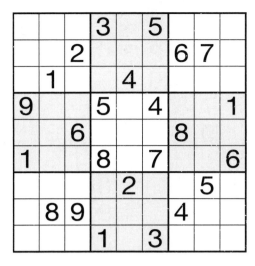

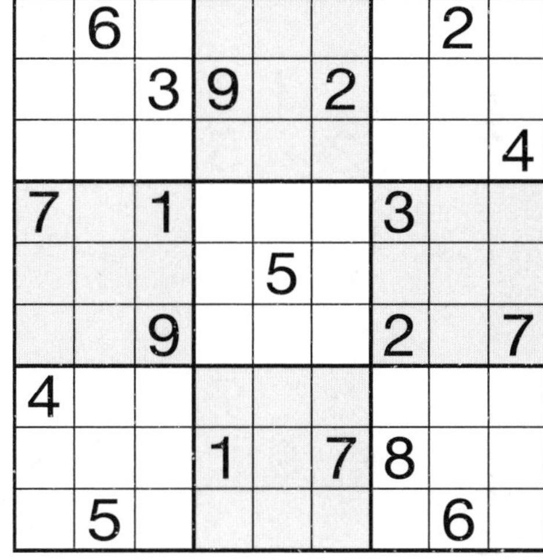

	6						2	
		3	9		2			
								4
7		1				3		
				5				
		9				2		7
4								
			1		7	8		
	5						6	

PUZZLE / 478 Time:_______

				8				1
			3	6		7		
		5	2				6	
	8	6						5
3						8	2	
	7				2	3		
		1		4	5			
4				7				

PUZZLE / 479 Time:_______

		3				9		
	4		2	1			8	
5								7
	6				5			
8	7						5	6
			7				4	
9								3
	1			8	9		2	
		2				1		

PUZZLE / 480 Time:_______

	5	1	6					
						8	7	
				9			2	
			4					9
8								3
2					1			
	6			2				
	4	9						
					7	5	1	

PUZZLE / 481 Time:_______

								9
		1	2	3				
	4	5	6					
	7	8						
	9			6			3	
						1	5	
					8	2	4	
				4	9	7		
3								

PUZZLE / 482 Time:_______

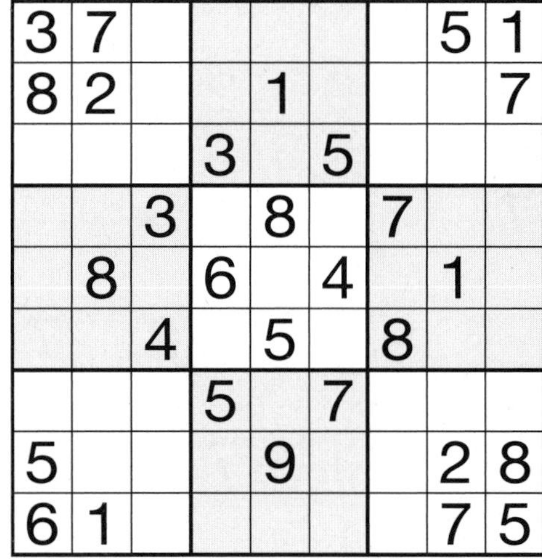

3	7						5	1
8	2			1				7
			3		5			
		3		8		7		
	8		6		4		1	
		4		5		8		
			5		7			
5				9			2	8
6	1						7	5

PUZZLE / 483 Time:_______

			1					
	3	2		5	6			
4						7		
5						8		
	7		4		3		1	
		6						2
		8						3
			7	8		6	4	
					1			

PUZZLE / 484 Time:_______

	3	1	8			2	5	
					4			
	7			6			8	
			1					
	5	3				7	6	
					9			
	6			5			4	
			7					
	8	4			6	9	3	

PUZZLE / 485 Time:_______

				5				
	4		8		7		3	
		1		2		7		
	1						6	
2		3				5		7
	6						9	
		7		6		3		
	9		4		5		8	
				1				

PUZZLE / 486 Time:_______

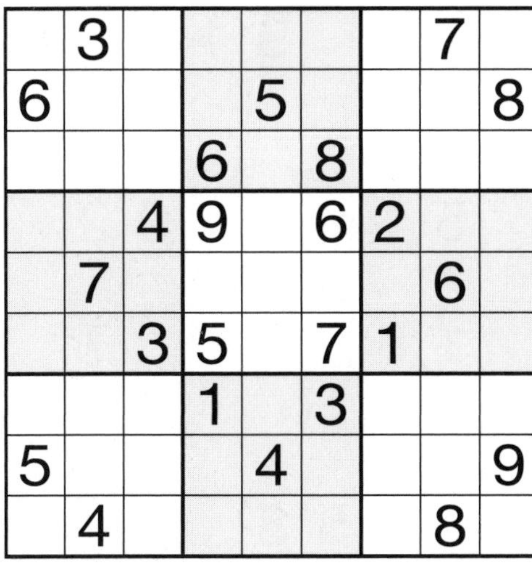

PUZZLE / 487 Time:_______

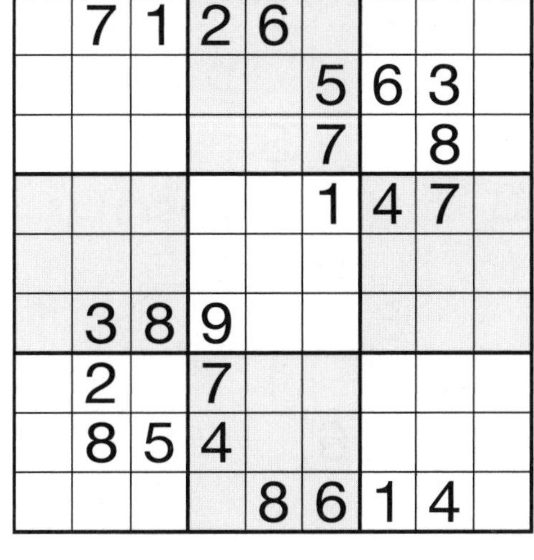

PUZZLE / 488 Time:_______

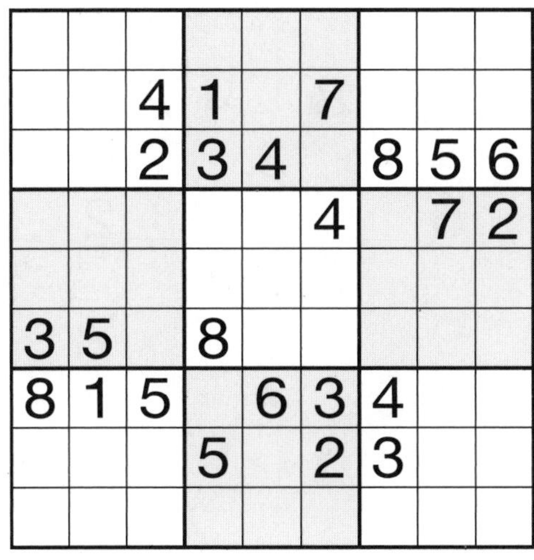

PUZZLE / 489 Time:_______

PUZZLE / 490 Time:_______

							1	9
	9	1	2	3				5
	6		4					
	1	7						
	3			5			9	
						3	7	
					6		3	
1				7	8	9	5	
8	2							

PUZZLE / 491 Time:_______

		1						4
	7			3			5	
9			2			3		
		8			2			
	3			5			8	
			3			2		
		9			8			1
	2			9			7	
4						9		

PUZZLE / 492 Time:_______

	6	8					9	
	7				2			
				3			6	
3						8		
			9		5			
		6						1
	4			1				
			6				5	
	5					2	7	

PUZZLE / 493 Time:_______

				9	1			8
2						4		
		6					5	
	5			8		9	2	
			3		4			
	1	8		6			7	
	9					3		
		4						7
8			5	3				

PUZZLE / 494 Time:_______

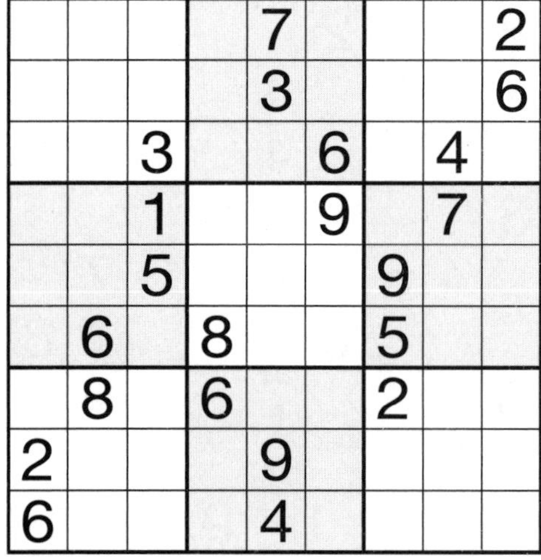

				7				2
				3				6
		3			6		4	
		1			9		7	
		5				9		
	6		8			5		
	8		6			2		
2				9				
6				4				

PUZZLE / 495 Time:_______

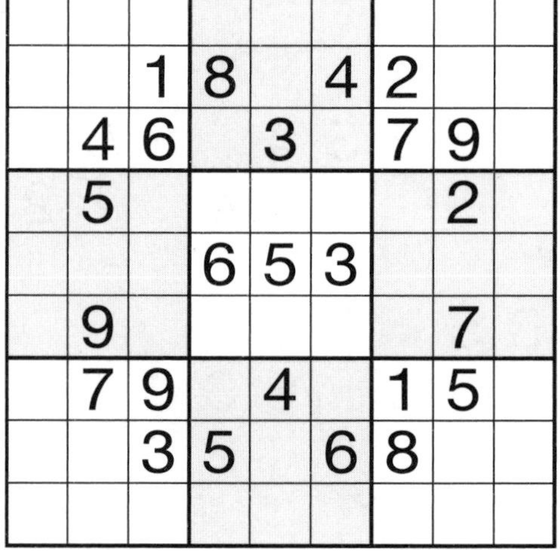

		1	8		4	2		
	4	6		3		7	9	
	5						2	
			6	5	3			
	9						7	
	7	9		4		1	5	
		3	5		6	8		

PUZZLE / 496 Time:_______

		3	4			7		
1	2			5			8	
				6				9
		8	7					
		9		1		4		
					6	5		
4				7				
	5			8			2	3
		6			9	1		

PUZZLE / 497 Time:_______

3				1	2			7
	4				6			
		5				8		
						5	9	
	6	7				3	2	
	1	4						
		9				1		
			3				5	
2			7	8				6

PUZZLE / 498 Time:_______

	1		5				6	
		3				1		9
		8		7			4	
				1			2	
			4		5			
	5			3				
	6			9		3		
1		7				6		
	2				8		7	

PUZZLE / 499 Time:_______

	4							
3	7				8	9		
		8	7		2			
			9				2	8
4				7				3
9	6				1			
			5		6	2		
		5	4				1	9
							5	

PUZZLE / 500 Time:_______

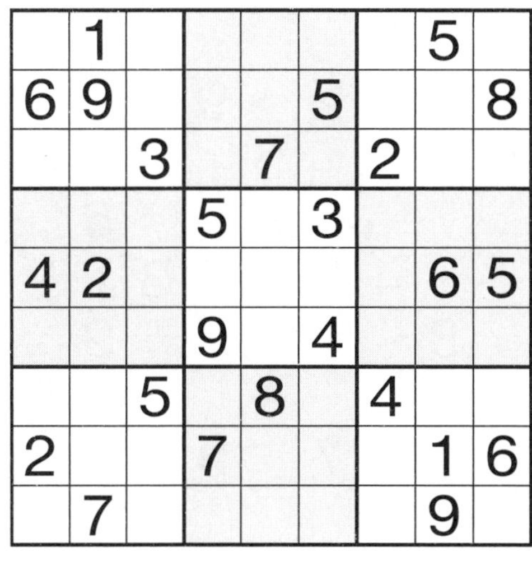

	1						5	
6	9				5			8
		3		7		2		
			5		3			
4	2						6	5
			9		4			
		5		8		4		
2			7				1	6
	7						9	

PUZZLE / 501 Time:_______

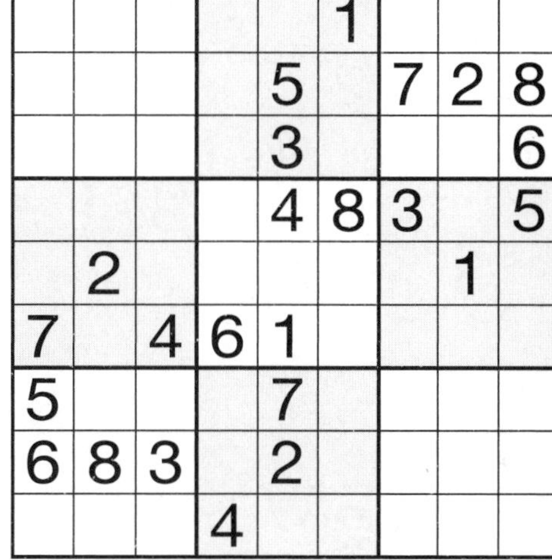

					1			
				5		7	2	8
				3				6
				4	8	3		5
	2						1	
7		4	6	1				
5				7				
6	8	3		2				
			4					

PUZZLE / 502 Time:_______

					6	4	1	
2			8					
9			7	3				
6						3	9	
		4				8		
	2	3						7
				7	5			9
					4			5
	8	5	6					

PUZZLE / 503 Time:_______

5		8						9
	6		8				4	
				9				1
			3		6		7	
		7				5		
	4		1		5			
4				6				
	9				2		5	
6						2		8

PUZZLE / 504 Time:_______

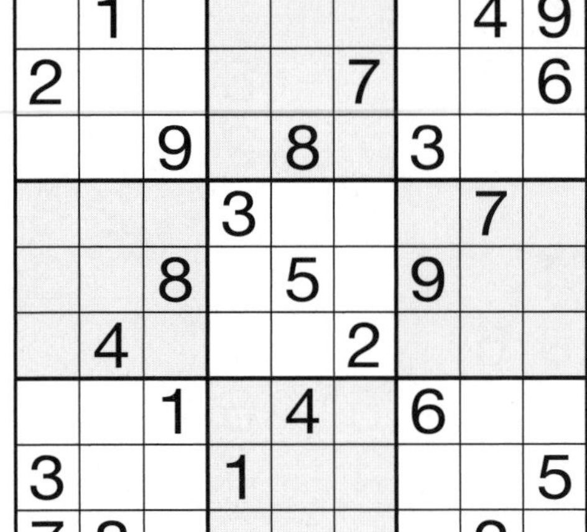

	1						4	9
2					7			6
		9		8		3		
			3				7	
		8		5		9		
	4				2			
		1		4		6		
3			1					5
7	8						2	

PUZZLE / 505 Time:_______

			9					
		4	8	6			1	
			4				5	
	9				6			3
	7			2			9	
6			7				8	
	2				5			
	5			9	3	2		
					4			

PUZZLE / 506 Time:_______

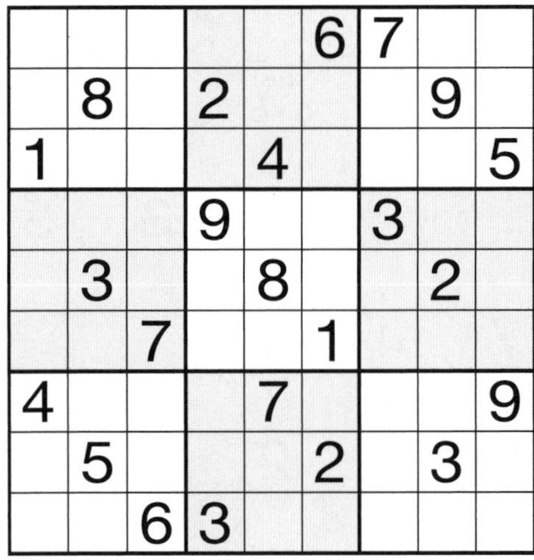

					6	7		
	8		2				9	
1				4				5
			9			3		
	3			8			2	
		7			1			
4				7				9
	5				2		3	
		6	3					

PUZZLE / 507 Time:_______

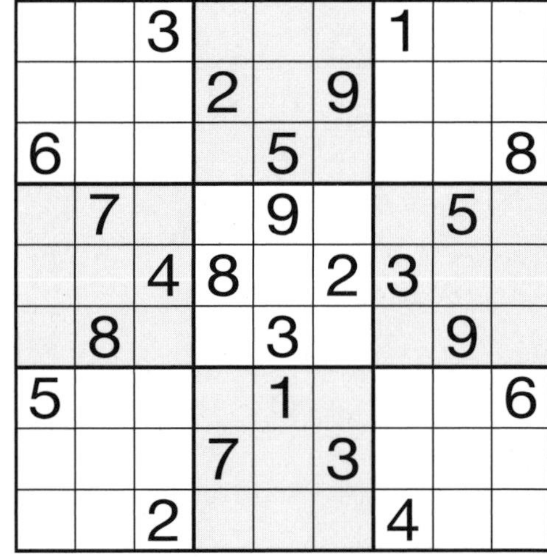

		3				1		
			2		9			
6				5				8
	7			9			5	
		4	8		2	3		
	8			3			9	
5				1				6
			7		3			
		2				4		

PUZZLE / 508 Time:_______

8			2	1			5	
		6						7
	1				3	6		
4							7	
5				2				6
	3							1
		8	7				2	
6						8		
	2			4	9			5

PUZZLE / 509 Time:_______

4		9			7	6		
	5		4					
					5	1	7	
					2	3	9	
3								5
	8	6	9					
	6	8	2					
					9		2	
		4	8			5		9

PUZZLE / 510 Time:_______

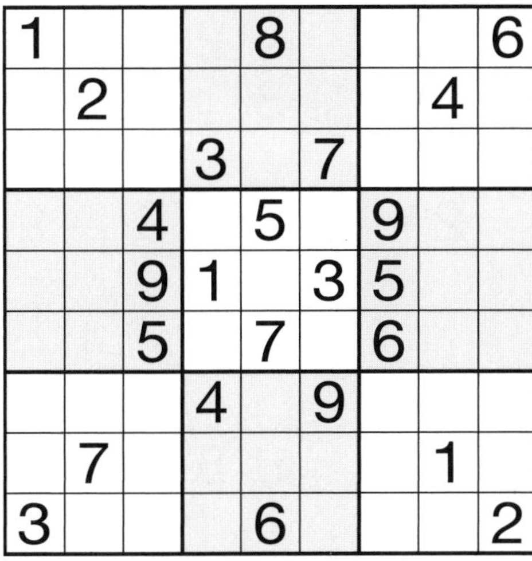

1				8				6
	2						4	
			3		7			
		4		5		9		
		9	1		3	5		
		5		7		6		
			4		9			
	7						1	
3				6				2

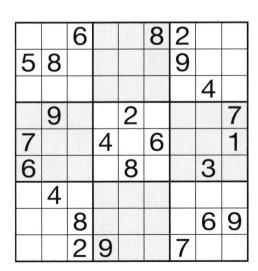

PUZZLE / 511 Time:_______

		9	5	3				
	1	8	7					
2	6	3						
1	3							
7								9
							8	5
						6	7	3
					3	8	2	
				1	6	9		

PUZZLE / 512 Time:_______

	6						7	
5			1		2			8
		1				2		
	1			6			2	
			8	3	9			
	4			7			3	
		4				3		
2			4		3			1
	7						5	

PUZZLE / 513 Time:_______

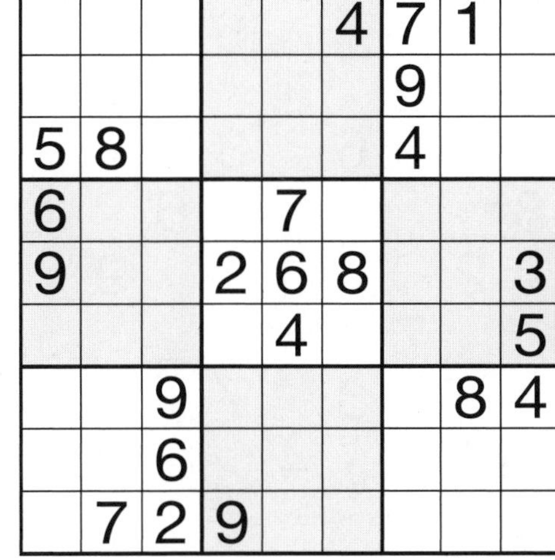

					4	7	1	
						9		
5	8					4		
6				7				
9			2	6	8			3
				4				5
		9					8	4
		6						
	7	2	9					

PUZZLE / 514 Time:_______

		6			8	2		
5	8					9		
							4	
	9			2				7
7			4		6			1
6				8			3	
	4							
		8					6	9
		2	9			7		

PUZZLE / 515 Time:_______

8			3				5	6
5	9			4			3	
			8		6			
	1			2			7	
			5		1			
	2			3			6	4
9	7				8			3

PUZZLE / 516 Time:_______

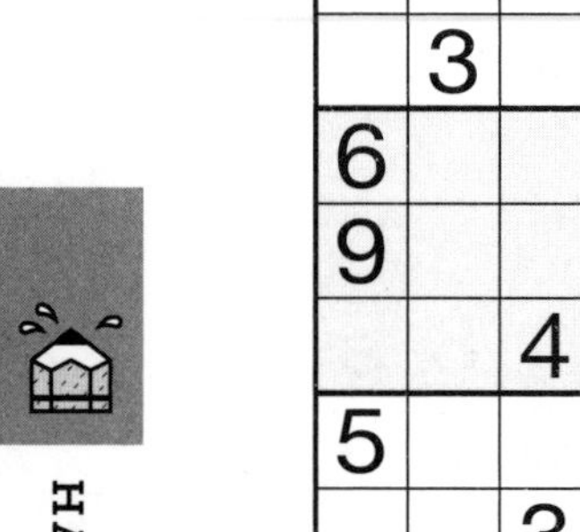

		7		8	3			
						2		
	3		7					1
6						5		
9				2				4
		4						6
5					6		9	
		3						
			4	1		8		

PUZZLE / 517 Time:_______

		4			2		9	
			1	3		5		
6								7
	2		9			3		
		9			1		4	
5								6
		7		9	8			
	8		7			1		

PUZZLE / 518 Time:_______

	4							7
		9		1			6	
			6		8	1		
8						6		
	2			5			9	
		7						5
		5	3		7			
	1			4		2		
3							8	

PUZZLE / 519 Time:_______

				4				
		6			9			5
9			5			3		7
3			7			2		
1								4
		7			1			6
6		4			8			1
2			6			5		
				2				

PUZZLE / 520 Time:_______

5					2	8		
		9	5					
	2			3				5
	4				7			3
		6				7		
8			4				9	
2				7			5	
					5	3		
		8	6					4

PUZZLE / 521 Time:_______

		9	7	5			3	
			3				6	8
3			9					
	7				2			
		4		9		1		
			1				5	
					3			5
6	8				4			
	4			8	9	3		

PUZZLE / 522 Time:_______

								9
		7	1			5	3	8
	3	6				4		
	2			5				
			2	6	7			
				1			9	
		2				7	8	
1	9	4			3	6		
7								

PUZZLE / 523 Time:______

	6			5		3		
		8	1				2	9
2					7			
			5					4
	4						3	
7					6			
			7					5
4	3				2	6		
		2		1			8	

PUZZLE / 524 Time:______

			2		7			
		3		6		2		
	8						3	
2								9
	4						5	
5								3
	9						4	
		8		2		7		
			1		8			

PUZZLE / 525 Time:______

		3	7					
					2	5		
8	4				5	1		
5	6							
							7	6
		7	3				9	4
		2	9					
					6	8		

PUZZLE / 526 Time:______

3								8
					7		1	
		2		4				
	8				6		9	
	1						5	
	7		3				4	
				5		2		
	5		4					
8								3

PUZZLE / 527 Time:______

		8		9			3	
			4					2
4					3	1		
					6		2	
	4	5				9	7	
	9		8					
		6	3					1
1					8			
	2			7		3		

PUZZLE / 528 Time:______

HARD PUZZLES

				4		9		
3	2		1				8	
		4		5				6
	8		7					9
		2				4		
6					1		5	
5				1		8		
	6				9		3	1
		3		7				

PUZZLE / 529 Time:_______

					4	2	9	
								1
	1	2	6					3
				1				6
				7				
8				5				
5					9	4	8	
7								
	9	3	5					

PUZZLE / 530 Time:_______

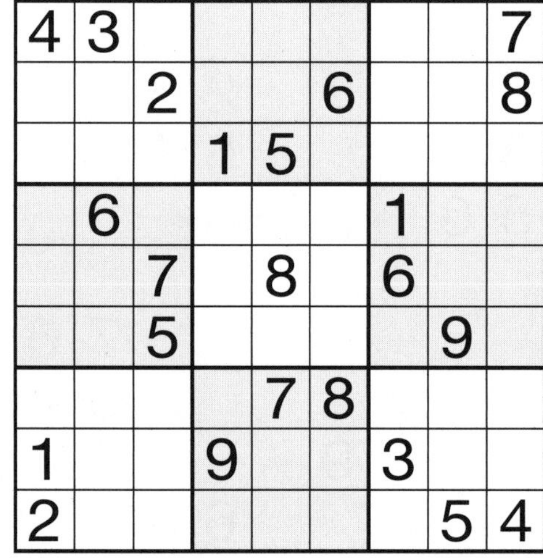

4	3							7
		2			6			8
			1	5				
	6					1		
		7		8		6		
		5					9	
				7	8			
1			9			3		
2							5	4

PUZZLE / 531 Time:_______

		8			1	4		
9	1			8				
			3					7
						2		
	4		6		8		9	
		7						
2					9			
				6			3	5
		4	5			6		

PUZZLE / 532 Time:_______

	5	3	7					
				9	5	4	6	
	8				9	6	1	
	6	4				5	3	
	9	1	5				7	
	4	9	3	8				
					7	9	2	

PUZZLE / 533 Time:_______

			3				2	
8				9		6		
	1			7				4
			4			5		
2								7
		3			6			
4				2			3	
		6		5				1
	9				8			

PUZZLE / 534 Time:_______

			2				1	
		2	1	6			8	
9		3				7		6
	8			5			4	
4		7				3		8
	4			9	6	5		
	9				3			

PUZZLE / 535 Time:______

2				3	6			
		4				5		
6			1					2
	5		8					
		7				9		
					9		4	
3					8			1
		6				7		
			7	2				4

PUZZLE / 536 Time:______

	7	6						
1	8	5	2					
8	1	4	7					
	2	3				7	6	
					9	3	4	8
					5	6	3	9
						5	7	

PUZZLE / 537 Time:______

	4		7			2		
5							9	
		3		2	6			
3			4			1		
	1						6	
		6			2			4
			1	9		8		
	8							5
		9			3		4	

PUZZLE / 538 Time:______

			1		8			
		3				6		
	7			2			8	
4			6					3
		7		9		4		
1					5			9
	8			4			2	
		9				1		
			3		2			

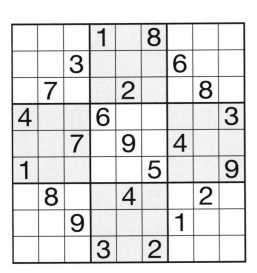

PUZZLE / 539 Time:______

	3	5	1		7		6	
					9		8	
	8	2	3		1		7	
	1		6		4	8	3	
	7		2					
	6		5		8	4	1	

PUZZLE / 540 Time:______

HARD PUZZLES

	3	5						
7	2	6	5	4				
8				9	6			
					8	3		
		7				2		
		4	6					
			9	5				3
				6	7	1	8	2
						4	5	

PUZZLE / 541 Time:_______

					6	5		
		2		8			6	
9							3	
	6		1		4			
7								9
			3		2		8	
	4							1
	9			5		7		
		8	9					

PUZZLE / 542 Time:_______

	7		9					2
6			5				3	
			8			1		
9	3	5			2			
				4				
			1			2	5	8
		1			8			
	5				7			3
4					9		6	

PUZZLE / 543 Time:_______

8		1				2		5
	2			9			3	
7		4				6		1
			3		8			
	6						2	
			6		2			
9		5				1		6
	1			4			5	
2		8				9		3

PUZZLE / 544 Time:_______

		9	4			8		
	1						4	
2				1				
			9		3			7
	2						6	
8			7		5			
				3				2
	4						7	
		5			1	3		

PUZZLE / 545 Time:_______

	1		2		3		4	
5		3			9		7	
	6		7			8		4
3		7			2		6	
	2		8			7		3
	9		4		6		5	

PUZZLE / 546 Time:_______

				8			9	7
3	7				6			
		1						2
			9			5		
	6						3	
		4			7			
5						1		
			8				2	6
9	4			7				

PUZZLE / 547 Time:_______

			9					
		8					6	
	5			8	1		9	
	2	7		1			5	
			3	2	7			
	9			6		7	3	
	6		5	3			7	
	1					4		
					2			

PUZZLE / 548 Time:_______

9	3							
2						5		
			6	1				3
					3	9		
	5	4		9		7	8	
		6	1					
8				5	2			
		7						5
							1	7

PUZZLE / 549 Time:_______

				1	9	3		
		1	2					
3		7				4		
			8		5			4
	2						6	
4			3		1			
		8				7		5
					2	8		
		3	9	8				

PUZZLE / 550 Time:_______

								2
	2	1	9	5				
	3				7			
	9				3	5		
	7			2			9	
		5	4				1	
			8				4	
				4	1	7	5	
7								

PUZZLE / 551 Time:_______

							7	
6								5
3				2	8			
			6			3		
		7				2		
		1			4			
			5	7				1
8								4
	2							

PUZZLE / 552 Time:_______

1	6						9	
			3					8
		4		8		2		
	9					8		
	2			5			7	
		6					1	
		5		6		7		
3					9			
	7						4	1

PUZZLE / 553 Time:______

					6			5
	2			1			3	
1			4					
					9			7
	1			2			8	
5			1					
					5			4
	9			3			6	
4			6					

PUZZLE / 554 Time:______

	1						4	
9			1					
		3		4		8		
					5			2
	2						7	
5			6					
		4		2		5		
					9			6
	5						8	

PUZZLE / 555 Time:______

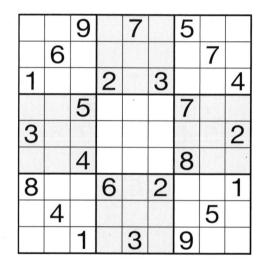

		9		7		5		
	6						7	
1			2		3			4
		5				7		
3								2
		4				8		
8			6		2			1
	4						5	
		1		3		9		

PUZZLE / 556 Time:______

						6	3	
4			8	3	1			
2								
	8		2		9		4	
	9						8	
	3		1		4		7	
								3
			4	6	2			5
	4	8						

PUZZLE / 557 Time:______

			1					
		2					7	
	3		4			8		
		5			7			
	6						9	
			8			1		
		9			2		5	
	1					4		
					5			

PUZZLE / 558 Time:______

		1	7			5	2	
2								
9					1			3
		8	5		6			4
6			8		7	9		
3			1					6
								7
	4	5			9	2		

PUZZLE / 559 Time:_______

		2			5		3	
	4					9		
1				8				7
		5			3		7	
4								1
	6		9			2		
6				5				8
		3					9	
	2		6			5		

PUZZLE / 560 Time:_______

		4	6					
		7					3	8
				2				5
								3
			1		6			
8								
5				8				
1	4					6		
					2	7		

PUZZLE / 561 Time:_______

		6	3				5	
	4			7				2
1					4			
			4					
	9	2				8	6	
					6			
			8					5
2				1			3	
	1				7	6		

PUZZLE / 562 Time:_______

	1	2	3					
								6
						7		9
				6		1		8
		8		2		9		
9		7		5				
8		5						
4								
					7	6	3	

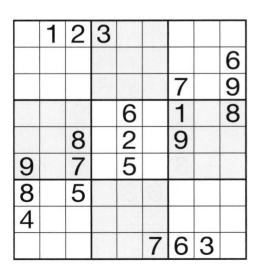

PUZZLE / 563 Time:_______

	9			3				
	1				2	7	3	
	2							1
		3	6	4				5
6				5	1	2		
7							8	
	5	8	2				6	
				6			4	

PUZZLE / 564 Time:_______

		4	6				1	
	5			7			3	
	8			4				
		6	3					
					5	8		
				8			9	
	7			5			6	
	4				2	1		

PUZZLE / 565 Time:_______

8	6			5				
7	1		6		2			
		9		7		8		
	8		2		3		4	
		2		1		3		
			4		6		2	1
				9			5	7

PUZZLE / 566 Time:_______

		6		1		7		
			9		5			
3				4				2
	1						8	
2		3		5		9		6
	5						4	
8				2				7
			1		6			
		7		9		3		

PUZZLE / 567 Time:_______

5				1				8
		4				6		
	7		2		5		4	
		9				4		
1				3				6
		5				9		
	4		6		1		9	
		7				1		
2				4				3

PUZZLE / 568 Time:_______

	6	1						
	4						9	2
			2	6				4
			3		2	4		
		4				1		
		8	5		4			
3				9	7			
8	7						5	
						3	6	

PUZZLE / 569 Time:_______

	4							
	1							7
				9	8	6		5
				5	7	9		
		3	2	1				
8		9	6	3				
5							2	
							4	

PUZZLE / 570 Time:_______

			8					
		5	3	1				
		4						9
							7	5
8								6
3	1							
2						3		
				9	5	2		
					6			

PUZZLE / 571 Time:_______

6							4	8
			3	8	1			5
			7					
	8					4		
	5		6		9		3	
		6					9	
					2			
9			1	6	3			
7	3							1

PUZZLE / 572 Time:_______

6	4						2	7
8		3				1		4
	7						6	
			1	2	3			
			4	5	6			
			7	8	9			
	1						5	
9		7				6		8
4	6						1	3

PUZZLE / 573 Time:_______

		7			8		1	9
	9		7					2
5				1		7		
	4		8					
		6		7		5		
					2		8	
		9		3				4
7					1		6	
3	5		6			9		

PUZZLE / 574 Time:_______

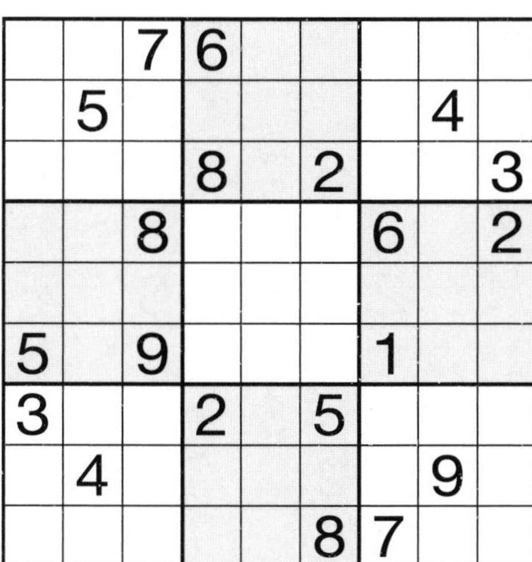

		7	6					
	5						4	
			8		2			3
		8				6		2
5		9				1		
3			2		5			
	4						9	
					8	7		

PUZZLE / 575 Time:_______

9				8				
	6				3		1	
		4	7				9	
	1							2
		5		2		8		
7							4	
	2				7	9		
	8		6				7	
				5				1

PUZZLE / 576 Time:_______

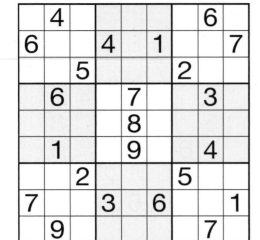

HARD PUZZLES

	4						6	
6			4		1			7
		5				2		
	6			7			3	
				8				
	1			9			4	
		2				5		
7			3		6			1
	9						7	

PUZZLE / 577 Time:_______

		8		5		2		
1			4		9			
2								4
	3			7			5	
		4				6		
	5			8			7	
6								8
			2		8			9
		3		9		7		

PUZZLE / 578 Time:_______

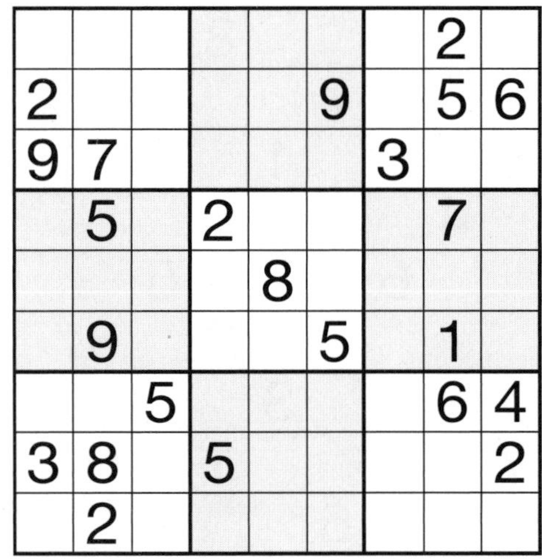

							2	
2					9		5	6
9	7					3		
	5		2				7	
				8				
	9				5		1	
		5					6	4
3	8		5					2
	2							

PUZZLE / 579 Time:_______

6			2				4	
1				4			3	
	7			9				5
		8						4
		3				9		
5						7		
2				1			5	
	5			3				8
	6				5			2

PUZZLE / 580 Time:_______

				5	9	4		
				2	1	6		
5	8	1						
4	3	6						
						3	8	7
						5	3	9
		2	9	7				
		5	1	6				

PUZZLE / 581 Time:_______

9						5		
	1				4		7	
			6	7				4
7			9					
		2		8		3		
					3			8
4				5	9			
	8		2				1	
		3						6

PUZZLE / 582 Time:_______

			7					
		2			1			
	9			5		3		
6			8				4	
		5		3		2		
	7				6			1
		6		2			9	
			1			4		
					5			

PUZZLE / 583 Time:_______

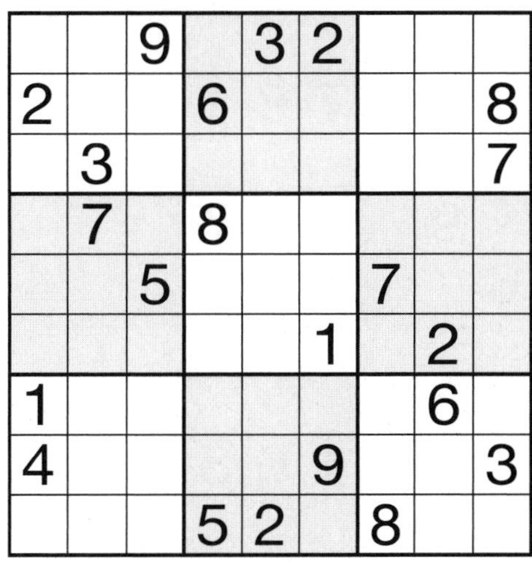

		9		3	2			
2			6					8
	3							7
	7		8					
		5				7		
					1		2	
1							6	
4					9			3
			5	2		8		

PUZZLE / 584 Time:_______

			1	8				9
		7					2	
	3			6	2			
3			4				5	
		2				1		
	9				7			4
			8	2			3	
	1					6		
7				4	9			

PUZZLE / 585 Time:_______

4					9			
			3			7	8	
		2		4				6
		1					3	
6				5				2
	2					9		
5				6		8		
	9	8			7			
			4					5

PUZZLE / 586 Time:_______

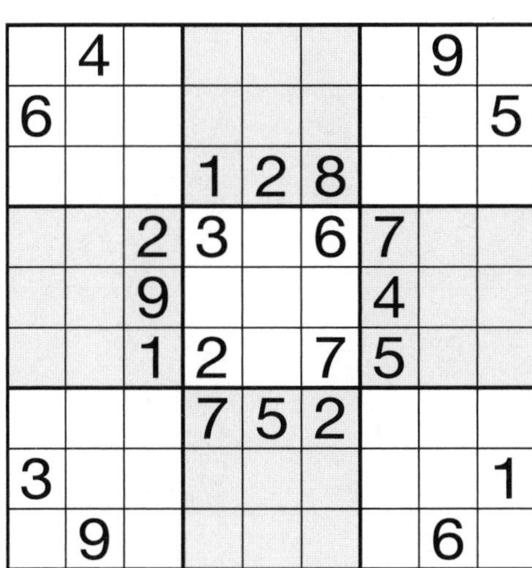

	4						9	
6								5
			1	2	8			
		2	3		6	7		
		9				4		
		1	2		7	5		
			7	5	2			
3								1
	9						6	

PUZZLE / 587 Time:_______

		3			9			
			6	4				
1		9		2	3			
	4				6	8		
	9	8				5	7	
		5	2				1	
			3	8		1		2
				5	2			
			9			4		

PUZZLE / 588 Time:_______

			7	8	1			
		8				3	2	5
	9				7			
6				9				4
			3				7	
4	8	5				1		
			1	6	3			

PUZZLE / 589 Time:_______

1						3		
		9	3				8	
	7			2				4
					3			1
	8	6				7	2	
9			6					
2				7			5	
	5				6	4		
		1						8

PUZZLE / 590 Time:_______

					1		3	
		5			8		4	
	6		9			7		
	1		8					
	9		7		6		8	
					5		2	
		3			4		9	
	4		3			6		
	8		1					

PUZZLE / 591 Time:_______

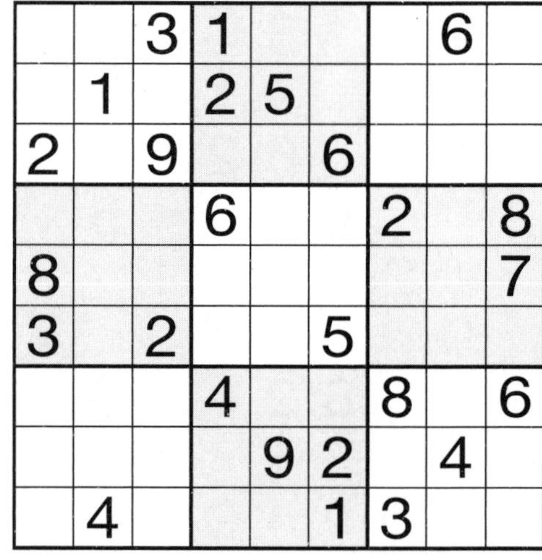

		3	1				6	
	1		2	5				
2		9			6			
			6			2		8
8								7
3		2			5			
			4			8		6
				9	2		4	
	4				1	3		

PUZZLE / 592 Time:_______

								8
							5	2
			5	7		9	6	
		6	7			5	1	
		1	6		3	7		
	2	4			5	8		
	8	7		3	4			
3	4							
1								

PUZZLE / 593 Time:_______

		7	3					
		4	5			8	6	
			4		8	7	5	
	9	3	1		6			
	3	8			2	1		
					9	3		

PUZZLE / 594 Time:_______

	6	7			2			
		3		1				9
							5	1
5		9						
	7			8			6	
						7		3
4	8							
7				9		5		
			6			4	3	

PUZZLE / 595 Time:_______

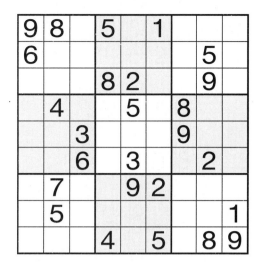

9	8		5		1			
6							5	
			8	2			9	
	4			5		8		
		3				9		
		6		3			2	
	7			9	2			
	5							1
			4		5		8	9

PUZZLE / 596 Time:_______

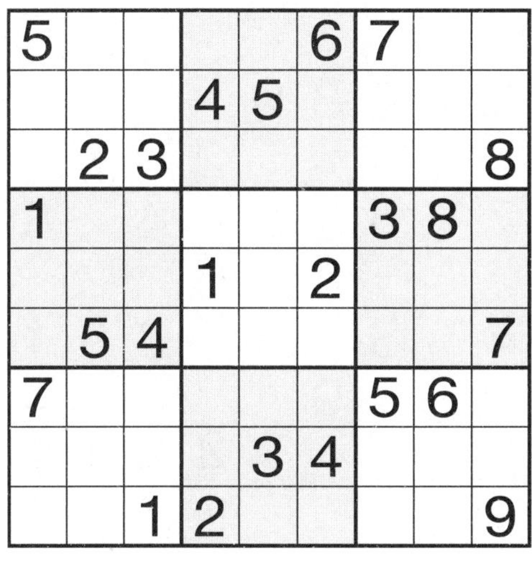

5					6	7		
			4	5				
	2	3						8
1						3	8	
			1		2			
	5	4						7
7						5	6	
				3	4			
		1	2					9

PUZZLE / 597 Time:_______

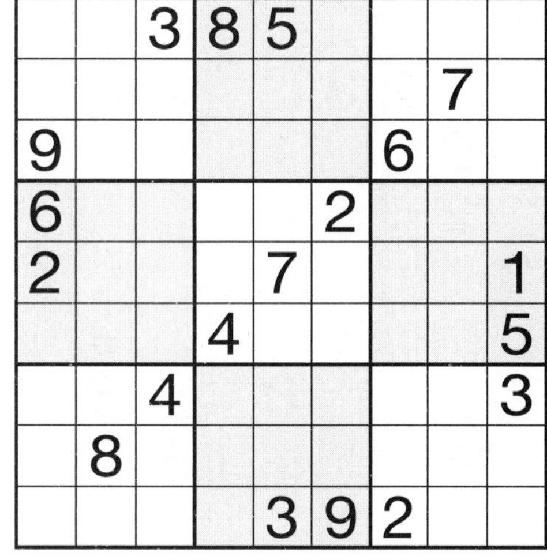

		3	8	5				
							7	
9						6		
6					2			
2				7				1
			4					5
		4						3
	8							
				3	9	2		

PUZZLE / 598 Time:_______

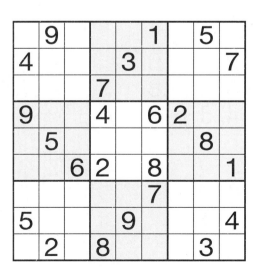

	9				1		5	
4				3				7
			7					
9			4		6	2		
	5						8	
		6	2		8			1
					7			
5				9				4
	2		8				3	

PUZZLE / 599 Time:_______

					8		7	
1		2		9		3		
	3				1		2	
4		5						
	6						3	
						1		5
	4		5				6	
		7		6		9		8
	8		9					

PUZZLE / 600 Time:_______

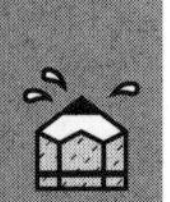

9				3				
2	3		9	5				
		8	1		9	3		
		1				7		
		6	5		7	2		
				4	2		8	7
				7				4

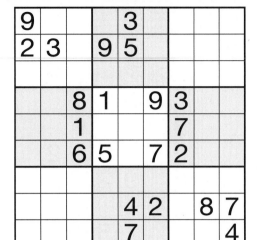

PUZZLE / 601 Time:_______

		8		3				
	1		9			5		
4					2		8	
	9					7		
2								3
		6					2	
	3		4					2
		4			8		6	
				1		3		

PUZZLE / 602 Time:_______

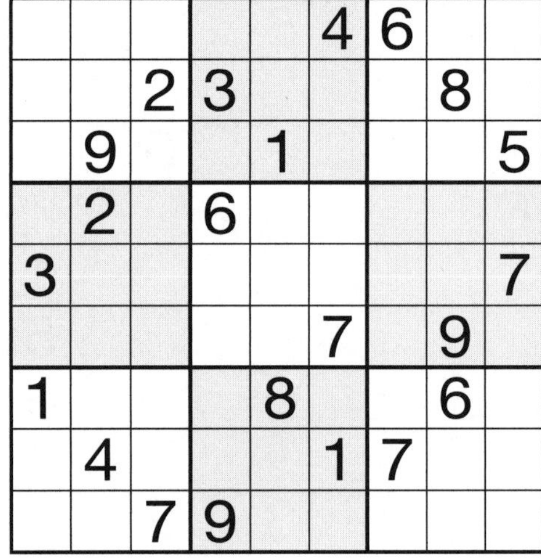

					4	6		
		2	3				8	
	9			1				5
	2		6					
3								7
					7		9	
1				8			6	
	4				1	7		
		7	9					

PUZZLE / 603 Time:_______

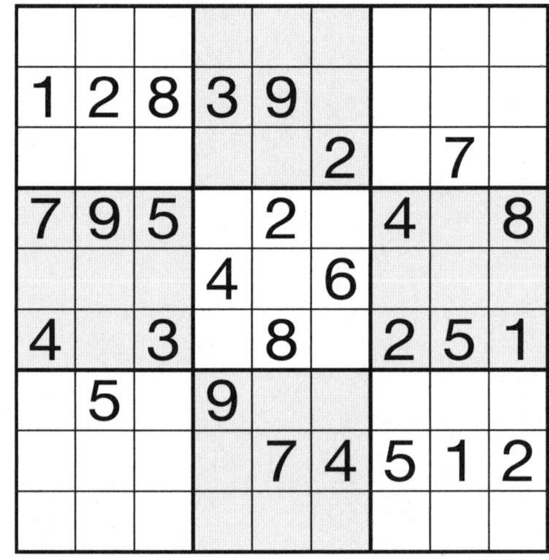

1	2	8	3	9				
					2		7	
7	9	5		2		4		8
			4		6			
4		3		8		2	5	1
	5		9					
				7	4	5	1	2

PUZZLE / 604 Time:_______

4	6				3	1		
1	8				2	6		
							7	4
2	4						9	1
8	3							
		4	5				1	6
		9	7				5	8

PUZZLE / 605 Time:_______

	1					8		
2			9				6	
3			8					1
4	5	6	7					
					3	4	5	6
9					2			7
	4				1			8
		5					9	

PUZZLE / 606 Time:_______

					1	4	2	3
								9
	4	2	5	3			1	
				4		2		
			2		8			
		1		9				
	8			6	7	5	3	
1								
7	5	6	8					

PUZZLE / 607 Time:_______

		7		3				6
8					1			
	3		4				9	
				1				
3		5				8		4
				6				
	9				3		6	
			5					7
2				7		1		

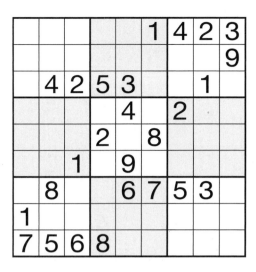

PUZZLE / 608 Time:_______

7			5			4		2
8					7		3	
		6		1				
	7		2			6		
1								5
		3			9		7	
				7		3		
	2		6					1
5		8			3			7

PUZZLE / 609 Time:_______

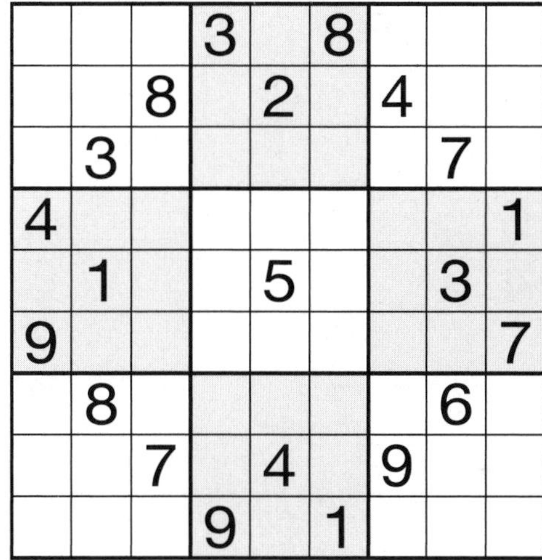

			3		8			
		8		2		4		
	3						7	
4								1
	1			5			3	
9								7
	8						6	
		7		4		9		
			9		1			

PUZZLE / 610 Time:_______

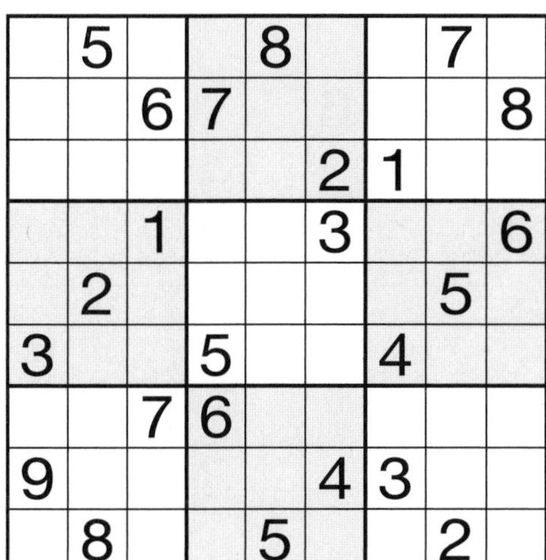

	5			8			7	
		6	7					8
					2	1		
		1			3			6
	2						5	
3			5			4		
		7	6					
9					4	3		
	8			5			2	

PUZZLE / 611 Time:_______

9		5						
	1							
				3	8	7		
						5	4	6
				7				
3	2	8						
		6	5	2				
							1	
						3		9

PUZZLE / 612 Time:_______

					5	4		
	8						7	
7				1				
3				7				
		5	1		4	8		
				6				9
				3				2
	4						3	
		8	9					

PUZZLE / 613 Time:_______

7			8			3		
4			5			1		
	1			2			4	
	6			3			5	
	3			8			2	
	7			9			1	
		5			7			6
		9			3			7

PUZZLE / 614 Time:_______

		2	3	8				
	5							
1		7			4	9	2	
5					1			
4								6
			9					7
	4	8	7			6		2
							5	
				2	8	4		

PUZZLE / 615 Time:_______

7				9		2		
	8		5				7	
					2		1	
			9			6	8	
3				2				7
	4	7			1			
	5		8					
	9				7		6	
		4		6				5

PUZZLE / 616 Time:_______

		4			7			
	5		3			1		
3				9			6	
2			1				3	
		7				8		
	8				4			5
	2			3				9
		9			5		1	
			8			5		

PUZZLE / 617 Time:_______

1				3			2	
	3		6			7		
		8			4		5	
4					9		1	
	7		2					6
	4		7			3		
		6			8		9	
	2			1				5

PUZZLE / 618 Time:_______

5	6							
		3	4	5	9			
9						1		
	8		1			6		
	5						9	
		6			7		4	
		5						2
			6	3	8	7		
							3	6

PUZZLE / 619 Time:_______

	1	2	4		7	3	5	
	3	4			5		9	
			8					2
3				1				8
1					2			
	5		9			4	6	
	6	7	5		4	2	1	

PUZZLE / 620 Time:_______

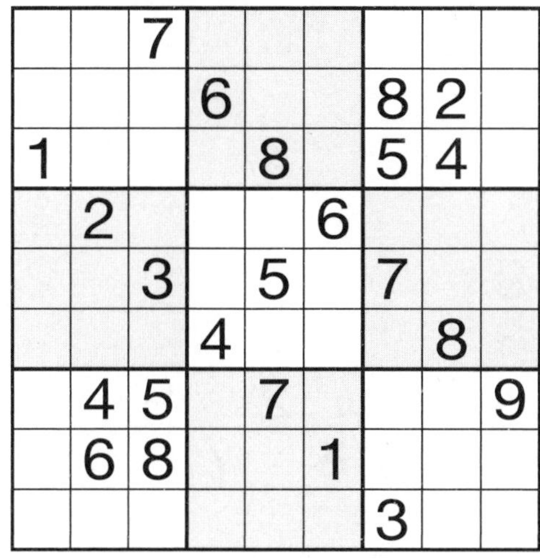

		7						
			6			8	2	
1				8		5	4	
	2				6			
		3		5		7		
			4				8	
	4	5		7				9
	6	8			1			
						3		

PUZZLE / 621 Time:_______

	9					7		
8		1			6			
				2				4
			7				3	
		6				5		
	4				8			
7				9				
			5			1		8
		8					6	

PUZZLE / 622 Time:_______

	9							2
1		8		5			7	
	7					3		
					2			
	6			3			5	
			9					
		5					3	
	2			6		7		5
4							1	

PUZZLE / 623 Time:_______

9	1				4			
		7				1		3
			8				5	
	2			8				
7				9				6
				5			7	
	3				7			
8		9				3		
			2				4	7

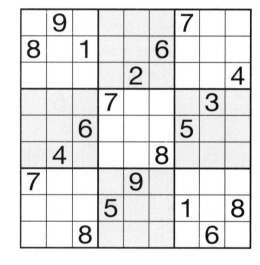

PUZZLE / 624 Time:_______

						7	8	
		9		5				2
		3			4			
			9					
2	5			4			6	9
					1			
			1			3		
8				2		5		
	6	5						

PUZZLE / 625 Time:_______

		1	3	8				
				6				
4	5	9		1				
		8						
1		3				9		2
						5		
				2		1	3	9
				3				
				5	4	2		

PUZZLE / 626 Time:_______

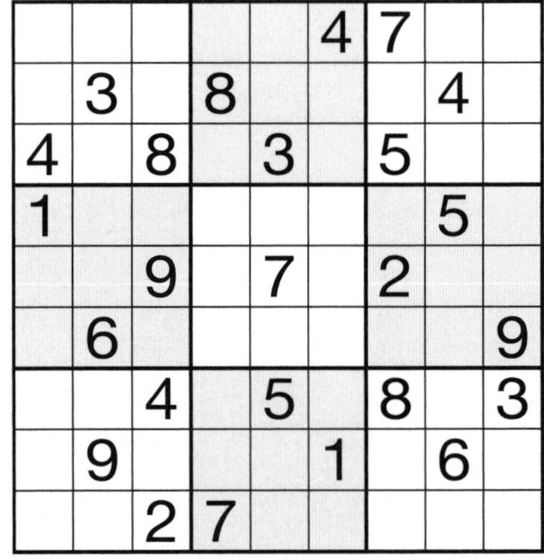

					4	7		
	3		8				4	
4		8		3		5		
1							5	
		9		7		2		
	6							9
		4		5		8		3
	9				1		6	
		2	7					

PUZZLE / 627 Time:_______

	9							6
	5				3	1		
		2		4			9	
			8					4
8								2
3					7			
	7			2		9		
		4	6				5	
1							4	

PUZZLE / 628 Time:_______

			3		4			
	9	6					1	
	2		7					
9		1						8
				9				
4						3		2
					3		7	
	6					5	2	
			2		1			

PUZZLE / 629 Time:_______

		7	3					
		2	5			7	9	
						6	3	
5	9							
6	2						7	8
							5	2
	5	3						
	8	9			6	1		
					4	5		

PUZZLE / 630 Time:_______

2	3		4	5				
1	4		6	3				
		7						1
	5						9	
3						5		
				7	6		8	9
				8	9		1	7

PUZZLE / 631 Time:_______

	4					3		
5			1	2			6	
					3			9
	1				4			
4				5				8
			6				5	
1			7					
	3			8	9			2
		7					3	

PUZZLE / 632 Time:_______

4	9				8			
			6	3				1
		2						9
			9				1	
		5				7		
	3				6			
3						6		
2				7	5			
			4				8	5

PUZZLE / 633 Time:_______

	2		3		1		7	
6								8
8				2				1
			7		9			
4				8				6
2								4
	5		9		7		3	

PUZZLE / 634 Time:_______

					8	5	7	
								6
	1	2	3					4
	3	4	5					2
8					6	4	5	
5					4	7	6	
4								
	9	3	1					

PUZZLE / 635 Time:_______

				8				3
		9	2		3	8		
	4						6	
4				1				5
		7	5		2	3		
5				7				6
	3						9	
		2	7		8	1		
1				2				

PUZZLE / 636 Time:_______

	3	1	2					
		4						2
			5			4		
	7	6			9			
	8			7			1	
			4			9	6	
		9			8			
5						7		
					1	2	3	

PUZZLE / 637 Time:_______

	8	2					9	
			3					6
					5	8		
6			9				2	
4				6				7
	3				7			9
		1	6					
9					3			
	5					2	1	

PUZZLE / 638 Time:_______

			1	6				
		9		5	2			
	5				9			
3						5	4	
4	1						3	6
	2	5						1
			2				1	
			5	3		8		
				4	6			

PUZZLE / 639 Time:_______

	3	7	5	9	8	4		
	2					7		
	7				6	2		
		2	1				3	
		1					5	
		3	4	2	7	8	9	

PUZZLE / 640 Time:_______

	9	8	6		7	4	3	
	5		1		8		9	
	4		2		9		1	
	2		8		1		5	
	8		9		6		4	
	1	3	5		2	7	8	

PUZZLE / 641 Time:_______

				7	3	1		
	9	2						
6								
7						3	5	
9				2				4
	1	5						6
								1
						2	7	
		9	4	6				

PUZZLE / 642 Time:_______

			4	5				
2	3				7			
		6				1		
8			2			9		
5								7
		4			9			3
		7				4		
			1				8	2
				3	6			

PUZZLE / 643 Time:_______

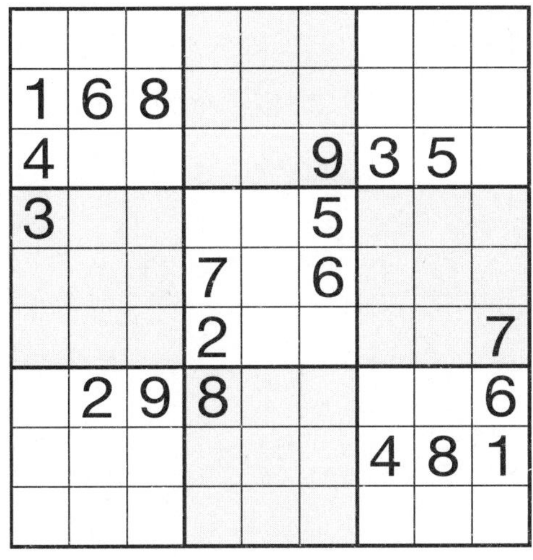

PUZZLE / 644 Time:_______

	6	2						9
1			8				2	
3			5			4		
	3	5			4			
				3				
			9			3	7	
		1			2			4
	4				6			1
2						7	8	

PUZZLE / 645 Time:_______

		3	4				9	6
	2			5				3
1			6					
	8	7				3	4	
					2			5
8				1			6	
9	4				8	7		

PUZZLE / 646 Time:_______

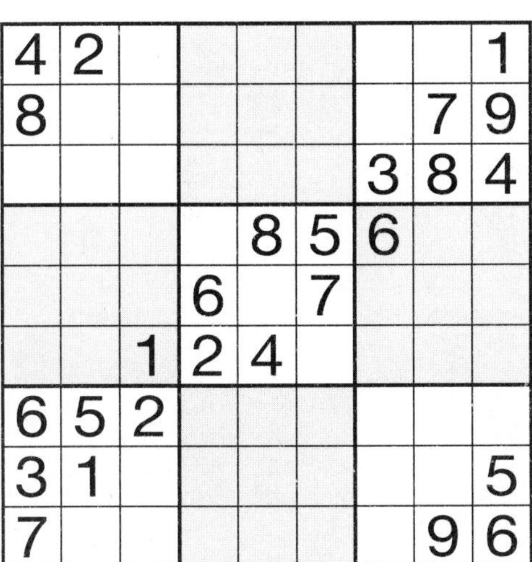

PUZZLE / 647 Time:_______

	9	5						
6	8		3					
7		4	9					
	5	2		4				
			6		3			
				8		7	3	
					8	1		4
					2		6	5
						3	7	

PUZZLE / 648 Time:_______

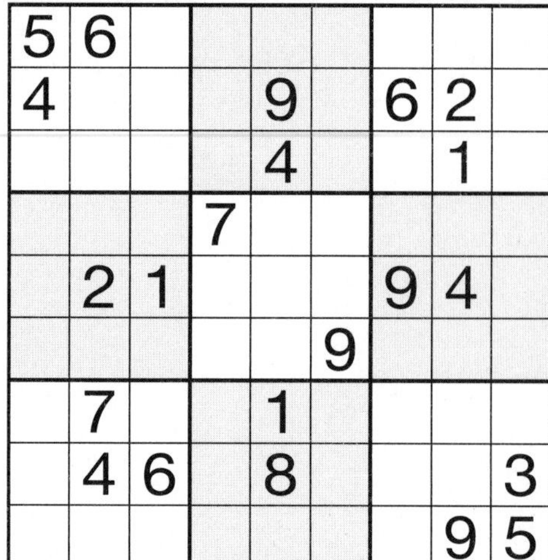

5	6							
4				9		6	2	
				4			1	
			7					
	2	1				9	4	
					9			
	7			1				
	4	6		8				3
							9	5

PUZZLE / 649 Time:_______

		3				6		
		2			4		9	
1				9				5
	8		5					
		7		6		1		
					2		3	
6				1				4
	7		4			8		
		8				7		

PUZZLE / 650 Time:_______

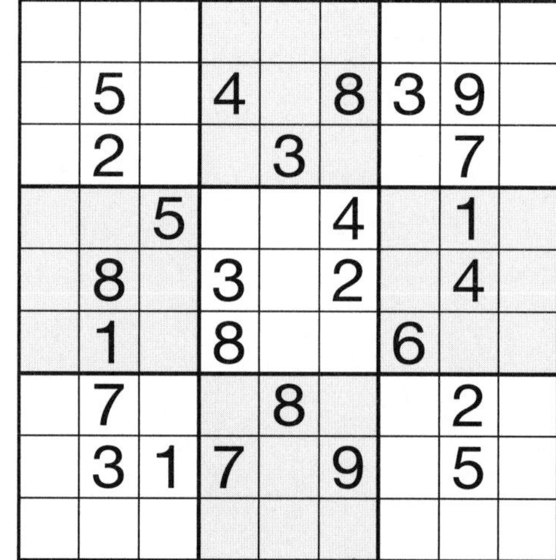

	5		4		8	3	9	
	2			3			7	
		5			4		1	
	8		3		2		4	
	1		8			6		
	7			8			2	
	3	1	7		9		5	

PUZZLE / 651 Time:_______

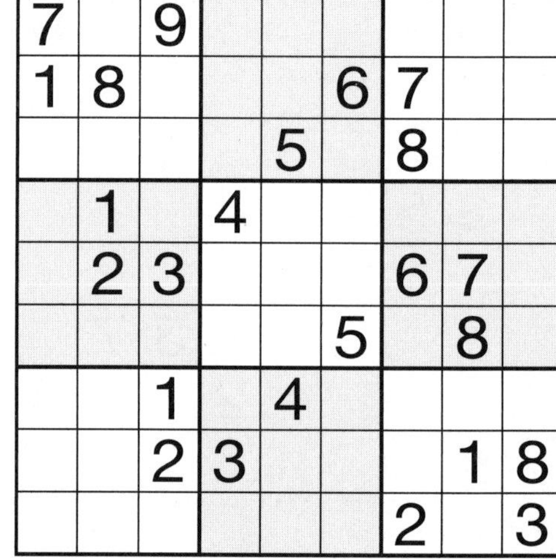

7		9						
1	8				6	7		
				5		8		
	1		4					
	2	3				6	7	
					5		8	
		1		4				
		2	3				1	8
						2		3

PUZZLE / 652 Time:_______

4			3		5			
	8			4			1	
		2				6		4
			1					
	7			6			3	
					9			
1		9				2		
	6			1			5	
			8		7			9

PUZZLE / 653 Time:_______

	3	6			2	5		
			1	9				3
2								1
7							4	
	2						3	
	5							8
8								9
3				5	6			
		2	8			1	7	

PUZZLE / 654 Time:_______

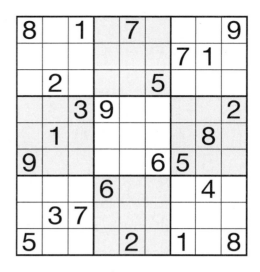

1				6				4
		5				9		
			8		2			
		3				8		
9				7				1
		2				5		
			1		8			
		7				3		
6				4				9

PUZZLE / 655 Time:_______

8		1		7				9
						7	1	
	2				5			
		3	9					2
	1						8	
9					6	5		
			6				4	
	3	7						
5				2		1		8

PUZZLE / 656 Time:_______

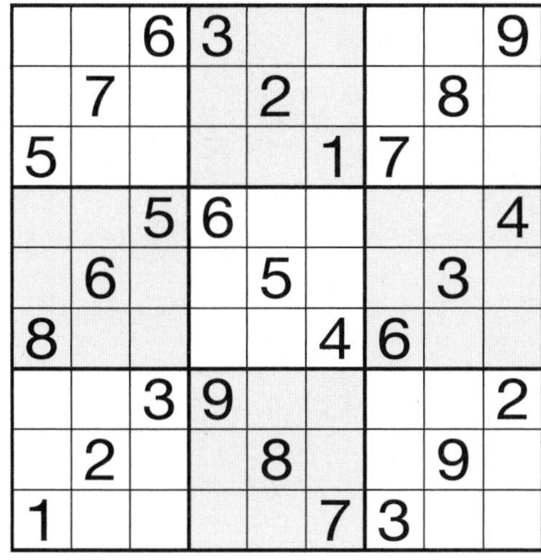

		6	3					9
	7			2			8	
5					1	7		
		5	6					4
	6			5			3	
8					4	6		
		3	9					2
	2			8			9	
1					7	3		

PUZZLE / 657 Time:_______

		9	1					6
				4	5	7		
7	5						3	
			6				9	
		5				2		
	6				8			
	4						2	7
		6	8	7				
9					2	1		

PUZZLE / 658 Time:_______

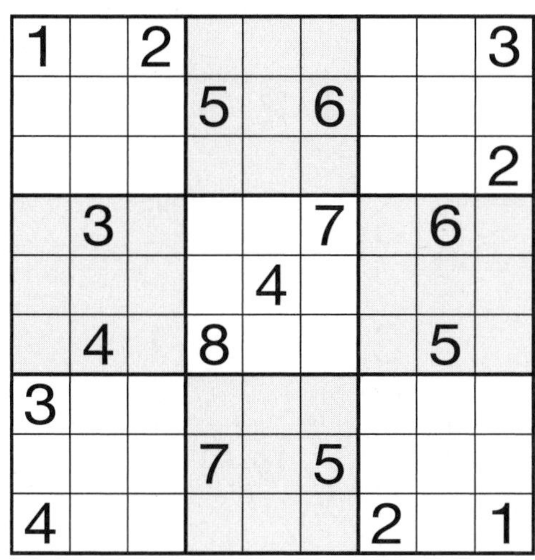

1		2						3
			5		6			
								2
	3				7		6	
				4				
	4		8				5	
3								
			7		5			
4						2		1

PUZZLE / 659 Time:_______

				3	9	6		
5			8	2	4			
8		3				9		
4		5				7		1
		2				3		6
			1	6	8			2
		1	2	7				

PUZZLE / 660 Time:_______

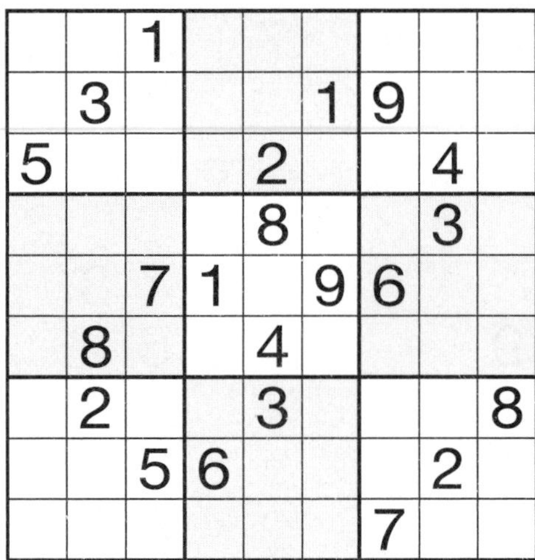

		1						
	3				1	9		
5				2			4	
				8			3	
		7	1		9	6		
	8			4				
	2			3				8
		5	6				2	
						7		

PUZZLE / 661 Time:_______

		6	5					
	2				7		8	
	3			2		9		
4					2			
1								5
			6					1
		1		7			4	
	7		8				2	
					3	8		

PUZZLE / 662 Time:_______

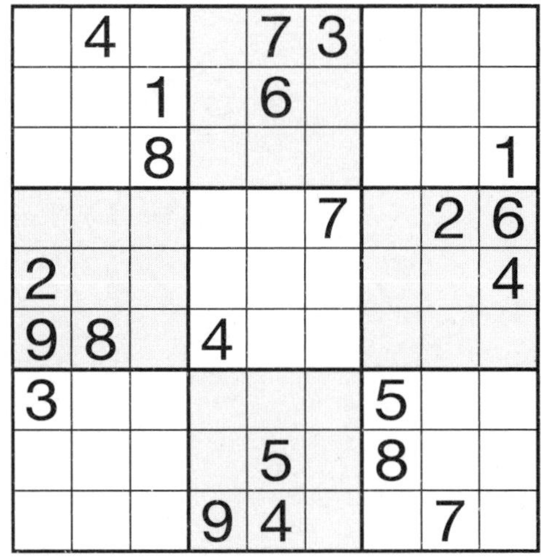

	4			7	3			
		1		6				
		8						1
					7		2	6
2								4
9	8		4					
3						5		
				5		8		
			9	4			7	

PUZZLE / 663 Time:_______

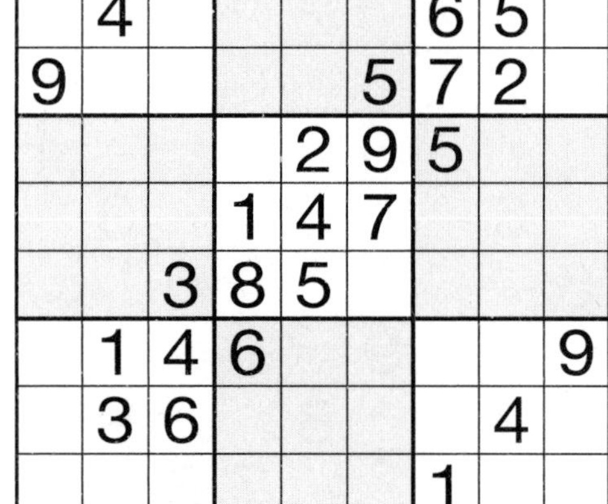

		8						
	4					6	5	
9					5	7	2	
				2	9	5		
			1	4	7			
		3	8	5				
	1	4	6					9
	3	6					4	
						1		

PUZZLE / 664 Time:_______

	1	2	3					
3				4		1		
6				5				
			5			3		
		6				5		
		7			8			
				3				8
		8		2				7
					7	6	2	

PUZZLE / 665 Time:_______

7								5
			1	2	3			
		4				8		
		3				2		
			4	5	6			
		6				1		
		2				6		
			7	8	9			
5								4

PUZZLE / 666 Time:_______

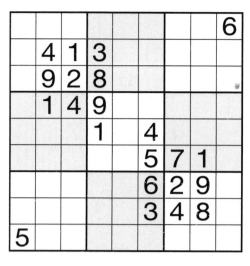

								6
	4	1	3					
	9	2	8					
	1	4	9					
			1		4			
					5	7	1	
					6	2	9	
					3	4	8	
5								

PUZZLE / 667 Time:_______

	1	2	9					
			6	1	2			5
								1
	3						1	4
	2						6	
8	7						5	
7								
4			3	9	8			
					4	8	3	

PUZZLE / 668 Time:_______

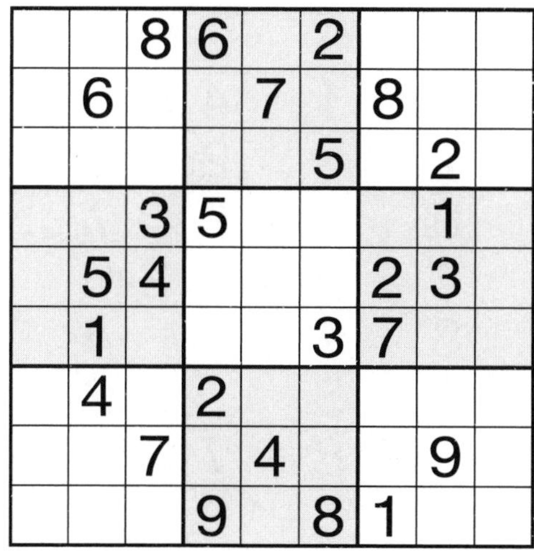

		8	6		2			
	6			7		8		
					5		2	
		3	5				1	
	5	4				2	3	
	1				3	7		
	4		2					
		7		4			9	
			9		8	1		

PUZZLE / 669 Time:_______

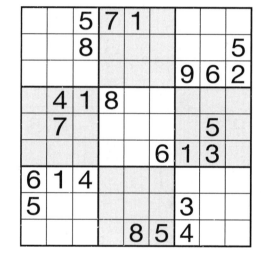

		5	7	1				
		8						5
						9	6	2
	4	1	8					
	7						5	
					6	1	3	
6	1	4						
5						3		
				8	5	4		

PUZZLE / 670 Time:_______

					3	4	2	
	6	4	2			5	3	
		3	5				7	
			4		6			
	8				1	9		
	9	6			5	3	1	
	4	5	9					

PUZZLE / 671 Time:_______

	2	3						
1			4					
			5		1	2	3	4
		6			9			5
	7						6	
8			6			7		
9	3	2	1		4			
					5			9
						8	4	

PUZZLE / 672 Time:_______

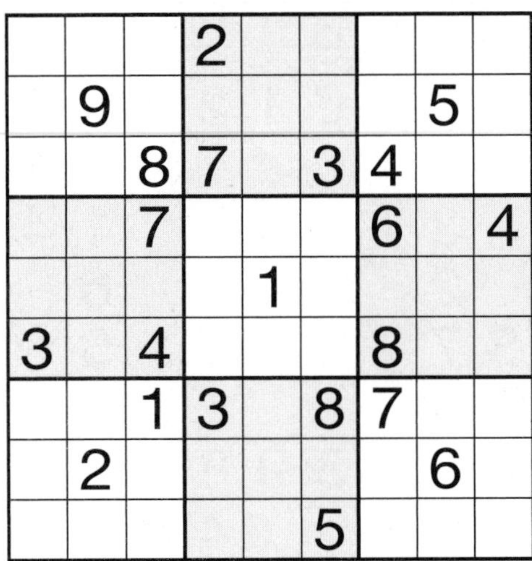

			2					
	9						5	
		8	7		3	4		
		7				6		4
				1				
3		4				8		
		1	3		8	7		
	2						6	
					5			

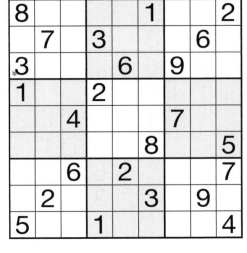

PUZZLE / 673 Time:_______

8					1			2
	7		3				6	
3				6		9		
1			2					
		4				7		
					8			5
		6		2				7
	2				3		9	
5			1					4

PUZZLE / 674 Time:_______

							9	6
					8	7	3	
		2		7	3			
		6	3					
9	3						6	5
					5	1		
			1	3		4		
	2	8	4					
4	7							

PUZZLE / 675 Time:_______

		6	1		4	5		
	7				2		3	
	6				9		7	
	4	1				2	6	
	8		3				4	
	3		5				2	
		9	8		7	4		

PUZZLE / 676 Time:_______

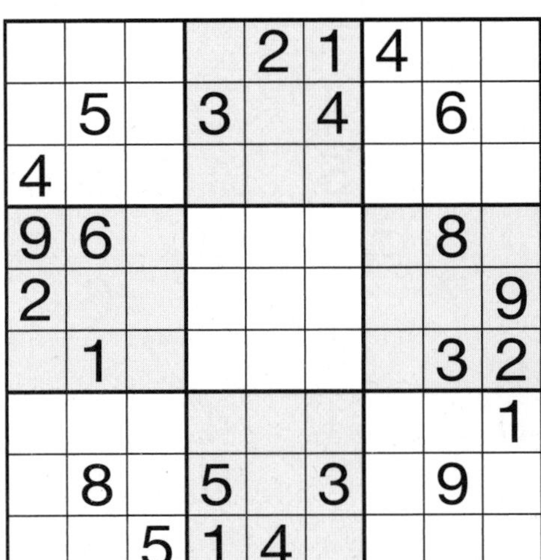

				2	1	4		
	5		3		4		6	
4								
9	6						8	
2								9
	1						3	2
								1
	8		5		3		9	
		5	1	4				

PUZZLE / 677 Time:_______

	4	8					7	
3			9			1		
				6	5			
6						7		
	9						4	
		4						2
			5	8				
		1			6			9
	3					8	2	

PUZZLE / 678 Time:_______

			2					1
				7			2	
5	4				8			
8	3				2			
1				5				2
			9				4	6
			5				9	7
	6			1				
4					3			

PUZZLE / 679 Time:_______

		4				3		
	6				4			
1				9				
			3				9	
		8	2	5	6	4		
	2				8			
				1				7
			6				1	
		2				8		

PUZZLE / 680 Time:_______

		8						1
	4			3	6			
9								
		7			9		3	2
				2				
1	6		7			4		
								8
			2	8			9	
4						1		

PUZZLE / 681 Time:_______

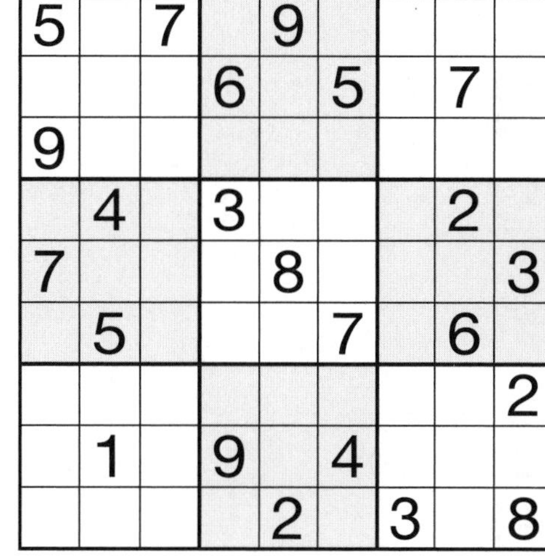

5		7		9				
			6		5		7	
9								
	4		3				2	
7				8				3
	5				7		6	
								2
	1		9		4			
				2		3		8

PUZZLE / 682 Time:_______

6								9
	7						4	
			1	2	3			
		3				7		
			4	5	6			
		9				8		
			7	8	9			
	2						5	
4								3

PUZZLE / 683 Time:_______

			1					
		1			7	5	3	
		9		4			7	
		4		2			1	
	6						8	
	5			8		2		
	4			9		6		
	3	6	5			9		
					4			

PUZZLE / 684 Time:_______

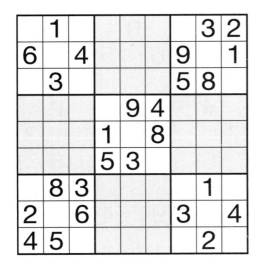

		2				9		
	4			7		8	2	
6	7	3					5	1
			9		8			
	8			4			9	
			7		6			
2	6					5	7	9
	1	5		2			4	
		4				2		

PUZZLE / 685 Time:_______

			3	9				4
		8			2	3	9	
		4						
	7				9	5		
	2			8			1	
		9	7				6	
						4		
	5	2	6			8		
1				7	5			

PUZZLE / 686 Time:_______

	1						3	2
6		4				9		1
	3					5	8	
				9	4			
			1		8			
			5	3				
	8	3					1	
2		6				3		4
4	5						2	

PUZZLE / 687 Time:_______

					7	8	1	
	2	5				4		
1			8					
9			1					
	8	2				6	9	
					4			8
					5			2
		9				7	6	
	6	4	7					

PUZZLE / 688 Time:_______

					3	6		
	9						8	
8			9	1				
7			4		2	5		
		2				7		
		4	5		6			2
				2	8			1
	5						4	
		3	6					

PUZZLE / 689 Time:_______

			1					
		5	7					
	9				5	8		
8	3				2	1		
		1	6				4	5
		6	4				1	
					9	2		
					7			

PUZZLE / 690 Time:_______

	4						3	1
	8		4					5
6					3			
								6
	3		2	7	1		9	
9								
			6					8
3					2		1	
8	9						5	

PUZZLE / 691 Time:_______

1							8	
	3			6			7	4
		8	9					
		5	7					
	4			1			9	
					6	4		
					3	5		
3	7			2			1	
	8							6

PUZZLE / 692 Time:_______

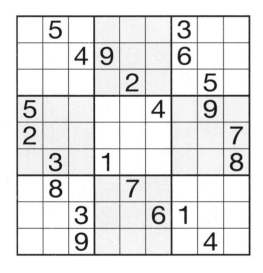

	5					3		
		4	9			6		
				2			5	
5					4		9	
2								7
	3		1					8
	8			7				
		3			6	1		
		9					4	

PUZZLE / 693 Time:_______

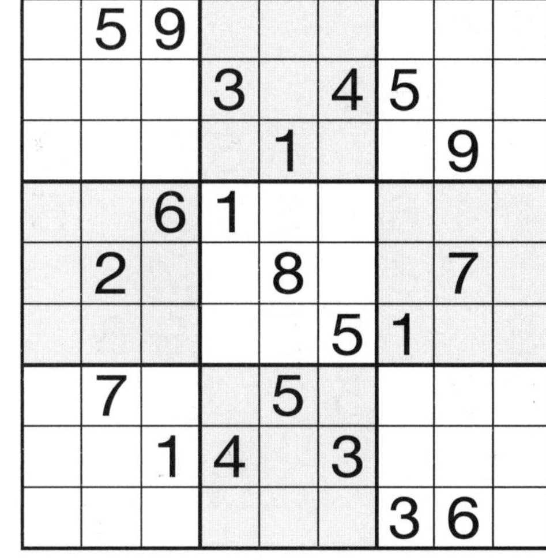

	5	9						
			3		4	5		
				1			9	
		6	1					
	2			8			7	
					5	1		
	7			5				
		1	4		3			
						3	6	

PUZZLE / 694 Time:_______

					6		4	
9		7				1		2
				3				
			2		4			6
		1				5		
3			5		1			
				6				
8		4				7		5
	2		9					

PUZZLE / 695 Time:_______

				5	7	1		
			2				4	
		1						8
	5		4					3
3				7				9
2					9		1	
7						4		
	2				8			
		6	9	3				

PUZZLE / 696 Time:_______

		8	6	1				
		6	4	7				
1	9							
9	8							
5	3						6	2
							4	7
							5	9
				8	6	7		
				5	3	4		

PUZZLE / 697 Time:_______

					7	5		
	8			4			9	
6		4			8	7		
2		3						
	9						1	
						4		5
		2	8			6		9
	6			1			3	
		5	3					

PUZZLE / 698 Time:_______

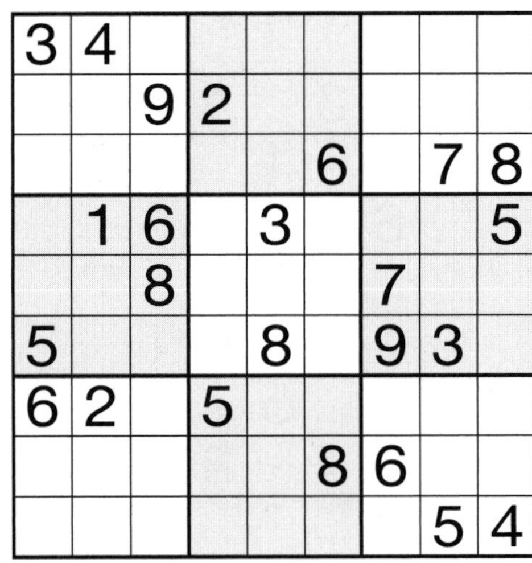

3	4							
		9	2					
					6		7	8
	1	6		3				5
		8				7		
5				8		9	3	
6	2		5					
					8	6		
							5	4

PUZZLE / 699 Time:_______

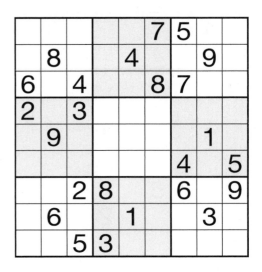

				1				
			4	9		7	5	
		2					9	
	9				3			
1	7			2			4	9
			7				6	
	5					6		
	8	3		6	2			
				5				

PUZZLE / 700 Time:_______

	1				6			
2				3		1		
					9		8	
						8		9
	2						6	
4		7						
	5		8					
		6		9				3
			2				4	

PUZZLE / 701 Time:_______

								4
		9	8				5	
	5			3		7		
	7			4				
		1	5		6	8		
				9			6	
		6		2			9	
	8				9	3		
1								

PUZZLE / 702 Time:_______

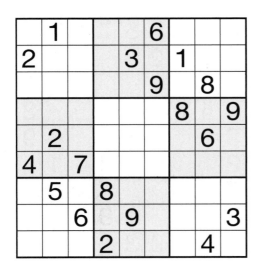

		3	4					
5								1
			8	9		5		
	7	8					1	
2			1		7			3
	3					9	6	
		6		1	9			
3								6
					8	2		

PUZZLE / 703 Time:_______

		1	2	3				
		4	5			7		8
						4		7
3								1
6		2						
2		5			4	6		
				8	7	3		

PUZZLE / 704 Time:_______

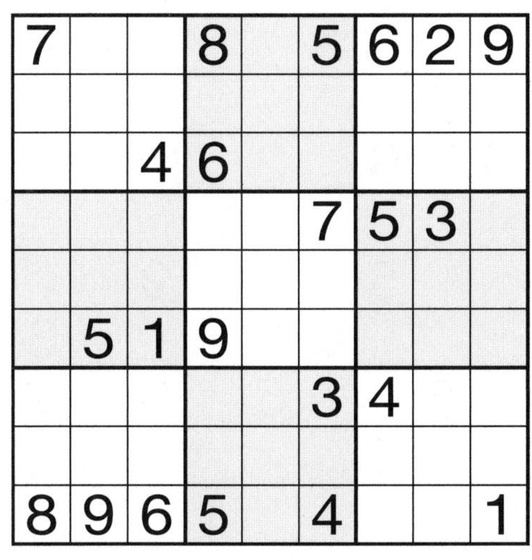

7			8		5	6	2	9
		4	6					
					7	5	3	
	5	1	9					
					3	4		
8	9	6	5		4			1

PUZZLE / 705 Time:_______

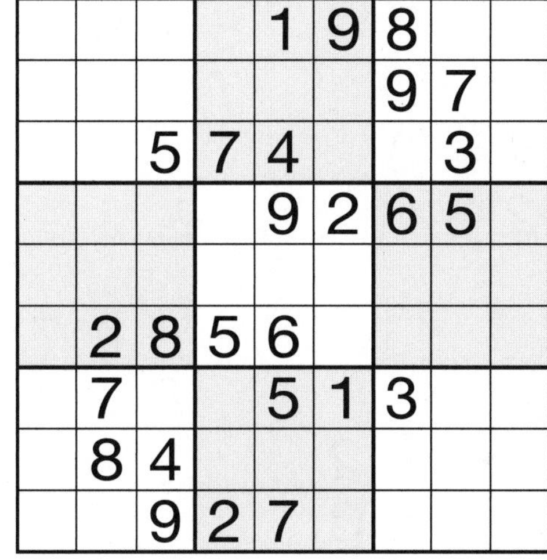

				1	9	8		
						9	7	
		5	7	4			3	
				9	2	6	5	
	2	8	5	6				
	7			5	1	3		
	8	4						
		9	2	7				

PUZZLE / 706 Time:_______

				7				
	9		5		8		3	
		3		4		2		
	4						7	
7		2				1		4
	8						5	
		7		1		5		
	5		2		9		4	
				6				

PUZZLE / 707 Time:_______

6							2	
	2		3	4				1
8			2			4		
	4		1			9		
5								7
		6			3		5	
		1			7			9
7				1	9		6	
	9							8

PUZZLE / 708 Time:_______

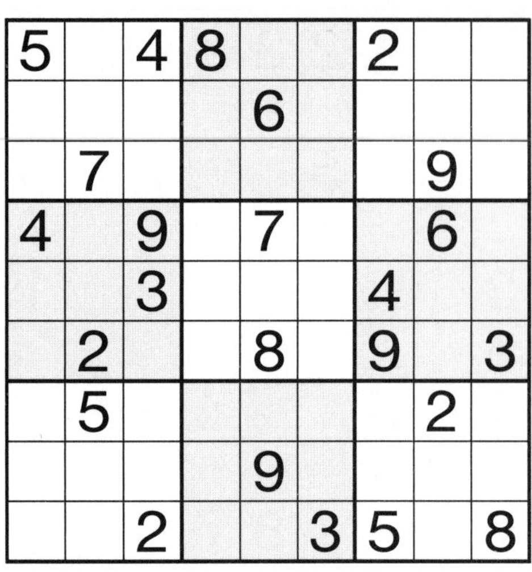

5		4	8			2		
				6				
	7						9	
4		9		7			6	
		3				4		
	2			8		9		3
	5						2	
				9				
		2			3	5		8

PUZZLE / 709 Time:_______

7				2				
	8		6					
		5			3		6	
		1				8		
		6		8		2		
		4				7		
	5		4			9		
					6		3	
				7				1

PUZZLE / 710 Time:_______

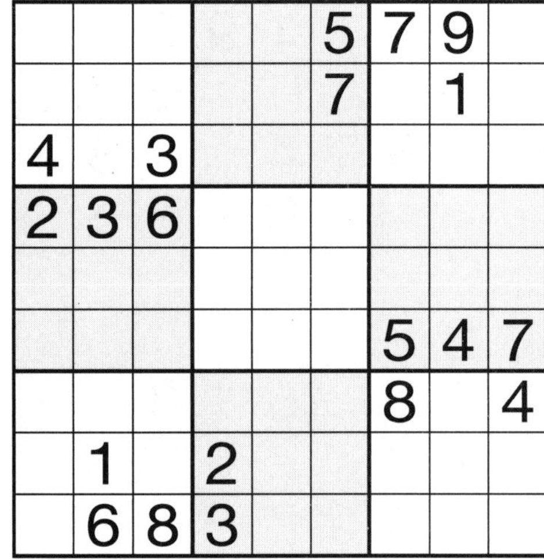

					5	7	9	
					7		1	
4		3						
2	3	6						
						5	4	7
						8		4
	1		2					
	6	8	3					

PUZZLE / 711 Time:_______

		3	5					6
	2					1		
5		9		2			4	
4					2			
		5		7		9		
			6					3
	5			6		3		9
		8					6	
6					1	8		

PUZZLE / 712 Time:_______

								6
	1	2	3					
	4	5	6					
	7	8	1					
					5	9	4	
					9	4	8	
					7	2	5	
3								

PUZZLE / 713 Time:_______

6					3		1	
				2		4		
		8	1				5	
			8					6
	2			6			7	
3					9			
	4				8	9		
		5		7				
	9		6					8

PUZZLE / 714 Time:_______

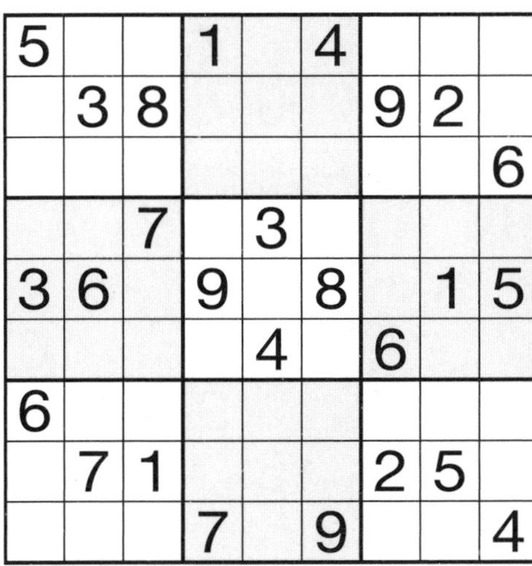

5			1		4			
	3	8				9	2	
								6
		7		3				
3	6		9		8		1	5
				4		6		
6								
	7	1				2	5	
			7		9			4

PUZZLE / 715 Time:_______

					2	1	3	
		1	4	6				8
								9
						2	5	
			7	9	3			
	6	8						
7								
2				8	9	3		
	5	4	1					

PUZZLE / 716 Time:_______

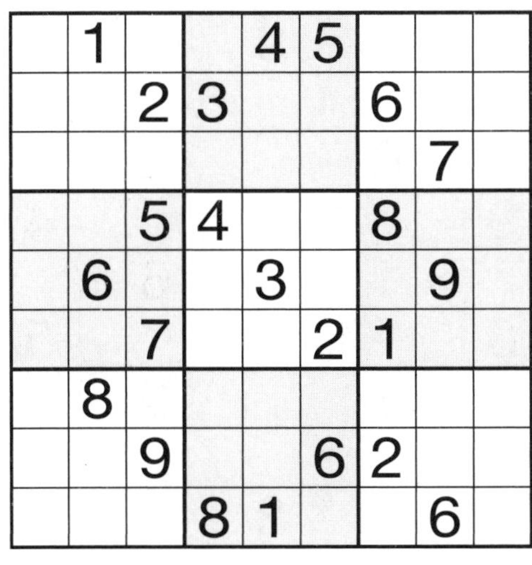

	1			4	5			
		2	3			6		
							7	
		5	4			8		
	6			3			9	
		7			2	1		
	8							
		9			6	2		
			8	1			6	

PUZZLE / 717 Time:_______

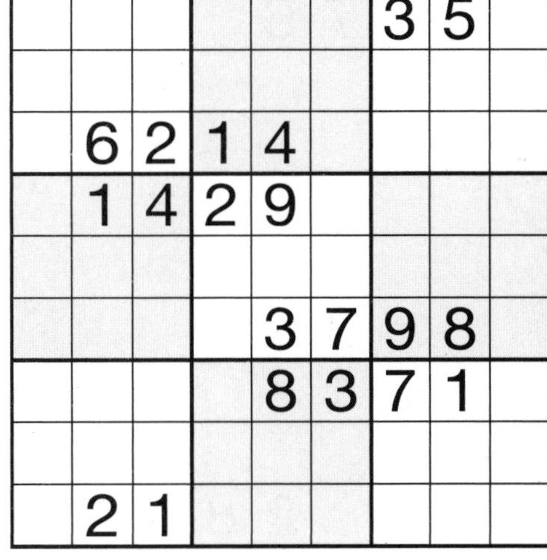

						3	5	
	6	2	1	4				
	1	4	2	9				
				3	7	9	8	
				8	3	7	1	
	2	1						

PUZZLE / 718 Time:_______

			3	4	9	6		
		9	5					
	5							1
4	7							2
1								8
5							3	4
3							8	
					6	1		
		1	2	8	7			

PUZZLE / 719 Time:_______

8				6				3
			2		7			
		1				2		
	5			1			6	
		4		2		5		
	9			3			7	
		2				8		
			5		9			
7				8				9

PUZZLE / 720 Time:_______

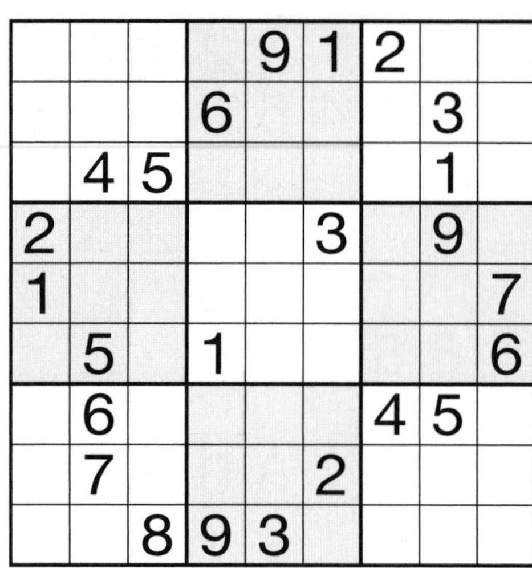

				9	1	2		
			6				3	
	4	5					1	
2					3		9	
1								7
	5		1					6
	6					4	5	
	7				2			
		8	9	3				

PUZZLE / 721 Time:_______

					7			
				9		1		
	5	6	4			9		
1						7		
	8			2			3	
		4						6
		7			9	4	6	
		1		5				
			3					

PUZZLE / 722 Time:_______

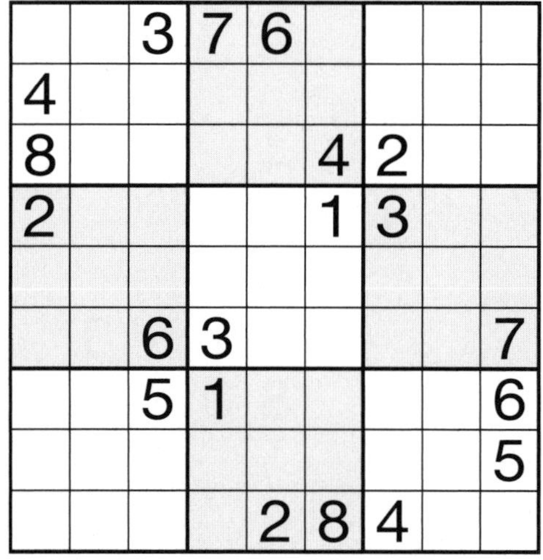

		3	7	6				
4								
8					4	2		
2					1	3		
		6	3					7
		5	1					6
								5
				2	8	4		

PUZZLE / 723 Time:_______

				9				
			4		5			
		6				2		
9			8		6			4
	5	1		3		6	8	
3			9		1			5
		2				5		
			3		7			
				8				

PUZZLE / 724 Time:_______

		7	4		1	2		
	6	8				9	4	
				4				
5	1			7			8	6
				2				
	2	6				1	5	
		4	9		2	3		

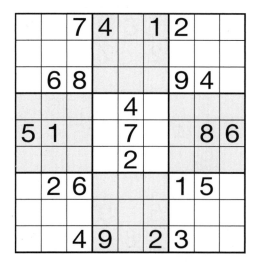

PUZZLE / 725 Time:_______

	6				9	3		
7			3				2	
		4		8			9	
			7					2
5								8
6					1			
	3			9		5		
	4				3			1
		5	1				8	

PUZZLE / 726 Time:_______

		5		2		1		
			7					6
7	9				4		3	
2			5					
		6				9		
					3			4
	7		9				5	8
3					6			
		4		8		2		

PUZZLE / 727 Time:_______

				1		4		
			9		3			
		8		5				2
	4		2				9	
		9		6		8		
	2				7		6	
6				2		7		
			8		5			
		1		4				

PUZZLE / 728 Time:_______

2								3
				4	2			
		5		3	1			
						5	6	
	8	6				4	3	
	7	1						
			7	5		8		
			6	8				
7								4

PUZZLE / 729 Time:_______

	5							
2		8				6	3	
	1				5		7	
				6		2		
			7		1			
		9		2				
	7		5				4	
	4	3				9		6
							1	

PUZZLE / 730 Time:_______

			3		5			2
				7		6	9	
					8			1
	9	3				1		
4								8
		7				4	5	
2			5					
	7	1		6				
5			8		1			

PUZZLE / 731 Time:_______

						1	5	4
2	6	3						
					6	9		
		4	1		5	3		
		1	2					
						4	8	7
5	9	6						

PUZZLE / 732 Time:_______

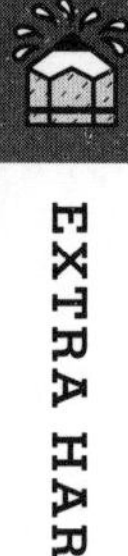

2			8				5	
		9						7
		3		9	1			
7			3			2		
	4						6	
		8			2			5
			5	4		3		
6						7		
	9				7			1

PUZZLE / 733 Time:_______

3		8	9		5			6
			2		6			4
8		2				3		5
		9				6		
6		5				4		1
7			3		2			
1			5		4	8		2

PUZZLE / 734 Time:_______

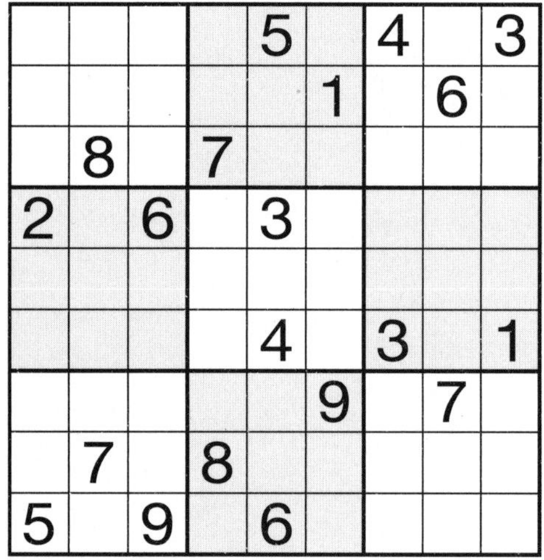

				5		4		3
					1		6	
	8		7					
2		6		3				
				4		3		1
					9		7	
	7		8					
5		9		6				

PUZZLE / 735 Time:_______

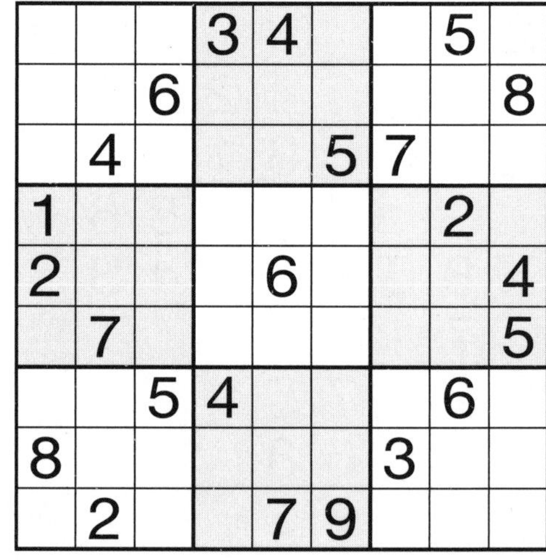

			3	4			5	
		6						8
	4				5	7		
1							2	
2				6				4
	7							5
		5	4				6	
8						3		
	2			7	9			

PUZZLE / 736 Time:_______

						9		
	5				8			
				3		6		2
			1				4	
		6				3		
	1				7			
6		2		9				
			5				8	
		3						

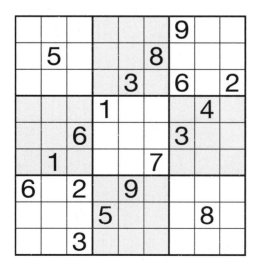

PUZZLE / 737 Time:_______

	2	8						
	7	5		1	6			
				8	4		7	5
							8	1
3	9							
6	5		3	7				
			6	5		2	4	
						3	5	

PUZZLE / 738 Time:_______

1					6	8		
	2						9	
		3	4					2
5					1	2		
	6			2			3	
		7	8					4
9					5	6		
	4						7	
		1	7					8

PUZZLE / 739 Time:______

		2						8
	1				5	6		
7				3			1	
			2				7	
3								4
	6				1			
	9			4				2
		7	8				5	
5						1		

PUZZLE / 740 Time:______

9								1
	2	5		1		9	4	
	6						7	
			2		3			
	4						5	
			6		7			
	8						6	
	7	1		8		5	9	
5								7

PUZZLE / 741 Time:______

		1	7		5	8		
9								
7		2	3		8	9		
5								
		6	2		1	7		
								3
		8	4		6	1		7
								4
		3	1		7	2		

PUZZLE / 742 Time:______

			3		9			
1								8
	5			2			1	
		6		8		3		
		5	1		6	9		
		2		5		7		
	3			4			5	
8								6
			7		1			

PUZZLE / 743 Time:______

			2	8	4	9		
		3						
	6					1		
9					5		8	
4				9				5
	7		3					2
		5					3	
						8		
		2	9	1	6			

PUZZLE / 744 Time:______

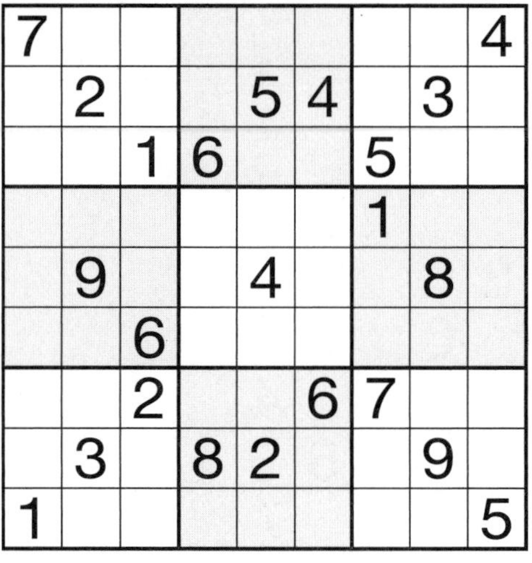

7								4
	2			5	4		3	
		1	6			5		
						1		
	9			4			8	
		6						
		2			6	7		
	3		8	2			9	
1								5

PUZZLE / 745 Time:_______

	4	7	1	8				
					2	6	9	
	1	8	4					
					6	9	3	
	2	1	7					
				5	3	7	6	

PUZZLE / 746 Time:_______

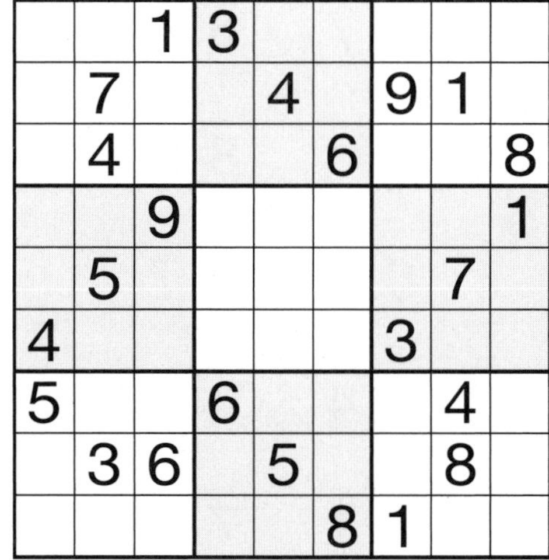

		1	3					
	7			4		9	1	
	4				6			8
		9						1
	5						7	
4						3		
5			6				4	
	3	6		5			8	
					8	1		

PUZZLE / 747 Time:_______

2	5							
7				2			5	
					8	6		
					1	4		
	6						8	
		8	9					
		9	6					
	3			8				2
							7	5

PUZZLE / 748 Time:_______

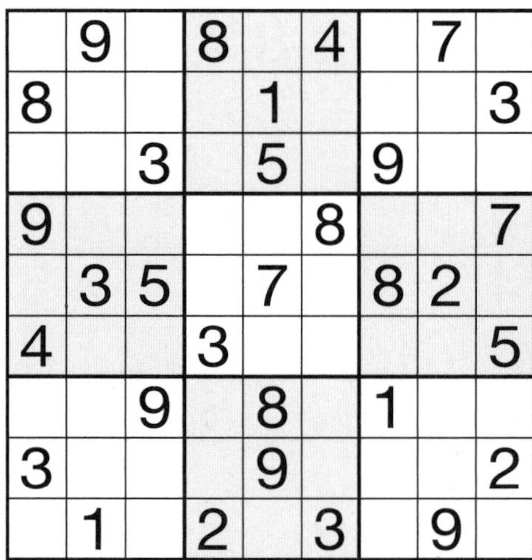

	9		8		4		7	
8				1				3
		3		5		9		
9					8			7
	3	5		7		8	2	
4			3					5
		9		8		1		
3				9				2
	1		2		3		9	

PUZZLE / 749 Time:_______

	2	1	4					5
	7	6	1					3
	8	9	2					6
3					8	7	5	
6					9	2	4	
8					5	3	6	

PUZZLE / 750 Time:_______

3		5		8				1
	6		1				2	
7		1				3		
	1				4			
2				5				7
			6				9	
		7				9		2
	8				9		3	
9				3		4		8

PUZZLE / 751 Time:_______

				1		3		
			9		2		4	
		7		5		6		8
			7				5	
	6				9			
4		5		6		7		
	1		5		4			
		3		7				

PUZZLE / 752 Time:_______

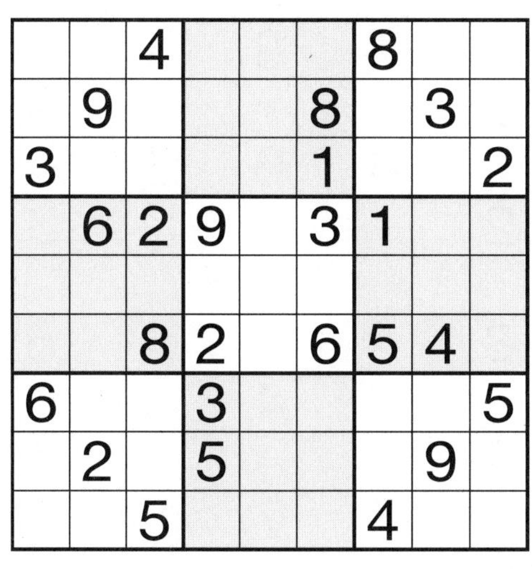

		4				8		
	9				8		3	
3					1			2
	6	2	9		3	1		
		8	2		6	5	4	
6			3					5
	2		5				9	
		5				4		

PUZZLE / 753 Time:_______

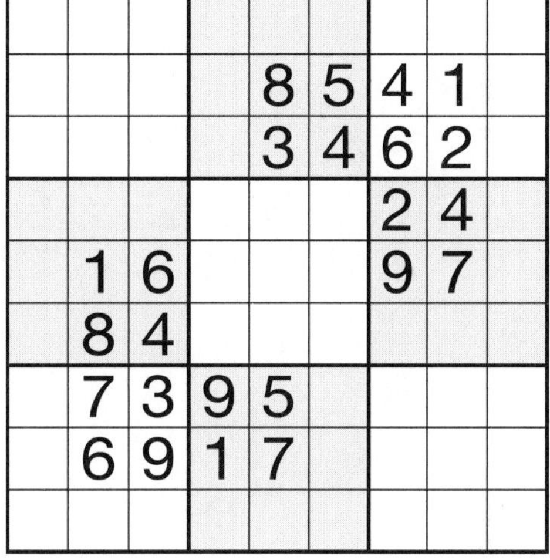

				8	5	4	1	
				3	4	6	2	
						2	4	
	1	6				9	7	
	8	4						
	7	3	9	5				
	6	9	1	7				

PUZZLE / 754 Time:_______

	7			2			8	
3		8			5			
			4			6		
5			6					
	2						1	
					8			9
		9			3			
			2			5		4
	3			1			2	

PUZZLE / 755 Time:_______

8					7			5
				1			9	
			9			3		
		7			6			3
	2			9			1	
3			1			4		
		8			5			
	7			3				
6			4					8

PUZZLE / 756 Time:_______

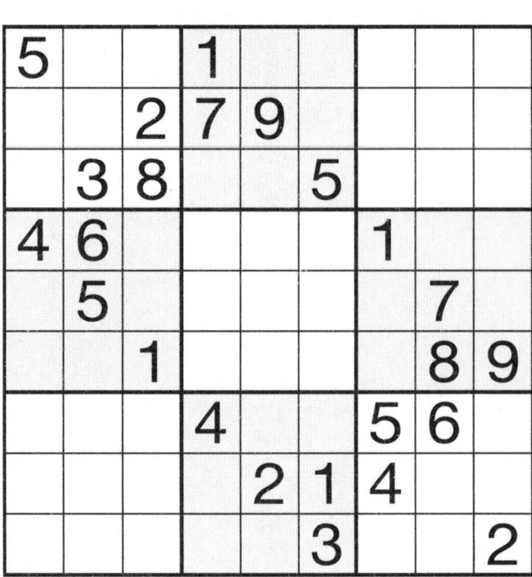

5			1					
		2	7	9				
	3	8			5			
4	6					1		
	5						7	
		1					8	9
			4			5	6	
				2	1	4		
					3			2

PUZZLE / 757 Time:_______

		1	9		6	2		
	8			2			4	
	6		2		8		9	
		2				1		
	4		1		9		7	
	7			6			5	
		6	3		4	9		

PUZZLE / 758 Time:_______

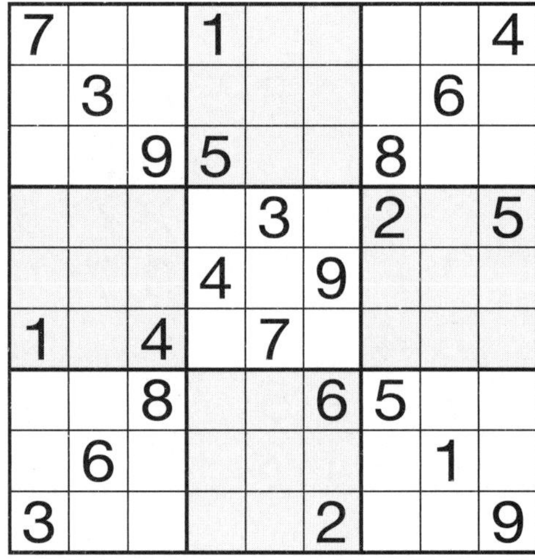

7			1					4
	3						6	
		9	5			8		
				3		2		5
			4		9			
1		4		7				
		8			6	5		
	6						1	
3					2			9

PUZZLE / 759 Time:_______

		7		8		1		
3								9
		4		6		2		
2								3
			9		5			
8								5
		3		4		8		
5								1
		6		7		5		

PUZZLE / 760 Time:_______

		1						
	5		1				7	
		2		9		3		8
			6		7		2	
		6				1		
	3		8		5			
8		9		2		6		
	7				1		4	
						7		

PUZZLE / 761 Time:_______

		2		4				7
	4				3		1	
8				5				
			8				4	
5		9				6		3
	3				6			
				9				2
	1		5				8	
4				6		5		

PUZZLE / 762 Time:_______

	5			9			1	
1								3
		2				8		
			3		2			
6								5
			8		4			
		8				2		
3								7
	4			1			8	

PUZZLE / 763 Time:_______

		7					1	8
		6				7		
	2				3			
5			1	7				
1								9
				6	4			2
			3				8	
		1				6		
4	3					9		

PUZZLE / 764 Time:_______

	7			8				2
8		9					6	
			5		2			
		5			4	2		
2				3				8
		6	9			4		
			6		8			
	5					7		1
1				5			3	

PUZZLE / 765 Time:_______

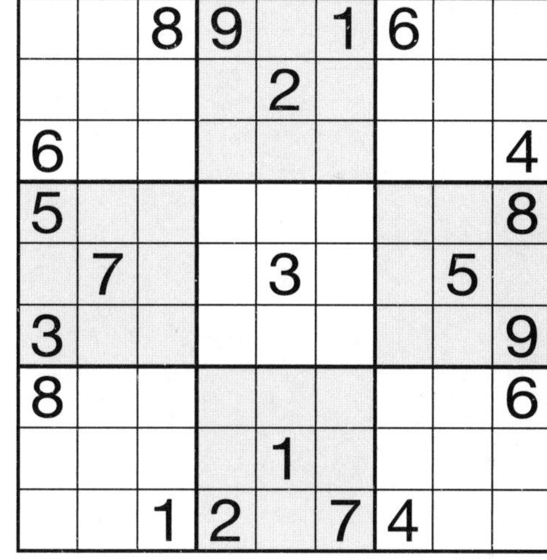

		8	9		1	6		
				2				
6								4
5								8
	7			3			5	
3								9
8								6
				1				
		1	2		7	4		

PUZZLE / 766 Time:_______

	3		8		2		4	
	2		6		4		8	
		5				3		
1				9				7
		2				1		
	6		4		7		3	
	9		5		1		2	

PUZZLE / 767 Time:_______

								3
				2	3	5	4	
			4			6	7	
		1	7				8	
	6						9	
	5				6	3		
	4	3			7			
	1	2	9	8				
7								

PUZZLE / 768 Time:_______

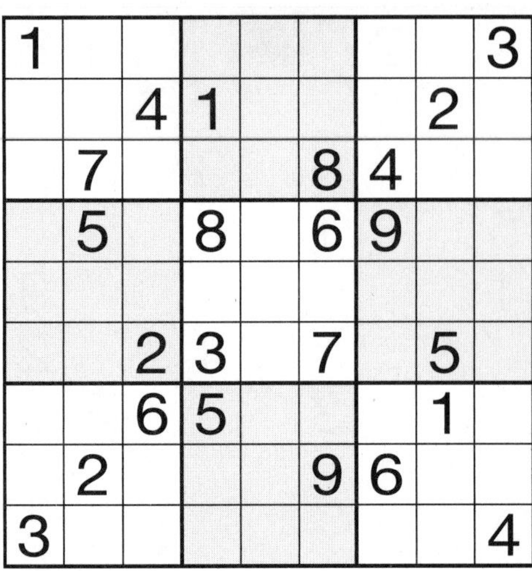

PUZZLE / 769 Time:______

			4	7				
		3			5	8	4	
	4							6
		4	2			3	5	
	6	8			9	2		
7							9	
	5	2	3			4		
				6	7			

PUZZLE / 770 Time:______

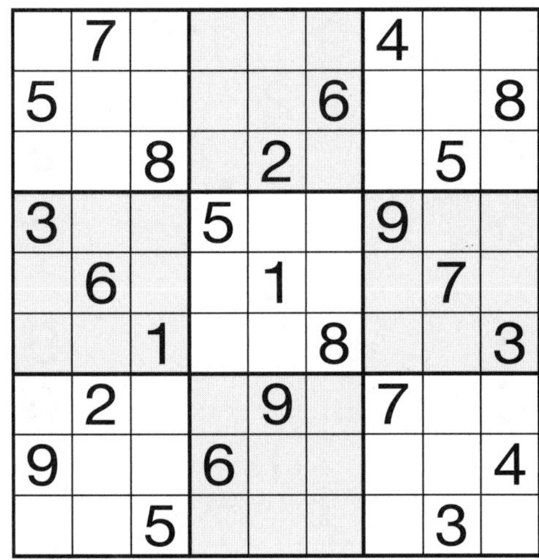

PUZZLE / 771 Time:______

9				3				5
		2					4	
	6		1			8		
		9			7			
3								1
			9			2		
		8			4		7	
	2					6		
7				1				8

PUZZLE / 772 Time:______

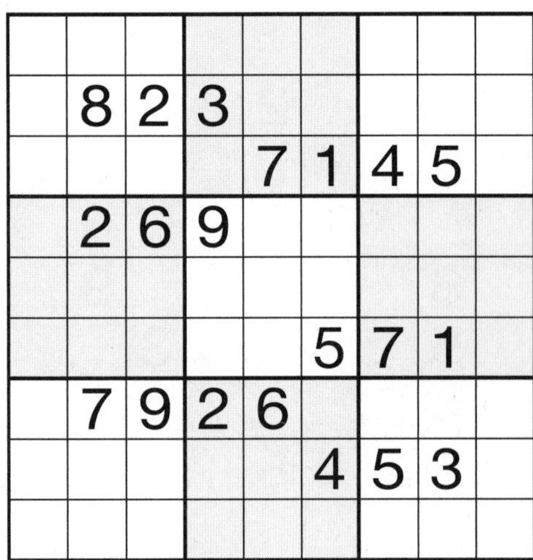

PUZZLE / 773 Time:______

	7			8			5	
		6	5					4
	9			1			3	
4					8	2		
	5			7			9	
		3	2					1
	4			9			8	
9					5	7		
	3			2			4	

PUZZLE / 774 Time:______

		5		7	8		9	
	6		1			8		
1							4	
	9							3
8								1
6							2	
	7							2
		6			3		1	
	1		9	4		3		

PUZZLE / 775 Time:_______

5				8				7
		2				1		
	9		5		1		4	
		9				8		
4				5				9
		3				2		
	6		1		2		3	
		4				6		
7				6				2

PUZZLE / 776 Time:_______

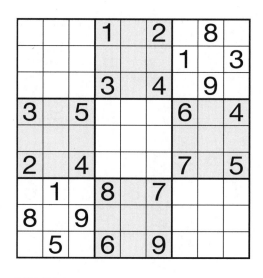

			1		2		8	
						1		3
			3		4		9	
3		5				6		4
2		4				7		5
	1		8		7			
8		9						
	5		6		9			

PUZZLE / 777 Time:_______

		8	1					
			6					
4	9	5	3					
3								
7	6						2	4
								9
					4	6	7	3
					2			
					5	1		

PUZZLE / 778 Time:_______

		2	7	3				
			4					5
			9					6
							5	7
5	4						3	8
6	8							
7					9			
8					1			
				2	3	9		

PUZZLE / 779 Time:_______

	1	8						7
					9		6	
2					4			
5				3		6	4	
	6	7		8				5
			1					3
	4		7					
9						2	5	

PUZZLE / 780 Time:_______

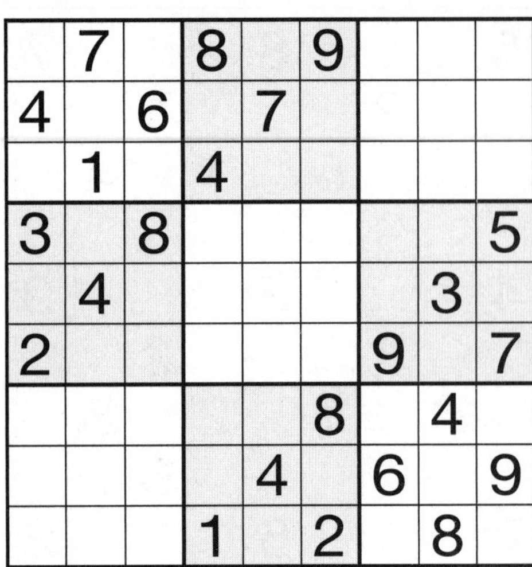

PUZZLE / 781 Time:_______

	8				6		9	
4				9	7			8
					3	4		
						8	4	5
	4			2			3	
1	3	8						
		1	9					
3			5	7				4
	2		6				7	

PUZZLE / 782 Time:_______

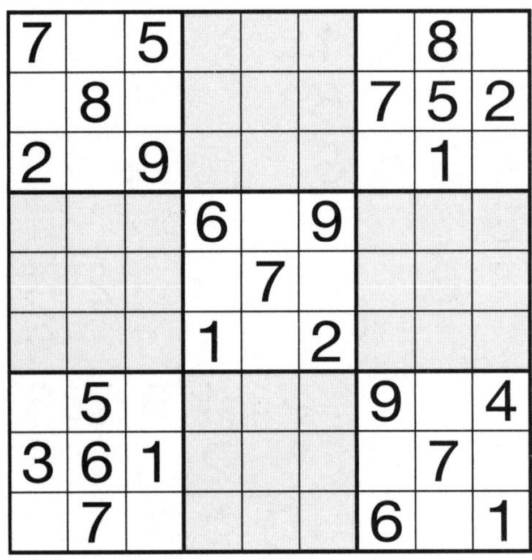

PUZZLE / 783 Time:_______

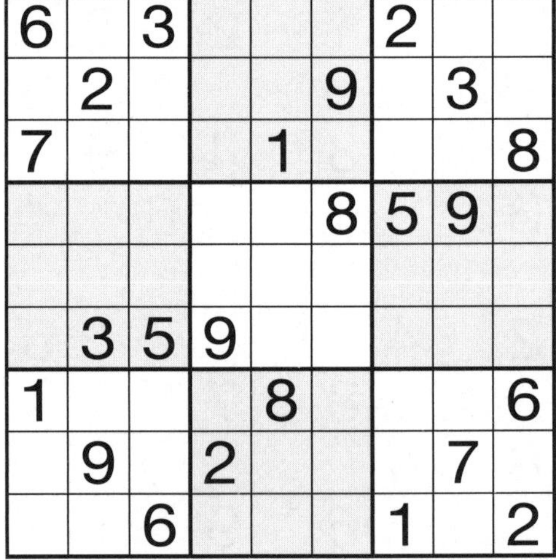

PUZZLE / 784 Time:_______

		2						
	4			8			6	
			1		9			7
		3				4		
	8			2			3	
		7				1		
5			8		4			
	6			5			2	
						3		

PUZZLE / 785 Time:_______

			3		7		9	
4		8						
	1					5		
			9				6	
7				3				2
	8				4			
		9					7	
						4		1
	5		1		8			

PUZZLE / 786 Time:_______

7	4						9	
	1	2				4		
		6	9		4			7
			2	7			5	
		5				9		
	8			6	9			
5			3		8	2		
		4				5	6	
	2						8	9

PUZZLE / 787 Time:_______

4					2			6
	9			3			7	
		2				8		
			6		5			1
	5						2	
6			4		3			
		8				1		
	7			8			9	
3			2					5

PUZZLE / 788 Time:_______

					2	3		
		8	5				4	
	5			6			1	
	1			7				4
3								9
2				4			5	
	6			8			7	
	7				1	6		
		5	6					

PUZZLE / 789 Time:_______

				4	9			
	3	7				6	1	
	9	2		7			5	
	7		9			1	8	
				8				
	1	6			4		7	
	8			5		7	9	
	2	1				5	3	
			3	1				

PUZZLE / 790 Time:_______

			5					
		2		3		1		
	4				7		5	
	3		4				6	
		1				2		
	8				5		7	
	6		3				8	
		8		2		9		
					1			

PUZZLE / 791 Time:_______

		6	2				7	
	8			9				2
1				5				
5			9					
	6	2				1	4	
					3			7
				1				6
6				3			8	
	5				4	3		

PUZZLE / 792 Time:_______

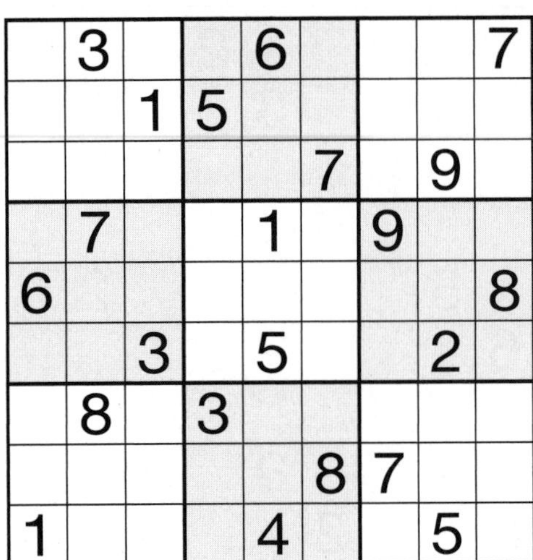

PUZZLE / 793 Time:_______

		9			6			
			4			5		
6				3			2	
	4				7			6
		1				3		
2			5				7	
	5			1				9
		7			2			
			8			4		

PUZZLE / 794 Time:_______

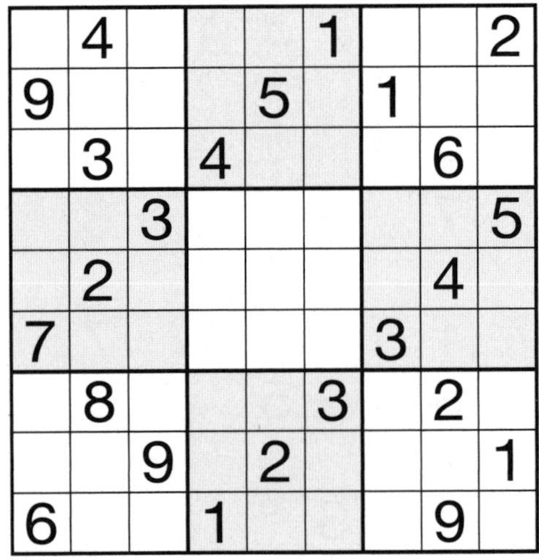

PUZZLE / 795 Time:_______

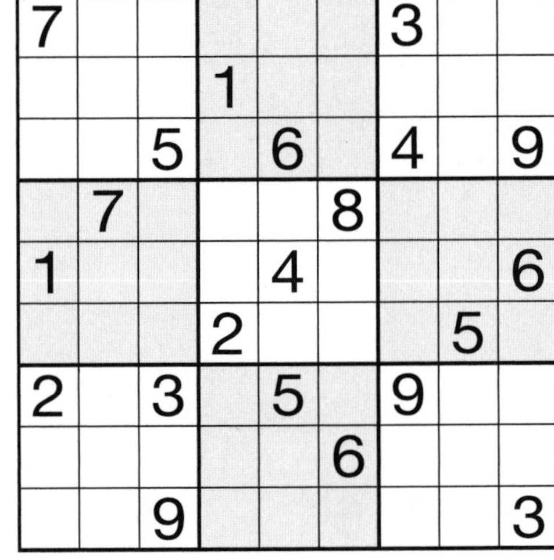

PUZZLE / 796 Time:_______

		7	6				5	
	9					3		1
8					3			
	2		3			6		
		8		6		7		
		6			7		9	
			5					2
5		4					8	
	7				1	4		

PUZZLE / 797 Time:_______

4	5		6	2				
3		2		7		1		
	8		4			6		
		3				7		
		6			1		2	
		5		1		3		4
				9	8		1	5

PUZZLE / 798 Time:_______

	2		5					
5				9			1	
		8						4
			8			9		
	7						3	
		1			4			
9						8		
	3			2				9
					3		2	

PUZZLE / 799 Time:_______

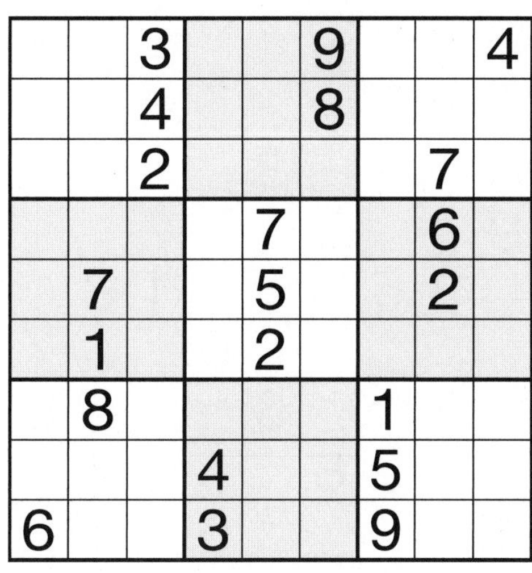

		3			9			4
		4			8			
		2					7	
				7			6	
	7			5			2	
	1			2				
	8					1		
			4			5		
6			3			9		

PUZZLE / 800 Time:_______

					6	7	8	
		8				3		
	2		4					
					4		5	
		3				1		
	1		5					
					8		4	
		9				6		
	3	7	1					

PUZZLE / 801 Time:_______

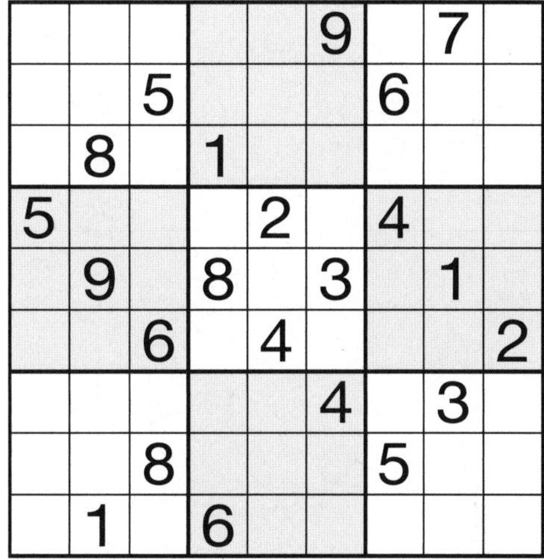

					9		7	
		5				6		
	8		1					
5				2		4		
	9		8		3		1	
		6		4				2
					4		3	
		8				5		
	1		6					

PUZZLE / 802 Time:_______

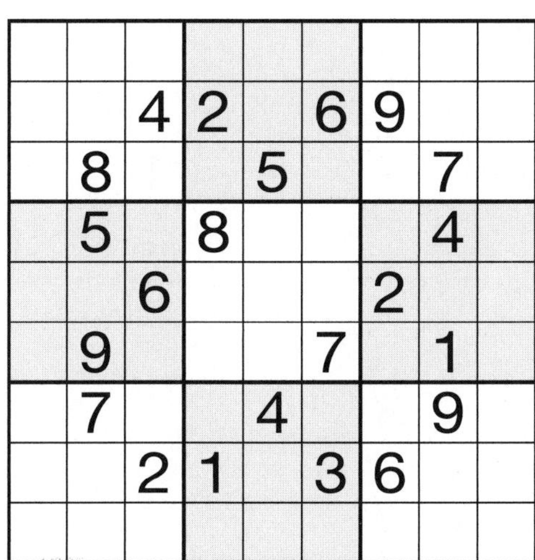

		4	2		6	9		
	8			5			7	
	5		8				4	
		6				2		
	9				7		1	
	7			4			9	
		2	1		3	6		

PUZZLE / 803 Time:_______

			7	8			4	6
				9				5
					1	2		
4						3		
6	5						7	8
		3						9
		2	8					
7				6				
8	6			7	5			

PUZZLE / 804 Time:_______

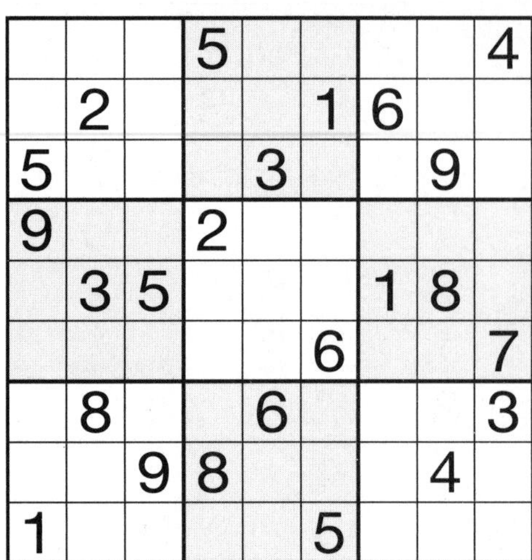

PUZZLE / 805 Time:_______

8						7	4	9
6			1					
9					2			
		4					3	
				5				
	7					6		
			8					2
					9			5
5	6	2						3

PUZZLE / 806 Time:_______

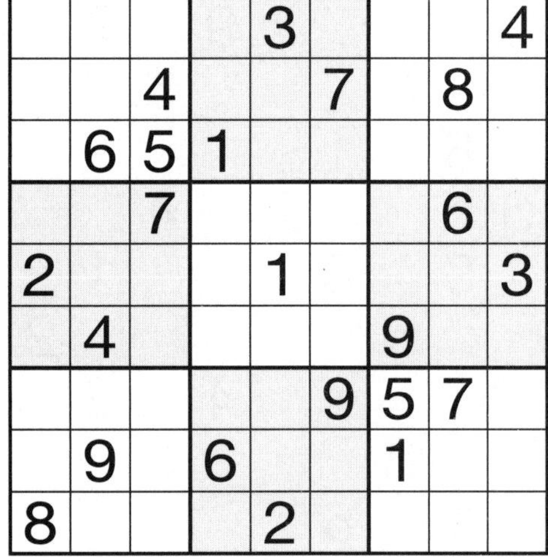

PUZZLE / 807 Time:_______

PUZZLE / 808 Time:_______

					5	1		
		9	2					
							4	3
5	6			1	7			
			9	4			2	8
1	5							
					1	6		
		4	3					

PUZZLE / 809 Time:_______

						9		
	3				5		6	
				9		1		8
					2		3	
		7				4		
	9		3					
1		8		4				
	5		6				2	
		4						

PUZZLE / 810 Time:_______

8				5				1
						9		
	2	6	3			8		
			8		7	1		
9								4
		5	1		4			
		7			1	2	3	
		1						
5				8				9

PUZZLE / 811 Time:_______

2	3						4	5
1								6
			9		8			
		3	2		1	4		
		5	6		4	1		
			7		9			
5								7
4	6						9	8

PUZZLE / 812 Time:_______

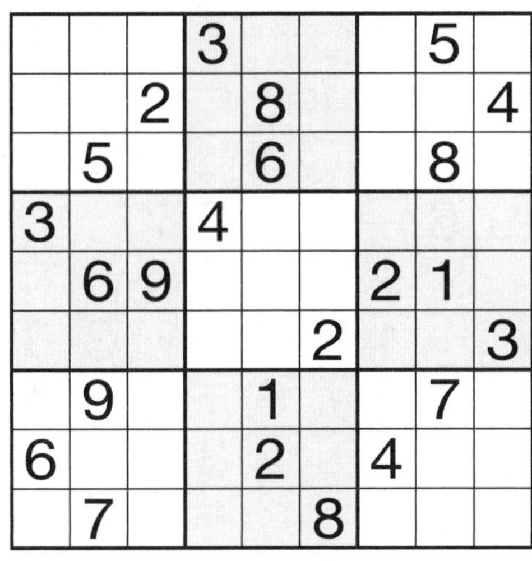

			3				5	
		2		8				4
	5			6			8	
3			4					
	6	9				2	1	
					2			3
	9			1			7	
6				2		4		
	7				8			

PUZZLE / 813 Time:_______

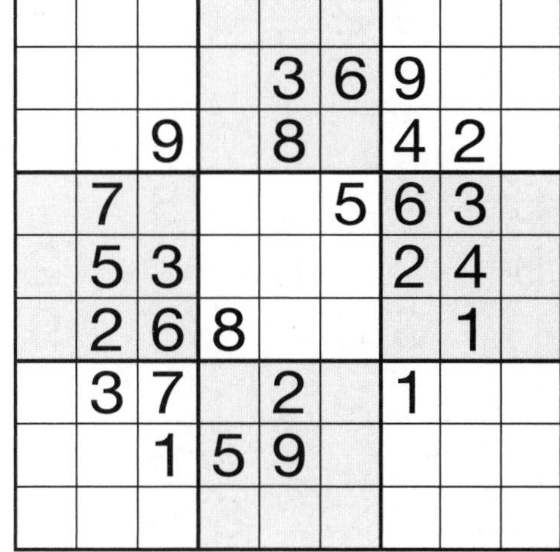

				3	6	9		
		9		8		4	2	
	7				5	6	3	
	5	3				2	4	
	2	6	8				1	
	3	7		2		1		
		1	5	9				

PUZZLE / 814 Time:_______

	2		5			7		
		9			8		5	
				6				1
	9				3			
6		3				8		2
			1				3	
3				2				
	6		7			5		
		8			4		6	

PUZZLE / 815 Time:_______

		2	8			3	9	
	9				4			
8				6				
	8				9			
		4				8		
			3				6	
				2				7
			6				3	
	7	6			5	2		

PUZZLE / 816 Time:_______

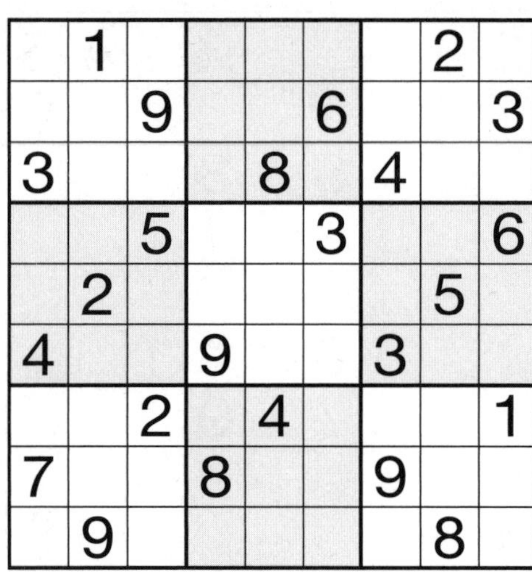

	1						2	
		9			6			3
3				8		4		
		5			3			6
	2						5	
4			9			3		
		2		4				1
7			8			9		
	9						8	

PUZZLE / 817 Time:_______

	8	7			4	2		
1	4				2		6	
3				6	5			4
8				7				9
6			9	4				7
	5		1				9	6
		1	4			8	7	

PUZZLE / 818 Time:_______

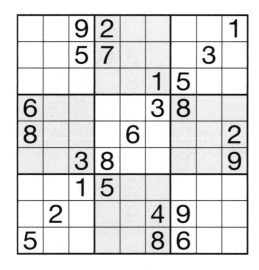

		9	2					1
		5	7				3	
					1	5		
6					3	8		
8				6				2
		3	8					9
		1	5					
	2				4	9		
5					8	6		

PUZZLE / 819 Time:_______

							1	2
			1	5				3
1				4				
9	6				3	7		
		2				4		
		1	2				3	6
				6				4
7				2	8			
8	9							

PUZZLE / 820 Time:_______

					2	3	4	
	5	9	7					
							6	
							8	
	6		1	5	7		3	
	2							
	8							
					3	4	2	
	7	1	5					

PUZZLE / 821 Time:_______

	9	5	8	2	6	3	7	
	3						8	
	5		6		8		9	
	6						3	
	1		4		9		2	
	7						6	
	8	6	7	5	3	9	1	

PUZZLE / 822 Time:_______

				2	3			1
	1						5	
8			6					4
		3			6	7		
	4						3	
		6	7			4		
4					5			2
	8						4	
9			8	6				

PUZZLE / 823 Time:_______

					3	1		
			7		2			
		5						8
	9						2	4
				8				
7	3						5	
1						3		
			2		9			
		8	5					

PUZZLE / 824 Time:_______

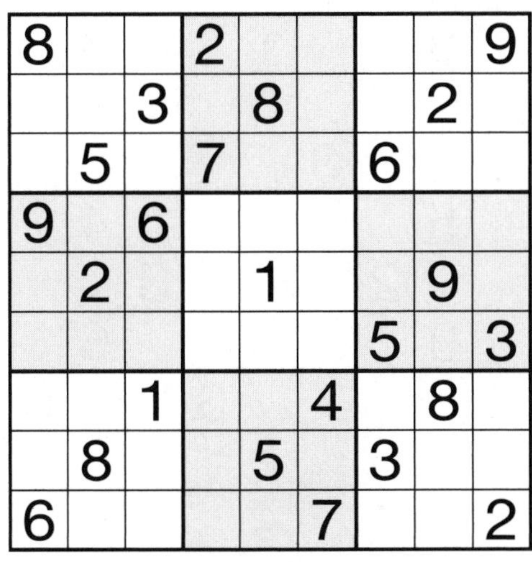

8			2					9
		3		8			2	
	5		7			6		
9		6						
	2			1			9	
						5		3
		1			4		8	
	8			5		3		
6					7			2

PUZZLE / 825 Time:_______

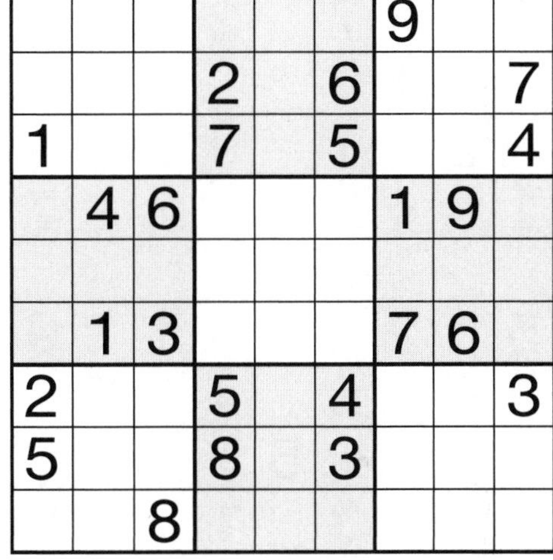

						9		
			2		6			7
1			7		5			4
	4	6				1	9	
	1	3				7	6	
2			5		4			3
5			8		3			
		8						

PUZZLE / 826 Time:_______

		4				8	5	
8				5				4
			4		9			2
		1	8		7	3		
				3				
		2	6		5	4		
5			9		1			
3				6				7
	6	9				5		

PUZZLE / 827 Time:_______

								5
	5						2	
		6	9		2	3		
		5	2		9	6		
				3				
		3	1		6	9		
		2	3		5	4		
	8						1	
9								

PUZZLE / 828 Time:_______

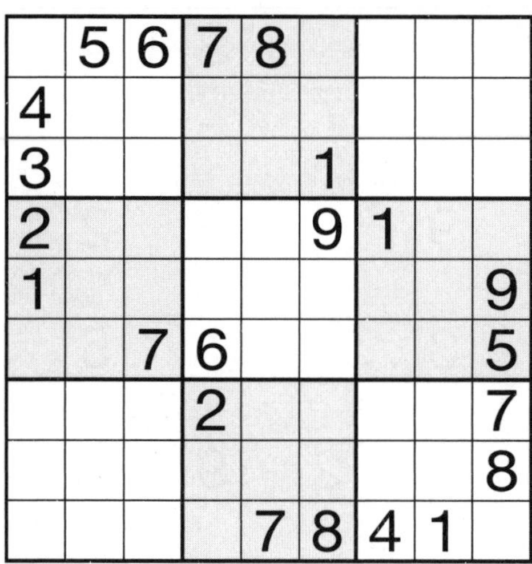

	5	6	7	8				
4								
3					1			
2					9	1		
1								9
		7	6					5
			2					7
								8
				7	8	4	1	

PUZZLE / 829 Time:______

1				8				5
	3				2		6	
		7				4		
			1	4				
5		6		3		8		1
				6	9			
		1				6		
	6		8				9	
2				5				3

PUZZLE / 830 Time:______

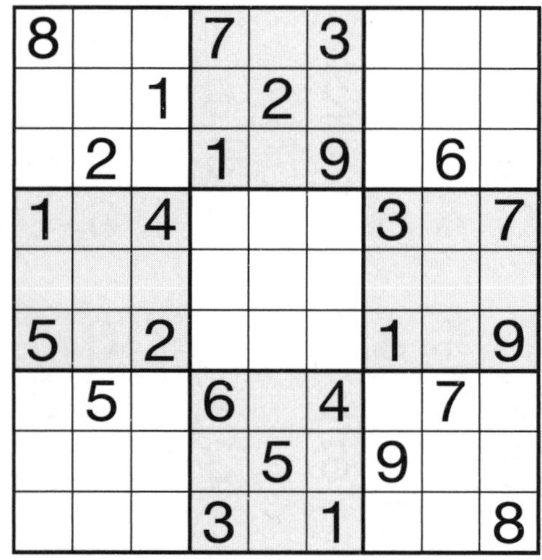

8			7		3			
		1		2				
	2		1		9		6	
1		4				3		7
5		2				1		9
	5		6		4		7	
				5		9		
			3		1			8

PUZZLE / 831 Time:______

	8			1			3	
		7				1		
1			6		2			7
	5						4	
		2				3		
	9						5	
4			7		3			6
		6				4		
	1			4			9	

PUZZLE / 832 Time:______

1	4							9
		8	9			7		4
	7					1	2	
			5	2			9	
			6		8			
	6			4	3			
	9	6					8	
3		2			4	9		
8							3	6

PUZZLE / 833 Time:______

			2			8		
		4			8		5	
	2				9		6	
					5		4	
		2				3		
	7		6					
	9		5				7	
	6		9			2		
		8			7			

PUZZLE / 834 Time:______

4			2					3
		1			5		9	
	3			9		1		
7		6						2
	8						5	
2						6		1
		4		2			1	
	5		4			3		
1					8			7

PUZZLE / 835 Time:_______

	3	7		6		4	1	
			5		3			
	5	2	1	8		6	4	
	6						7	
	1	3		2	6	5	8	
			3		4			
	4	8		1		7	3	

PUZZLE / 836 Time:_______

		4				5		
	8						6	
5		6		3		7		8
			1		7			
		5				4		
			5		2			
3		8		9		6		7
	2						1	
		7				8		

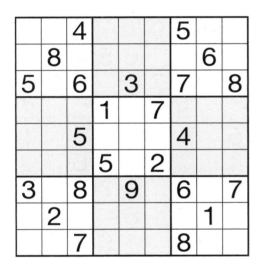

PUZZLE / 837 Time:_______

	2		3		5		6	
1		3		4		5		7
3		2			9			
4			5		7			3
			8			6		4
8		1		2		3		5
	9		1		3		4	

PUZZLE / 838 Time:_______

6					1	4		
	5			8			2	
		2	3					6
1						7		
	2						8	
		3						9
4					7	6		
	8			2			5	
		6	9					1

PUZZLE / 839 Time:_______

					3	4		
	3			2			5	
4			1			6		
					7			2
	9			8			3	
8			9					
		1			6			8
	2			5			7	
		3	4					

PUZZLE / 840 Time:_______

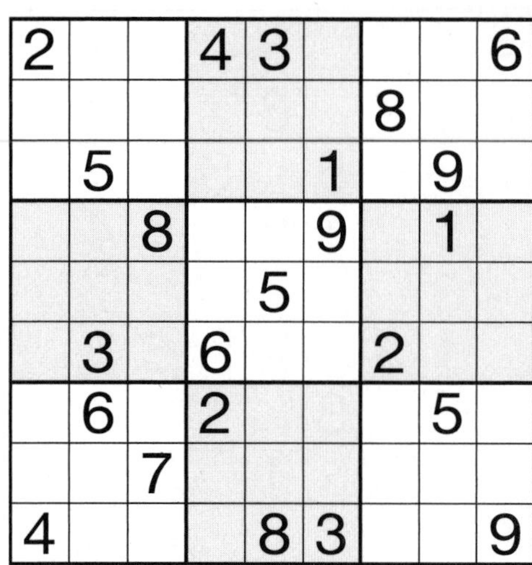

2			4	3				6
						8		
	5				1		9	
		8			9		1	
				5				
	3		6			2		
	6		2				5	
		7						
4				8	3			9

PUZZLE / 841 Time:_______

				9	8		5	1
		1			4	6	9	
		9			2	5	6	
	7	4	8			1		
	4	2	1			7		
9	8		7	3				

PUZZLE / 842 Time:_______

						5		
					6	1		
				8	9		4	3
			9	6		3	8	
		5	1		3	2		
	9	3		2	4			
5	6		2	9				
		1	3					
		2						

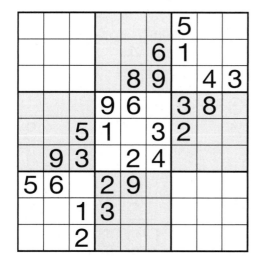

PUZZLE / 843 Time:_______

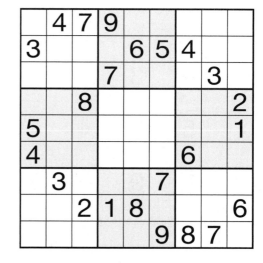

	4	7	9					
3				6	5	4		
			7				3	
		8						2
5								1
4						6		
	3				7			
		2	1	8				6
					9	8	7	

PUZZLE / 844 Time:_______

5			8	9			2	
		7			3			9
	4					7		
	5				1			
		6				1		
			7				5	
		8					3	
2			5			9		
	7			8	4			2

PUZZLE / 845 Time:_______

				5	1			
1		8	7				5	
	6					2		
			3					5
	8			9			7	
9					4			
		2					1	
	4				2	9		6
			6	8				

PUZZLE / 846 Time:_______

		7	6					
					3	4		
9				2			5	
4			1				6	
		2				7		
	3				8			5
	4			9				6
		8	7					
					2	1		

PUZZLE / 847 Time:_______

1	9			8	6			
3					2			
		6						
			3				4	7
6								1
8	2				9			
						9		
			8					4
			7	5			6	3

PUZZLE / 848 Time:_______

	7						5	
8		9				3		7
	3				4		6	
		5		9				
			6		8			
				1		2		
	2		5				1	
5		1				6		4
	6						9	

PUZZLE / 849 Time:_______

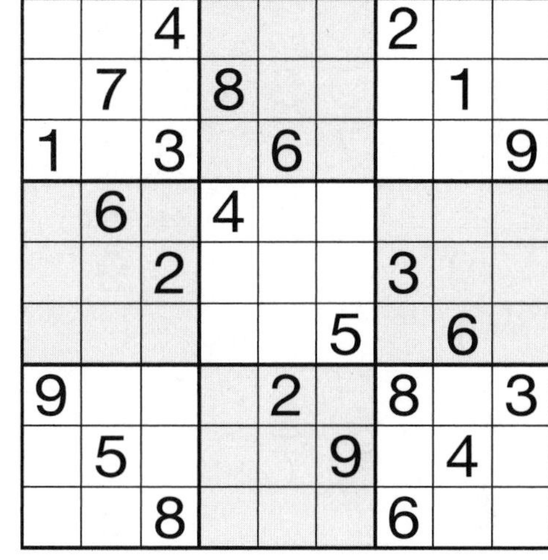

		4				2		
	7		8				1	
1		3		6				9
	6		4					
		2				3		
					5		6	
9				2		8		3
	5				9		4	
		8				6		

PUZZLE / 850 Time:_______

	2		3				6	
1				4		5		2
		5					1	
9				6				
	8		7		9		2	
				8				3
	9					1		
5		8		7				4
	7				6		5	

PUZZLE / 851 Time:_______

	6	3	1					
8								
1		7	2	5				
2		5						
		9				4		
						6		3
				7	4	8		6
								9
					8	7	5	

PUZZLE / 852 Time:_______

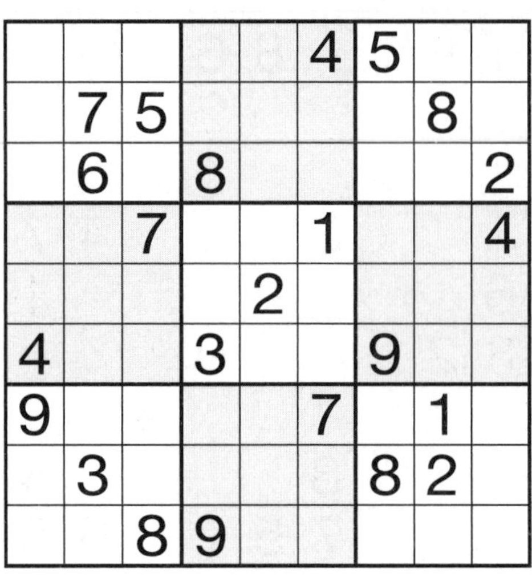

PUZZLE / 853 Time:_______

					1			
				9		4	2	
		8	2			7	1	
		1	5		8			4
	5						6	
3			9		6	2		
	2	6			7	5		
	7	4		3				
			6					

PUZZLE / 854 Time:_______

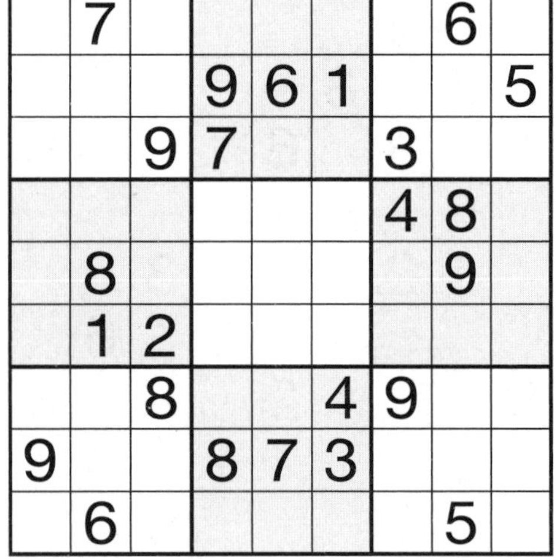

PUZZLE / 855 Time:_______

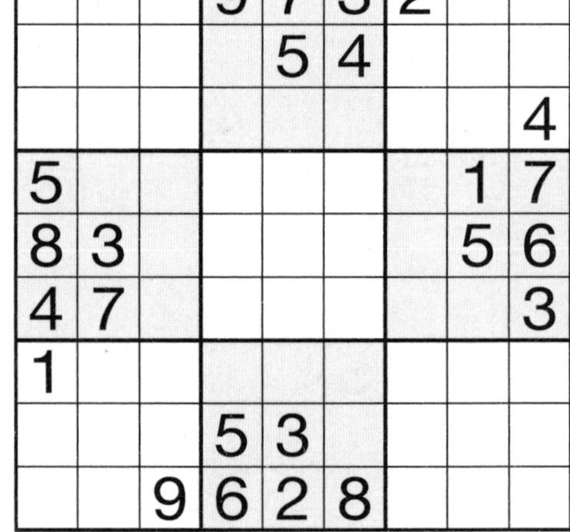

PUZZLE / 856 Time:_______

					4	1		
		5						
		6	2				5	
			6				2	3
8								4
9	3				7			
	4				9	8		
						4		
		3	5					

PUZZLE / 857 Time:_______

	3							
	5		9		6			
		4			1		2	
		2			4		8	
		1				6		
	9		6			5		
	4		7			8		
			5		8		7	
							3	

PUZZLE / 858 Time:_______

	3			1	4		5	
2								
		4	6			8		
7					5		1	
	6			3			7	
	1		7					8
		9			6	1		
								2
	5		3	7			6	

PUZZLE / 859 Time:_______

		8		3				
			4		6			
9				8				
	5				1		2	
8		2				6		3
	6		2				4	
				9				4
			3		2			
				5		7		

PUZZLE / 860 Time:_______

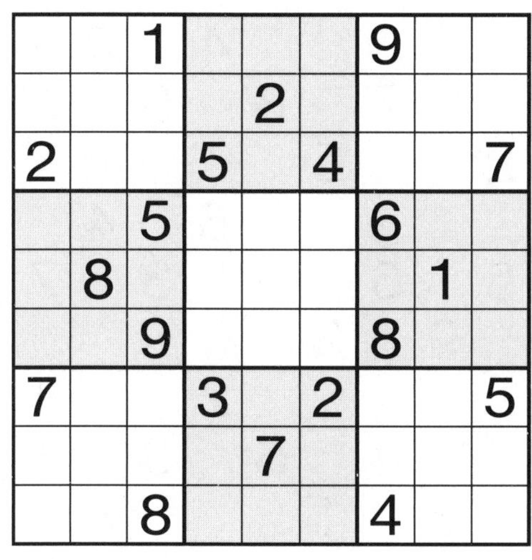

		1				9		
				2				
2			5		4			7
		5				6		
	8						1	
		9				8		
7			3		2			5
				7				
		8				4		

PUZZLE / 861 Time:_______

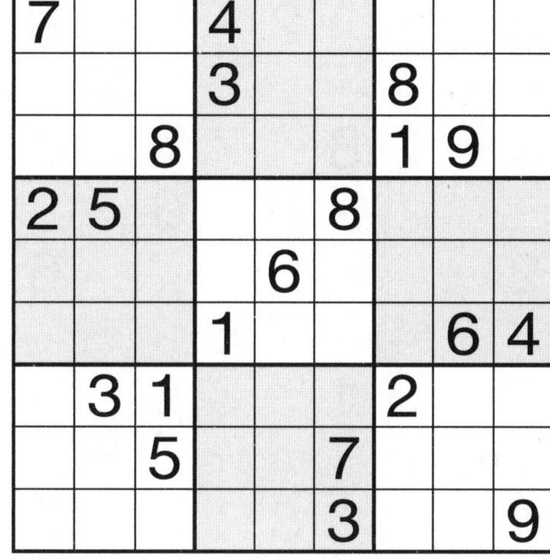

7			4					
			3			8		
		8				1	9	
2	5				8			
				6				
			1				6	4
	3	1				2		
		5			7			
					3			9

PUZZLE / 862 Time:_______

6		5			3			
1		9			7		4	
9		4			2		7	
	7		6			2		8
	2		5			3		6
			3			8		5

PUZZLE / 863 Time:_______

7	1							
		5	9		3			4
		9		8			5	
			8			7	6	
				6				
	5	3			1			
	6			9		4		
8			5		4	3		
							2	8

PUZZLE / 864 Time:_______

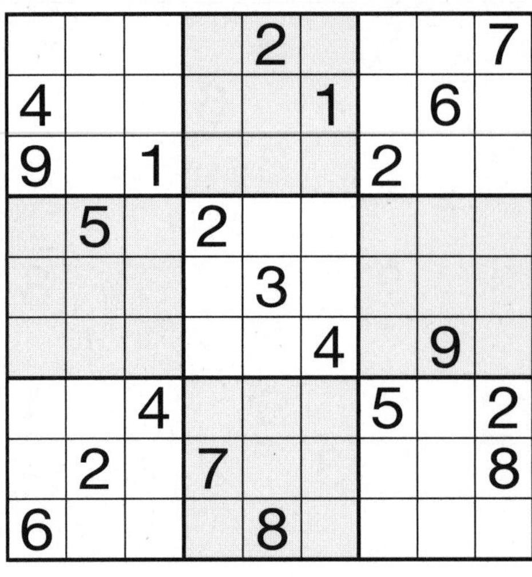

				2				7
4					1		6	
9		1				2		
	5		2					
				3				
					4		9	
		4				5		2
	2		7					8
6				8				

PUZZLE / 865 Time:_______

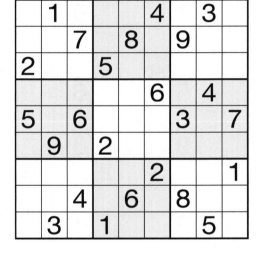

			9					1
		2		8			6	
	3				5	4		
6					4	8		
	1						3	
		7	6					5
		6	2				4	
	5			3		2		
1					6			

PUZZLE / 866 Time:_______

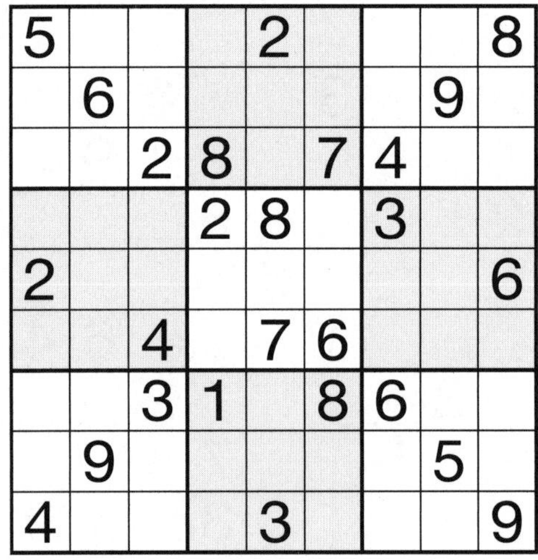

5				2				8
	6						9	
		2	8		7	4		
			2	8		3		
2								6
		4		7	6			
		3	1		8	6		
	9						5	
4				3				9

PUZZLE / 867 Time:_______

	1				4		3	
		7		8		9		
2			5					
					6		4	
5		6				3		7
	9		2					
					2			1
		4		6		8		
	3		1				5	

PUZZLE / 868 Time:_______

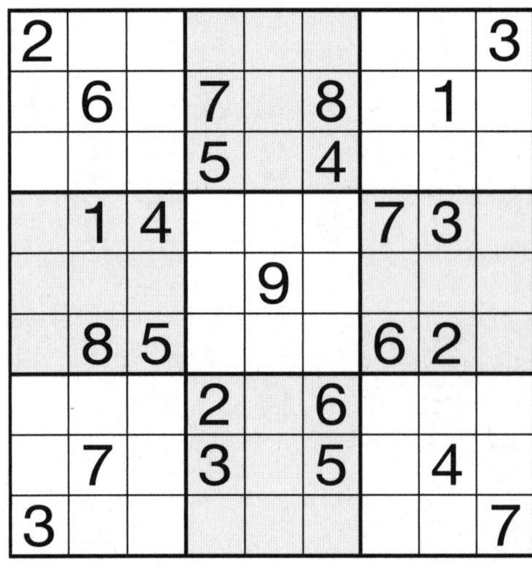

2								3
	6		7		8		1	
			5		4			
	1	4				7	3	
				9				
	8	5				6	2	
			2		6			
	7		3		5		4	
3								7

PUZZLE / 869 Time:_______

			9	4				
		4			8	2		
	6						3	
3			1					8
9		2				3		7
5					4			6
	8						6	
		3	6			5		
				1	7			

PUZZLE / 870 Time:_______

	7	5					4	
3				6				
2	8		7					3
			8	4				2
		2				1		
4				7	2			
1					7		9	8
				9				7
	9					6	3	

PUZZLE / 871 Time:_______

	5	7						
				1	5			
	6	2					4	1
				9	1			
3	1						9	6
			5	7				
9	8					4	3	
			8	5				
						2	7	

PUZZLE / 872 Time:_______

			9			1		
5				8		2		
	2				7		3	
1					6		4	
		6				5		
	5		4					8
	7		1				6	
		8		2				7
		9			3			

PUZZLE / 873 Time:_______

		8				5	9	
6			1					
2				4				7
			9		6		3	
		6				1		
	9		3		1			
8				1				4
					2			6
	3	5				2		

PUZZLE / 874 Time:_______

					9	1		
	2	5					6	
3			8				2	
9				6		4		
			5		3			
		7		4				5
	1				7			3
	6					9	4	
		8	1					

PUZZLE / 875 Time:_______

	9	3				1		
6			9	1			5	
4			2	5			8	
		8		4		7		
	2			8	9			4
	4			2	8			3
		9				5	4	

PUZZLE / 876 Time:_______

EXTRA HARD PUZZLES

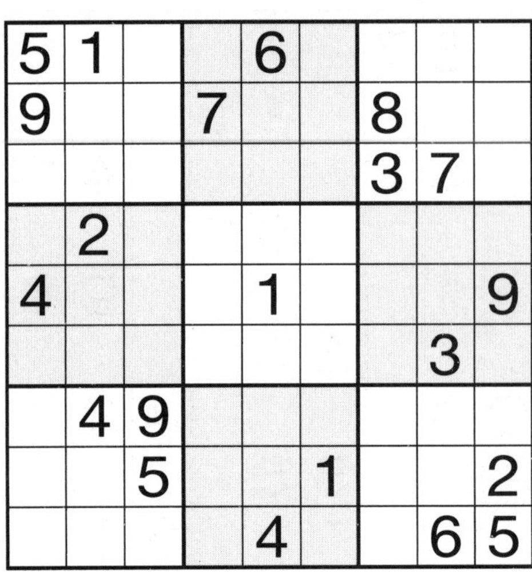

PUZZLE / 877 Time:_______

	2	8	4	7				
4					8			
3					6			
	9	7	6	3				
				4	2	5	3	
			1					6
			5					7
				8	3	9	4	

PUZZLE / 878 Time:_______

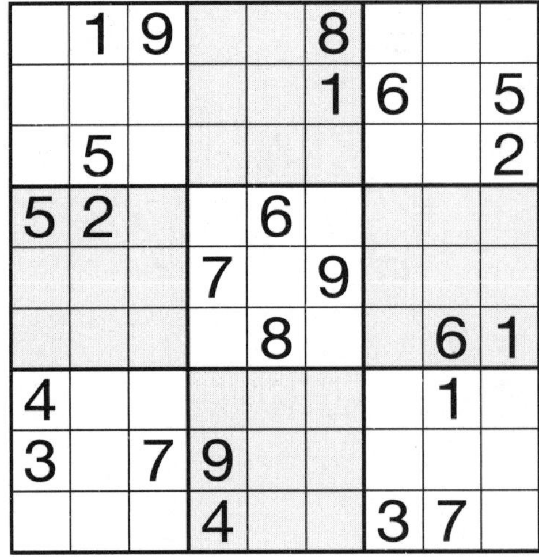

PUZZLE / 879 Time:_______

		5				1	2	
	9			4				3
			7		6			
		3						4
	6			2			1	
8						7		
			4		3			
4				6			9	
	8	9				3		

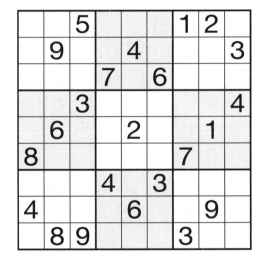

PUZZLE / 880 Time:_______

2					6			5
	4		7				9	
		8		5		1		
7						5		
	3			9			8	
		4						2
		3		1		2		
	9				7		3	
8			5					4

PUZZLE / 881 Time:_______

				4				
		3	2					9
		5	9			6	3	
				7		8	2	
6								1
	4	8		1				
	8	9			5	4		
3					6	7		
				2				

PUZZLE / 882 Time:_______

2	3						4	5
1								6
			7		8			
		8	4		1	7		
		6	9		5	1		
			1		6			
4								8
7	1						5	2

PUZZLE / 883 Time:_______

				5	4	9	3	
				9	8	2	5	
						4	2	
	4	5				3	6	
	1	8						
	5	6	4	1				
	9	4	3	8				

PUZZLE / 884 Time:_______

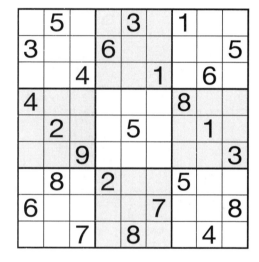

	1		5					
5				8				
	4		1			3		
		9			4		6	
4				1				7
	5		3			8		
		2			1		9	
				7				6
					6		7	

PUZZLE / 885 Time:_______

	5			3		1		
3			6					5
		4			1		6	
4						8		
	2			5			1	
		9						3
	8		2			5		
6					7			8
		7		8			4	

PUZZLE / 886 Time:_______

2				8		3		6
	1	9						
					6		1	
	8		2			5		4
				1				
7		3			4		9	
	3		6					
						2	4	
9		1		5				8

PUZZLE / 887 Time:_______

6						9		
				3	1			
			2					7
		2			9		1	
	7						2	
	9		4			5		
1					8			
			6	4				
		3						2

PUZZLE / 888 Time:_______

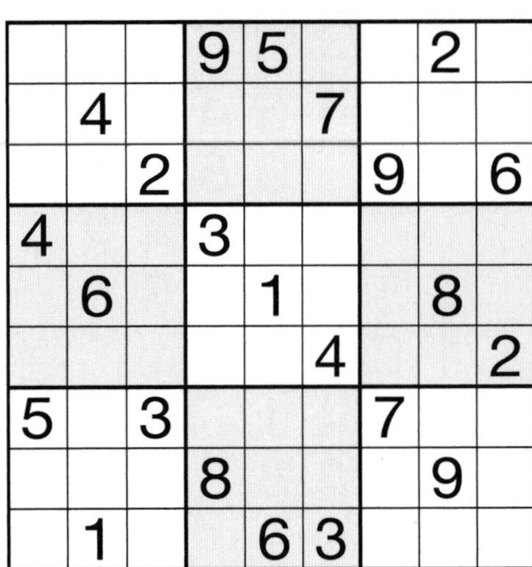

			9	5			2	
	4				7			
		2				9		6
4			3					
	6			1			8	
					4			2
5		3				7		
			8				9	
	1			6	3			

PUZZLE / 889 Time:_______

5								
3	8				5	4		
			1			7		
	2			3				
	4	9		7		1	2	
				2			8	
		5			4			
		8	3				7	2
								6

PUZZLE / 890 Time:_______

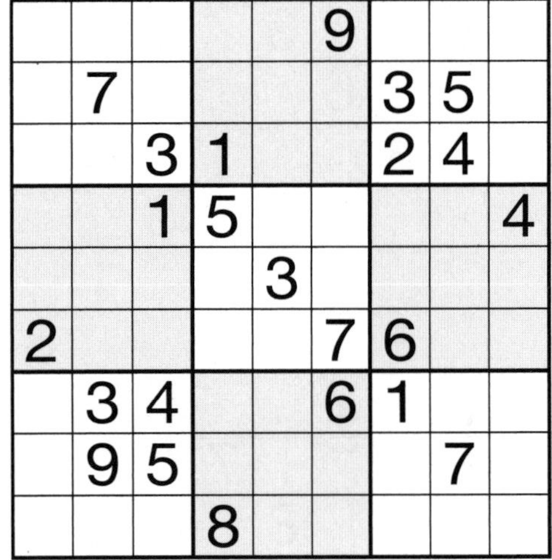

					9			
	7					3	5	
		3	1			2	4	
		1	5					4
				3				
2					7	6		
	3	4			6	1		
	9	5					7	
			8					

PUZZLE / 891 Time:_______

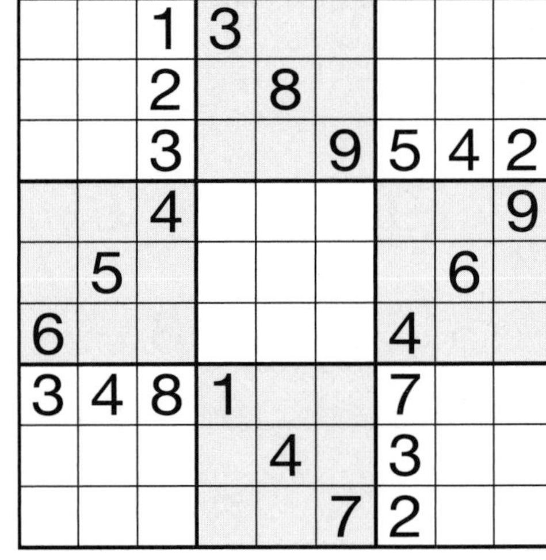

		1	3					
		2		8				
		3			9	5	4	2
		4						9
	5						6	
6						4		
3	4	8	1			7		
				4		3		
					7	2		

PUZZLE / 892 Time:_______

	6		7		2		8	
				3				
			9		6			
7								4
9		1	6		7	5		3
3								9
			3		9			
				8				
	1		5		4		7	

PUZZLE / 893 Time:_______

		2	4	6	5			
			1	8				
4								
1	4							2
9	8						3	5
3							4	8
								6
				4	9			
			6	1	3	4		

PUZZLE / 894 Time:_______

1	4				5			
2				4	1	3		
3	1				2			
			5				8	6
		4	6	8				7
			7				6	8

PUZZLE / 895 Time:_______

6			9			8		1
		7			8		5	
				2				
1			4				3	
		4				1		
	9				5			2
				4				
	5		2			4		
3		2			7			9

PUZZLE / 896 Time:_______

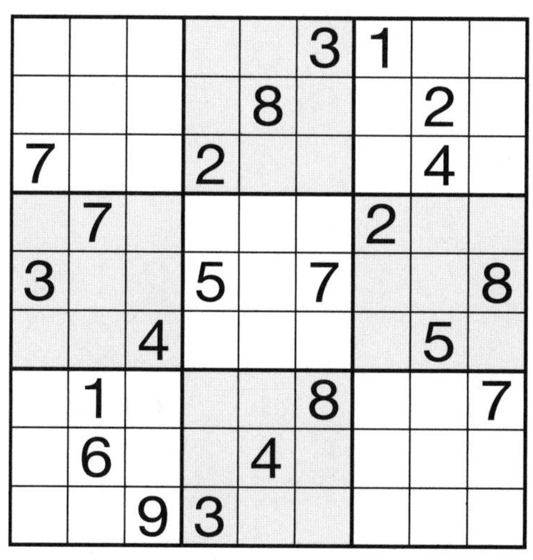

					3	1		
				8			2	
7			2				4	
	7					2		
3			5		7			8
		4					5	
	1				8			7
	6			4				
		9	3					

PUZZLE / 897 Time:_______

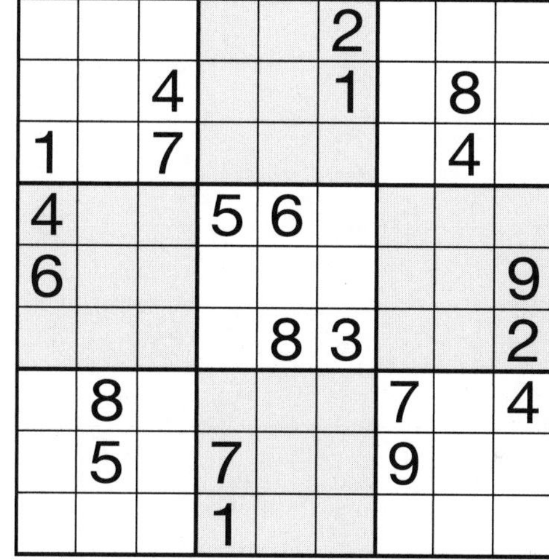

					2			
		4			1		8	
1		7					4	
4			5	6				
6								9
				8	3			2
	8					7		4
	5		7			9		
			1					

PUZZLE / 898 Time:_______

6								1
		3			5			
	5	7			9	3		
					6	9	4	
	2	8	3					
		5	8			1	3	
			2			5		
4								6

PUZZLE / 899 Time:_______

1						2	6	8
						9	3	4
		4	8			1	7	5
		7	5					
					9	6		
9	5	6			2	3		
2	7	8						
3	4	1						7

PUZZLE / 900 Time:_______

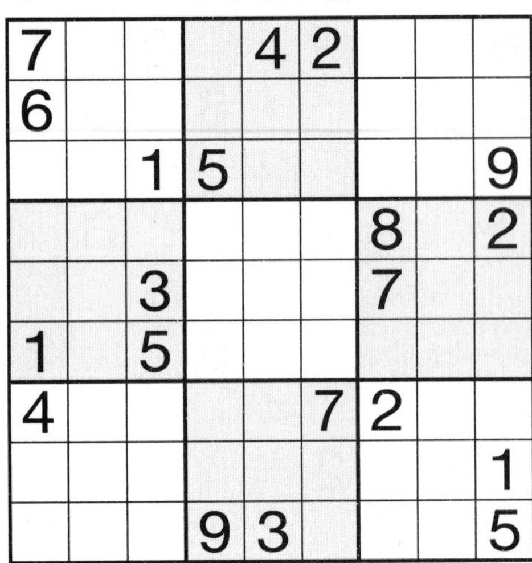

7				4	2			
6								
		1	5					9
						8		2
		3				7		
1		5						
4					7	2		
								1
			9	3				5

PUZZLE / 901 Time:______

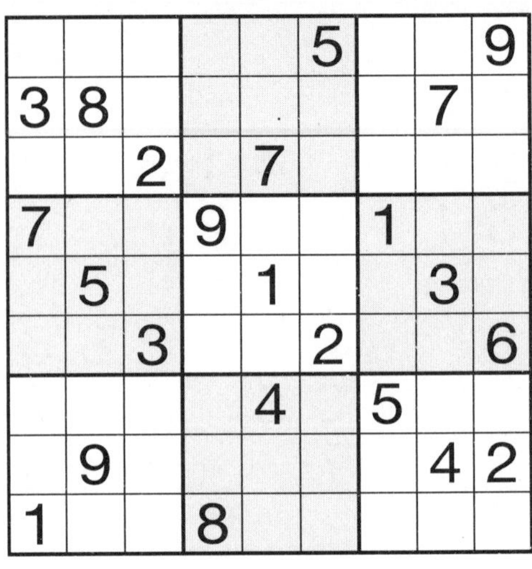

					5			9
3	8						7	
		2		7				
7			9			1		
	5			1			3	
		3			2			6
				4		5		
	9						4	2
1			8					

PUZZLE / 902 Time:______

					1	4		
						7	2	
		1	2				6	5
		5	7					3
9					4	6		
2	6				9	8		
	5	3						
		7	3					

PUZZLE / 903 Time:______

		7		5				
	9		6		3			
8				4				
	6						7	
7		1		8		2		4
	5						3	
				1				6
			5		7		4	
				3		9		

PUZZLE / 904 Time:______

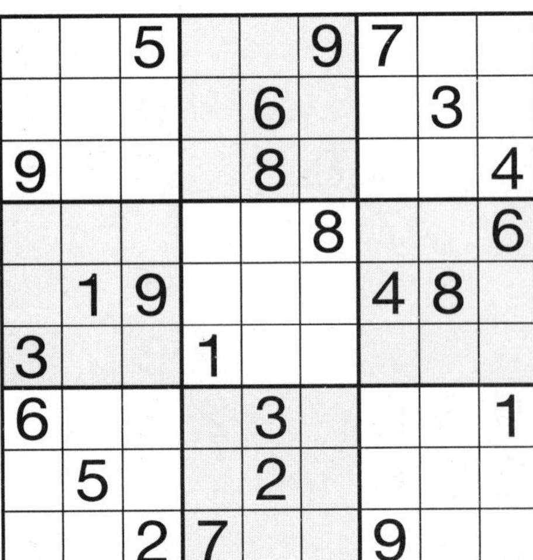

		5			9	7		
				6			3	
9				8				4
					8			6
	1	9				4	8	
3			1					
6				3				1
	5			2				
		2	7			9		

PUZZLE / 905 Time:______

		7				1		
	6		8				2	
5				2				3
	4				7			
		6		5		4		
			2				6	
3				4				1
	2				8		5	
		1				3		

PUZZLE / 906 Time:______

					3	5		
8			6					
	1	4					9	
		7			2			9
	4			7			8	
2			1			6		
	9					4	5	
					6			2
		1	2					

PUZZLE / 907 Time:_______

		3				7		
2			1		9			4
5				8				1
		4				6		
	6		5		7		4	
		5				2		
3				6				9
4			8		5			2
		7				4		

PUZZLE / 908 Time:_______

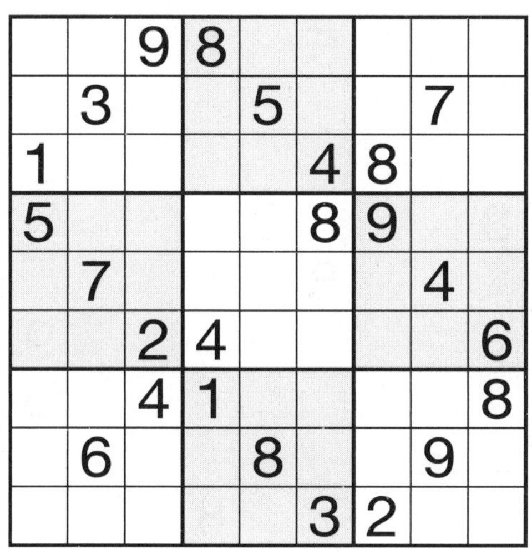

		9	8					
	3			5			7	
1					4	8		
5					8	9		
	7						4	
		2	4					6
		4	1					8
	6			8			9	
					3	2		

PUZZLE / 909 Time:_______

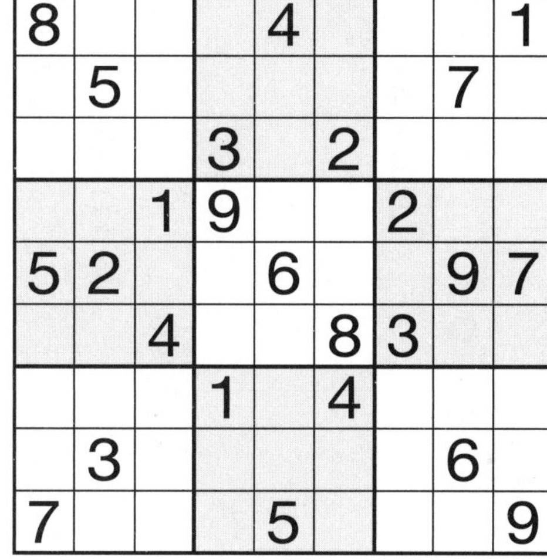

8				4				1
	5						7	
			3		2			
		1	9			2		
5	2			6			9	7
		4			8	3		
			1		4			
	3						6	
7				5				9

PUZZLE / 910 Time:_______

					7		6	
					6	8	3	
		7				2		
	5	6	9					
		4				5		
					8	3	1	
		2				1		
	4	5	3					
	9		8					

PUZZLE / 911 Time:_______

					7	9		
					2	8		
			5	4				7
			3	2		4	9	
	6	1				2	3	
	3	4		1	5			
7				6	9			
		5	8					
		8	2					

PUZZLE / 912 Time:_______

8				6				9
	3		8		5		4	
	4						3	
6								7
	1						5	
	5		6		3		1	
9				8				6

PUZZLE / 913 Time:_______

		4		9		6		
			4		8			
8								1
	8		7		4		3	
9				1				8
	7		3		9		1	
1								2
			2		3			
		6		4		5		

PUZZLE / 914 Time:_______

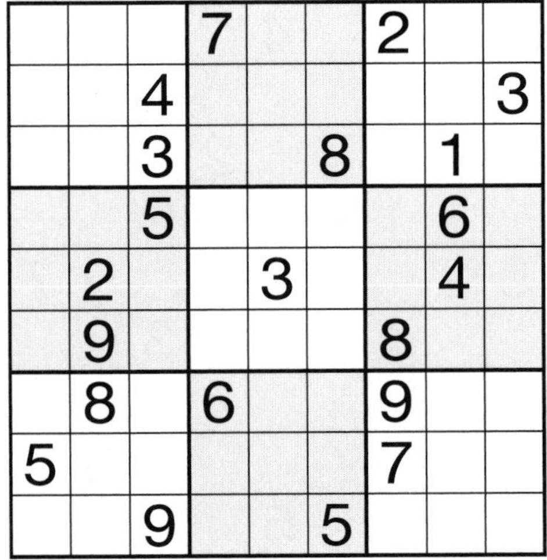

			7			2		
		4						3
		3			8		1	
		5					6	
	2			3			4	
	9					8		
	8		6			9		
5						7		
		9			5			

PUZZLE / 915 Time:_______

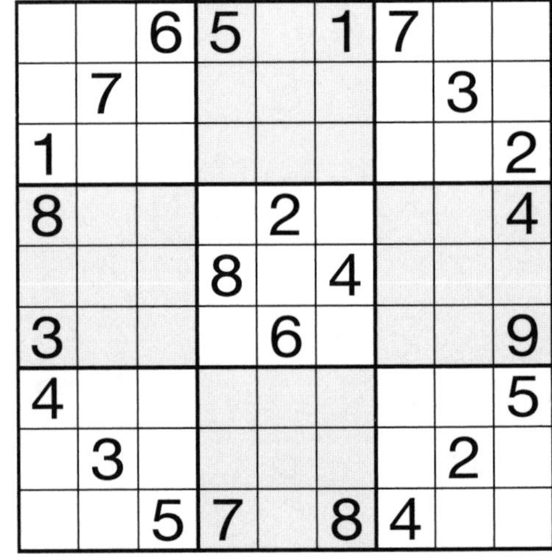

		6	5		1	7		
	7						3	
1								2
8				2				4
			8		4			
3				6				9
4								5
	3						2	
		5	7		8	4		

PUZZLE / 916 Time:_______

	1	2	5			4	3	
	3	4	6			8	7	
						7	9	
	6	5						
	2	8			7	5	4	
	7	1			9	3	8	

PUZZLE / 917 Time:_______

	4	2		8	9		5	6
6			5			3		
3			4			8		
	6			1			4	
		4			2			7
		1			4			9
4	3		9	5		2	1	

PUZZLE / 918 Time:_______

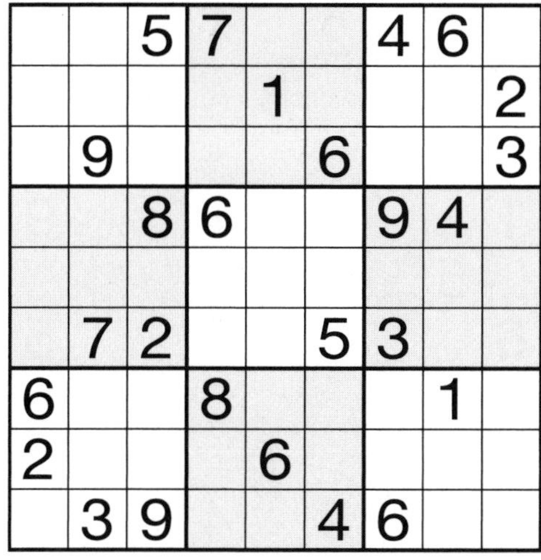

		5	7			4	6	
				1				2
	9				6			3
		8	6			9	4	
	7	2			5	3		
6			8				1	
2				6				
	3	9			4	6		

PUZZLE / 919 Time:_______

	7	4	3					
		9	6			1	2	
			5			4	1	
	9	1	8		4	3	6	
	6	5			3			
	5	8			9	7		
					2	8	4	

PUZZLE / 920 Time:_______

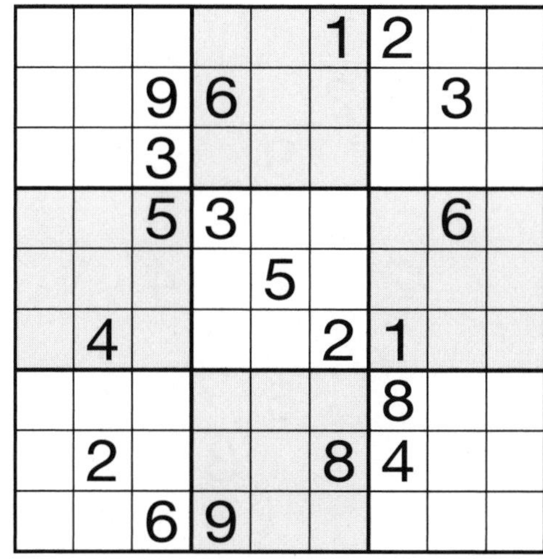

					1	2		
		9	6				3	
		3						
		5	3				6	
				5				
	4				2	1		
						8		
	2				8	4		
		6	9					

PUZZLE / 921 Time:_______

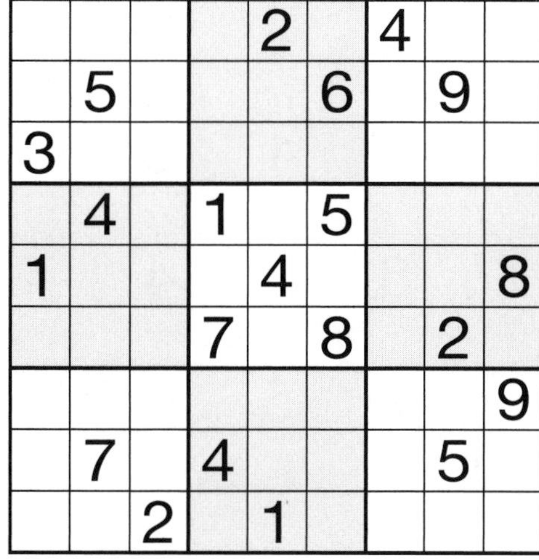

				2		4		
	5				6		9	
3								
	4		1		5			
1				4				8
			7		8		2	
								9
	7		4				5	
		2		1				

PUZZLE / 922 Time:_______

4								3
	3			4			9	
		7			2	5		
		3	4		9			
	6			3			7	
			7		6	8		
		9	5			3		
	1			6			8	
5								9

PUZZLE / 923 Time:_______

			3		2			
	3			8			4	
			9		6			
5		2				6		1
	7						9	
8		1				5		7
			8		7			
	8			9			7	
			6		1			

PUZZLE / 924 Time:_______

		8	6					
			3	9				
4				1	8			
1	5				7	4		
	6	9				5	3	
		3	9				2	1
			5	2				6
				8	6			
					9	1		

PUZZLE / 925 Time:_______

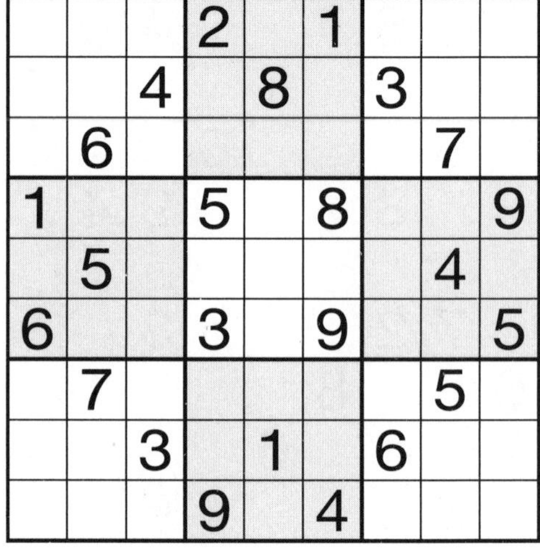

			2		1			
		4		8		3		
	6						7	
1			5		8			9
	5						4	
6			3		9			5
	7						5	
		3		1		6		
			9		4			

PUZZLE / 926 Time:_______

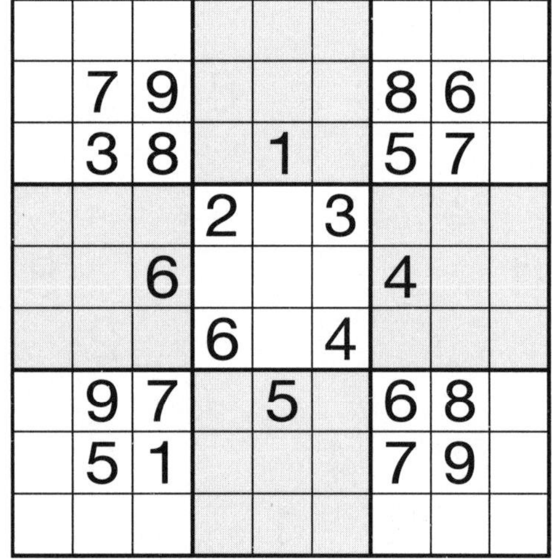

	7	9				8	6	
	3	8		1		5	7	
			2		3			
		6				4		
			6		4			
	9	7		5		6	8	
	5	1				7	9	

PUZZLE / 927 Time:_______

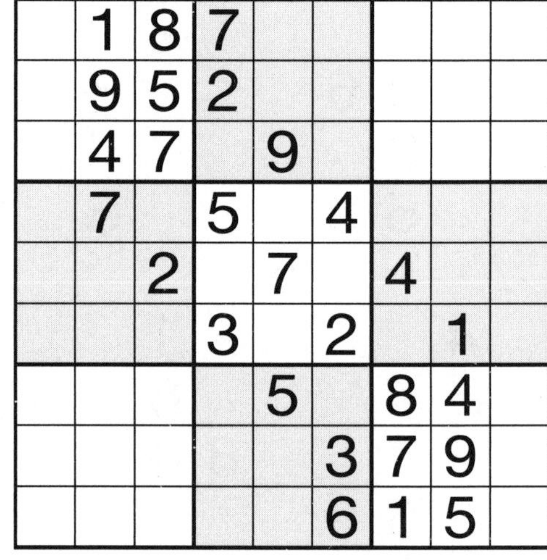

	1	8	7					
	9	5	2					
	4	7		9				
	7		5		4			
		2		7		4		
			3		2		1	
				5		8	4	
					3	7	9	
					6	1	5	

PUZZLE / 928 Time:_______

5				4				
	3		5		2			
		1				6		
	8		6				4	
4				8				7
	2				3		5	
		7				5		
			2		9		1	
				1				9

PUZZLE / 929 Time:_______

				7				
				9	1	2	7	5
		5						6
		9						1
		1	7	6	3	9		
8						4		
2						8		
1	4	6	5	8				
				3				

PUZZLE / 930 Time:_______

	5	6				2	9	
8		9				4		3
	3						8	7
			4	9	2			
			1		3			
			5	6	7			
9	8						3	
5		3				1		2
	2	4				9	5	

PUZZLE / 931 Time:_______

	2		8		1		3	
7				9				5
3				6				4
	4						5	
6				2				9
2				4				6
	8		6		5		1	

PUZZLE / 932 Time:_______

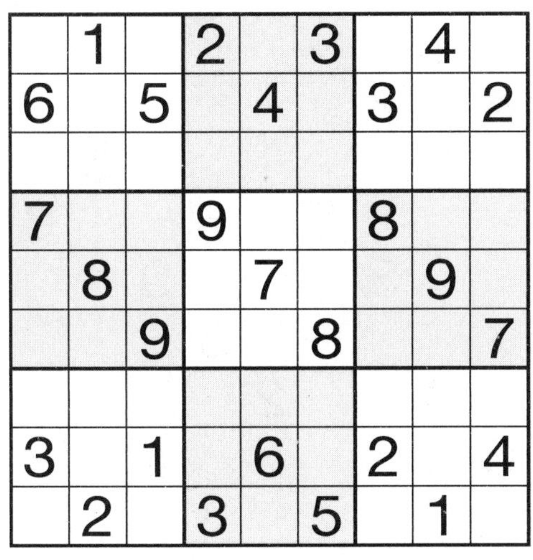

	1		2		3		4	
6		5		4		3		2
7			9			8		
	8			7			9	
		9			8			7
3		1		6		2		4
	2		3		5		1	

PUZZLE / 933 Time:_______

	2	8	4				5	
								6
	6		7			4		
		1			9			
6				8				7
			5			8		
		5			6		8	
4								
	9				3	5	1	

PUZZLE / 934 Time:_______

EXTRA EXTRA HARD PUZZLES

					9	5	7	
				2				9
			8					3
		3			2			6
	5						9	
7			6			2		
5					7			
2				5				
	4	6	3					

PUZZLE / 935 Time:_______

			7			8		5
				8			9	
			2		1			4
6		2				1		
	9						4	
		1				7		3
4			1		3			
	6			9				
7		3			2			

PUZZLE / 936 Time:_______

		8	9					
	4		6			3		
3		2					9	
4	3		5					
				1				
					8		5	3
	1					4		6
		9			6		2	
					2	9		

PUZZLE / 937 Time:_______

		2		9			8	
			8			4		
3							5	
	1		5		7			
6								8
			1		2		4	
	8							9
		1			9			
	7			3		6		

PUZZLE / 938 Time:_______

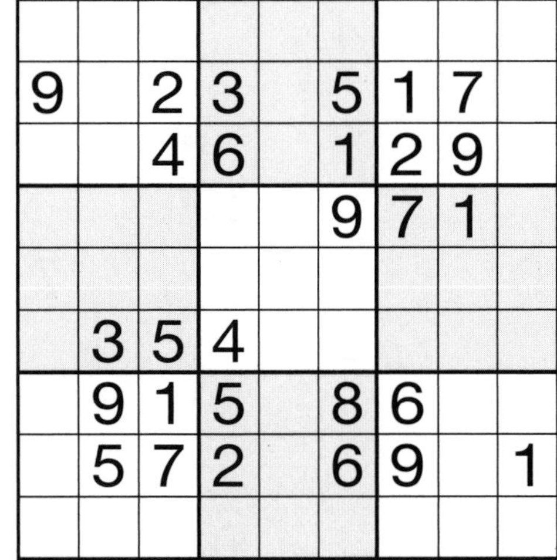

9		2	3		5	1	7	
		4	6		1	2	9	
					9	7	1	
	3	5	4					
	9	1	5		8	6		
	5	7	2		6	9		1

PUZZLE / 939 Time:_______

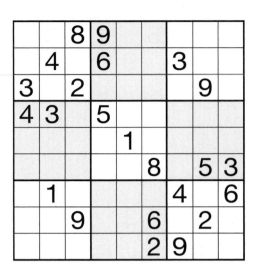

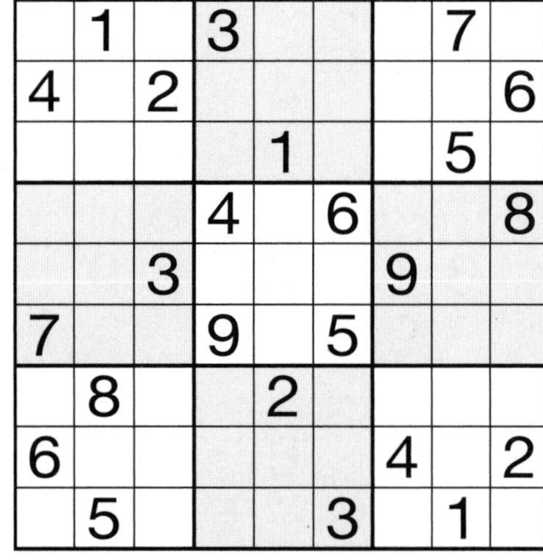

	1		3				7	
4		2						6
				1			5	
			4		6			8
		3				9		
7			9		5			
	8			2				
6						4		2
	5				3		1	

PUZZLE / 940 Time:_______

			7					
		5			9			
	1			2			6	
	2		5			8		
1			9		3			6
		7			1		4	
	5			1			7	
			3			1		
					5			

PUZZLE / 941 Time:_______

1		2				3		
					8			5
	6			2			8	
9			6					1
		3		8		5		
8					7			9
	9			7			4	
2			4					
		5				9		7

PUZZLE / 942 Time:_______

		6	5	8				
3								
8					2	1		
4					3	2		
1								5
		5	4					6
		4	6					7
								4
				2	4	3		

PUZZLE / 943 Time:_______

				1			3	6
							7	4
		1	2					
		5	8					
3								1
					2	8		
					5	9		
1	5							
4	6			3				

PUZZLE / 944 Time:_______

6				2		4		
	2		5				1	
		5			8			3
			1				6	
		4		3		9		
	9				7			
8			4			5		
	4				9		7	
		3		6				1

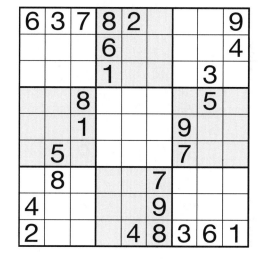

PUZZLE / 945 Time:_______

6	3	7	8	2				9
			6					4
			1				3	
		8					5	
		1				9		
	5					7		
	8				7			
4					9			
2				4	8	3	6	1

PUZZLE / 946 Time:_______

3				4		8		
	5		6				7	
		2						3
	1				9			
4				2				9
			7				6	
8						7		
	4				1		5	
		3		9				1

PUZZLE / 947 Time:_______

		8	1		6	3		
	3			9			1	
	5		7		4		9	
		1				4		
	9		6		2		7	
	7			5			2	
		4	8		3	1		

PUZZLE / 948 Time:_______

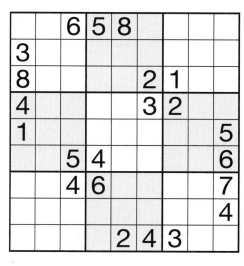

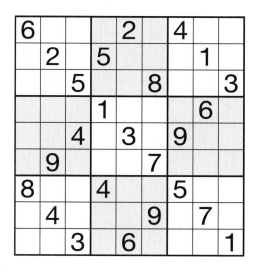

					5	6		
		4	3					
3					9		1	
6		2	4		1		3	
	9		5		6	8		4
	2		9					8
					4	9		
		8	2					

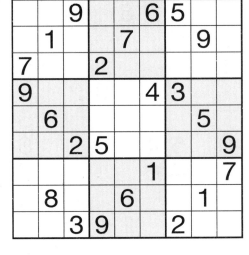

PUZZLE / 949 Time:_______

		9			6	5		
	1			7			9	
7			2					
9					4	3		
	6						5	
		2	5					9
					1			7
	8			6			1	
		3	9			2		

PUZZLE / 950 Time:_______

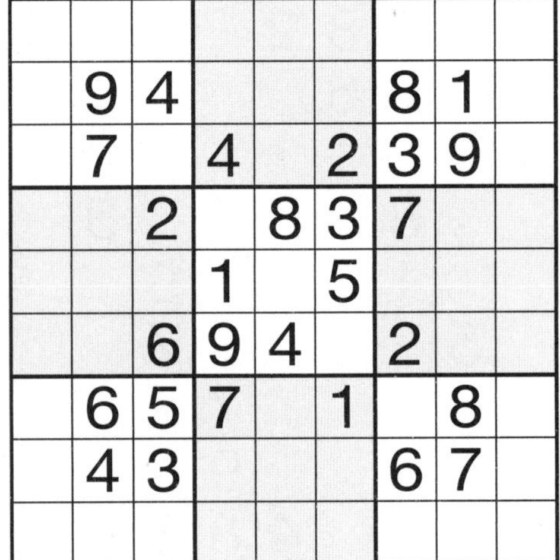

	9	4				8	1	
	7		4		2	3	9	
		2		8	3	7		
			1		5			
		6	9	4		2		
	6	5	7		1		8	
	4	3				6	7	

PUZZLE / 951 Time:_______

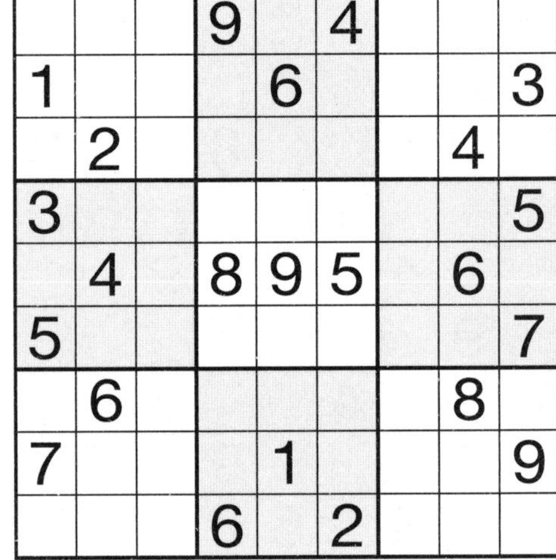

			9		4			
1				6				3
	2						4	
3								5
	4		8	9	5		6	
5								7
	6						8	
7				1				9
			6		2			

PUZZLE / 952 Time:_______

					4	8	5	
					1	9	2	
	1	9	7					
	7	4	3					
					8	7	1	
					9	4	6	
	4	5	2					
	3	6	4					

PUZZLE / 953 Time:_______

						3		
	4				8		1	
1		9		4		2		
	5		1		3			
		2				9		
			7		9		5	
		8		6		5		4
	7		5				8	
		5						

PUZZLE / 954 Time:_______

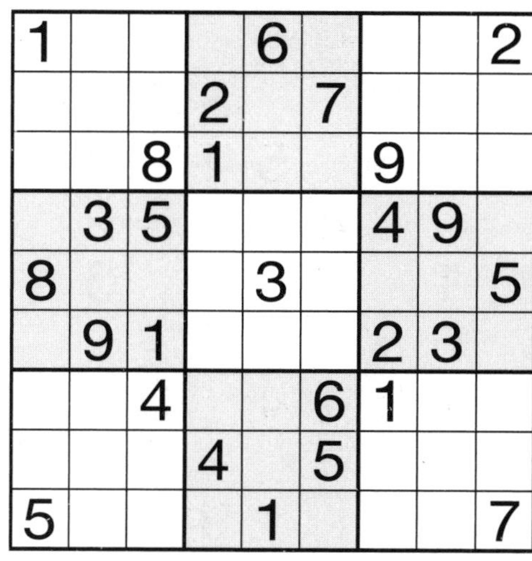

1				6				2
			2		7			
		8	1			9		
	3	5				4	9	
8				3				5
	9	1				2	3	
		4			6	1		
			4		5			
5				1				7

PUZZLE / 955 Time:_______

		5	2	3				
	7							
2				8	7	6		
7			9				5	
6								4
	5				1			6
		4	3	2				8
							2	
				1	4	9		

PUZZLE / 956 Time:_______

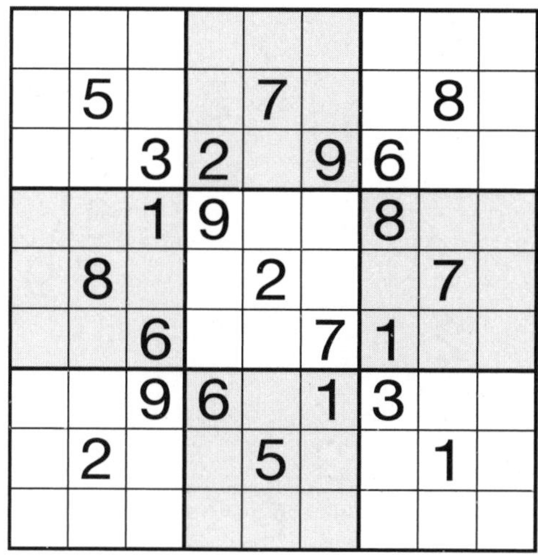

	5			7			8	
		3	2		9	6		
		1	9			8		
	8			2			7	
		6			7	1		
		9	6		1	3		
	2			5			1	

PUZZLE / 957 Time:_______

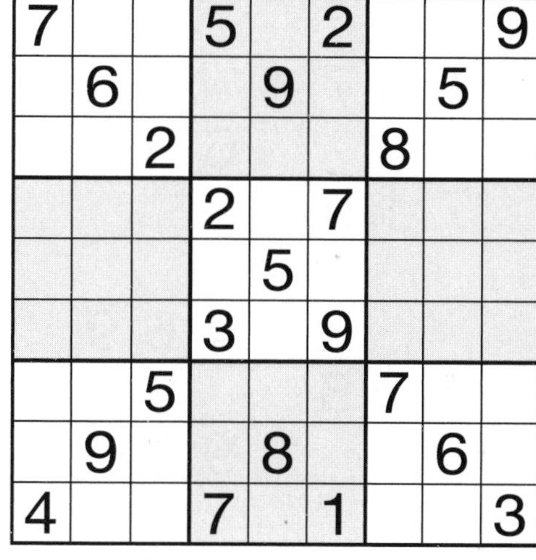

7			5		2			9
	6			9			5	
		2				8		
			2		7			
				5				
			3		9			
		5				7		
	9			8			6	
4			7		1			3

PUZZLE / 958 Time:_______

9				3				4
		7				2		
	3				5			8
		8		4		7		6
6		4		9		1		
7			3				5	
		9				8		
2				5				9

PUZZLE / 959 Time:_______

			7					3
		1		8		9		
3	9							5
	8				5	4		
	7						5	
		3	2				1	
6							8	9
		8		6		7		
4					1			

PUZZLE / 960 Time:_______

1								7
4				8				6
	6		4		9		2	
		4		2		3		
			9		5			
		5		4		7		
	4		2		1		9	
9				7				3
2								4

PUZZLE / 961 Time:_______

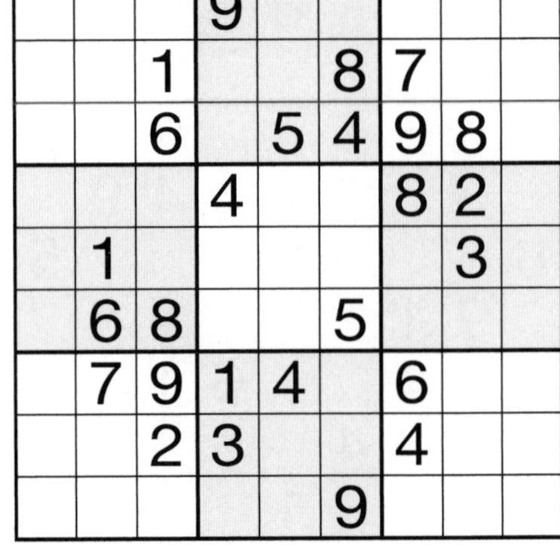

PUZZLE / 962 Time:_______

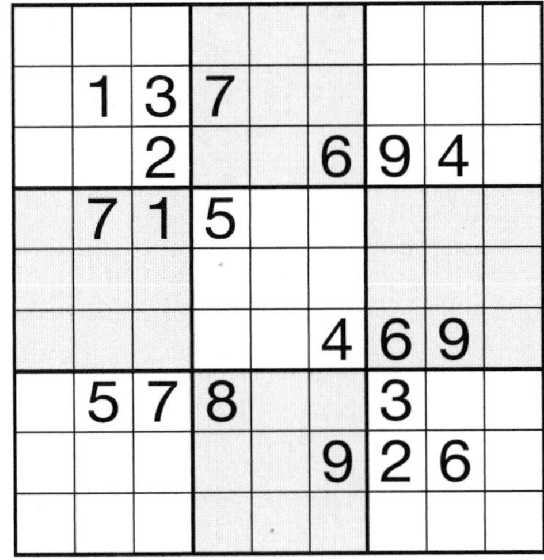

PUZZLE / 963 Time:_______

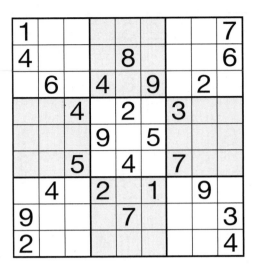

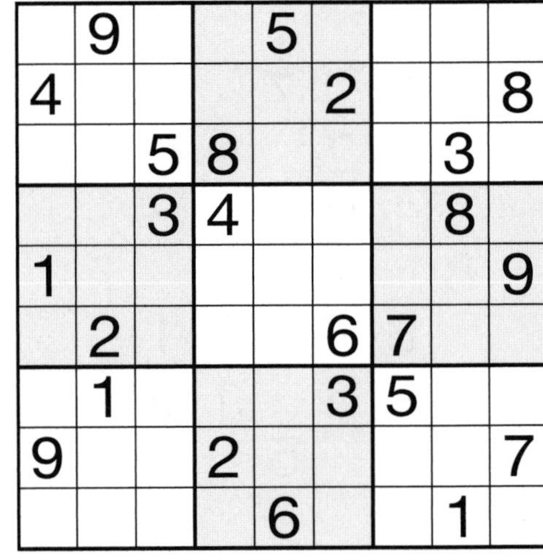

PUZZLE / 964 Time:_______

3	8	9				5	1	
5		4			3	6		
4	9	8		7	5			
				1				
			3	2		4	9	7
		5	2			1		6
	3	2				9	5	8

PUZZLE / 965 Time:_______

					8			
		7		9		6		
	4		5		3		8	
6		2				8		
	8						4	
		1				2		7
	3		9		2		5	
		6		3		1		
			8					

PUZZLE / 966 Time:_______

					3			
		1		2		9		
	3		6				7	
1						4		
	6						5	
		2						1
	8				5		3	
		4		1		2		
			7					

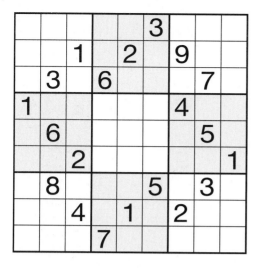

PUZZLE / 967 Time:_______

			6	8				
		1			2	9		
	3			4			5	
	4							5
6		2				8		9
9							1	
	1			5			3	
		4	3			1		
				6	1			

PUZZLE / 968 Time:_______

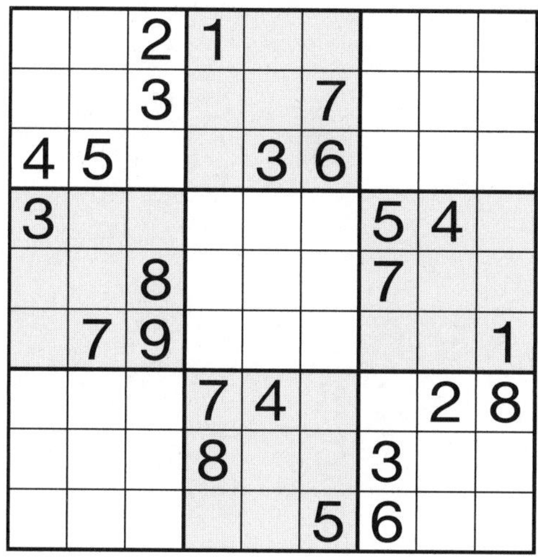

		2	1					
		3			7			
4	5			3	6			
3						5	4	
		8				7		
	7	9						1
			7	4			2	8
			8			3		
					5	6		

PUZZLE / 969 Time:_______

		1	6		5	9		
		6	9		3	2		
9	3						7	6
8	7						9	2
6	2						4	3
5	1						2	9
		7	8		2	3		
		2	1		9	7		

PUZZLE / 970 Time:_______

			9	6				
	6	2			4	3		
3							8	
7				5	1		2	
		5				1		
	8		4	2				3
	2							7
		7	1			5	9	
				4	6			

PUZZLE / 971 Time:_______

				6	2			
					4	1		
	3	8						9
		7	2				8	4
6								5
1	4				8	9		
7						8	5	
		6	5					
			3	2				

PUZZLE / 972 Time:_______

				5				2
					4		7	
		8				9		
	2		9			6		
	5		7		3		4	
		9			5		2	
		7				8		
	3		2					
4				7				

PUZZLE / 973 Time:_______

		4				6		
	9			5			1	
8			7		1			4
		8				2		
	7						9	
		9				4		
4			6		2			5
	5			1			6	
		2				8		

PUZZLE / 974 Time:_______

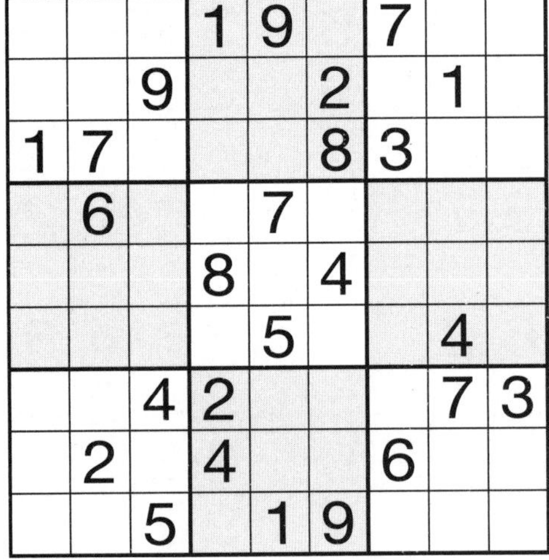

			1	9		7		
		9			2		1	
1	7				8	3		
	6			7				
			8		4			
				5			4	
		4	2				7	3
	2		4			6		
		5		1	9			

PUZZLE / 975 Time:_______

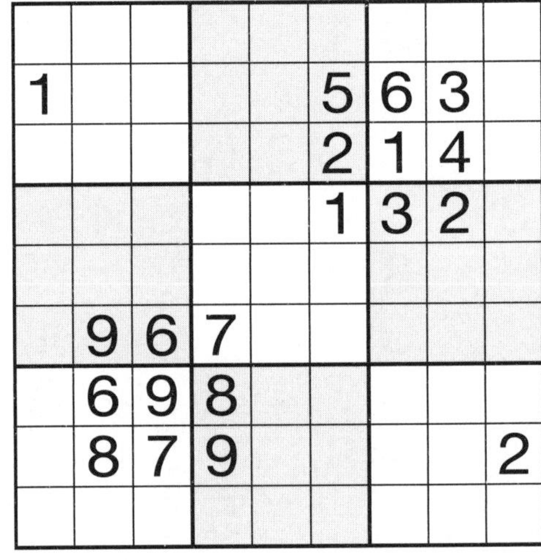

1					5	6	3	
					2	1	4	
					1	3	2	
	9	6	7					
	6	9	8					
	8	7	9					2

PUZZLE / 976 Time:_______

	9	8					6	
4			5					9
7				3				
	8			2				
		5	3		4	8		
				6			3	
				4				3
5					9			6
	7					1	2	

PUZZLE / 977 Time:_______

1		2		3		4		5
4				6				3
			2		7			
5		1				7		2
			9		6			
2				8				1
8		3		2		9		4

PUZZLE / 978 Time:_______

						7	8	
					6	5	4	
		5	3					
	1	2	4					
					7	8	9	
					8	6		
	4	3	2					
	2	1						

PUZZLE / 979 Time:_______

3					7	4		
	5			9			8	
		6	2					9
								6
	8	5				1	9	
7								
4					1	9		
	9			8			5	
		3	7					2

PUZZLE / 980 Time:_______

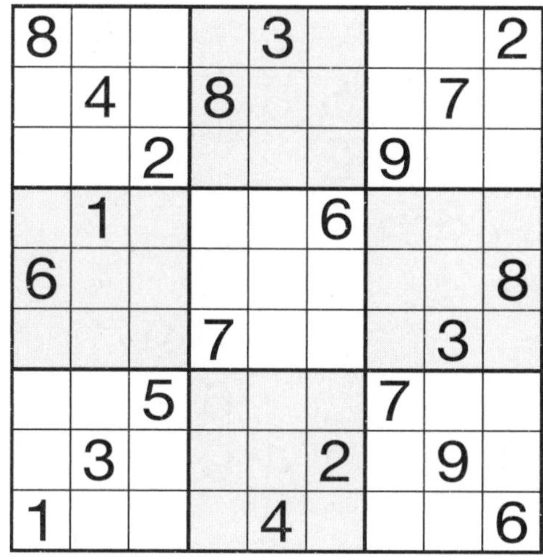

8				3				2
	4		8				7	
		2				9		
	1				6			
6								8
			7				3	
		5				7		
	3				2		9	
1				4				6

PUZZLE / 981 Time:_______

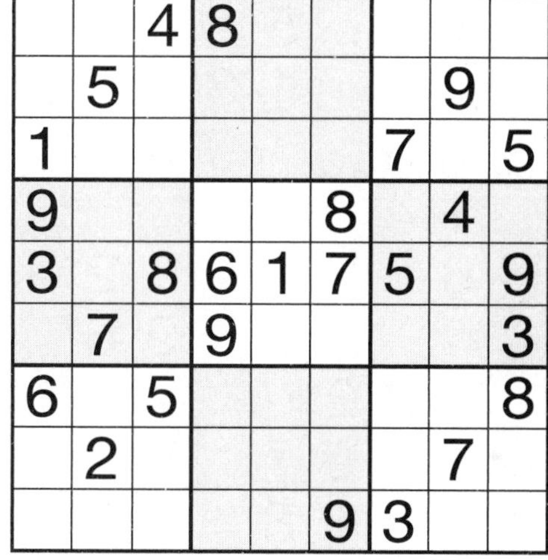

		4	8					
	5						9	
1						7		5
9					8		4	
3		8	6	1	7	5		9
	7		9					3
6		5						8
	2						7	
					9	3		

PUZZLE / 982 Time:_______

		6				1		
			1		4			
4				7				8
	4			9			1	
	7						6	
	2			3			5	
1				4				3
			7		5			
		8				2		

PUZZLE / 983 Time:_______

					2			
				1		9	2	
		2	3			5	4	
		7	5					1
	4						7	
3					9	8		
	2	3			8	6		
	7	4		2				
			6					

PUZZLE / 984 Time:_______

		3	2					
		9			4	6		
6	1						9	
9				1			7	
			4		8			
	6			7				5
	7						2	9
		4	3			8		
					1	4		

PUZZLE / 985 Time:_______

			9	6				
					1			
	2	7				5		
			3				7	4
				2				
9	6				7			
		4				7	2	
			6					
				5	9			

PUZZLE / 986 Time:_______

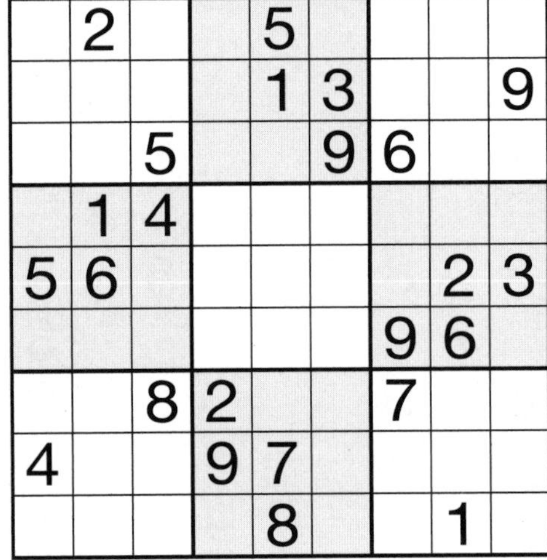

	2			5				
				1	3			9
		5			9	6		
	1	4						
5	6						2	3
						9	6	
		8	2			7		
4			9	7				
				8			1	

PUZZLE / 987 Time:_______

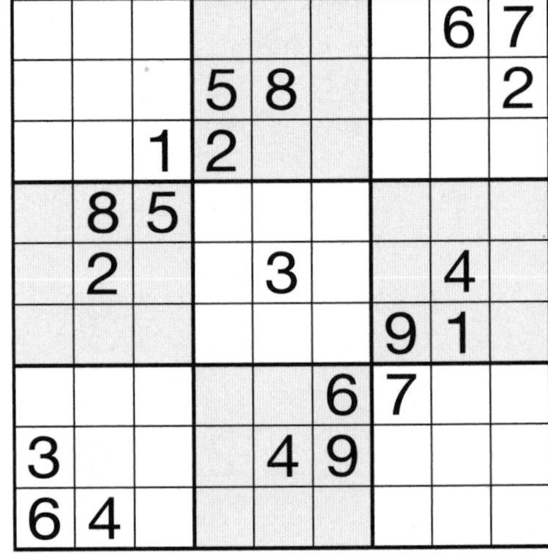

							6	7
			5	8				2
		1	2					
	8	5						
	2			3			4	
						9	1	
					6	7		
3				4	9			
6	4							

PUZZLE / 988 Time:_______

	1						4	
8								3
		2				5		
	5		2		9		1	
6				5				4
	9		8		1		6	
		3				9		
2								8
	6						5	

PUZZLE / 989 Time:_______

			4		5			
	2	3				4	8	
	1			6			3	
3			6		7			9
		6				8		
4			9		2			3
	4			2			1	
	3	2				5	6	
			5		3			

PUZZLE / 990 Time:_______

	9			6	3			
		1						4
			1				8	
2				3		5		
9			6		5			1
		4		7				9
	5				7			
8						9		
			3	1			6	

PUZZLE / 991 Time:_______

		4			3			7
		9			2			5
		6			5			1
		3			8			4
5			6			2		
9			5			7		
6			9			1		
1			2			9		

PUZZLE / 992 Time:_______

8			5			9		4
	2			8			1	
3					9			
		2						7
	1						2	
6						5		
			7					9
	4			3			8	
9		8			5			6

PUZZLE / 993 Time:_______

	6						5	
1			6		9			3
		7				8		
	5			2			8	
			3		4			
	7			1			2	
		4				9		
9			5		1			4
	3						6	

PUZZLE / 994 Time:_______

		3			8			1
5				2		6		
			4				5	
	1				3			8
				6				
2			7				4	
	4				1			
		9		8				3
8			2			5		

PUZZLE / 995 Time:_______

	6						2	
3								6
		9	5		2	1		
		6	9		5	7		
		1	4		8	9		
		7	8		6	3		
4								1
	8						4	

PUZZLE / 996 Time:_______

5	9				6			
6				5		7		
			4				8	
		3						9
	2						5	
1						6		
	8				2			
		6		3				8
			5				1	2

PUZZLE / 997 Time:_______

6	7						8	4
2	5						6	3
				2				
			7		3			
		8		5		9		
			1		9			
				6				
7	3						9	2
4	9						5	8

PUZZLE / 998 Time:_______

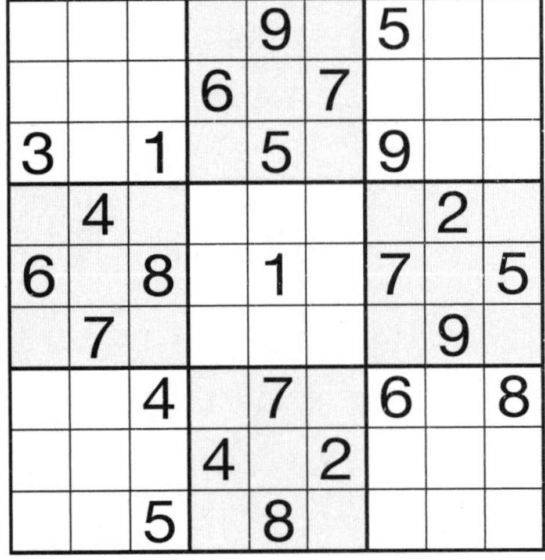

				9		5		
			6		7			
3		1		5		9		
	4						2	
6		8		1		7		5
	7						9	
		4		7		6		8
			4		2			
		5		8				

PUZZLE / 999 Time:_______

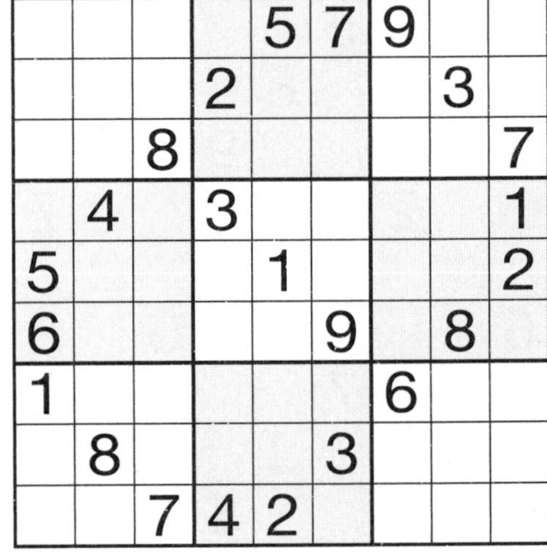

				5	7	9		
			2				3	
		8						7
	4		3					1
5				1				2
6					9		8	
1						6		
	8				3			
		7	4	2				

PUZZLE / 1000 Time:_______

4		3			5		2	
2		7			3		6	
5		1			6		9	
	6		8			1		4
	4		1			2		6
	7		6			9		1

PUZZLE / 1001 Time:_______

2				8				9
	7						2	
			9		5			
		3	4		1	2		
5				6				7
		2	3		7	6		
			1		6			
	3						1	
9				7				3

PUZZLE / 1002 Time:_______

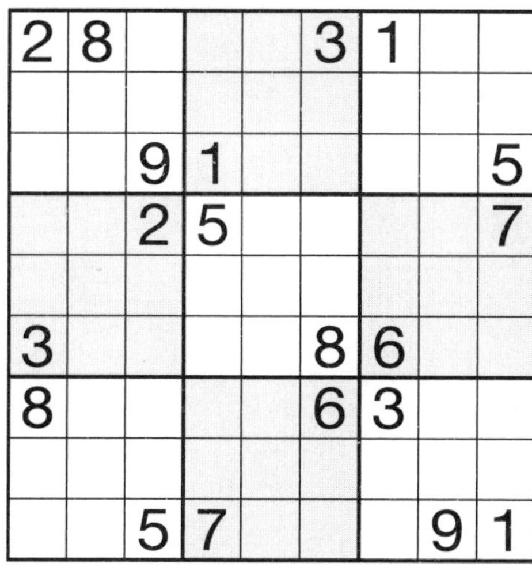

PUZZLE / 1003 Time:_______

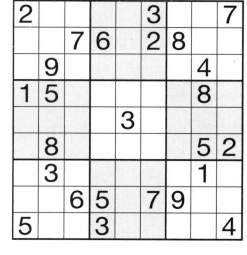

2					3			7
		7	6		2	8		
	9						4	
1	5						8	
				3				
	8						5	2
	3						1	
		6	5		7	9		
5			3					4

PUZZLE / 1004 Time:_______

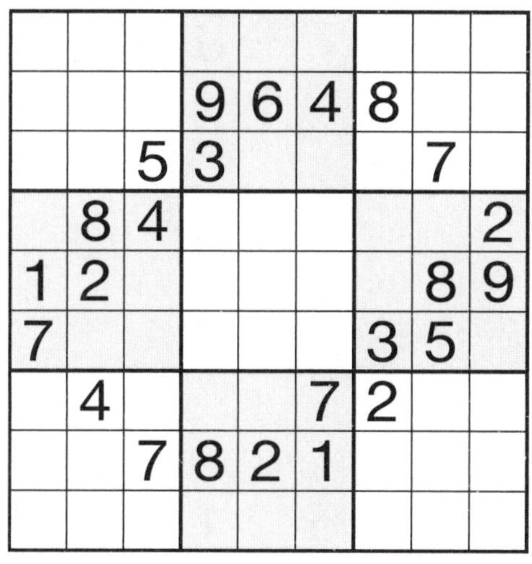

PUZZLE / 1005 Time:_______

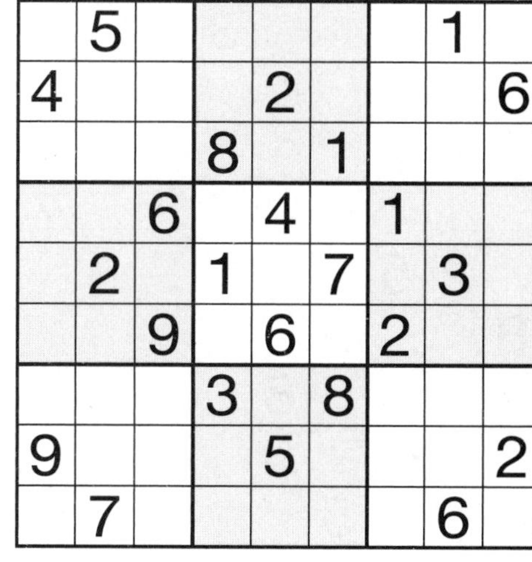

PUZZLE / 1006 Time:_______

		2	4					
	6			9			3	
	4			7			9	
		8	1		6	4		
	7			5			6	
	9			3			7	
					1	8		

PUZZLE / 1007 Time:_______

					6	8		
	5	3					2	
1			3				5	
			1		5			7
		4				3		
2			4		7			
	2				4			1
	3					5	8	
		6	2					

PUZZLE / 1008 Time:_______

		1						
	7			5			4	
			6		4			5
		6		9		7		
	3		5		6		2	
		2		4		8		
2			4		9			
	1			7			8	
						9		

PUZZLE / 1009 Time:_______

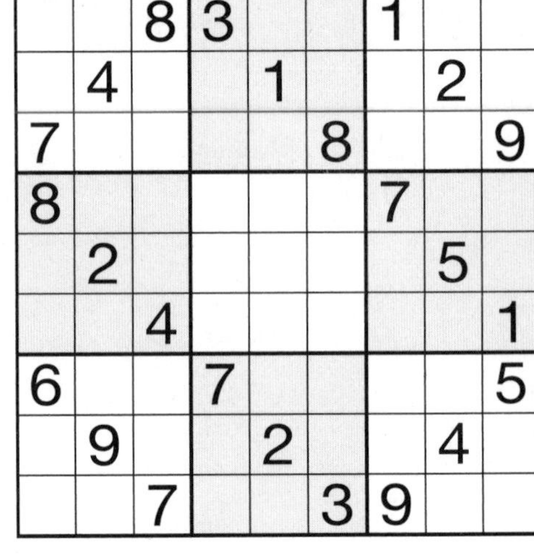

		8	3			1		
	4			1			2	
7					8			9
8						7		
	2						5	
		4						1
6			7					5
	9			2			4	
		7			3	9		

PUZZLE / 1010 Time:_______

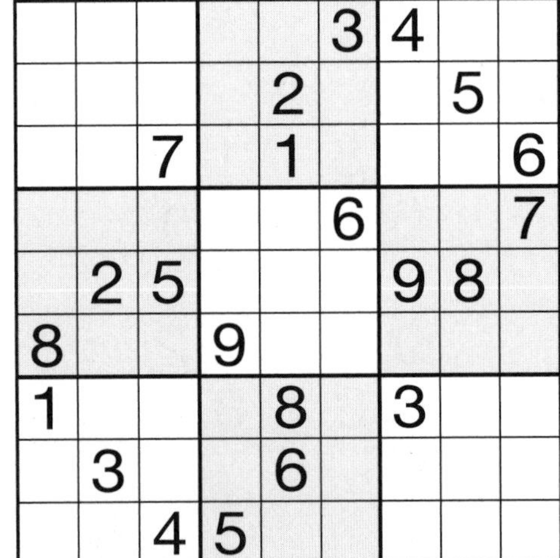

					3	4		
				2			5	
		7		1				6
					6			7
	2	5				9	8	
8			9					
1				8		3		
	3			6				
		4	5					

PUZZLE / 1011 Time:_______

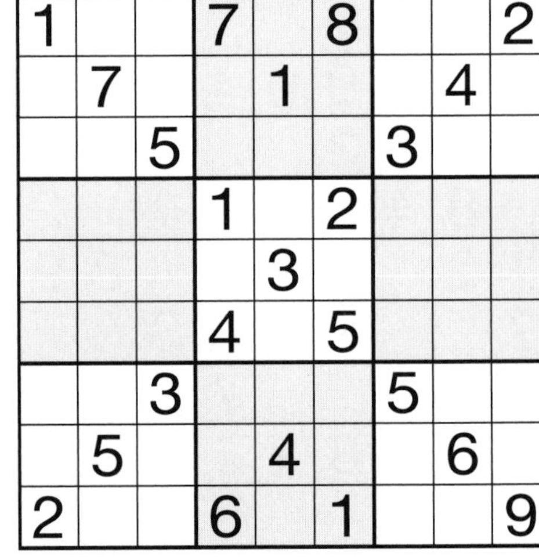

1			7		8			2
	7			1			4	
		5				3		
			1		2			
				3				
			4		5			
		3				5		
	5			4			6	
2			6		1			9

PUZZLE / 1012 Time:_______

6				4				2
	5		9				1	
		1				9		
	6				2			
7				3				4
			7				3	
		4				3		
	1				9		7	
5				2				6

PUZZLE / 1013 Time:_______

		4	1		2	3		
	7			4			5	
	2			1			3	
		1	3		6	9		
	5			7			8	
	3			8			4	
		6	9		4	2		

PUZZLE / 1014 Time:_______

Solutions

7	4	5	9	1	6	3	8	2
2	9	1	7	8	3	5	4	6
3	8	6	5	4	2	9	1	7
8	1	2	3	6	9	7	5	4
5	7	9	4	2	1	6	3	8
6	3	4	8	7	5	2	9	1
9	2	8	6	5	4	1	7	3
4	6	3	1	9	7	8	2	5
1	5	7	2	3	8	4	6	9

PUZZLE / 1

4	9	3	1	2	6	5	8	7
1	5	8	3	7	9	6	2	4
7	6	2	8	4	5	9	1	3
5	1	4	2	6	3	7	9	8
6	3	7	9	5	8	1	4	2
8	2	9	7	1	4	3	5	6
9	7	5	4	3	2	8	6	1
3	4	6	5	8	1	2	7	9
2	8	1	6	9	7	4	3	5

PUZZLE / 2

9	3	7	8	2	4	6	1	5
2	6	8	9	5	1	7	3	4
1	5	4	3	6	7	2	8	9
5	1	9	4	8	2	3	7	6
8	7	2	5	3	6	9	4	1
3	4	6	1	7	9	8	5	2
7	9	5	6	1	8	4	2	3
6	8	1	2	4	3	5	9	7
4	2	3	7	9	5	1	6	8

PUZZLE / 3

9	5	2	4	8	6	7	3	1
1	7	8	3	5	9	2	6	4
4	6	3	2	1	7	8	9	5
5	1	6	9	4	8	3	2	7
3	2	9	5	7	1	4	8	6
7	8	4	6	3	2	1	5	9
6	4	7	8	2	5	9	1	3
2	9	1	7	6	3	5	4	8
8	3	5	1	9	4	6	7	2

PUZZLE / 4

8	4	3	5	7	9	2	1	6
9	6	5	3	1	2	8	4	7
1	7	2	6	4	8	3	5	9
2	9	7	4	6	5	1	8	3
5	3	6	9	8	1	7	2	4
4	8	1	2	3	7	9	6	5
6	1	8	7	9	4	5	3	2
3	5	9	1	2	6	4	7	8
7	2	4	8	5	3	6	9	1

PUZZLE / 5

4	9	2	6	1	5	3	7	8
7	1	3	9	8	4	6	2	5
6	5	8	7	3	2	4	1	9
2	4	6	8	9	3	7	5	1
1	3	9	5	2	7	8	4	6
8	7	5	1	4	6	2	9	3
3	6	7	4	5	9	1	8	2
9	8	4	2	6	1	5	3	7
5	2	1	3	7	8	9	6	4

PUZZLE / 6

9	1	2	8	6	5	4	3	7
5	8	4	7	2	3	9	1	6
7	3	6	1	4	9	8	5	2
3	7	5	6	9	8	1	2	4
6	4	1	2	3	7	5	8	9
2	9	8	5	1	4	6	7	3
8	6	9	3	5	2	7	4	1
4	5	3	9	7	1	2	6	8
1	2	7	4	8	6	3	9	5

PUZZLE / 7

5	1	8	9	2	6	7	4	3
4	2	9	7	3	8	6	1	5
3	7	6	4	1	5	8	2	9
8	5	3	2	6	1	4	9	7
7	9	1	3	8	4	5	6	2
6	4	2	5	9	7	1	3	8
1	3	5	6	7	2	9	8	4
9	8	4	1	5	3	2	7	6
2	6	7	8	4	9	3	5	1

PUZZLE / 8

2	4	1	5	9	3	7	6	8
8	3	7	4	1	6	9	5	2
5	6	9	2	7	8	1	3	4
4	7	8	6	3	5	2	1	9
9	5	3	1	8	2	4	7	6
1	2	6	7	4	9	5	8	3
3	8	2	9	5	1	6	4	7
6	1	4	8	2	7	3	9	5
7	9	5	3	6	4	8	2	1

PUZZLE / 9

5	9	2	6	1	8	4	7	3
3	1	6	7	4	5	2	8	9
4	7	8	2	3	9	5	6	1
7	2	3	5	9	1	6	4	8
8	4	9	3	6	2	1	5	7
6	5	1	8	7	4	3	9	2
1	3	4	9	5	7	8	2	6
2	6	7	4	8	3	9	1	5
9	8	5	1	2	6	7	3	4

PUZZLE / 10

9	1	4	6	7	5	2	3	8
3	5	6	8	9	2	4	1	7
8	7	2	1	3	4	6	9	5
7	2	5	3	6	1	8	4	9
4	8	1	2	5	9	3	7	6
6	3	9	7	4	8	1	5	2
5	4	3	9	8	6	7	2	1
2	6	7	5	1	3	9	8	4
1	9	8	4	2	7	5	6	3

PUZZLE / 11

1	3	9	7	8	4	5	2	6
7	2	5	6	9	3	8	1	4
4	8	6	1	5	2	3	7	9
6	4	2	8	1	9	7	5	3
5	9	7	2	3	6	1	4	8
8	1	3	4	7	5	6	9	2
2	6	1	5	4	8	9	3	7
9	7	8	3	2	1	4	6	5
3	5	4	9	6	7	2	8	1

PUZZLE / 12

1	4	6	7	3	5	9	8	2
2	7	5	9	1	8	3	4	6
8	9	3	2	6	4	1	5	7
7	5	9	3	8	1	6	2	4
4	3	2	5	9	6	8	7	1
6	8	1	4	7	2	5	9	3
9	1	4	6	5	7	2	3	8
5	6	7	8	2	3	4	1	9
3	2	8	1	4	9	7	6	5

PUZZLE / 13

2	5	7	6	8	1	9	4	3
9	1	4	7	5	3	2	8	6
6	8	3	9	4	2	5	1	7
7	4	6	8	3	5	1	9	2
5	2	8	1	9	6	3	7	4
3	9	1	4	2	7	8	6	5
4	3	9	5	7	8	6	2	1
8	6	2	3	1	4	7	5	9
1	7	5	2	6	9	4	3	8

PUZZLE / 14

3	1	2	4	7	5	8	6	9
4	7	8	6	9	3	5	1	2
5	9	6	1	2	8	7	3	4
6	2	3	8	1	4	9	5	7
7	4	5	9	6	2	3	8	1
1	8	9	5	3	7	2	4	6
9	5	4	7	8	1	6	2	3
8	3	7	2	4	6	1	9	5
2	6	1	3	5	9	4	7	8

PUZZLE / 15

5	1	2	8	7	4	3	6	9
4	3	9	6	5	2	8	7	1
6	7	8	1	3	9	4	5	2
7	8	5	9	2	3	6	1	4
1	9	4	5	8	6	7	2	3
2	6	3	7	4	1	5	9	8
3	4	6	2	1	5	9	8	7
9	2	7	4	6	8	1	3	5
8	5	1	3	9	7	2	4	6

PUZZLE / 16

1	4	7	3	9	5	6	2	8
5	9	8	2	7	6	3	1	4
6	3	2	8	4	1	5	9	7
8	6	5	7	1	3	9	4	2
3	1	4	9	8	2	7	5	6
7	2	9	6	5	4	1	8	3
2	5	3	1	6	8	4	7	9
4	7	6	5	2	9	8	3	1
9	8	1	4	3	7	2	6	5

PUZZLE / 17

7	4	9	2	5	6	1	3	8
8	6	1	4	9	3	5	7	2
5	2	3	1	7	8	9	6	4
9	8	6	7	2	4	3	5	1
2	3	5	6	1	9	4	8	7
4	1	7	3	8	5	6	2	9
1	9	8	5	6	7	2	4	3
3	5	2	8	4	1	7	9	6
6	7	4	9	3	2	8	1	5

PUZZLE / 18

7	6	9	5	1	8	4	3	2
4	3	1	6	9	2	5	8	7
2	5	8	4	3	7	1	6	9
1	7	3	8	4	9	6	2	5
8	2	6	3	5	1	9	7	4
9	4	5	2	7	6	3	1	8
3	1	2	9	8	5	7	4	6
6	9	4	7	2	3	8	5	1
5	8	7	1	6	4	2	9	3

PUZZLE / 19

7	5	2	3	4	6	1	9	8
8	4	1	7	9	2	3	6	5
6	9	3	8	5	1	2	7	4
9	6	4	2	1	7	8	5	3
2	3	5	6	8	9	4	1	7
1	7	8	4	3	5	6	2	9
5	8	9	1	6	3	7	4	2
4	2	6	5	7	8	9	3	1
3	1	7	9	2	4	5	8	6

PUZZLE / 20

7	6	2	8	3	5	1	4	9
5	8	9	1	4	7	6	3	2
4	3	1	2	6	9	7	5	8
1	5	8	4	9	3	2	7	6
2	7	4	6	5	8	3	9	1
3	9	6	7	1	2	5	8	4
9	2	3	5	8	6	4	1	7
8	4	7	3	2	1	9	6	5
6	1	5	9	7	4	8	2	3

PUZZLE / 21

3	7	2	8	5	1	6	9	4
4	1	5	9	6	2	7	8	3
8	6	9	7	4	3	2	5	1
7	2	6	4	1	9	8	3	5
9	4	3	2	8	5	1	6	7
1	5	8	3	7	6	9	4	2
5	9	7	6	2	4	3	1	8
2	3	1	5	9	8	4	7	6
6	8	4	1	3	7	5	2	9

PUZZLE / 22

3	9	1	4	5	6	2	8	7
6	2	5	8	1	7	9	4	3
7	4	8	3	9	2	1	5	6
9	3	6	5	7	1	4	2	8
2	8	4	6	3	9	5	7	1
5	1	7	2	8	4	3	6	9
8	6	3	1	2	5	7	9	4
4	7	2	9	6	3	8	1	5
1	5	9	7	4	8	6	3	2

PUZZLE / 23

6	4	7	1	9	5	8	3	2
9	1	5	2	8	3	4	7	6
8	2	3	7	4	6	9	1	5
4	3	2	8	6	1	5	9	7
5	9	8	4	3	7	6	2	1
1	7	6	9	5	2	3	8	4
7	8	9	6	2	4	1	5	3
3	6	1	5	7	8	2	4	9
2	5	4	3	1	9	7	6	8

PUZZLE / 24

1	8	9	4	7	2	3	5	6
6	3	4	1	8	5	2	7	9
5	7	2	3	6	9	4	8	1
3	6	1	7	5	8	9	4	2
7	2	8	9	4	6	5	1	3
4	9	5	2	3	1	7	6	8
9	1	7	8	2	4	6	3	5
8	5	3	6	9	7	1	2	4
2	4	6	5	1	3	8	9	7

PUZZLE / 25

4	2	9	5	6	3	1	8	7
3	1	5	9	7	8	6	2	4
6	8	7	2	4	1	9	3	5
7	4	1	6	8	5	3	9	2
9	5	3	7	1	2	8	4	6
2	6	8	4	3	9	5	7	1
1	3	2	8	5	7	4	6	9
8	9	4	1	2	6	7	5	3
5	7	6	3	9	4	2	1	8

PUZZLE / 26

4	2	7	5	3	1	6	9	8
3	1	9	4	8	6	5	7	2
6	5	8	2	9	7	3	4	1
8	9	5	7	1	2	4	3	6
2	3	6	9	4	5	8	1	7
7	4	1	3	6	8	9	2	5
1	7	4	6	5	9	2	8	3
9	6	2	8	7	3	1	5	4
5	8	3	1	2	4	7	6	9

PUZZLE / 27

3	6	9	5	2	7	1	4	8
1	5	2	9	8	4	7	6	3
7	4	8	1	3	6	5	9	2
2	9	3	8	6	1	4	5	7
5	8	1	4	7	3	9	2	6
4	7	6	2	9	5	3	8	1
6	3	5	7	4	2	8	1	9
8	1	7	6	5	9	2	3	4
9	2	4	3	1	8	6	7	5

PUZZLE / 28

7	6	5	9	8	1	2	3	4
4	2	9	5	3	6	1	7	8
1	3	8	4	2	7	6	9	5
5	1	6	3	9	4	8	2	7
8	4	2	6	7	5	9	1	3
9	7	3	8	1	2	4	5	6
2	8	7	1	6	3	5	4	9
3	9	4	2	5	8	7	6	1
6	5	1	7	4	9	3	8	2

PUZZLE / 29

3	2	7	5	9	8	1	4	6
1	8	5	7	6	4	2	3	9
6	9	4	1	2	3	8	7	5
7	6	1	3	4	9	5	2	8
2	5	8	6	7	1	4	9	3
4	3	9	2	8	5	6	1	7
8	1	3	4	5	7	9	6	2
5	7	2	9	1	6	3	8	4
9	4	6	8	3	2	7	5	1

PUZZLE / 30

6	8	4	9	5	3	7	1	2
9	2	1	4	6	7	8	3	5
7	5	3	8	1	2	9	6	4
8	6	7	3	2	4	5	9	1
1	3	9	7	8	5	2	4	6
5	4	2	1	9	6	3	7	8
2	7	6	5	3	1	4	8	9
3	1	8	2	4	9	6	5	7
4	9	5	6	7	8	1	2	3

PUZZLE / **31**

6	4	7	5	8	1	9	2	3
1	3	9	7	6	2	5	4	8
8	2	5	4	9	3	6	7	1
2	5	8	9	1	6	7	3	4
7	9	1	2	3	4	8	5	6
3	6	4	8	5	7	2	1	9
9	8	3	1	2	5	4	6	7
4	1	2	6	7	8	3	9	5
5	7	6	3	4	9	1	8	2

PUZZLE / **32**

2	7	5	3	6	8	1	4	9
4	1	6	7	5	9	8	3	2
8	3	9	2	1	4	5	7	6
1	4	7	6	8	2	3	9	5
6	9	2	5	4	3	7	8	1
3	5	8	1	9	7	2	6	4
7	6	1	9	3	5	4	2	8
5	8	3	4	2	6	9	1	7
9	2	4	8	7	1	6	5	3

PUZZLE / **33**

9	6	1	7	4	2	8	5	3
4	3	5	1	8	6	2	7	9
2	8	7	5	3	9	1	4	6
6	5	3	8	2	4	9	1	7
7	9	4	3	1	5	6	2	8
8	1	2	6	9	7	4	3	5
3	4	8	9	5	1	7	6	2
1	7	9	2	6	3	5	8	4
5	2	6	4	7	8	3	9	1

PUZZLE / **34**

8	2	1	7	6	4	3	5	9
7	4	5	8	3	9	6	1	2
9	3	6	5	2	1	7	8	4
5	6	3	2	4	7	8	9	1
4	9	8	1	5	3	2	7	6
1	7	2	9	8	6	4	3	5
3	5	7	4	1	2	9	6	8
6	8	4	3	9	5	1	2	7
2	1	9	6	7	8	5	4	3

PUZZLE / **35**

5	1	2	7	3	8	4	6	9
6	4	9	5	2	1	8	7	3
3	8	7	6	9	4	2	1	5
4	5	3	2	6	7	9	8	1
2	9	6	8	1	3	5	4	7
8	7	1	4	5	9	6	3	2
1	3	4	9	8	5	7	2	6
9	2	8	1	7	6	3	5	4
7	6	5	3	4	2	1	9	8

PUZZLE / **36**

3	5	9	8	6	4	1	2	7
4	6	2	5	1	7	9	8	3
7	1	8	9	3	2	4	6	5
9	3	6	4	7	8	5	1	2
8	2	7	1	9	5	3	4	6
5	4	1	3	2	6	7	9	8
2	8	3	7	4	9	6	5	1
1	9	5	6	8	3	2	7	4
6	7	4	2	5	1	8	3	9

PUZZLE / **37**

6	9	3	2	7	4	5	8	1
5	8	7	9	1	6	3	4	2
2	1	4	8	5	3	9	7	6
4	3	5	6	2	9	8	1	7
7	2	9	4	8	1	6	3	5
8	6	1	7	3	5	2	9	4
9	4	2	1	6	8	7	5	3
1	5	6	3	9	7	4	2	8
3	7	8	5	4	2	1	6	9

PUZZLE / **38**

9	6	7	8	3	4	1	5	2
3	4	5	2	6	1	9	7	8
8	2	1	5	9	7	4	6	3
7	1	8	3	4	5	6	2	9
4	9	6	7	1	2	3	8	5
5	3	2	6	8	9	7	4	1
6	5	9	4	2	3	8	1	7
1	7	4	9	5	8	2	3	6
2	8	3	1	7	6	5	9	4

PUZZLE / **39**

1	7	3	6	8	4	5	2	9
2	9	6	5	3	1	4	7	8
8	5	4	9	7	2	6	1	3
7	8	5	4	2	9	3	6	1
4	6	2	3	1	8	9	5	7
3	1	9	7	6	5	8	4	2
5	2	1	8	4	3	7	9	6
9	3	7	2	5	6	1	8	4
6	4	8	1	9	7	2	3	5

PUZZLE / **40**

7	3	9	4	1	2	5	8	6
6	1	4	7	5	8	3	9	2
2	8	5	6	9	3	4	1	7
9	6	7	5	2	1	8	3	4
4	2	3	8	7	9	6	5	1
8	5	1	3	4	6	7	2	9
3	9	6	1	8	4	2	7	5
5	4	2	9	3	7	1	6	8
1	7	8	2	6	5	9	4	3

PUZZLE / **41**

8	5	6	9	4	3	2	7	1
7	2	9	8	1	6	5	4	3
4	1	3	7	2	5	8	9	6
6	4	1	3	8	7	9	5	2
2	8	5	6	9	4	3	1	7
3	9	7	1	5	2	4	6	8
5	3	8	4	7	1	6	2	9
1	6	2	5	3	9	7	8	4
9	7	4	2	6	8	1	3	5

PUZZLE / **42**

1	5	4	6	7	3	2	8	9
9	2	7	4	8	1	6	5	3
8	3	6	9	5	2	4	7	1
7	6	3	1	4	9	8	2	5
5	1	8	2	6	7	9	3	4
2	4	9	5	3	8	1	6	7
4	8	5	3	9	6	7	1	2
3	7	1	8	2	4	5	9	6
6	9	2	7	1	5	3	4	8

PUZZLE / **43**

2	8	3	5	4	6	9	7	1
5	4	1	9	7	3	8	2	6
6	7	9	8	1	2	3	4	5
1	2	8	7	5	9	4	6	3
3	9	6	4	2	1	7	5	8
7	5	4	3	6	8	1	9	2
4	3	2	1	9	5	6	8	7
9	1	5	6	8	7	2	3	4
8	6	7	2	3	4	5	1	9

PUZZLE / **44**

9	1	6	3	5	8	7	2	4
5	4	8	7	2	1	6	9	3
2	7	3	4	9	6	8	5	1
3	5	2	1	8	9	4	6	7
4	9	1	5	6	7	2	3	8
8	6	7	2	3	4	5	1	9
7	2	4	6	1	3	9	8	5
6	3	9	8	4	5	1	7	2
1	8	5	9	7	2	3	4	6

PUZZLE / **45**

7	4	3	9	6	5	8	2	1
2	8	6	1	4	3	9	5	7
9	5	1	7	8	2	6	4	3
4	1	8	2	3	6	5	7	9
3	2	9	5	7	8	4	1	6
5	6	7	4	9	1	2	3	8
8	3	2	6	5	7	1	9	4
6	9	5	3	1	4	7	8	2
1	7	4	8	2	9	3	6	5

PUZZLE / 46

9	2	7	5	6	8	3	4	1
4	6	8	7	1	3	5	2	9
5	1	3	9	2	4	7	6	8
1	5	6	8	9	2	4	7	3
8	7	9	3	4	6	2	1	5
3	4	2	1	7	5	9	8	6
7	8	5	2	3	1	6	9	4
6	9	1	4	5	7	8	3	2
2	3	4	6	8	9	1	5	7

PUZZLE / 47

9	1	8	3	4	2	5	6	7
6	2	4	7	1	5	8	9	3
3	5	7	8	9	6	2	4	1
1	7	6	5	8	3	4	2	9
4	8	9	1	2	7	3	5	6
5	3	2	4	6	9	1	7	8
8	9	5	6	3	4	7	1	2
7	6	3	2	5	1	9	8	4
2	4	1	9	7	8	6	3	5

PUZZLE / 48

4	9	3	2	6	1	8	7	5
7	1	6	5	4	8	2	3	9
5	8	2	9	3	7	4	6	1
9	4	1	6	7	5	3	2	8
6	2	8	3	9	4	5	1	7
3	7	5	1	8	2	6	9	4
2	6	4	7	5	9	1	8	3
8	3	9	4	1	6	7	5	2
1	5	7	8	2	3	9	4	6

PUZZLE / 49

5	2	9	4	1	3	7	6	8
8	1	6	7	2	9	5	3	4
7	3	4	6	5	8	2	9	1
6	4	3	5	9	1	8	7	2
2	5	7	8	6	4	3	1	9
1	9	8	2	3	7	4	5	6
4	8	5	9	7	6	1	2	3
9	7	1	3	4	2	6	8	5
3	6	2	1	8	5	9	4	7

PUZZLE / 50

4	2	1	7	5	9	6	8	3
7	8	3	4	1	6	2	9	5
9	6	5	3	8	2	7	1	4
6	1	9	5	7	3	8	4	2
8	3	2	6	4	1	9	5	7
5	4	7	2	9	8	1	3	6
2	7	8	1	3	5	4	6	9
3	9	6	8	2	4	5	7	1
1	5	4	9	6	7	3	2	8

PUZZLE / 51

3	1	9	5	2	7	8	4	6
6	2	7	1	8	4	3	5	9
8	4	5	3	6	9	2	1	7
2	8	4	6	3	1	7	9	5
1	7	3	9	4	5	6	2	8
9	5	6	8	7	2	1	3	4
5	6	1	7	9	3	4	8	2
7	9	2	4	1	8	5	6	3
4	3	8	2	5	6	9	7	1

PUZZLE / 52

6	3	9	4	7	2	5	1	8
4	1	7	8	5	9	3	2	6
8	2	5	3	1	6	7	4	9
9	6	4	2	3	7	1	8	5
3	7	2	1	8	5	9	6	4
1	5	8	6	9	4	2	3	7
7	4	1	9	2	8	6	5	3
2	9	6	5	4	3	8	7	1
5	8	3	7	6	1	4	9	2

PUZZLE / 53

4	3	7	6	5	9	8	1	2
2	5	9	4	1	8	7	6	3
1	8	6	3	7	2	4	5	9
5	7	3	1	9	4	2	8	6
6	4	2	7	8	5	3	9	1
9	1	8	2	6	3	5	7	4
8	2	1	5	3	6	9	4	7
3	6	5	9	4	7	1	2	8
7	9	4	8	2	1	6	3	5

PUZZLE / 54

6	5	3	8	2	4	1	7	9
9	1	2	5	6	7	4	3	8
8	7	4	9	3	1	6	2	5
3	2	7	1	4	8	5	9	6
5	4	6	2	7	9	8	1	3
1	9	8	3	5	6	7	4	2
7	6	9	4	8	3	2	5	1
4	3	5	6	1	2	9	8	7
2	8	1	7	9	5	3	6	4

PUZZLE / 55

8	1	4	6	5	3	9	2	7
9	6	3	7	1	2	4	8	5
2	7	5	9	4	8	3	6	1
4	8	6	1	2	5	7	3	9
3	2	9	4	6	7	1	5	8
1	5	7	3	8	9	2	4	6
6	3	2	8	9	1	5	7	4
5	4	1	2	7	6	8	9	3
7	9	8	5	3	4	6	1	2

PUZZLE / 56

8	2	9	4	5	3	6	1	7
3	1	4	8	6	7	2	9	5
7	6	5	9	2	1	8	4	3
5	8	6	3	4	9	7	2	1
9	3	7	5	1	2	4	8	6
1	4	2	6	7	8	5	3	9
4	9	3	7	8	6	1	5	2
6	5	1	2	3	4	9	7	8
2	7	8	1	9	5	3	6	4

PUZZLE / 57

8	4	2	3	6	5	1	7	9
7	3	9	4	1	8	5	2	6
6	1	5	7	2	9	3	4	8
3	2	6	8	5	4	7	9	1
1	5	7	6	9	3	2	8	4
9	8	4	1	7	2	6	5	3
4	7	8	2	3	1	9	6	5
2	9	3	5	4	6	8	1	7
5	6	1	9	8	7	4	3	2

PUZZLE / 58

8	3	2	4	7	5	9	6	1
6	7	9	3	1	8	2	4	5
5	4	1	9	6	2	3	7	8
2	5	3	1	8	6	4	9	7
1	9	8	2	4	7	5	3	6
4	6	7	5	3	9	8	1	2
7	1	4	8	2	3	6	5	9
9	2	6	7	5	4	1	8	3
3	8	5	6	9	1	7	2	4

PUZZLE / 59

2	3	4	9	5	6	8	1	7
7	6	9	8	1	2	5	3	4
1	8	5	4	7	3	2	9	6
9	4	2	7	6	8	1	5	3
6	1	3	2	9	5	7	4	8
5	7	8	1	3	4	6	2	9
3	9	1	6	2	7	4	8	5
8	2	6	5	4	9	3	7	1
4	5	7	3	8	1	9	6	2

PUZZLE / 60

3	5	7	2	6	8	4	1	9
2	1	6	7	4	9	5	3	8
8	9	4	5	1	3	2	7	6
7	2	5	6	3	4	9	8	1
9	6	1	8	2	7	3	4	5
4	3	8	1	9	5	7	6	2
5	7	2	4	8	1	6	9	3
1	4	9	3	5	6	8	2	7
6	8	3	9	7	2	1	5	4

PUZZLE / 61

4	2	1	9	3	8	7	5	6
9	3	5	6	2	7	4	1	8
7	6	8	4	1	5	9	2	3
6	5	3	7	8	4	1	9	2
1	7	4	2	9	3	6	8	5
8	9	2	1	5	6	3	7	4
3	8	7	5	6	1	2	4	9
2	1	6	8	4	9	5	3	7
5	4	9	3	7	2	8	6	1

PUZZLE / 62

7	3	9	8	2	6	4	5	1
4	6	8	5	1	7	2	9	3
5	1	2	9	3	4	8	6	7
2	5	3	6	4	9	1	7	8
6	9	7	3	8	1	5	2	4
1	8	4	7	5	2	9	3	6
8	7	5	1	9	3	6	4	2
9	2	6	4	7	8	3	1	5
3	4	1	2	6	5	7	8	9

PUZZLE / 63

4	8	5	9	3	1	7	2	6
9	7	1	2	6	4	5	8	3
3	6	2	5	7	8	1	4	9
6	1	7	8	2	5	9	3	4
5	2	3	4	9	7	6	1	8
8	4	9	6	1	3	2	7	5
7	5	8	1	4	6	3	9	2
2	3	4	7	5	9	8	6	1
1	9	6	3	8	2	4	5	7

PUZZLE / 64

6	7	2	1	5	4	9	3	8
8	5	9	3	2	7	1	6	4
3	1	4	6	8	9	5	2	7
5	3	7	8	6	2	4	9	1
4	6	8	9	3	1	7	5	2
9	2	1	7	4	5	3	8	6
7	4	6	2	9	3	8	1	5
1	8	3	5	7	6	2	4	9
2	9	5	4	1	8	6	7	3

PUZZLE / 65

7	1	2	5	8	3	6	4	9
5	6	3	1	4	9	7	8	2
9	8	4	6	7	2	5	3	1
1	9	8	3	5	7	2	6	4
4	2	7	8	6	1	9	5	3
3	5	6	9	2	4	8	1	7
8	7	1	4	9	5	3	2	6
6	4	9	2	3	8	1	7	5
2	3	5	7	1	6	4	9	8

PUZZLE / 66

9	3	1	7	8	4	5	6	2
4	2	7	5	3	6	1	8	9
8	5	6	1	2	9	7	3	4
3	1	2	9	5	7	8	4	6
6	7	4	2	1	8	3	9	5
5	8	9	6	4	3	2	7	1
1	9	8	3	6	5	4	2	7
7	4	5	8	9	2	6	1	3
2	6	3	4	7	1	9	5	8

PUZZLE / 67

6	2	7	9	3	5	4	1	8
9	4	1	6	8	7	2	5	3
3	8	5	4	2	1	6	7	9
8	9	2	1	5	3	7	4	6
1	3	4	2	7	6	9	8	5
5	7	6	8	9	4	1	3	2
4	1	9	3	6	8	5	2	7
2	5	3	7	1	9	8	6	4
7	6	8	5	4	2	3	9	1

PUZZLE / 68

3	7	4	2	8	5	6	1	9
6	2	9	4	7	1	8	3	5
1	8	5	6	3	9	4	7	2
9	5	6	8	4	7	3	2	1
2	3	8	1	5	6	7	9	4
7	4	1	9	2	3	5	6	8
8	9	7	3	1	4	2	5	6
4	1	3	5	6	2	9	8	7
5	6	2	7	9	8	1	4	3

PUZZLE / 69

8	9	6	2	4	5	1	3	7
5	2	3	7	9	1	8	6	4
1	7	4	8	3	6	2	9	5
9	8	5	3	1	7	4	2	6
6	3	2	4	5	8	9	7	1
4	1	7	9	6	2	5	8	3
7	4	8	1	2	3	6	5	9
2	6	1	5	7	9	3	4	8
3	5	9	6	8	4	7	1	2

PUZZLE / 70

9	3	7	6	8	1	4	5	2
2	6	5	9	7	4	3	1	8
4	8	1	2	5	3	7	9	6
6	5	2	1	9	7	8	4	3
1	4	8	5	3	2	9	6	7
7	9	3	8	4	6	1	2	5
3	2	4	7	1	5	6	8	9
5	1	9	3	6	8	2	7	4
8	7	6	4	2	9	5	3	1

PUZZLE / 71

1	8	7	4	3	6	2	9	5
4	3	9	5	7	2	1	8	6
5	2	6	9	8	1	7	3	4
9	7	8	2	4	5	3	6	1
3	4	2	6	1	8	9	5	7
6	1	5	7	9	3	8	4	2
7	5	4	8	2	9	6	1	3
8	6	3	1	5	7	4	2	9
2	9	1	3	6	4	5	7	8

PUZZLE / 72

1	9	6	7	2	8	4	3	5
4	3	8	1	6	5	9	7	2
7	5	2	9	3	4	6	8	1
3	4	5	6	8	1	7	2	9
2	6	7	5	4	9	8	1	3
8	1	9	3	7	2	5	4	6
6	2	1	8	5	7	3	9	4
9	7	3	4	1	6	2	5	8
5	8	4	2	9	3	1	6	7

PUZZLE / 73

7	9	3	6	2	1	8	5	4
6	8	4	5	9	3	2	1	7
2	5	1	8	4	7	9	3	6
9	3	5	1	8	4	6	7	2
1	2	8	3	7	6	5	4	9
4	6	7	9	5	2	1	8	3
5	4	6	7	1	9	3	2	8
3	1	2	4	6	8	7	9	5
8	7	9	2	3	5	4	6	1

PUZZLE / 74

7	3	6	4	9	5	2	8	1
5	8	2	3	7	1	9	6	4
1	9	4	8	2	6	7	5	3
8	1	7	2	3	9	6	4	5
2	5	9	6	1	4	3	7	8
6	4	3	7	5	8	1	2	9
3	6	1	5	4	7	8	9	2
4	2	8	9	6	3	5	1	7
9	7	5	1	8	2	4	3	6

PUZZLE / 75

6	3	4	7	1	9	8	2	5
8	9	1	2	5	4	7	6	3
2	7	5	6	8	3	1	9	4
5	2	7	4	6	1	9	3	8
4	8	6	3	9	2	5	7	1
9	1	3	5	7	8	6	4	2
3	5	9	1	2	6	4	8	7
7	6	2	8	4	5	3	1	9
1	4	8	9	3	7	2	5	6

PUZZLE / **76**

4	7	5	8	6	9	2	1	3
3	2	6	4	7	1	9	8	5
1	8	9	2	3	5	7	4	6
6	4	1	3	5	7	8	2	9
2	9	7	6	4	8	3	5	1
8	5	3	1	9	2	6	7	4
9	1	4	7	8	6	5	3	2
5	3	8	9	2	4	1	6	7
7	6	2	5	1	3	4	9	8

PUZZLE / **77**

7	5	2	1	3	6	8	9	4
1	9	4	7	2	8	3	6	5
6	3	8	4	5	9	1	2	7
8	4	1	9	7	5	6	3	2
5	6	7	3	8	2	9	4	1
9	2	3	6	4	1	5	7	8
2	7	9	8	1	3	4	5	6
3	8	5	2	6	4	7	1	9
4	1	6	5	9	7	2	8	3

PUZZLE / **78**

6	9	4	2	7	5	8	1	3
8	2	3	6	4	1	5	9	7
1	7	5	3	8	9	2	4	6
9	5	1	7	3	4	6	2	8
7	3	8	1	2	6	9	5	4
4	6	2	5	9	8	3	7	1
5	8	6	4	1	2	7	3	9
3	4	9	8	5	7	1	6	2
2	1	7	9	6	3	4	8	5

PUZZLE / **79**

4	7	2	1	3	5	8	9	6
5	9	6	2	8	7	3	1	4
3	1	8	4	6	9	2	5	7
8	5	1	9	4	6	7	3	2
7	3	9	8	1	2	6	4	5
2	6	4	7	5	3	9	8	1
9	8	7	5	2	1	4	6	3
1	2	3	6	9	4	5	7	8
6	4	5	3	7	8	1	2	9

PUZZLE / **80**

6	4	9	2	1	7	5	3	8
7	1	8	4	3	5	6	2	9
3	5	2	8	9	6	7	1	4
4	6	3	7	5	8	1	9	2
8	2	5	1	4	9	3	7	6
1	9	7	3	6	2	4	8	5
2	8	1	6	7	4	9	5	3
5	7	4	9	2	3	8	6	1
9	3	6	5	8	1	2	4	7

PUZZLE / **81**

7	2	8	9	6	5	4	3	1
9	3	6	7	4	1	8	5	2
5	1	4	8	2	3	7	9	6
8	7	9	6	5	4	2	1	3
2	4	1	3	9	7	5	6	8
3	6	5	2	1	8	9	4	7
4	9	2	1	7	6	3	8	5
6	8	7	5	3	9	1	2	4
1	5	3	4	8	2	6	7	9

PUZZLE / **82**

3	4	2	6	7	8	9	1	5
8	6	9	3	5	1	4	7	2
7	1	5	2	9	4	8	3	6
5	2	1	9	8	3	6	4	7
4	7	3	5	2	6	1	8	9
6	9	8	4	1	7	2	5	3
1	5	6	7	4	9	3	2	8
9	8	7	1	3	2	5	6	4
2	3	4	8	6	5	7	9	1

PUZZLE / **83**

9	7	5	4	1	8	3	6	2
6	2	4	7	3	5	8	9	1
3	1	8	9	2	6	7	4	5
5	4	6	2	9	7	1	8	3
7	3	9	8	5	1	6	2	4
1	8	2	3	6	4	9	5	7
8	6	3	5	7	2	4	1	9
4	5	7	1	8	9	2	3	6
2	9	1	6	4	3	5	7	8

PUZZLE / **84**

3	6	7	4	5	1	2	8	9
9	5	1	8	2	3	6	7	4
4	2	8	6	9	7	3	5	1
5	4	6	7	3	8	9	1	2
8	7	3	9	1	2	4	6	5
2	1	9	5	4	6	8	3	7
6	9	4	3	7	5	1	2	8
1	8	5	2	6	9	7	4	3
7	3	2	1	8	4	5	9	6

PUZZLE / **85**

5	6	4	3	2	8	7	9	1
3	2	1	7	4	9	8	6	5
9	7	8	1	6	5	2	4	3
8	1	6	5	7	3	4	2	9
2	5	3	9	8	4	1	7	6
4	9	7	2	1	6	3	5	8
1	3	2	6	9	7	5	8	4
7	4	9	8	5	1	6	3	2
6	8	5	4	3	2	9	1	7

PUZZLE / **86**

5	9	3	7	4	2	1	6	8
8	2	7	9	6	1	5	3	4
6	4	1	8	5	3	2	7	9
7	8	6	1	3	4	9	5	2
4	5	9	2	7	8	6	1	3
3	1	2	6	9	5	8	4	7
9	7	8	3	1	6	4	2	5
1	3	4	5	2	9	7	8	6
2	6	5	4	8	7	3	9	1

PUZZLE / **87**

3	4	7	8	9	5	1	2	6
2	6	5	4	1	7	8	9	3
1	9	8	3	6	2	7	4	5
4	1	2	7	8	6	5	3	9
6	8	3	5	4	9	2	1	7
7	5	9	2	3	1	6	8	4
8	3	1	6	7	4	9	5	2
5	7	4	9	2	8	3	6	1
9	2	6	1	5	3	4	7	8

PUZZLE / **88**

6	3	5	2	1	7	9	8	4
7	4	2	9	8	3	1	6	5
1	9	8	6	5	4	3	2	7
4	8	7	1	2	5	6	9	3
9	1	6	3	4	8	5	7	2
2	5	3	7	9	6	8	4	1
8	6	4	5	3	2	7	1	9
3	7	1	4	6	9	2	5	8
5	2	9	8	7	1	4	3	6

PUZZLE / **89**

5	9	3	8	1	6	7	2	4
6	8	2	9	4	7	3	1	5
1	7	4	3	2	5	6	8	9
8	4	7	2	9	3	5	6	1
9	2	1	6	5	4	8	7	3
3	6	5	7	8	1	4	9	2
7	5	6	1	3	9	2	4	8
2	3	9	4	6	8	1	5	7
4	1	8	5	7	2	9	3	6

PUZZLE / **90**

1	6	5	3	7	9	2	8	4
7	9	2	8	4	1	5	3	6
3	4	8	5	6	2	7	9	1
8	3	1	2	9	6	4	5	7
4	2	9	7	3	5	1	6	8
5	7	6	4	1	8	3	2	9
9	8	7	1	5	3	6	4	2
6	1	3	9	2	4	8	7	5
2	5	4	6	8	7	9	1	3

PUZZLE / 91

1	4	6	5	7	8	3	9	2
5	7	8	9	2	3	1	6	4
3	9	2	1	6	4	7	8	5
4	6	7	3	1	5	8	2	9
2	8	3	7	4	9	5	1	6
9	1	5	6	8	2	4	7	3
7	5	4	8	9	6	2	3	1
6	2	1	4	3	7	9	5	8
8	3	9	2	5	1	6	4	7

PUZZLE / 92

2	5	3	1	6	9	7	4	8
9	6	7	4	8	2	1	5	3
8	1	4	3	5	7	9	6	2
1	8	5	6	2	4	3	9	7
4	3	2	7	9	5	6	8	1
7	9	6	8	3	1	4	2	5
6	7	1	2	4	8	5	3	9
3	2	9	5	7	6	8	1	4
5	4	8	9	1	3	2	7	6

PUZZLE / 93

6	9	1	5	4	8	3	2	7
5	4	7	6	2	3	8	9	1
8	2	3	1	9	7	5	4	6
1	5	6	9	3	2	7	8	4
2	8	9	7	1	4	6	3	5
7	3	4	8	5	6	9	1	2
3	7	2	4	6	9	1	5	8
9	6	5	2	8	1	4	7	3
4	1	8	3	7	5	2	6	9

PUZZLE / 94

7	3	6	8	4	1	5	9	2
5	1	4	2	9	3	8	6	7
2	8	9	6	7	5	1	4	3
8	7	1	5	3	9	6	2	4
4	2	5	7	8	6	3	1	9
9	6	3	1	2	4	7	5	8
3	5	8	9	6	2	4	7	1
6	9	7	4	1	8	2	3	5
1	4	2	3	5	7	9	8	6

PUZZLE / 95

4	7	5	6	9	8	1	3	2
1	9	6	2	3	7	8	4	5
8	3	2	4	5	1	7	6	9
3	2	8	1	7	4	9	5	6
7	6	1	5	2	9	4	8	3
5	4	9	8	6	3	2	7	1
9	8	3	7	1	6	5	2	4
6	5	7	9	4	2	3	1	8
2	1	4	3	8	5	6	9	7

PUZZLE / 96

2	1	6	3	5	9	8	7	4
3	9	5	7	8	4	2	1	6
7	8	4	2	6	1	9	3	5
9	4	8	6	3	7	5	2	1
1	2	7	5	9	8	6	4	3
5	6	3	4	1	2	7	9	8
4	3	2	8	7	6	1	5	9
6	5	9	1	2	3	4	8	7
8	7	1	9	4	5	3	6	2

PUZZLE / 97

2	3	8	9	5	7	6	4	1
1	7	4	8	2	6	9	3	5
5	9	6	1	3	4	2	7	8
6	4	3	5	7	1	8	9	2
7	2	1	3	8	9	5	6	4
9	8	5	6	4	2	7	1	3
8	1	9	2	6	3	4	5	7
4	6	2	7	1	5	3	8	9
3	5	7	4	9	8	1	2	6

PUZZLE / 98

1	4	7	9	8	5	2	6	3
6	5	8	7	2	3	4	1	9
9	3	2	4	6	1	5	7	8
2	7	1	6	4	9	3	8	5
5	8	3	1	7	2	9	4	6
4	9	6	3	5	8	7	2	1
8	1	5	2	3	7	6	9	4
3	2	4	8	9	6	1	5	7
7	6	9	5	1	4	8	3	2

PUZZLE / 99

4	2	1	8	9	6	5	3	7
5	6	7	3	2	4	1	9	8
9	8	3	7	5	1	6	4	2
3	1	6	4	8	9	2	7	5
8	7	9	5	1	2	3	6	4
2	4	5	6	3	7	8	1	9
7	5	4	2	6	3	9	8	1
6	9	2	1	4	8	7	5	3
1	3	8	9	7	5	4	2	6

PUZZLE / 100

1	5	9	6	7	4	3	2	8
7	2	8	1	3	9	4	6	5
3	6	4	8	5	2	9	7	1
9	7	6	5	8	1	2	4	3
4	3	5	2	9	6	1	8	7
2	8	1	3	4	7	6	5	9
8	4	3	9	6	5	7	1	2
6	9	2	7	1	8	5	3	4
5	1	7	4	2	3	8	9	6

PUZZLE / 101

6	8	5	2	9	1	4	3	7
2	7	9	3	6	4	8	1	5
3	1	4	7	5	8	2	6	9
8	2	6	4	1	5	9	7	3
4	3	1	9	7	6	5	8	2
9	5	7	8	2	3	6	4	1
1	6	2	5	4	7	3	9	8
5	4	8	1	3	9	7	2	6
7	9	3	6	8	2	1	5	4

PUZZLE / 102

4	8	2	7	3	9	5	6	1
6	7	3	1	5	4	8	9	2
1	9	5	2	8	6	4	7	3
8	4	7	5	1	2	9	3	6
5	1	9	3	6	8	2	4	7
2	3	6	9	4	7	1	8	5
7	5	8	4	2	3	6	1	9
9	6	1	8	7	5	3	2	4
3	2	4	6	9	1	7	5	8

PUZZLE / 103

4	9	6	7	5	8	3	2	1
1	8	3	6	4	2	5	9	7
5	7	2	3	1	9	8	4	6
3	4	9	5	2	1	7	6	8
6	1	7	8	3	4	2	5	9
2	5	8	9	6	7	4	1	3
9	3	1	4	7	5	6	8	2
7	2	5	1	8	6	9	3	4
8	6	4	2	9	3	1	7	5

PUZZLE / 104

8	1	3	7	9	5	4	2	6
2	5	9	3	6	4	8	1	7
4	7	6	2	8	1	3	5	9
6	9	2	5	1	3	7	4	8
1	8	5	6	4	7	9	3	2
7	3	4	9	2	8	5	6	1
3	2	8	4	7	6	1	9	5
9	4	1	8	5	2	6	7	3
5	6	7	1	3	9	2	8	4

PUZZLE / 105

7	4	9	3	6	5	2	1	8
2	1	8	7	9	4	6	5	3
5	3	6	1	2	8	9	4	7
8	5	7	4	3	9	1	2	6
1	9	2	8	7	6	4	3	5
4	6	3	2	5	1	7	8	9
3	2	5	9	4	7	8	6	1
9	8	4	6	1	3	5	7	2
6	7	1	5	8	2	3	9	4

PUZZLE / 106

7	3	2	5	6	1	9	4	8
6	1	9	8	2	4	7	5	3
8	5	4	7	9	3	6	2	1
3	2	5	9	4	7	1	8	6
9	8	7	6	1	2	4	3	5
1	4	6	3	8	5	2	9	7
2	7	8	4	5	6	3	1	9
4	9	3	1	7	8	5	6	2
5	6	1	2	3	9	8	7	4

PUZZLE / 107

9	8	5	7	2	6	4	3	1
4	1	7	8	9	3	2	5	6
6	3	2	4	1	5	9	7	8
8	2	6	9	3	1	5	4	7
5	9	1	6	4	7	8	2	3
7	4	3	5	8	2	6	1	9
2	5	9	1	7	8	3	6	4
3	7	8	2	6	4	1	9	5
1	6	4	3	5	9	7	8	2

PUZZLE / 108

7	8	2	1	4	6	3	9	5
3	5	6	2	7	9	4	1	8
4	1	9	5	8	3	2	7	6
5	2	7	3	6	4	9	8	1
8	4	3	9	5	1	6	2	7
6	9	1	7	2	8	5	4	3
2	6	4	8	3	7	1	5	9
9	7	5	6	1	2	8	3	4
1	3	8	4	9	5	7	6	2

PUZZLE / 109

2	3	7	1	8	9	4	6	5
5	9	8	7	6	4	1	2	3
1	4	6	5	2	3	7	9	8
9	8	4	2	1	6	5	3	7
6	5	2	3	7	8	9	1	4
3	7	1	4	9	5	2	8	6
8	2	5	6	4	1	3	7	9
4	1	9	8	3	7	6	5	2
7	6	3	9	5	2	8	4	1

PUZZLE / 110

2	7	8	1	9	3	4	6	5
5	4	6	7	2	8	1	9	3
3	9	1	5	4	6	2	8	7
8	6	5	2	3	1	7	4	9
9	1	3	4	5	7	6	2	8
7	2	4	6	8	9	5	3	1
4	8	2	9	7	5	3	1	6
6	3	7	8	1	4	9	5	2
1	5	9	3	6	2	8	7	4

PUZZLE / 111

7	6	3	1	9	4	8	2	5
8	9	2	6	5	3	1	4	7
5	4	1	8	7	2	9	6	3
6	3	9	2	1	7	4	5	8
1	7	8	5	4	6	2	3	9
2	5	4	3	8	9	7	1	6
4	8	6	7	3	1	5	9	2
9	2	5	4	6	8	3	7	1
3	1	7	9	2	5	6	8	4

PUZZLE / 112

3	1	2	7	5	8	4	6	9
4	8	7	6	9	1	3	2	5
6	9	5	4	2	3	8	1	7
5	2	3	1	4	9	6	7	8
7	4	1	5	8	6	2	9	3
8	6	9	2	3	7	1	5	4
1	3	6	8	7	5	9	4	2
2	7	8	9	1	4	5	3	6
9	5	4	3	6	2	7	8	1

PUZZLE / 113

3	4	1	2	8	5	7	6	9
2	6	9	7	4	1	3	8	5
7	8	5	6	3	9	2	1	4
9	1	6	3	7	8	4	5	2
4	7	2	1	5	6	9	3	8
5	3	8	4	9	2	1	7	6
1	5	3	9	6	4	8	2	7
8	9	7	5	2	3	6	4	1
6	2	4	8	1	7	5	9	3

PUZZLE / 114

8	3	9	6	5	1	4	7	2
2	6	4	3	8	7	9	5	1
7	5	1	9	2	4	3	6	8
9	8	5	2	7	3	1	4	6
1	2	3	4	9	6	5	8	7
6	4	7	5	1	8	2	9	3
5	7	6	1	4	2	8	3	9
4	1	8	7	3	9	6	2	5
3	9	2	8	6	5	7	1	4

PUZZLE / 115

4	3	1	5	6	9	2	8	7
7	8	5	2	4	3	9	6	1
6	9	2	1	7	8	3	4	5
8	5	4	3	9	2	1	7	6
1	2	7	6	5	4	8	3	9
9	6	3	8	1	7	4	5	2
5	1	9	4	8	6	7	2	3
3	4	6	7	2	1	5	9	8
2	7	8	9	3	5	6	1	4

PUZZLE / 116

1	8	7	9	4	6	2	5	3
5	3	6	7	8	2	1	4	9
9	2	4	1	5	3	8	7	6
4	6	1	2	7	5	3	9	8
8	9	5	3	6	1	4	2	7
3	7	2	8	9	4	5	6	1
7	1	9	5	2	8	6	3	4
2	4	8	6	3	9	7	1	5
6	5	3	4	1	7	9	8	2

PUZZLE / 117

2	3	5	8	6	1	7	9	4
4	7	6	2	3	9	1	8	5
9	8	1	5	7	4	6	2	3
8	2	3	9	4	7	5	1	6
1	4	9	6	5	8	2	3	7
5	6	7	3	1	2	9	4	8
7	9	8	4	2	6	3	5	1
6	5	2	1	8	3	4	7	9
3	1	4	7	9	5	8	6	2

PUZZLE / 118

2	4	3	1	9	8	6	7	5
1	5	9	6	7	4	2	3	8
7	6	8	5	2	3	4	1	9
3	1	4	9	5	2	7	8	6
6	9	5	3	8	7	1	4	2
8	2	7	4	1	6	5	9	3
5	8	1	7	6	9	3	2	4
4	7	2	8	3	5	9	6	1
9	3	6	2	4	1	8	5	7

PUZZLE / 119

3	4	1	6	7	8	9	2	5
6	7	5	9	1	2	4	8	3
2	9	8	4	5	3	1	6	7
1	5	6	7	4	9	8	3	2
9	2	7	3	8	6	5	4	1
8	3	4	1	2	5	7	9	6
5	1	9	2	6	4	3	7	8
4	8	2	5	3	7	6	1	9
7	6	3	8	9	1	2	5	4

PUZZLE / 120

4	2	1	8	9	3	7	6	5
6	8	7	5	4	2	1	9	3
9	3	5	7	1	6	4	8	2
3	7	8	1	6	5	9	2	4
2	6	9	3	7	4	5	1	8
1	5	4	9	2	8	3	7	6
5	9	6	4	8	7	2	3	1
8	1	3	2	5	9	6	4	7
7	4	2	6	3	1	8	5	9

PUZZLE / 121

7	2	6	1	9	8	5	4	3
8	4	1	5	3	6	7	9	2
5	3	9	2	4	7	8	1	6
3	5	4	6	2	9	1	8	7
1	9	2	8	7	3	4	6	5
6	7	8	4	1	5	2	3	9
2	1	5	9	6	4	3	7	8
4	6	3	7	8	2	9	5	1
9	8	7	3	5	1	6	2	4

PUZZLE / 122

8	2	6	9	3	5	1	4	7
5	4	3	7	6	1	8	2	9
7	1	9	4	8	2	3	5	6
6	3	5	1	4	8	7	9	2
1	9	7	2	5	6	4	8	3
4	8	2	3	7	9	6	1	5
9	6	4	8	2	7	5	3	1
3	5	1	6	9	4	2	7	8
2	7	8	5	1	3	9	6	4

PUZZLE / 123

4	6	9	1	7	2	3	8	5
3	8	7	9	5	4	2	1	6
5	1	2	3	8	6	4	7	9
8	5	6	2	1	9	7	4	3
1	9	3	5	4	7	6	2	8
2	7	4	8	6	3	9	5	1
9	2	5	7	3	1	8	6	4
7	4	1	6	9	8	5	3	2
6	3	8	4	2	5	1	9	7

PUZZLE / 124

5	6	4	7	3	8	2	1	9
9	7	1	2	6	5	4	8	3
2	3	8	4	1	9	6	5	7
7	4	3	9	2	1	8	6	5
8	2	5	3	7	6	9	4	1
1	9	6	5	8	4	7	3	2
3	5	2	6	4	7	1	9	8
6	1	9	8	5	2	3	7	4
4	8	7	1	9	3	5	2	6

PUZZLE / 125

9	8	6	4	1	2	7	5	3
5	7	3	9	6	8	2	4	1
2	1	4	7	5	3	6	9	8
4	5	1	8	9	7	3	6	2
6	9	8	2	3	1	5	7	4
3	2	7	5	4	6	1	8	9
7	6	2	3	8	4	9	1	5
8	3	9	1	7	5	4	2	6
1	4	5	6	2	9	8	3	7

PUZZLE / 126

8	9	2	7	3	1	6	4	5
7	5	1	4	2	6	9	3	8
6	3	4	9	8	5	7	1	2
3	2	8	5	6	7	1	9	4
1	6	5	8	9	4	2	7	3
9	4	7	3	1	2	5	8	6
2	7	6	1	4	8	3	5	9
4	1	3	6	5	9	8	2	7
5	8	9	2	7	3	4	6	1

PUZZLE / 127

4	3	6	8	9	2	1	7	5
1	8	2	4	7	5	3	6	9
5	7	9	6	1	3	4	8	2
8	1	4	9	6	7	5	2	3
7	2	3	5	8	4	6	9	1
6	9	5	2	3	1	7	4	8
9	5	8	1	4	6	2	3	7
3	4	1	7	2	9	8	5	6
2	6	7	3	5	8	9	1	4

PUZZLE / 128

6	3	2	5	8	9	7	1	4
8	4	5	1	3	7	2	9	6
1	9	7	4	2	6	5	3	8
7	5	3	9	4	2	6	8	1
9	6	1	3	7	8	4	5	2
4	2	8	6	1	5	3	7	9
2	8	6	7	5	1	9	4	3
3	7	9	8	6	4	1	2	5
5	1	4	2	9	3	8	6	7

PUZZLE / 129

1	5	2	6	4	3	8	7	9
8	4	6	7	1	9	2	5	3
3	9	7	2	5	8	6	4	1
9	1	3	8	7	5	4	6	2
6	8	4	9	2	1	7	3	5
2	7	5	4	3	6	1	9	8
5	2	1	3	6	7	9	8	4
7	3	9	1	8	4	5	2	6
4	6	8	5	9	2	3	1	7

PUZZLE / 130

7	1	2	5	9	4	3	6	8
3	8	4	7	6	2	9	1	5
9	6	5	3	8	1	7	4	2
8	2	3	9	5	6	4	7	1
5	9	1	4	3	7	8	2	6
6	4	7	2	1	8	5	9	3
1	7	6	8	4	5	2	3	9
2	3	8	6	7	9	1	5	4
4	5	9	1	2	3	6	8	7

PUZZLE / 131

9	4	1	6	2	8	3	7	5
2	6	7	9	5	3	1	8	4
5	3	8	1	4	7	9	6	2
3	7	6	2	9	1	4	5	8
8	2	5	3	7	4	6	9	1
4	1	9	5	8	6	2	3	7
7	5	3	4	1	9	8	2	6
1	9	2	8	6	5	7	4	3
6	8	4	7	3	2	5	1	9

PUZZLE / 132

9	6	4	5	2	1	7	8	3
8	1	7	4	9	3	6	2	5
5	2	3	8	6	7	1	4	9
4	5	6	7	3	2	8	9	1
1	9	8	6	5	4	2	3	7
3	7	2	1	8	9	5	6	4
7	3	1	2	4	8	9	5	6
6	8	9	3	7	5	4	1	2
2	4	5	9	1	6	3	7	8

PUZZLE / 133

4	5	7	2	3	6	9	8	1
3	9	1	8	4	5	7	6	2
2	8	6	1	7	9	3	4	5
1	3	8	6	5	7	2	9	4
5	7	2	9	8	4	1	3	6
6	4	9	3	1	2	5	7	8
9	6	3	4	2	1	8	5	7
7	2	4	5	9	8	6	1	3
8	1	5	7	6	3	4	2	9

PUZZLE / 134

5	8	4	9	1	2	3	7	6
1	7	3	6	8	5	2	4	9
9	6	2	3	7	4	1	8	5
7	2	6	8	9	3	5	1	4
4	1	9	5	2	7	8	6	3
3	5	8	4	6	1	9	2	7
6	9	5	2	4	8	7	3	1
2	3	7	1	5	6	4	9	8
8	4	1	7	3	9	6	5	2

PUZZLE / 135

7	6	9	2	5	1	8	3	4
2	5	4	6	8	3	7	1	9
1	8	3	7	9	4	2	6	5
9	3	1	5	6	7	4	2	8
8	7	2	1	4	9	6	5	3
5	4	6	8	3	2	9	7	1
6	9	8	3	7	5	1	4	2
4	2	5	9	1	6	3	8	7
3	1	7	4	2	8	5	9	6

PUZZLE / 136

6	9	7	2	1	4	5	8	3
4	5	8	9	6	3	7	1	2
2	1	3	7	8	5	6	4	9
1	7	2	4	5	6	3	9	8
3	6	4	8	2	9	1	5	7
9	8	5	3	7	1	4	2	6
8	3	1	6	4	2	9	7	5
5	2	9	1	3	7	8	6	4
7	4	6	5	9	8	2	3	1

PUZZLE / 137

5	3	6	4	7	8	2	1	9
9	1	7	5	3	2	4	8	6
2	8	4	1	9	6	3	5	7
7	5	1	2	6	4	9	3	8
8	2	9	7	1	3	5	6	4
6	4	3	8	5	9	7	2	1
3	7	8	6	4	5	1	9	2
1	6	5	9	2	7	8	4	3
4	9	2	3	8	1	6	7	5

PUZZLE / 138

9	7	5	6	4	8	2	3	1
8	6	3	9	1	2	4	5	7
1	4	2	5	3	7	6	9	8
4	8	1	2	9	5	3	7	6
5	3	6	8	7	1	9	4	2
7	2	9	4	6	3	8	1	5
6	1	7	3	8	4	5	2	9
3	5	8	1	2	9	7	6	4
2	9	4	7	5	6	1	8	3

PUZZLE / 139

6	1	2	4	5	8	3	9	7
7	4	8	3	1	9	6	2	5
5	9	3	2	6	7	1	4	8
8	5	9	6	2	4	7	1	3
2	6	1	7	3	5	9	8	4
3	7	4	8	9	1	2	5	6
9	2	6	5	8	3	4	7	1
1	8	7	9	4	6	5	3	2
4	3	5	1	7	2	8	6	9

PUZZLE / 140

3	7	8	2	4	6	5	1	9
6	4	5	1	9	3	7	8	2
2	9	1	8	7	5	6	3	4
4	8	9	6	1	2	3	7	5
1	6	7	5	3	4	9	2	8
5	2	3	7	8	9	4	6	1
8	5	4	3	2	7	1	9	6
9	3	2	4	6	1	8	5	7
7	1	6	9	5	8	2	4	3

PUZZLE / 141

5	9	8	7	6	3	1	2	4
7	2	6	1	9	4	3	8	5
4	3	1	2	8	5	9	7	6
2	7	4	8	5	9	6	3	1
8	1	5	6	3	2	7	4	9
9	6	3	4	1	7	2	5	8
6	4	7	5	2	1	8	9	3
3	8	2	9	4	6	5	1	7
1	5	9	3	7	8	4	6	2

PUZZLE / 142

3	8	9	5	1	2	4	7	6
2	7	5	6	4	8	1	9	3
4	1	6	7	9	3	8	2	5
7	2	1	9	3	4	6	5	8
5	6	8	2	7	1	3	4	9
9	3	4	8	5	6	7	1	2
8	9	3	1	2	7	5	6	4
1	4	2	3	6	5	9	8	7
6	5	7	4	8	9	2	3	1

PUZZLE / 143

1	9	5	3	6	4	2	8	7
7	3	2	9	1	8	4	6	5
4	8	6	5	7	2	3	1	9
2	6	9	8	5	3	1	7	4
8	4	7	1	9	6	5	3	2
3	5	1	4	2	7	6	9	8
5	2	8	7	3	1	9	4	6
9	7	3	6	4	5	8	2	1
6	1	4	2	8	9	7	5	3

PUZZLE / 144

1	3	4	2	8	5	9	6	7
7	9	2	4	6	3	1	8	5
5	6	8	9	1	7	2	4	3
4	7	5	1	9	6	3	2	8
3	2	6	7	4	8	5	1	9
9	8	1	3	5	2	6	7	4
6	4	9	8	3	1	7	5	2
8	1	7	5	2	9	4	3	6
2	5	3	6	7	4	8	9	1

PUZZLE / 145

6	9	5	4	3	8	1	2	7
3	4	7	1	2	5	8	9	6
8	1	2	6	9	7	3	5	4
9	7	6	8	5	2	4	1	3
1	3	4	9	7	6	5	8	2
5	2	8	3	4	1	7	6	9
2	5	9	7	1	4	6	3	8
7	6	3	5	8	9	2	4	1
4	8	1	2	6	3	9	7	5

PUZZLE / 146

4	6	7	5	2	9	1	3	8
9	2	5	1	8	3	7	4	6
3	1	8	7	6	4	9	5	2
8	5	3	9	4	1	6	2	7
6	4	9	2	7	5	3	8	1
2	7	1	6	3	8	5	9	4
5	9	6	4	1	2	8	7	3
1	3	2	8	9	7	4	6	5
7	8	4	3	5	6	2	1	9

PUZZLE / 147

9	5	6	2	7	1	4	8	3
8	2	4	6	3	5	1	9	7
3	1	7	4	8	9	6	5	2
7	8	3	1	5	4	9	2	6
2	9	5	8	6	3	7	1	4
6	4	1	9	2	7	8	3	5
4	3	9	7	1	2	5	6	8
1	6	2	5	4	8	3	7	9
5	7	8	3	9	6	2	4	1

PUZZLE / 148

7	5	6	4	1	2	8	9	3
3	4	2	5	8	9	6	7	1
1	9	8	7	3	6	4	5	2
2	6	9	8	5	1	7	3	4
4	7	5	2	9	3	1	6	8
8	1	3	6	4	7	5	2	9
5	3	4	9	7	8	2	1	6
6	8	1	3	2	5	9	4	7
9	2	7	1	6	4	3	8	5

PUZZLE / 149

4	2	5	7	9	1	3	6	8
1	3	9	6	2	8	4	5	7
7	8	6	5	4	3	1	9	2
6	1	4	8	3	2	5	7	9
9	7	3	1	6	5	8	2	4
8	5	2	4	7	9	6	1	3
5	4	1	2	8	7	9	3	6
3	6	7	9	5	4	2	8	1
2	9	8	3	1	6	7	4	5

PUZZLE / 150

3	4	5	2	6	1	8	7	9
9	6	8	3	4	7	1	2	5
1	7	2	5	9	8	4	6	3
6	3	4	7	8	9	5	1	2
5	8	9	6	1	2	3	4	7
7	2	1	4	5	3	9	8	6
8	9	6	1	2	5	7	3	4
4	1	7	9	3	6	2	5	8
2	5	3	8	7	4	6	9	1

PUZZLE / 151

7	8	2	9	3	6	4	1	5
3	4	6	1	5	7	2	9	8
1	9	5	8	4	2	6	3	7
6	5	9	2	1	3	7	8	4
4	3	1	7	8	5	9	2	6
2	7	8	6	9	4	3	5	1
8	6	7	3	2	1	5	4	9
9	2	4	5	7	8	1	6	3
5	1	3	4	6	9	8	7	2

PUZZLE / 152

1	3	5	9	4	7	8	6	2
9	8	2	6	5	1	7	3	4
7	4	6	8	3	2	5	1	9
2	1	4	3	7	5	9	8	6
5	6	7	2	9	8	1	4	3
8	9	3	4	1	6	2	5	7
4	5	1	7	6	9	3	2	8
3	2	9	1	8	4	6	7	5
6	7	8	5	2	3	4	9	1

PUZZLE / 153

3	9	6	8	5	1	7	4	2
1	4	7	2	3	6	5	8	9
5	2	8	9	4	7	3	1	6
6	5	4	1	8	9	2	7	3
8	1	9	7	2	3	6	5	4
2	7	3	4	6	5	8	9	1
9	6	2	5	1	8	4	3	7
7	3	5	6	9	4	1	2	8
4	8	1	3	7	2	9	6	5

PUZZLE / 154

4	5	9	7	1	8	3	2	6
7	6	1	4	2	3	9	5	8
2	3	8	9	6	5	7	1	4
9	1	6	3	5	2	8	4	7
5	8	7	1	4	9	2	6	3
3	2	4	8	7	6	5	9	1
1	4	3	2	9	7	6	8	5
6	7	2	5	8	4	1	3	9
8	9	5	6	3	1	4	7	2

PUZZLE / 155

7	4	5	8	6	1	9	2	3
2	9	8	7	3	5	4	6	1
6	3	1	9	4	2	8	5	7
9	7	3	5	1	6	2	8	4
8	6	2	4	7	3	1	9	5
1	5	4	2	9	8	7	3	6
4	8	7	3	5	9	6	1	2
3	2	6	1	8	7	5	4	9
5	1	9	6	2	4	3	7	8

PUZZLE / 156

5	1	7	3	8	6	4	2	9
4	3	6	5	2	9	8	1	7
8	2	9	1	4	7	6	3	5
1	7	4	8	3	5	9	6	2
2	9	3	6	7	4	1	5	8
6	5	8	2	9	1	7	4	3
9	8	2	4	1	3	5	7	6
3	6	1	7	5	8	2	9	4
7	4	5	9	6	2	3	8	1

PUZZLE / 157

4	6	1	7	3	9	8	5	2
8	7	3	2	5	4	1	9	6
9	2	5	6	1	8	7	3	4
3	9	2	1	7	6	4	8	5
6	1	4	5	8	2	9	7	3
5	8	7	9	4	3	2	6	1
1	5	8	3	2	7	6	4	9
2	4	9	8	6	5	3	1	7
7	3	6	4	9	1	5	2	8

PUZZLE / 158

4	2	9	7	1	5	8	6	3
3	5	6	4	2	8	9	7	1
8	1	7	6	3	9	4	2	5
6	9	8	2	5	7	1	3	4
1	4	3	9	8	6	2	5	7
2	7	5	1	4	3	6	9	8
5	8	1	3	9	2	7	4	6
9	6	4	5	7	1	3	8	2
7	3	2	8	6	4	5	1	9

PUZZLE / 159

3	4	2	5	1	9	6	7	8
6	9	7	8	3	4	2	5	1
5	1	8	2	6	7	3	9	4
2	5	3	9	4	6	1	8	7
1	8	4	3	7	2	5	6	9
9	7	6	1	5	8	4	3	2
8	6	9	4	2	3	7	1	5
7	2	1	6	9	5	8	4	3
4	3	5	7	8	1	9	2	6

PUZZLE / 160

6	5	2	4	9	3	8	1	7
4	8	1	2	6	7	9	5	3
9	3	7	8	1	5	4	2	6
2	4	6	9	5	8	3	7	1
3	1	5	7	4	2	6	8	9
8	7	9	6	3	1	2	4	5
5	9	4	1	8	6	7	3	2
7	6	3	5	2	4	1	9	8
1	2	8	3	7	9	5	6	4

PUZZLE / 161

3	7	8	6	9	4	5	2	1
1	9	2	8	3	5	4	7	6
4	5	6	7	1	2	8	3	9
7	8	1	4	6	3	9	5	2
2	3	4	9	5	8	1	6	7
5	6	9	2	7	1	3	8	4
9	2	3	5	4	7	6	1	8
8	4	5	1	2	6	7	9	3
6	1	7	3	8	9	2	4	5

PUZZLE / 162

2	3	6	5	4	7	8	9	1
5	9	7	8	1	6	2	3	4
8	4	1	3	2	9	7	6	5
1	6	5	9	7	8	3	4	2
9	2	3	4	6	5	1	7	8
7	8	4	1	3	2	6	5	9
4	1	2	6	5	3	9	8	7
3	7	9	2	8	4	5	1	6
6	5	8	7	9	1	4	2	3

PUZZLE / 163

2	4	3	9	5	1	7	6	8
6	1	7	3	2	8	4	5	9
5	9	8	7	6	4	3	2	1
1	6	4	8	7	3	2	9	5
3	5	2	6	1	9	8	4	7
7	8	9	2	4	5	1	3	6
8	2	6	5	3	7	9	1	4
4	7	5	1	9	2	6	8	3
9	3	1	4	8	6	5	7	2

PUZZLE / 164

4	9	8	3	7	1	5	2	6
6	3	5	9	2	4	7	8	1
7	1	2	8	6	5	9	3	4
8	5	7	1	9	6	3	4	2
3	4	9	2	8	7	1	6	5
1	2	6	4	5	3	8	7	9
2	8	4	5	3	9	6	1	7
9	7	3	6	1	2	4	5	8
5	6	1	7	4	8	2	9	3

PUZZLE / 165

6	2	4	9	3	1	8	5	7
1	5	3	6	7	8	4	2	9
8	9	7	5	4	2	3	6	1
7	1	5	3	9	6	2	4	8
3	4	9	8	2	7	5	1	6
2	6	8	1	5	4	7	9	3
9	8	2	7	6	5	1	3	4
5	7	6	4	1	3	9	8	2
4	3	1	2	8	9	6	7	5

PUZZLE / 166

5	7	3	9	8	1	2	4	6
4	9	2	6	3	7	5	1	8
1	8	6	4	2	5	3	7	9
3	2	5	1	7	9	8	6	4
8	1	4	3	5	6	7	9	2
9	6	7	8	4	2	1	3	5
6	3	9	5	1	8	4	2	7
2	4	8	7	6	3	9	5	1
7	5	1	2	9	4	6	8	3

PUZZLE / 167

5	8	6	1	9	3	4	2	7
4	1	2	7	8	5	3	9	6
9	3	7	6	2	4	5	8	1
2	4	5	3	6	1	8	7	9
1	7	9	4	5	8	6	3	2
3	6	8	9	7	2	1	5	4
7	9	4	8	3	6	2	1	5
6	2	3	5	1	7	9	4	8
8	5	1	2	4	9	7	6	3

PUZZLE / 168

7	5	6	8	3	4	9	2	1
1	4	8	2	9	5	3	6	7
2	3	9	1	7	6	5	8	4
5	2	7	3	6	9	4	1	8
8	9	1	7	4	2	6	5	3
3	6	4	5	1	8	2	7	9
4	1	3	6	2	7	8	9	5
9	8	2	4	5	1	7	3	6
6	7	5	9	8	3	1	4	2

PUZZLE / 169

9	3	5	1	4	2	7	8	6
1	4	6	5	7	8	9	3	2
8	2	7	6	9	3	4	1	5
6	7	9	2	5	1	3	4	8
2	1	8	4	3	6	5	7	9
4	5	3	9	8	7	2	6	1
3	8	1	7	2	5	6	9	4
5	6	4	3	1	9	8	2	7
7	9	2	8	6	4	1	5	3

PUZZLE / 170

6	8	4	3	7	1	2	5	9
5	9	7	8	2	4	3	1	6
1	2	3	5	9	6	8	7	4
2	7	5	6	1	9	4	8	3
8	4	6	2	3	7	5	9	1
9	3	1	4	5	8	7	6	2
4	1	8	7	6	3	9	2	5
3	5	9	1	8	2	6	4	7
7	6	2	9	4	5	1	3	8

PUZZLE / 171

5	8	3	4	1	9	7	2	6
6	1	2	3	7	8	4	5	9
4	9	7	2	6	5	3	1	8
1	7	6	5	9	4	2	8	3
9	4	8	1	2	3	5	6	7
3	2	5	7	8	6	1	9	4
8	3	4	9	5	1	6	7	2
7	5	9	6	4	2	8	3	1
2	6	1	8	3	7	9	4	5

PUZZLE / 172

6	4	2	9	3	8	7	1	5
1	7	5	4	2	6	9	8	3
9	3	8	7	5	1	6	4	2
4	8	9	5	7	3	1	2	6
7	2	1	6	8	9	5	3	4
3	5	6	2	1	4	8	9	7
8	1	7	3	4	5	2	6	9
2	9	4	8	6	7	3	5	1
5	6	3	1	9	2	4	7	8

PUZZLE / 173

3	6	8	5	4	7	2	9	1
9	7	4	6	2	1	5	3	8
5	1	2	3	8	9	6	4	7
1	4	5	8	6	3	7	2	9
6	2	9	7	5	4	8	1	3
7	8	3	1	9	2	4	5	6
2	3	6	4	1	8	9	7	5
4	5	1	9	7	6	3	8	2
8	9	7	2	3	5	1	6	4

PUZZLE / 174

1	4	6	9	8	2	7	5	3
7	8	5	1	6	3	2	9	4
3	2	9	5	4	7	8	1	6
4	1	8	3	7	6	5	2	9
9	6	7	2	5	8	4	3	1
2	5	3	4	1	9	6	7	8
5	3	2	8	9	4	1	6	7
6	9	4	7	2	1	3	8	5
8	7	1	6	3	5	9	4	2

PUZZLE / 175

5	4	8	9	7	6	2	3	1
1	7	6	3	2	4	5	9	8
9	3	2	1	8	5	4	6	7
8	6	1	5	3	2	7	4	9
7	2	5	8	4	9	6	1	3
4	9	3	7	6	1	8	2	5
3	5	4	2	1	7	9	8	6
2	1	7	6	9	8	3	5	4
6	8	9	4	5	3	1	7	2

PUZZLE / 176

3	1	8	2	9	6	5	7	4
9	5	7	3	8	4	6	2	1
2	6	4	1	7	5	3	9	8
6	2	9	7	5	8	1	4	3
5	8	3	4	1	2	7	6	9
4	7	1	6	3	9	2	8	5
7	4	5	8	6	3	9	1	2
8	3	6	9	2	1	4	5	7
1	9	2	5	4	7	8	3	6

PUZZLE / 177

1	8	9	7	2	4	6	3	5
5	3	7	1	6	8	2	9	4
2	6	4	3	9	5	7	8	1
6	5	8	4	7	1	3	2	9
7	2	3	8	5	9	1	4	6
4	9	1	6	3	2	5	7	8
3	1	6	9	8	7	4	5	2
8	7	5	2	4	6	9	1	3
9	4	2	5	1	3	8	6	7

PUZZLE / 178

3	7	9	1	2	5	8	4	6
5	4	2	7	6	8	3	1	9
1	8	6	4	9	3	2	7	5
8	2	5	3	7	6	4	9	1
7	1	4	9	5	2	6	8	3
6	9	3	8	1	4	5	2	7
2	3	1	6	8	9	7	5	4
4	5	7	2	3	1	9	6	8
9	6	8	5	4	7	1	3	2

PUZZLE / 179

9	7	5	3	1	6	8	2	4
8	4	2	7	9	5	6	1	3
6	1	3	8	4	2	5	9	7
1	9	4	6	5	8	7	3	2
5	3	8	2	7	9	4	6	1
7	2	6	1	3	4	9	5	8
4	5	1	9	8	3	2	7	6
3	6	9	4	2	7	1	8	5
2	8	7	5	6	1	3	4	9

PUZZLE / 180

3	5	4	9	8	2	6	1	7
6	9	1	5	3	7	8	4	2
2	8	7	1	6	4	9	3	5
8	4	9	3	7	6	5	2	1
1	7	2	8	5	9	3	6	4
5	6	3	4	2	1	7	8	9
4	3	5	7	1	8	2	9	6
7	1	6	2	9	3	4	5	8
9	2	8	6	4	5	1	7	3

PUZZLE / 181

4	6	3	8	9	7	1	5	2
1	8	2	6	3	5	9	4	7
5	9	7	2	4	1	3	6	8
8	1	4	3	7	2	6	9	5
2	3	9	4	5	6	7	8	1
6	7	5	1	8	9	4	2	3
9	4	8	5	1	3	2	7	6
3	5	6	7	2	4	8	1	9
7	2	1	9	6	8	5	3	4

PUZZLE / 182

5	4	9	1	2	7	8	6	3
6	8	1	4	9	3	5	2	7
3	7	2	6	8	5	4	1	9
2	6	3	7	4	8	1	9	5
4	5	8	3	1	9	6	7	2
9	1	7	2	5	6	3	4	8
8	3	4	9	7	1	2	5	6
7	2	5	8	6	4	9	3	1
1	9	6	5	3	2	7	8	4

PUZZLE / 183

6	4	5	1	2	9	8	7	3
8	9	2	7	3	6	4	5	1
1	3	7	5	8	4	9	2	6
2	8	9	6	7	1	3	4	5
5	1	4	3	9	8	2	6	7
7	6	3	2	4	5	1	8	9
4	5	8	9	6	3	7	1	2
3	7	6	4	1	2	5	9	8
9	2	1	8	5	7	6	3	4

PUZZLE / 184

2	6	3	1	8	4	9	7	5
8	7	5	3	9	6	2	4	1
1	4	9	5	2	7	6	3	8
5	8	6	2	7	9	4	1	3
9	3	7	6	4	1	5	8	2
4	2	1	8	3	5	7	9	6
3	9	8	4	6	2	1	5	7
7	5	2	9	1	8	3	6	4
6	1	4	7	5	3	8	2	9

PUZZLE / 185

5	7	9	8	6	2	1	3	4
6	3	2	4	9	1	8	7	5
8	1	4	7	5	3	6	9	2
4	9	1	3	8	5	7	2	6
3	6	7	2	1	9	4	5	8
2	5	8	6	4	7	3	1	9
7	2	6	5	3	8	9	4	1
9	8	3	1	2	4	5	6	7
1	4	5	9	7	6	2	8	3

PUZZLE / 186

1	3	8	2	7	9	5	6	4
7	4	6	1	5	3	8	2	9
2	9	5	8	4	6	7	3	1
5	8	4	3	6	1	9	7	2
6	7	2	4	9	8	1	5	3
9	1	3	7	2	5	6	4	8
4	2	1	6	8	7	3	9	5
3	5	7	9	1	2	4	8	6
8	6	9	5	3	4	2	1	7

PUZZLE / 187

1	9	6	5	7	2	8	4	3
2	5	8	3	4	9	1	6	7
3	4	7	1	8	6	9	2	5
7	6	4	9	2	3	5	8	1
5	8	3	6	1	4	2	7	9
9	1	2	7	5	8	6	3	4
8	2	1	4	3	5	7	9	6
4	7	9	8	6	1	3	5	2
6	3	5	2	9	7	4	1	8

PUZZLE / 188

1	8	6	9	4	2	5	3	7
5	7	2	8	3	6	1	4	9
3	4	9	1	7	5	2	6	8
8	6	1	3	2	7	9	5	4
9	5	3	4	8	1	6	7	2
7	2	4	5	6	9	3	8	1
2	3	5	7	1	4	8	9	6
6	9	7	2	5	8	4	1	3
4	1	8	6	9	3	7	2	5

PUZZLE / 189

4	2	6	8	3	9	5	7	1
8	7	1	2	5	4	3	9	6
5	3	9	6	7	1	2	4	8
9	8	2	1	6	3	4	5	7
3	5	4	7	8	2	1	6	9
1	6	7	9	4	5	8	3	2
7	4	8	3	1	6	9	2	5
6	9	5	4	2	8	7	1	3
2	1	3	5	9	7	6	8	4

PUZZLE / 190

3	7	9	4	5	6	1	2	8
4	2	6	7	1	8	5	9	3
8	1	5	3	2	9	7	4	6
1	6	2	8	9	4	3	7	5
5	4	3	2	6	7	9	8	1
7	9	8	1	3	5	2	6	4
9	8	7	5	4	1	6	3	2
6	3	1	9	8	2	4	5	7
2	5	4	6	7	3	8	1	9

PUZZLE / 191

6	9	5	4	7	3	1	8	2
1	4	2	9	6	8	7	3	5
7	8	3	1	2	5	9	6	4
2	7	9	6	8	4	5	1	3
5	6	8	3	1	9	2	4	7
4	3	1	2	5	7	6	9	8
3	1	7	8	9	2	4	5	6
8	5	6	7	4	1	3	2	9
9	2	4	5	3	6	8	7	1

PUZZLE / 192

8	6	9	2	5	7	1	4	3
5	4	2	6	3	1	8	7	9
1	3	7	4	8	9	5	2	6
2	5	1	7	4	6	9	3	8
9	7	3	8	2	5	4	6	1
4	8	6	1	9	3	2	5	7
6	2	8	9	7	4	3	1	5
3	1	4	5	6	8	7	9	2
7	9	5	3	1	2	6	8	4

PUZZLE / 193

7	6	1	5	2	4	3	8	9
8	2	9	7	6	3	1	4	5
3	4	5	8	9	1	6	7	2
2	5	6	9	4	8	7	1	3
1	3	4	2	7	6	9	5	8
9	7	8	3	1	5	2	6	4
5	8	2	6	3	7	4	9	1
6	1	3	4	8	9	5	2	7
4	9	7	1	5	2	8	3	6

PUZZLE / 194

2	9	7	5	1	3	8	6	4
5	3	6	4	8	9	1	7	2
1	8	4	7	6	2	3	9	5
3	6	8	2	9	1	5	4	7
7	5	1	6	3	4	9	2	8
4	2	9	8	7	5	6	1	3
6	7	5	9	4	8	2	3	1
9	1	2	3	5	7	4	8	6
8	4	3	1	2	6	7	5	9

PUZZLE / 195

4	6	9	5	8	2	7	3	1
2	3	5	1	7	4	9	8	6
8	1	7	6	3	9	2	4	5
6	7	2	3	4	1	8	5	9
3	8	1	9	5	6	4	7	2
5	9	4	7	2	8	1	6	3
7	2	6	8	9	5	3	1	4
9	5	3	4	1	7	6	2	8
1	4	8	2	6	3	5	9	7

PUZZLE / **196**

3	4	8	1	7	5	6	9	2
6	2	7	8	9	3	1	5	4
9	1	5	2	6	4	8	3	7
8	6	4	5	3	2	7	1	9
5	7	9	6	1	8	2	4	3
1	3	2	7	4	9	5	8	6
2	9	1	4	8	7	3	6	5
4	5	6	3	2	1	9	7	8
7	8	3	9	5	6	4	2	1

PUZZLE / **197**

6	9	2	3	8	5	7	4	1
8	4	7	2	1	9	6	3	5
1	5	3	6	4	7	9	2	8
2	7	4	9	6	1	8	5	3
5	3	1	7	2	8	4	6	9
9	6	8	4	5	3	2	1	7
3	8	6	5	7	4	1	9	2
7	2	9	1	3	6	5	8	4
4	1	5	8	9	2	3	7	6

PUZZLE / **198**

1	5	4	8	3	7	6	9	2
6	9	7	5	1	2	8	4	3
3	8	2	6	4	9	1	5	7
9	3	1	2	6	8	5	7	4
4	7	5	3	9	1	2	8	6
8	2	6	4	7	5	3	1	9
5	1	9	7	2	6	4	3	8
7	6	3	1	8	4	9	2	5
2	4	8	9	5	3	7	6	1

PUZZLE / **199**

2	7	4	3	9	6	5	8	1
1	3	8	5	7	4	2	6	9
5	9	6	2	8	1	4	3	7
7	4	3	9	1	5	8	2	6
6	8	1	7	3	2	9	4	5
9	2	5	6	4	8	7	1	3
4	5	9	1	2	3	6	7	8
3	6	2	8	5	7	1	9	4
8	1	7	4	6	9	3	5	2

PUZZLE / **200**

5	7	1	3	9	2	6	8	4
9	6	3	4	8	7	1	2	5
2	4	8	6	5	1	9	3	7
1	5	9	8	7	3	2	4	6
7	8	2	5	4	6	3	1	9
4	3	6	1	2	9	7	5	8
3	2	4	7	6	5	8	9	1
6	9	5	2	1	8	4	7	3
8	1	7	9	3	4	5	6	2

PUZZLE / **201**

2	7	6	5	8	1	4	9	3
5	1	8	9	4	3	6	7	2
3	9	4	7	2	6	8	5	1
1	6	7	4	5	9	2	3	8
9	8	3	6	7	2	1	4	5
4	5	2	1	3	8	7	6	9
8	2	9	3	6	7	5	1	4
6	3	5	2	1	4	9	8	7
7	4	1	8	9	5	3	2	6

PUZZLE / **202**

6	2	9	4	3	7	5	1	8
8	4	7	9	5	1	3	2	6
5	1	3	2	8	6	4	9	7
4	8	5	6	9	3	1	7	2
7	9	2	1	4	8	6	3	5
3	6	1	5	7	2	9	8	4
9	3	6	7	2	5	8	4	1
2	5	4	8	1	9	7	6	3
1	7	8	3	6	4	2	5	9

PUZZLE / **203**

7	6	1	9	4	2	5	8	3
5	8	3	7	1	6	9	2	4
2	9	4	8	3	5	6	1	7
3	5	9	1	7	4	8	6	2
8	7	2	6	9	3	1	4	5
4	1	6	5	2	8	7	3	9
1	3	7	4	6	9	2	5	8
6	2	8	3	5	7	4	9	1
9	4	5	2	8	1	3	7	6

PUZZLE / **204**

5	7	4	3	8	2	1	6	9
6	8	3	1	9	4	7	5	2
9	2	1	6	7	5	8	4	3
7	6	5	2	4	3	9	1	8
4	3	8	9	1	7	5	2	6
1	9	2	8	5	6	4	3	7
8	5	6	7	3	1	2	9	4
3	4	7	5	2	9	6	8	1
2	1	9	4	6	8	3	7	5

PUZZLE / 205

4	2	7	5	1	9	8	3	6
3	8	5	4	7	6	1	2	9
9	6	1	3	2	8	7	5	4
1	9	3	2	5	7	4	6	8
7	4	8	6	3	1	2	9	5
2	5	6	9	8	4	3	1	7
6	7	9	1	4	3	5	8	2
5	1	4	8	9	2	6	7	3
8	3	2	7	6	5	9	4	1

PUZZLE / 206

7	6	1	8	9	3	4	5	2
9	8	5	2	4	7	3	1	6
3	2	4	5	1	6	8	7	9
2	5	9	4	6	8	1	3	7
6	4	7	1	3	5	9	2	8
1	3	8	9	7	2	5	6	4
8	9	6	7	5	1	2	4	3
4	1	3	6	2	9	7	8	5
5	7	2	3	8	4	6	9	1

PUZZLE / 207

2	8	7	9	5	1	3	4	6
6	9	4	3	2	7	5	8	1
3	1	5	6	8	4	2	9	7
5	6	2	8	4	3	1	7	9
1	4	3	2	7	9	6	5	8
8	7	9	1	6	5	4	3	2
7	3	6	5	9	2	8	1	4
4	5	8	7	1	6	9	2	3
9	2	1	4	3	8	7	6	5

PUZZLE / 208

9	1	3	4	8	6	2	7	5
6	5	2	1	7	9	3	8	4
4	7	8	3	5	2	9	1	6
7	3	6	2	1	4	8	5	9
1	8	4	5	9	7	6	2	3
5	2	9	6	3	8	7	4	1
3	9	5	8	2	1	4	6	7
2	4	1	7	6	3	5	9	8
8	6	7	9	4	5	1	3	2

PUZZLE / 209

9	8	2	5	6	4	1	7	3
5	7	4	1	2	3	8	9	6
6	1	3	9	7	8	4	2	5
3	4	9	8	1	6	2	5	7
7	6	8	3	5	2	9	1	4
2	5	1	4	9	7	3	6	8
8	9	6	2	4	5	7	3	1
1	3	5	7	8	9	6	4	2
4	2	7	6	3	1	5	8	9

PUZZLE / 210

2	6	8	7	3	1	9	5	4
3	5	9	8	4	2	6	7	1
4	7	1	6	9	5	8	2	3
5	8	6	2	1	4	3	9	7
7	1	2	9	6	3	5	4	8
9	3	4	5	8	7	1	6	2
6	9	7	3	2	8	4	1	5
8	4	5	1	7	9	2	3	6
1	2	3	4	5	6	7	8	9

PUZZLE / 211

7	1	4	3	8	5	6	9	2
6	5	2	9	4	1	8	3	7
3	8	9	7	6	2	1	5	4
1	9	8	4	2	6	3	7	5
5	7	6	8	9	3	2	4	1
2	4	3	1	5	7	9	6	8
9	3	1	5	7	8	4	2	6
8	2	7	6	3	4	5	1	9
4	6	5	2	1	9	7	8	3

PUZZLE / 212

2	6	4	1	7	9	3	5	8
5	9	3	8	4	2	7	6	1
8	7	1	5	3	6	9	2	4
1	8	7	2	9	4	6	3	5
6	4	9	7	5	3	1	8	2
3	5	2	6	1	8	4	7	9
7	2	8	4	6	1	5	9	3
9	1	6	3	2	5	8	4	7
4	3	5	9	8	7	2	1	6

PUZZLE / 213

4	2	7	6	1	5	8	9	3
8	3	6	7	9	4	2	5	1
1	5	9	8	2	3	4	7	6
5	9	2	1	3	7	6	4	8
3	7	8	4	5	6	1	2	9
6	1	4	2	8	9	7	3	5
7	8	5	3	6	2	9	1	4
9	4	1	5	7	8	3	6	2
2	6	3	9	4	1	5	8	7

PUZZLE / 214

6	7	4	8	9	3	5	1	2
3	9	1	7	2	5	8	6	4
8	5	2	6	1	4	9	7	3
4	8	5	3	7	6	1	2	9
9	3	6	2	4	1	7	8	5
2	1	7	9	5	8	4	3	6
1	6	9	4	3	7	2	5	8
5	4	3	1	8	2	6	9	7
7	2	8	5	6	9	3	4	1

PUZZLE / 215

2	4	3	5	6	1	9	7	8
1	5	8	7	2	9	6	3	4
9	7	6	8	4	3	1	5	2
7	1	2	6	9	5	8	4	3
6	3	4	2	8	7	5	9	1
5	8	9	1	3	4	7	2	6
3	2	7	9	1	8	4	6	5
4	9	1	3	5	6	2	8	7
8	6	5	4	7	2	3	1	9

PUZZLE / 216

8	3	7	2	5	6	4	9	1
4	2	1	8	9	3	7	6	5
6	5	9	1	4	7	3	2	8
3	1	2	9	8	5	6	7	4
9	6	8	7	3	4	1	5	2
7	4	5	6	1	2	8	3	9
2	8	6	4	7	9	5	1	3
1	7	3	5	2	8	9	4	6
5	9	4	3	6	1	2	8	7

PUZZLE / 217

3	8	4	2	5	9	6	7	1
1	9	6	4	8	7	3	2	5
2	5	7	3	6	1	4	8	9
7	4	1	8	9	3	2	5	6
8	6	3	5	4	2	9	1	7
9	2	5	1	7	6	8	3	4
6	1	9	7	2	8	5	4	3
4	3	8	9	1	5	7	6	2
5	7	2	6	3	4	1	9	8

PUZZLE / 218

5	3	1	7	4	6	8	9	2
7	8	9	3	2	5	6	4	1
6	4	2	8	1	9	3	7	5
9	1	4	5	7	8	2	3	6
8	7	3	6	9	2	1	5	4
2	5	6	4	3	1	9	8	7
1	9	8	2	5	7	4	6	3
3	6	5	1	8	4	7	2	9
4	2	7	9	6	3	5	1	8

PUZZLE / 219

6	1	2	3	4	7	9	5	8
9	8	7	5	1	2	4	6	3
4	3	5	8	6	9	2	7	1
2	6	9	1	3	4	5	8	7
3	4	1	7	5	8	6	9	2
7	5	8	9	2	6	1	3	4
8	2	4	6	9	3	7	1	5
5	9	3	4	7	1	8	2	6
1	7	6	2	8	5	3	4	9

PUZZLE / 220

4	1	6	5	7	3	9	2	8
7	2	8	4	1	9	6	3	5
9	3	5	8	2	6	1	7	4
8	7	3	1	6	2	5	4	9
5	4	2	7	9	8	3	1	6
6	9	1	3	5	4	7	8	2
1	6	4	2	3	5	8	9	7
3	8	9	6	4	7	2	5	1
2	5	7	9	8	1	4	6	3

PUZZLE / 221

6	8	5	4	1	7	2	9	3
2	4	3	9	6	8	1	5	7
9	7	1	5	2	3	4	8	6
5	3	7	2	9	1	8	6	4
4	6	2	8	3	5	9	7	1
8	1	9	6	7	4	3	2	5
7	5	4	1	8	2	6	3	9
3	2	6	7	4	9	5	1	8
1	9	8	3	5	6	7	4	2

PUZZLE / 222

5	3	4	6	2	1	7	9	8
2	7	6	5	9	8	4	3	1
9	8	1	4	7	3	6	2	5
7	5	9	8	4	2	3	1	6
4	6	2	1	3	7	8	5	9
3	1	8	9	5	6	2	7	4
6	9	3	2	1	4	5	8	7
1	4	7	3	8	5	9	6	2
8	2	5	7	6	9	1	4	3

PUZZLE / 223

7	1	3	5	6	2	4	8	9
6	9	4	7	1	8	2	3	5
5	2	8	9	4	3	6	7	1
9	8	5	2	7	6	1	4	3
2	7	1	4	3	9	8	5	6
3	4	6	8	5	1	7	9	2
8	5	2	1	9	4	3	6	7
1	3	9	6	8	7	5	2	4
4	6	7	3	2	5	9	1	8

PUZZLE / 224

4	2	3	9	8	1	6	5	7
7	9	6	5	3	4	2	8	1
8	1	5	6	7	2	4	9	3
9	3	1	7	2	5	8	6	4
5	4	8	1	6	3	9	7	2
6	7	2	8	4	9	3	1	5
2	5	9	4	1	8	7	3	6
1	6	4	3	9	7	5	2	8
3	8	7	2	5	6	1	4	9

PUZZLE / 225

9	2	7	1	8	4	6	3	5
6	3	1	2	7	5	4	9	8
5	8	4	6	3	9	1	7	2
2	9	5	3	4	1	7	8	6
7	4	6	8	9	2	3	5	1
8	1	3	7	5	6	2	4	9
1	5	8	4	6	3	9	2	7
4	6	9	5	2	7	8	1	3
3	7	2	9	1	8	5	6	4

PUZZLE / 226

2	3	4	9	6	5	1	7	8
6	5	1	7	4	8	3	2	9
8	7	9	2	1	3	4	5	6
7	9	6	1	5	2	8	3	4
3	4	5	8	9	6	7	1	2
1	8	2	3	7	4	6	9	5
4	2	7	6	3	9	5	8	1
5	1	8	4	2	7	9	6	3
9	6	3	5	8	1	2	4	7

PUZZLE / 227

9	8	1	7	4	5	3	2	6
5	6	3	2	8	1	7	9	4
4	2	7	3	9	6	1	5	8
7	1	5	6	2	3	8	4	9
8	9	2	5	1	4	6	3	7
6	3	4	8	7	9	5	1	2
1	7	9	4	5	8	2	6	3
2	4	6	1	3	7	9	8	5
3	5	8	9	6	2	4	7	1

PUZZLE / 228

3	2	9	1	4	5	6	8	7
8	1	5	7	6	2	3	4	9
6	7	4	9	8	3	5	2	1
4	9	7	8	5	1	2	3	6
2	5	8	3	9	6	1	7	4
1	6	3	4	2	7	9	5	8
9	3	6	2	7	4	8	1	5
7	8	2	5	1	9	4	6	3
5	4	1	6	3	8	7	9	2

PUZZLE / 229

1	8	6	7	5	2	9	4	3
7	2	9	3	4	6	1	8	5
4	5	3	8	1	9	7	2	6
3	9	8	4	7	5	6	1	2
5	7	1	6	2	8	4	3	9
2	6	4	9	3	1	5	7	8
8	3	7	5	6	4	2	9	1
9	1	5	2	8	7	3	6	4
6	4	2	1	9	3	8	5	7

PUZZLE / 230

1	2	9	6	7	3	8	5	4
7	8	4	5	2	1	3	6	9
3	5	6	8	9	4	2	1	7
9	4	5	7	6	2	1	3	8
6	7	1	3	8	9	4	2	5
2	3	8	1	4	5	9	7	6
8	1	2	4	5	7	6	9	3
5	6	3	9	1	8	7	4	2
4	9	7	2	3	6	5	8	1

PUZZLE / 231

5	1	7	6	4	8	3	9	2
4	9	3	2	1	5	6	8	7
8	6	2	7	3	9	5	1	4
7	4	6	1	8	3	9	2	5
9	8	5	4	2	7	1	3	6
3	2	1	5	9	6	7	4	8
1	5	8	3	7	2	4	6	9
6	3	9	8	5	4	2	7	1
2	7	4	9	6	1	8	5	3

PUZZLE / 232

4	8	6	3	1	7	5	9	2
3	2	7	5	9	4	8	1	6
9	1	5	2	6	8	7	4	3
2	4	3	6	8	5	9	7	1
6	5	1	9	7	2	4	3	8
7	9	8	1	4	3	6	2	5
1	6	2	7	5	9	3	8	4
5	7	4	8	3	1	2	6	9
8	3	9	4	2	6	1	5	7

PUZZLE / 233

8	3	4	9	1	6	7	2	5
6	2	7	3	8	5	4	1	9
9	5	1	7	2	4	8	3	6
5	1	3	4	7	2	6	9	8
7	6	8	5	9	3	2	4	1
2	4	9	1	6	8	3	5	7
1	8	6	2	4	9	5	7	3
4	7	5	6	3	1	9	8	2
3	9	2	8	5	7	1	6	4

PUZZLE / 234

1	8	4	6	2	3	9	5	7
9	2	7	1	5	4	6	8	3
6	3	5	7	9	8	1	4	2
3	7	6	2	8	1	5	9	4
2	9	1	4	6	5	3	7	8
5	4	8	3	7	9	2	1	6
4	6	2	5	1	7	8	3	9
8	1	3	9	4	2	7	6	5
7	5	9	8	3	6	4	2	1

PUZZLE / **235**

1	2	7	6	9	3	5	8	4
3	8	5	4	2	1	9	7	6
9	6	4	8	5	7	1	3	2
6	1	2	3	4	9	8	5	7
5	3	8	2	7	6	4	1	9
4	7	9	5	1	8	2	6	3
8	9	1	7	6	2	3	4	5
7	5	3	9	8	4	6	2	1
2	4	6	1	3	5	7	9	8

PUZZLE / **236**

4	3	2	6	9	5	7	1	8
8	5	1	2	4	7	9	6	3
7	9	6	3	1	8	4	2	5
3	2	9	7	5	1	6	8	4
1	4	7	8	3	6	2	5	9
5	6	8	9	2	4	3	7	1
9	8	3	5	6	2	1	4	7
6	7	4	1	8	3	5	9	2
2	1	5	4	7	9	8	3	6

PUZZLE / **237**

2	1	6	8	4	5	9	7	3
7	4	5	9	3	2	6	1	8
8	9	3	7	1	6	4	2	5
3	6	2	1	9	4	8	5	7
1	8	9	3	5	7	2	6	4
5	7	4	6	2	8	3	9	1
9	2	8	4	7	1	5	3	6
6	5	7	2	8	3	1	4	9
4	3	1	5	6	9	7	8	2

PUZZLE / **238**

5	6	7	8	9	4	2	3	1
4	1	2	3	6	7	5	8	9
3	8	9	1	5	2	7	4	6
2	5	6	7	1	3	4	9	8
1	9	4	2	8	5	3	6	7
8	7	3	9	4	6	1	2	5
9	2	8	5	3	1	6	7	4
7	4	1	6	2	9	8	5	3
6	3	5	4	7	8	9	1	2

PUZZLE / **239**

8	2	6	7	1	3	9	5	4
1	3	4	5	9	8	7	2	6
7	9	5	2	6	4	8	1	3
3	1	7	9	8	5	4	6	2
5	6	8	4	7	2	3	9	1
2	4	9	6	3	1	5	7	8
9	8	3	1	2	7	6	4	5
6	5	2	3	4	9	1	8	7
4	7	1	8	5	6	2	3	9

PUZZLE / **240**

7	8	9	2	6	5	3	4	1
4	1	2	3	9	8	6	7	5
6	3	5	7	1	4	8	2	9
8	7	6	5	4	1	2	9	3
5	2	1	6	3	9	4	8	7
9	4	3	8	7	2	5	1	6
2	6	8	9	5	7	1	3	4
3	9	4	1	2	6	7	5	8
1	5	7	4	8	3	9	6	2

PUZZLE / **241**

2	6	4	8	1	3	9	7	5
1	5	7	4	2	9	3	6	8
3	8	9	7	6	5	2	4	1
7	4	1	6	9	8	5	3	2
5	2	8	1	3	7	4	9	6
6	9	3	2	5	4	1	8	7
4	1	6	3	7	2	8	5	9
9	3	2	5	8	6	7	1	4
8	7	5	9	4	1	6	2	3

PUZZLE / **242**

5	4	6	8	9	1	2	3	7
9	7	8	2	3	4	1	6	5
2	3	1	5	6	7	4	8	9
3	9	4	7	1	5	8	2	6
1	5	7	6	8	2	9	4	3
8	6	2	3	4	9	5	7	1
7	8	9	1	2	3	6	5	4
4	2	5	9	7	6	3	1	8
6	1	3	4	5	8	7	9	2

PUZZLE / **243**

6	5	9	8	4	1	3	2	7
3	4	8	7	5	2	1	6	9
2	7	1	9	3	6	4	8	5
1	6	2	5	8	3	7	9	4
5	3	7	6	9	4	2	1	8
8	9	4	1	2	7	6	5	3
7	8	3	2	1	9	5	4	6
9	2	6	4	7	5	8	3	1
4	1	5	3	6	8	9	7	2

PUZZLE / **244**

7	6	9	3	4	8	5	1	2
3	4	2	5	9	1	6	8	7
8	5	1	6	2	7	4	9	3
9	2	6	1	3	4	8	7	5
5	7	4	2	8	9	3	6	1
1	8	3	7	6	5	2	4	9
4	1	5	8	7	2	9	3	6
2	3	8	9	1	6	7	5	4
6	9	7	4	5	3	1	2	8

PUZZLE / **245**

7	2	8	9	1	3	5	6	4
4	5	3	6	8	2	1	7	9
1	6	9	5	7	4	3	2	8
6	7	1	2	4	5	9	8	3
8	3	4	7	9	1	2	5	6
5	9	2	3	6	8	7	4	1
3	1	6	4	5	7	8	9	2
9	8	7	1	2	6	4	3	5
2	4	5	8	3	9	6	1	7

PUZZLE / **246**

6	2	4	8	1	9	5	3	7
9	7	1	6	3	5	2	8	4
3	8	5	2	4	7	1	9	6
1	5	6	7	9	8	4	2	3
4	3	2	1	5	6	9	7	8
8	9	7	4	2	3	6	5	1
5	6	3	9	8	4	7	1	2
2	4	9	3	7	1	8	6	5
7	1	8	5	6	2	3	4	9

PUZZLE / **247**

2	8	7	3	1	5	9	6	4
5	1	3	4	9	6	2	7	8
4	9	6	7	2	8	5	3	1
8	5	9	1	6	7	4	2	3
7	3	1	9	4	2	6	8	5
6	2	4	8	5	3	7	1	9
1	6	5	2	3	4	8	9	7
9	7	2	5	8	1	3	4	6
3	4	8	6	7	9	1	5	2

PUZZLE / **248**

6	2	3	5	8	9	7	4	1
4	5	8	6	1	7	2	3	9
7	9	1	4	3	2	8	5	6
1	8	2	3	5	6	9	7	4
5	6	9	7	4	1	3	8	2
3	4	7	2	9	8	1	6	5
8	1	6	9	7	4	5	2	3
2	7	5	1	6	3	4	9	8
9	3	4	8	2	5	6	1	7

PUZZLE / **249**

9	2	5	6	7	8	1	3	4
7	4	6	2	3	1	9	5	8
3	8	1	9	4	5	6	7	2
2	6	8	7	9	4	5	1	3
1	7	3	8	5	2	4	9	6
4	5	9	3	1	6	8	2	7
5	3	7	4	8	9	2	6	1
6	1	4	5	2	7	3	8	9
8	9	2	1	6	3	7	4	5

PUZZLE / **250**

3	9	1	7	5	8	4	2	6
4	6	2	9	1	3	5	7	8
8	7	5	2	4	6	1	3	9
9	2	3	5	7	1	6	8	4
7	5	6	8	2	4	9	1	3
1	4	8	6	3	9	7	5	2
2	8	4	1	9	7	3	6	5
6	1	9	3	8	5	2	4	7
5	3	7	4	6	2	8	9	1

PUZZLE / **251**

7	1	4	3	2	5	8	6	9
2	3	9	8	6	7	1	4	5
8	5	6	4	9	1	2	7	3
4	6	3	9	5	8	7	2	1
9	2	5	7	1	6	3	8	4
1	8	7	2	4	3	5	9	6
3	4	2	5	7	9	6	1	8
5	7	1	6	8	4	9	3	2
6	9	8	1	3	2	4	5	7

PUZZLE / **252**

1	5	4	3	2	9	6	7	8
8	6	7	5	4	1	3	2	9
9	3	2	8	7	6	5	4	1
4	9	5	2	6	8	1	3	7
3	7	6	4	1	5	9	8	2
2	1	8	7	9	3	4	6	5
7	2	1	9	3	4	8	5	6
6	8	3	1	5	2	7	9	4
5	4	9	6	8	7	2	1	3

PUZZLE / **253**

5	3	7	2	8	9	4	6	1
8	1	2	7	6	4	3	5	9
9	4	6	1	3	5	8	2	7
1	2	3	8	9	7	5	4	6
6	5	4	3	2	1	9	7	8
7	8	9	5	4	6	1	3	2
2	7	8	4	1	3	6	9	5
3	6	5	9	7	8	2	1	4
4	9	1	6	5	2	7	8	3

PUZZLE / **254**

8	7	1	9	2	4	5	3	6
2	9	3	5	8	6	4	1	7
4	6	5	7	3	1	2	8	9
9	5	8	1	4	7	3	6	2
6	3	4	2	5	8	9	7	1
1	2	7	3	6	9	8	5	4
7	8	9	4	1	5	6	2	3
5	1	2	6	9	3	7	4	8
3	4	6	8	7	2	1	9	5

PUZZLE / **255**

3	9	8	2	1	5	6	7	4
2	4	1	7	6	3	9	5	8
7	5	6	8	4	9	1	3	2
6	1	4	5	3	8	2	9	7
5	3	9	4	2	7	8	1	6
8	2	7	1	9	6	5	4	3
9	6	5	3	8	4	7	2	1
4	8	2	9	7	1	3	6	5
1	7	3	6	5	2	4	8	9

PUZZLE / **256**

5	2	3	4	7	1	9	6	8
9	1	8	5	6	2	3	7	4
6	7	4	3	9	8	5	2	1
4	5	7	6	1	9	8	3	2
8	3	2	7	5	4	6	1	9
1	6	9	2	8	3	4	5	7
7	8	5	1	4	6	2	9	3
2	9	1	8	3	5	7	4	6
3	4	6	9	2	7	1	8	5

PUZZLE / **257**

2	1	3	9	4	5	8	7	6
7	8	5	6	2	3	1	9	4
6	9	4	8	7	1	2	3	5
1	6	8	5	9	4	7	2	3
3	2	9	7	6	8	4	5	1
5	4	7	3	1	2	9	6	8
9	7	1	4	5	6	3	8	2
4	3	6	2	8	7	5	1	9
8	5	2	1	3	9	6	4	7

PUZZLE / **258**

8	3	4	6	1	5	2	9	7
6	9	2	7	3	4	5	1	8
5	1	7	9	8	2	6	4	3
4	6	9	8	7	1	3	2	5
3	7	1	2	5	9	4	8	6
2	8	5	3	4	6	9	7	1
1	5	6	4	9	8	7	3	2
7	4	8	5	2	3	1	6	9
9	2	3	1	6	7	8	5	4

PUZZLE / **259**

7	6	1	9	4	2	3	5	8
5	2	9	8	7	3	4	6	1
3	8	4	6	1	5	7	9	2
1	3	5	4	8	7	6	2	9
2	7	6	1	5	9	8	3	4
4	9	8	3	2	6	1	7	5
6	4	3	5	9	8	2	1	7
9	1	7	2	6	4	5	8	3
8	5	2	7	3	1	9	4	6

PUZZLE / **260**

9	4	3	7	6	2	1	8	5
6	5	8	3	1	4	7	9	2
2	7	1	8	9	5	4	6	3
5	9	6	1	4	3	8	2	7
1	8	4	2	7	9	3	5	6
3	2	7	5	8	6	9	4	1
8	3	5	9	2	7	6	1	4
4	1	2	6	3	8	5	7	9
7	6	9	4	5	1	2	3	8

PUZZLE / **261**

6	7	8	9	1	4	5	3	2
3	4	1	8	5	2	6	9	7
5	2	9	7	3	6	1	8	4
4	3	2	5	7	9	8	1	6
8	9	7	3	6	1	2	4	5
1	6	5	2	4	8	9	7	3
9	5	6	4	8	3	7	2	1
2	1	3	6	9	7	4	5	8
7	8	4	1	2	5	3	6	9

PUZZLE / **262**

7	3	5	2	8	1	9	6	4
1	8	6	5	4	9	3	7	2
4	9	2	7	3	6	5	1	8
5	6	8	3	1	4	2	9	7
9	2	7	6	5	8	1	4	3
3	1	4	9	7	2	6	8	5
8	4	9	1	2	3	7	5	6
2	5	1	4	6	7	8	3	9
6	7	3	8	9	5	4	2	1

PUZZLE / **263**

8	9	1	7	4	2	5	6	3
4	7	3	5	6	1	8	2	9
5	2	6	3	9	8	7	4	1
3	4	9	6	8	5	1	7	2
6	1	8	9	2	7	3	5	4
7	5	2	4	1	3	9	8	6
2	8	5	1	3	4	6	9	7
9	3	4	8	7	6	2	1	5
1	6	7	2	5	9	4	3	8

PUZZLE / **264**

7	9	5	6	1	2	4	3	8
4	1	3	8	5	9	2	6	7
6	2	8	4	3	7	5	9	1
5	4	7	9	8	1	6	2	3
3	6	9	7	2	4	1	8	5
2	8	1	3	6	5	7	4	9
9	5	6	1	4	3	8	7	2
8	7	2	5	9	6	3	1	4
1	3	4	2	7	8	9	5	6

PUZZLE / **265**

3	9	8	1	2	7	5	4	6
4	2	7	3	6	5	9	1	8
6	5	1	4	8	9	3	7	2
7	8	5	9	4	6	2	3	1
9	1	4	2	3	8	7	6	5
2	6	3	7	5	1	8	9	4
1	4	2	5	7	3	6	8	9
5	7	6	8	9	4	1	2	3
8	3	9	6	1	2	4	5	7

PUZZLE / **266**

9	5	1	3	8	6	7	2	4
6	7	2	9	1	4	8	5	3
8	4	3	2	5	7	1	6	9
4	1	9	6	2	8	3	7	5
2	3	6	7	4	5	9	1	8
7	8	5	1	3	9	6	4	2
5	9	4	8	6	1	2	3	7
1	2	7	5	9	3	4	8	6
3	6	8	4	7	2	5	9	1

PUZZLE / **267**

4	1	8	7	9	3	2	5	6
9	3	2	5	8	6	1	7	4
7	6	5	2	4	1	9	3	8
6	2	7	4	3	5	8	9	1
3	9	1	6	7	8	5	4	2
8	5	4	1	2	9	7	6	3
1	7	3	9	6	2	4	8	5
2	4	6	8	5	7	3	1	9
5	8	9	3	1	4	6	2	7

PUZZLE / **268**

3	6	8	9	4	1	2	7	5
2	7	4	5	6	3	8	1	9
1	5	9	2	7	8	4	6	3
5	4	3	7	2	6	9	8	1
8	1	6	3	5	9	7	2	4
9	2	7	1	8	4	3	5	6
4	8	5	6	9	7	1	3	2
7	3	2	4	1	5	6	9	8
6	9	1	8	3	2	5	4	7

PUZZLE / **269**

3	1	9	2	7	5	4	8	6
7	5	6	4	1	8	2	3	9
2	8	4	9	6	3	5	7	1
9	2	1	3	5	4	8	6	7
6	4	3	7	8	9	1	5	2
8	7	5	1	2	6	3	9	4
1	3	2	5	9	7	6	4	8
4	9	8	6	3	2	7	1	5
5	6	7	8	4	1	9	2	3

PUZZLE / **270**

9	7	2	5	4	8	3	1	6
4	3	6	7	1	9	5	2	8
8	5	1	2	3	6	4	7	9
6	8	9	4	7	5	2	3	1
2	4	7	3	8	1	9	6	5
3	1	5	6	9	2	7	8	4
7	9	4	1	6	3	8	5	2
1	2	3	8	5	4	6	9	7
5	6	8	9	2	7	1	4	3

PUZZLE / **271**

6	3	2	8	7	5	9	4	1
5	7	1	9	4	3	2	6	8
9	8	4	2	6	1	7	5	3
2	6	7	1	9	4	3	8	5
4	9	5	3	8	2	1	7	6
8	1	3	7	5	6	4	2	9
3	5	6	4	1	7	8	9	2
7	2	9	6	3	8	5	1	4
1	4	8	5	2	9	6	3	7

PUZZLE / **272**

3	5	4	9	8	2	1	7	6
9	7	6	4	1	3	5	2	8
2	8	1	7	6	5	9	3	4
8	6	9	1	3	4	7	5	2
7	3	2	6	5	9	8	4	1
1	4	5	2	7	8	3	6	9
4	2	3	8	9	7	6	1	5
6	9	7	5	4	1	2	8	3
5	1	8	3	2	6	4	9	7

PUZZLE / **273**

4	3	7	5	2	8	6	9	1
1	5	9	6	3	7	4	8	2
2	8	6	4	9	1	7	5	3
5	6	3	9	1	2	8	7	4
9	4	8	7	5	3	2	1	6
7	2	1	8	6	4	5	3	9
8	1	5	3	4	6	9	2	7
6	9	2	1	7	5	3	4	8
3	7	4	2	8	9	1	6	5

PUZZLE / **274**

1	3	2	4	6	7	9	5	8
9	5	8	2	1	3	6	7	4
6	4	7	5	8	9	3	1	2
8	9	5	6	4	2	1	3	7
7	6	3	8	9	1	4	2	5
4	2	1	7	3	5	8	9	6
2	8	9	3	7	6	5	4	1
5	1	4	9	2	8	7	6	3
3	7	6	1	5	4	2	8	9

PUZZLE / **275**

3	8	5	1	6	4	7	2	9
4	9	6	7	8	2	5	3	1
1	2	7	5	9	3	8	6	4
5	3	8	4	2	9	6	1	7
6	4	1	8	5	7	3	9	2
9	7	2	3	1	6	4	8	5
8	5	3	9	4	1	2	7	6
2	1	4	6	7	8	9	5	3
7	6	9	2	3	5	1	4	8

PUZZLE / **276**

3	1	7	4	2	5	8	6	9
6	8	4	1	3	9	5	7	2
5	9	2	7	6	8	1	3	4
7	3	5	9	1	4	2	8	6
8	2	9	6	5	7	3	4	1
1	4	6	3	8	2	7	9	5
2	6	8	5	4	3	9	1	7
9	5	1	8	7	6	4	2	3
4	7	3	2	9	1	6	5	8

PUZZLE / **277**

3	7	8	2	1	5	6	9	4
6	4	2	9	8	3	5	7	1
9	1	5	6	7	4	8	3	2
7	3	6	8	9	2	1	4	5
8	5	4	1	3	6	7	2	9
1	2	9	4	5	7	3	6	8
5	9	3	7	4	1	2	8	6
4	6	7	5	2	8	9	1	3
2	8	1	3	6	9	4	5	7

PUZZLE / **278**

4	8	9	2	3	7	1	5	6
6	1	2	9	8	5	7	4	3
7	3	5	6	4	1	9	2	8
3	6	8	1	7	4	5	9	2
2	5	1	8	6	9	3	7	4
9	4	7	3	5	2	6	8	1
8	9	6	5	2	3	4	1	7
5	2	4	7	1	6	8	3	9
1	7	3	4	9	8	2	6	5

PUZZLE / **279**

2	3	1	5	4	9	6	8	7
4	9	5	8	6	7	1	2	3
7	6	8	3	2	1	9	5	4
1	7	3	6	8	5	4	9	2
9	8	6	4	7	2	5	3	1
5	2	4	1	9	3	8	7	6
8	1	7	2	5	6	3	4	9
3	4	9	7	1	8	2	6	5
6	5	2	9	3	4	7	1	8

PUZZLE / 280

7	3	6	8	9	5	2	4	1
2	8	5	4	1	6	9	7	3
4	9	1	2	7	3	6	8	5
3	7	2	1	8	4	5	9	6
8	5	9	6	2	7	3	1	4
1	6	4	5	3	9	8	2	7
6	1	3	9	4	8	7	5	2
5	4	8	7	6	2	1	3	9
9	2	7	3	5	1	4	6	8

PUZZLE / 281

4	2	8	7	9	1	3	5	6
7	3	6	2	8	5	9	4	1
5	1	9	3	4	6	7	8	2
1	7	5	9	6	8	2	3	4
6	9	3	4	5	2	8	1	7
2	8	4	1	3	7	5	6	9
9	4	2	8	1	3	6	7	5
3	5	7	6	2	4	1	9	8
8	6	1	5	7	9	4	2	3

PUZZLE / 282

3	1	8	9	6	7	2	5	4
6	7	4	2	8	5	9	1	3
9	2	5	1	4	3	8	7	6
8	6	1	5	9	4	7	3	2
7	3	2	8	1	6	5	4	9
5	4	9	3	7	2	1	6	8
4	9	3	7	5	8	6	2	1
1	5	6	4	2	9	3	8	7
2	8	7	6	3	1	4	9	5

PUZZLE / 283

1	5	7	8	4	6	2	9	3
9	4	8	2	3	7	6	1	5
3	6	2	5	9	1	7	4	8
5	3	4	9	2	8	1	6	7
7	9	6	1	5	3	4	8	2
8	2	1	6	7	4	3	5	9
4	7	5	3	1	9	8	2	6
2	8	3	4	6	5	9	7	1
6	1	9	7	8	2	5	3	4

PUZZLE / 284

6	9	2	3	8	1	5	4	7
4	1	7	5	2	9	6	3	8
3	5	8	6	4	7	1	9	2
1	7	9	4	6	5	8	2	3
8	4	5	1	3	2	9	7	6
2	3	6	9	7	8	4	1	5
9	8	1	2	5	3	7	6	4
7	2	4	8	1	6	3	5	9
5	6	3	7	9	4	2	8	1

PUZZLE / 285

6	2	3	8	1	9	5	4	7
8	5	4	3	2	7	9	1	6
9	1	7	4	5	6	3	8	2
7	9	5	1	6	4	8	2	3
3	6	2	7	8	5	1	9	4
1	4	8	9	3	2	6	7	5
2	8	9	6	4	3	7	5	1
4	3	1	5	7	8	2	6	9
5	7	6	2	9	1	4	3	8

PUZZLE / 286

5	1	6	2	4	8	9	7	3
9	2	7	3	6	5	4	8	1
8	3	4	9	7	1	5	6	2
6	7	8	5	3	4	2	1	9
3	9	2	1	8	7	6	4	5
4	5	1	6	9	2	7	3	8
2	6	5	4	1	3	8	9	7
7	4	3	8	2	9	1	5	6
1	8	9	7	5	6	3	2	4

PUZZLE / 287

2	4	9	7	3	5	6	1	8
7	6	5	1	4	8	2	3	9
8	3	1	2	9	6	7	5	4
4	5	8	3	6	2	1	9	7
1	2	3	9	7	4	5	8	6
6	9	7	5	8	1	3	4	2
5	7	4	6	1	9	8	2	3
3	8	2	4	5	7	9	6	1
9	1	6	8	2	3	4	7	5

PUZZLE / 288

7	4	2	6	8	9	3	5	1
9	3	5	7	2	1	6	8	4
8	1	6	4	3	5	7	9	2
3	8	9	2	5	4	1	7	6
6	2	1	3	9	7	5	4	8
4	5	7	8	1	6	2	3	9
2	6	4	9	7	3	8	1	5
1	9	3	5	6	8	4	2	7
5	7	8	1	4	2	9	6	3

PUZZLE / 289

6	2	5	9	4	3	8	1	7
3	9	1	7	8	5	4	6	2
8	7	4	1	6	2	9	3	5
2	8	3	6	5	9	1	7	4
5	4	7	2	1	8	6	9	3
1	6	9	4	3	7	5	2	8
7	1	6	8	2	4	3	5	9
4	5	2	3	9	1	7	8	6
9	3	8	5	7	6	2	4	1

PUZZLE / 290

1	4	7	5	8	9	6	2	3
3	6	9	2	7	1	5	4	8
8	2	5	4	3	6	9	7	1
9	1	2	3	6	4	7	8	5
7	3	8	1	2	5	4	6	9
6	5	4	8	9	7	3	1	2
2	8	6	9	4	3	1	5	7
5	7	3	6	1	8	2	9	4
4	9	1	7	5	2	8	3	6

PUZZLE / 291

7	4	8	6	2	1	3	5	9
6	3	1	5	9	7	8	4	2
9	2	5	3	4	8	1	6	7
1	7	2	8	5	9	6	3	4
8	9	3	2	6	4	7	1	5
5	6	4	7	1	3	9	2	8
4	8	6	9	3	5	2	7	1
2	5	7	1	8	6	4	9	3
3	1	9	4	7	2	5	8	6

PUZZLE / 292

3	1	4	2	6	7	5	9	8
9	5	6	4	8	1	2	3	7
8	2	7	3	9	5	1	4	6
6	4	3	7	5	2	8	1	9
7	8	2	6	1	9	3	5	4
1	9	5	8	3	4	6	7	2
2	3	9	1	7	6	4	8	5
4	7	8	5	2	3	9	6	1
5	6	1	9	4	8	7	2	3

PUZZLE / 293

4	2	3	7	6	1	5	8	9
1	8	7	5	9	4	3	2	6
5	9	6	2	8	3	4	1	7
8	5	9	1	3	6	2	7	4
6	3	1	4	2	7	8	9	5
7	4	2	9	5	8	1	6	3
3	1	8	6	7	5	9	4	2
2	6	5	8	4	9	7	3	1
9	7	4	3	1	2	6	5	8

PUZZLE / 294

7	2	5	6	4	8	3	9	1
4	9	6	3	1	7	2	5	8
1	8	3	5	2	9	6	4	7
9	3	2	8	7	6	4	1	5
8	4	7	1	3	5	9	6	2
6	5	1	4	9	2	7	8	3
2	6	4	7	8	1	5	3	9
5	1	9	2	6	3	8	7	4
3	7	8	9	5	4	1	2	6

PUZZLE / **295**

9	6	4	2	8	7	5	3	1
1	7	8	5	9	3	4	2	6
2	5	3	1	6	4	7	8	9
5	8	2	3	4	1	9	6	7
3	4	7	9	2	6	8	1	5
6	1	9	8	7	5	2	4	3
7	2	5	6	1	8	3	9	4
4	9	6	7	3	2	1	5	8
8	3	1	4	5	9	6	7	2

PUZZLE / **296**

1	2	4	9	8	3	7	6	5
8	9	3	5	6	7	1	4	2
6	7	5	4	2	1	8	9	3
2	6	9	3	7	8	4	5	1
4	1	7	6	5	9	3	2	8
5	3	8	2	1	4	6	7	9
3	4	2	1	9	6	5	8	7
7	5	6	8	3	2	9	1	4
9	8	1	7	4	5	2	3	6

PUZZLE / **297**

8	9	2	6	1	7	5	4	3
5	7	3	8	2	4	9	1	6
1	6	4	5	3	9	8	7	2
7	5	1	2	4	8	6	3	9
2	3	6	9	5	1	7	8	4
4	8	9	7	6	3	2	5	1
9	4	5	3	7	6	1	2	8
6	1	7	4	8	2	3	9	5
3	2	8	1	9	5	4	6	7

PUZZLE / **298**

3	5	2	8	4	9	6	7	1
6	1	4	7	5	2	8	9	3
9	8	7	1	3	6	5	2	4
5	7	1	9	8	4	3	6	2
4	6	3	2	7	1	9	8	5
2	9	8	5	6	3	1	4	7
1	3	6	4	9	7	2	5	8
7	2	5	6	1	8	4	3	9
8	4	9	3	2	5	7	1	6

PUZZLE / **299**

7	8	1	2	9	3	4	6	5
5	9	2	4	6	1	7	3	8
3	4	6	8	5	7	9	1	2
9	2	3	5	4	8	1	7	6
4	1	8	3	7	6	5	2	9
6	5	7	9	1	2	3	8	4
2	3	9	7	8	4	6	5	1
1	7	5	6	2	9	8	4	3
8	6	4	1	3	5	2	9	7

PUZZLE / **300**

3	6	9	8	1	4	7	2	5
8	2	7	9	5	3	4	6	1
5	4	1	6	7	2	8	3	9
9	7	2	4	6	5	1	8	3
6	1	5	3	8	9	2	7	4
4	8	3	7	2	1	5	9	6
2	3	6	5	4	7	9	1	8
1	9	4	2	3	8	6	5	7
7	5	8	1	9	6	3	4	2

PUZZLE / **301**

3	9	8	7	2	5	4	6	1
1	4	7	6	9	8	3	5	2
5	2	6	4	3	1	8	7	9
4	5	9	1	8	7	6	2	3
2	8	1	3	6	9	7	4	5
6	7	3	2	5	4	1	9	8
7	1	5	8	4	2	9	3	6
9	6	4	5	1	3	2	8	7
8	3	2	9	7	6	5	1	4

PUZZLE / **302**

1	4	8	7	3	6	9	5	2
9	7	6	5	2	1	8	4	3
5	2	3	9	8	4	1	7	6
2	3	1	6	5	9	7	8	4
6	5	4	8	7	3	2	9	1
7	8	9	4	1	2	3	6	5
4	9	2	3	6	7	5	1	8
8	1	7	2	4	5	6	3	9
3	6	5	1	9	8	4	2	7

PUZZLE / **303**

3	4	9	6	7	2	1	5	8
2	6	8	4	5	1	7	3	9
1	5	7	8	9	3	6	2	4
4	1	3	5	2	7	8	9	6
9	8	5	3	4	6	2	1	7
6	7	2	1	8	9	3	4	5
7	2	4	9	1	8	5	6	3
5	3	1	7	6	4	9	8	2
8	9	6	2	3	5	4	7	1

PUZZLE / **304**

7	4	5	1	9	6	2	3	8
1	3	9	8	2	7	5	4	6
6	8	2	5	3	4	9	7	1
2	9	6	7	1	5	4	8	3
5	1	4	9	8	3	6	2	7
8	7	3	4	6	2	1	5	9
9	2	1	3	4	8	7	6	5
4	5	8	6	7	1	3	9	2
3	6	7	2	5	9	8	1	4

PUZZLE / **305**

6	8	1	2	4	9	5	7	3
3	2	7	5	1	6	4	9	8
9	5	4	7	3	8	6	1	2
2	9	5	8	6	4	1	3	7
7	3	6	1	9	5	8	2	4
1	4	8	3	7	2	9	5	6
8	1	3	4	5	7	2	6	9
5	6	2	9	8	3	7	4	1
4	7	9	6	2	1	3	8	5

PUZZLE / **306**

4	3	1	7	2	8	6	9	5
5	6	2	3	9	4	1	7	8
9	8	7	1	6	5	2	4	3
7	5	9	8	1	2	3	6	4
1	2	3	4	5	6	7	8	9
6	4	8	9	3	7	5	1	2
2	9	6	5	8	1	4	3	7
8	1	4	2	7	3	9	5	6
3	7	5	6	4	9	8	2	1

PUZZLE / **307**

8	6	9	4	7	2	1	3	5
3	1	2	9	8	5	6	4	7
7	5	4	6	1	3	2	8	9
6	9	8	2	5	1	3	7	4
1	4	7	3	9	6	5	2	8
5	2	3	7	4	8	9	1	6
9	8	6	1	3	7	4	5	2
2	3	5	8	6	4	7	9	1
4	7	1	5	2	9	8	6	3

PUZZLE / **308**

2	6	8	9	4	3	5	7	1
7	4	9	6	1	5	8	3	2
1	5	3	7	8	2	4	9	6
6	2	4	3	7	9	1	5	8
5	3	1	8	6	4	7	2	9
9	8	7	5	2	1	3	6	4
8	1	5	2	3	6	9	4	7
3	7	6	4	9	8	2	1	5
4	9	2	1	5	7	6	8	3

PUZZLE / **309**

9	7	6	8	5	1	2	3	4
1	4	8	3	2	6	7	9	5
2	5	3	4	9	7	1	8	6
4	1	2	5	3	8	9	6	7
7	3	5	6	1	9	8	4	2
8	6	9	7	4	2	5	1	3
5	8	7	9	6	4	3	2	1
3	2	4	1	8	5	6	7	9
6	9	1	2	7	3	4	5	8

PUZZLE / 310

8	6	2	5	4	9	1	3	7
3	5	1	6	2	7	9	4	8
7	9	4	3	8	1	2	6	5
6	8	9	4	1	5	3	7	2
1	4	5	7	3	2	6	8	9
2	7	3	8	9	6	5	1	4
9	3	8	1	5	4	7	2	6
4	2	6	9	7	3	8	5	1
5	1	7	2	6	8	4	9	3

PUZZLE / 311

9	5	2	1	6	3	8	7	4
8	7	6	4	2	9	5	3	1
1	3	4	8	5	7	9	2	6
2	4	9	5	7	8	1	6	3
5	8	7	6	3	1	4	9	2
6	1	3	2	9	4	7	5	8
7	6	1	3	4	5	2	8	9
3	9	8	7	1	2	6	4	5
4	2	5	9	8	6	3	1	7

PUZZLE / 312

1	4	8	6	9	7	2	3	5
5	2	6	3	4	1	8	9	7
9	7	3	5	2	8	6	1	4
7	9	2	4	8	3	1	5	6
8	6	1	7	5	9	4	2	3
3	5	4	2	1	6	9	7	8
6	8	9	1	3	5	7	4	2
4	3	7	9	6	2	5	8	1
2	1	5	8	7	4	3	6	9

PUZZLE / 313

7	1	8	6	9	5	2	3	4
9	4	5	3	2	1	6	7	8
6	2	3	4	8	7	1	9	5
4	7	1	9	5	8	3	6	2
5	8	6	7	3	2	4	1	9
3	9	2	1	6	4	8	5	7
1	3	7	8	4	9	5	2	6
2	6	4	5	7	3	9	8	1
8	5	9	2	1	6	7	4	3

PUZZLE / 314

6	5	8	9	7	2	4	3	1
9	4	2	6	3	1	8	5	7
1	7	3	4	8	5	6	9	2
5	2	6	1	9	8	7	4	3
4	3	1	7	2	6	5	8	9
7	8	9	5	4	3	2	1	6
2	9	5	3	6	4	1	7	8
3	6	4	8	1	7	9	2	5
8	1	7	2	5	9	3	6	4

PUZZLE / 315

4	5	1	9	3	6	2	8	7
3	8	9	5	2	7	6	4	1
6	7	2	1	4	8	9	5	3
7	2	4	6	1	3	8	9	5
5	9	3	8	7	4	1	6	2
1	6	8	2	9	5	3	7	4
9	1	5	4	8	2	7	3	6
8	3	6	7	5	1	4	2	9
2	4	7	3	6	9	5	1	8

PUZZLE / 316

7	2	6	5	8	1	3	4	9
4	5	8	9	6	3	7	1	2
3	1	9	4	7	2	8	6	5
6	4	7	2	3	9	5	8	1
2	3	5	8	1	4	9	7	6
9	8	1	7	5	6	4	2	3
1	6	4	3	9	7	2	5	8
5	9	2	1	4	8	6	3	7
8	7	3	6	2	5	1	9	4

PUZZLE / 317

5	7	2	8	6	4	1	3	9
4	3	8	9	7	1	2	5	6
9	6	1	2	3	5	4	7	8
6	9	5	1	4	3	8	2	7
3	2	4	7	8	9	5	6	1
8	1	7	5	2	6	9	4	3
7	5	3	4	1	8	6	9	2
2	8	9	6	5	7	3	1	4
1	4	6	3	9	2	7	8	5

PUZZLE / 318

9	6	5	8	2	7	3	4	1
2	7	4	3	6	1	5	9	8
8	3	1	4	9	5	6	2	7
1	9	8	6	5	4	2	7	3
6	4	7	2	3	9	8	1	5
3	5	2	1	7	8	9	6	4
7	2	6	5	4	3	1	8	9
5	8	9	7	1	6	4	3	2
4	1	3	9	8	2	7	5	6

PUZZLE / 319

3	7	2	4	6	8	9	1	5
8	1	4	9	3	5	2	7	6
5	9	6	2	7	1	4	8	3
9	2	5	3	1	7	6	4	8
4	3	8	6	9	2	7	5	1
7	6	1	5	8	4	3	2	9
6	5	7	8	2	9	1	3	4
2	8	9	1	4	3	5	6	7
1	4	3	7	5	6	8	9	2

PUZZLE / 320

1	3	4	9	2	5	6	7	8
8	9	2	7	6	1	3	4	5
5	7	6	4	3	8	1	2	9
2	1	7	3	9	4	5	8	6
9	6	5	2	8	7	4	3	1
3	4	8	5	1	6	7	9	2
4	8	9	1	5	3	2	6	7
7	2	1	6	4	9	8	5	3
6	5	3	8	7	2	9	1	4

PUZZLE / 321

7	4	3	8	6	1	2	5	9
9	6	1	2	3	5	4	7	8
2	5	8	4	7	9	3	6	1
3	9	5	7	1	2	8	4	6
1	2	4	6	5	8	7	9	3
8	7	6	3	9	4	1	2	5
5	8	2	9	4	3	6	1	7
6	3	9	1	2	7	5	8	4
4	1	7	5	8	6	9	3	2

PUZZLE / 322

7	1	6	2	9	3	5	4	8
8	9	2	5	7	4	3	6	1
4	3	5	1	6	8	7	2	9
5	7	8	3	4	1	2	9	6
2	6	3	8	5	9	4	1	7
9	4	1	7	2	6	8	5	3
6	8	4	9	3	5	1	7	2
1	5	7	6	8	2	9	3	4
3	2	9	4	1	7	6	8	5

PUZZLE / 323

7	1	3	9	4	8	5	2	6
2	8	9	1	6	5	7	3	4
5	6	4	2	7	3	8	9	1
8	2	6	5	3	4	1	7	9
1	4	5	8	9	7	3	6	2
3	9	7	6	2	1	4	8	5
9	3	8	4	1	2	6	5	7
6	7	1	3	5	9	2	4	8
4	5	2	7	8	6	9	1	3

PUZZLE / 324

8	7	3	5	1	2	4	6	9
1	9	6	3	8	4	5	7	2
4	5	2	7	6	9	3	8	1
9	3	4	2	7	6	8	1	5
6	8	7	9	5	1	2	4	3
5	2	1	4	3	8	7	9	6
2	4	8	1	9	5	6	3	7
3	6	9	8	2	7	1	5	4
7	1	5	6	4	3	9	2	8

PUZZLE / 325

8	5	9	3	7	4	2	6	1
2	3	4	1	6	8	5	9	7
6	7	1	2	5	9	3	8	4
1	9	8	7	2	6	4	5	3
5	4	3	8	9	1	7	2	6
7	6	2	5	4	3	9	1	8
3	2	5	6	8	7	1	4	9
4	1	6	9	3	5	8	7	2
9	8	7	4	1	2	6	3	5

PUZZLE / 326

7	8	5	3	4	1	2	6	9
2	4	1	9	6	5	7	3	8
6	9	3	7	8	2	1	5	4
1	3	2	6	9	8	4	7	5
4	6	7	2	5	3	9	8	1
9	5	8	4	1	7	6	2	3
8	2	4	1	3	6	5	9	7
5	7	9	8	2	4	3	1	6
3	1	6	5	7	9	8	4	2

PUZZLE / 327

5	9	3	4	1	7	2	6	8
4	6	2	9	5	8	3	1	7
7	1	8	3	6	2	9	4	5
6	3	1	7	2	4	5	8	9
8	4	7	6	9	5	1	2	3
2	5	9	1	8	3	4	7	6
9	7	6	5	4	1	8	3	2
1	2	5	8	3	6	7	9	4
3	8	4	2	7	9	6	5	1

PUZZLE / 328

1	2	3	5	6	8	4	9	7
7	6	8	2	9	4	3	1	5
4	9	5	3	7	1	8	6	2
8	5	2	4	1	9	6	7	3
6	3	7	8	5	2	9	4	1
9	1	4	7	3	6	2	5	8
3	4	9	1	8	7	5	2	6
5	7	6	9	2	3	1	8	4
2	8	1	6	4	5	7	3	9

PUZZLE / 329

3	2	6	8	4	1	5	9	7
1	5	9	3	6	7	2	4	8
7	4	8	9	5	2	6	3	1
8	1	3	6	7	5	9	2	4
9	6	2	4	8	3	7	1	5
5	7	4	1	2	9	3	8	6
6	3	1	7	9	8	4	5	2
2	8	7	5	3	4	1	6	9
4	9	5	2	1	6	8	7	3

PUZZLE / 330

3	7	6	4	8	2	9	5	1
8	2	5	1	6	9	3	4	7
4	9	1	7	5	3	2	8	6
7	8	2	3	4	6	5	1	9
9	5	3	8	2	1	7	6	4
1	6	4	5	9	7	8	3	2
2	4	8	6	7	5	1	9	3
5	3	7	9	1	4	6	2	8
6	1	9	2	3	8	4	7	5

PUZZLE / 331

4	6	2	1	3	9	5	7	8
8	1	9	5	7	4	2	6	3
5	3	7	6	8	2	4	9	1
6	7	8	2	5	3	9	1	4
2	5	4	9	1	8	6	3	7
3	9	1	7	4	6	8	5	2
7	4	3	8	6	5	1	2	9
9	8	5	3	2	1	7	4	6
1	2	6	4	9	7	3	8	5

PUZZLE / 332

7	2	6	3	5	1	9	4	8
5	3	9	8	4	7	6	2	1
4	1	8	9	2	6	5	3	7
1	9	7	4	8	2	3	6	5
2	6	4	1	3	5	8	7	9
3	8	5	7	6	9	4	1	2
6	5	3	2	1	8	7	9	4
8	7	2	6	9	4	1	5	3
9	4	1	5	7	3	2	8	6

PUZZLE / 333

1	9	5	7	3	6	2	8	4
7	8	3	1	4	2	5	9	6
4	2	6	9	8	5	7	1	3
6	7	8	2	9	1	4	3	5
9	5	4	3	6	7	1	2	8
3	1	2	4	5	8	9	6	7
5	3	9	8	2	4	6	7	1
2	6	7	5	1	3	8	4	9
8	4	1	6	7	9	3	5	2

PUZZLE / 334

9	4	8	7	1	2	5	6	3
3	2	5	9	6	8	4	1	7
1	6	7	4	5	3	9	2	8
2	1	6	5	9	7	8	3	4
5	7	4	8	3	6	2	9	1
8	9	3	1	2	4	6	7	5
7	5	1	6	8	9	3	4	2
4	3	9	2	7	5	1	8	6
6	8	2	3	4	1	7	5	9

PUZZLE / 335

1	6	8	2	7	5	9	4	3
7	5	4	9	6	3	8	2	1
9	3	2	1	8	4	5	6	7
6	4	5	8	3	1	2	7	9
3	8	7	4	9	2	6	1	5
2	9	1	6	5	7	3	8	4
5	2	3	7	1	6	4	9	8
4	1	9	5	2	8	7	3	6
8	7	6	3	4	9	1	5	2

PUZZLE / 336

3	7	6	5	4	2	1	9	8
5	2	4	1	9	8	3	7	6
8	9	1	3	6	7	2	4	5
2	8	3	7	1	9	5	6	4
4	5	9	6	2	3	8	1	7
6	1	7	8	5	4	9	3	2
1	3	2	4	8	6	7	5	9
7	4	8	9	3	5	6	2	1
9	6	5	2	7	1	4	8	3

PUZZLE / 337

9	4	7	2	8	3	6	1	5
6	8	1	4	5	7	2	9	3
5	3	2	6	9	1	8	4	7
8	6	5	7	4	9	1	3	2
2	1	9	8	3	6	5	7	4
4	7	3	1	2	5	9	8	6
7	2	6	3	1	8	4	5	9
1	9	4	5	7	2	3	6	8
3	5	8	9	6	4	7	2	1

PUZZLE / 338

8	6	3	5	7	9	2	1	4
4	7	2	6	1	8	5	9	3
1	5	9	3	4	2	6	7	8
7	4	5	9	8	1	3	2	6
2	3	6	4	5	7	9	8	1
9	1	8	2	3	6	7	4	5
5	9	7	1	6	4	8	3	2
3	8	4	7	2	5	1	6	9
6	2	1	8	9	3	4	5	7

PUZZLE / 339

8	9	1	3	5	2	6	4	7
2	7	3	4	6	1	5	9	8
4	5	6	7	8	9	1	2	3
7	1	4	2	9	5	3	8	6
5	2	9	8	3	6	4	7	1
3	6	8	1	4	7	9	5	2
9	4	7	6	2	3	8	1	5
1	3	5	9	7	8	2	6	4
6	8	2	5	1	4	7	3	9

PUZZLE / 340

2	7	5	3	4	8	6	1	9
9	4	8	1	6	2	7	5	3
3	6	1	9	7	5	2	8	4
8	2	3	6	9	4	5	7	1
4	1	6	7	5	3	9	2	8
5	9	7	2	8	1	4	3	6
7	5	4	8	1	6	3	9	2
6	8	2	5	3	9	1	4	7
1	3	9	4	2	7	8	6	5

PUZZLE / 341

7	6	2	9	5	8	4	3	1
3	9	5	1	6	4	7	8	2
8	1	4	3	2	7	6	5	9
2	7	6	5	8	1	9	4	3
5	3	9	4	7	6	2	1	8
1	4	8	2	9	3	5	7	6
6	2	3	8	4	5	1	9	7
9	5	1	7	3	2	8	6	4
4	8	7	6	1	9	3	2	5

PUZZLE / 342

9	1	6	7	4	3	2	8	5
7	8	4	1	2	5	3	6	9
2	3	5	6	9	8	1	7	4
1	7	3	5	8	4	6	9	2
4	6	2	9	3	1	7	5	8
8	5	9	2	7	6	4	3	1
6	2	7	4	5	9	8	1	3
3	9	1	8	6	2	5	4	7
5	4	8	3	1	7	9	2	6

PUZZLE / 343

8	5	1	2	4	6	9	3	7
2	3	9	7	1	5	4	8	6
6	4	7	9	8	3	1	2	5
1	2	6	4	5	8	3	7	9
5	7	4	1	3	9	2	6	8
9	8	3	6	2	7	5	1	4
4	6	2	8	9	1	7	5	3
7	9	5	3	6	2	8	4	1
3	1	8	5	7	4	6	9	2

PUZZLE / 344

5	3	9	2	7	1	8	4	6
6	7	2	8	4	5	3	1	9
4	8	1	3	6	9	5	7	2
3	5	7	6	1	2	4	9	8
1	2	8	4	9	7	6	3	5
9	6	4	5	8	3	1	2	7
8	9	5	1	2	4	7	6	3
2	4	3	7	5	6	9	8	1
7	1	6	9	3	8	2	5	4

PUZZLE / 345

5	2	4	9	6	3	8	1	7
6	1	8	2	4	7	5	3	9
3	9	7	8	5	1	2	4	6
7	4	1	5	8	9	3	6	2
8	3	6	7	1	2	4	9	5
2	5	9	6	3	4	1	7	8
1	6	2	4	9	8	7	5	3
9	8	3	1	7	5	6	2	4
4	7	5	3	2	6	9	8	1

PUZZLE / 346

8	3	2	7	5	9	6	1	4
7	6	1	4	3	8	5	9	2
5	4	9	2	6	1	7	8	3
6	9	8	1	4	2	3	5	7
3	5	7	9	8	6	2	4	1
1	2	4	5	7	3	9	6	8
2	7	5	6	1	4	8	3	9
4	8	6	3	9	7	1	2	5
9	1	3	8	2	5	4	7	6

PUZZLE / 347

7	6	2	3	8	1	9	5	4
4	9	8	2	6	5	7	1	3
1	5	3	4	9	7	6	2	8
8	1	7	6	4	9	2	3	5
9	4	5	1	2	3	8	6	7
2	3	6	5	7	8	4	9	1
3	7	9	8	5	6	1	4	2
5	8	4	9	1	2	3	7	6
6	2	1	7	3	4	5	8	9

PUZZLE / 348

8	3	9	7	5	4	1	6	2
2	1	7	6	3	9	5	8	4
5	6	4	2	8	1	3	9	7
6	2	3	8	9	5	4	7	1
4	8	1	3	7	6	2	5	9
9	7	5	4	1	2	6	3	8
7	9	6	1	2	3	8	4	5
3	5	2	9	4	8	7	1	6
1	4	8	5	6	7	9	2	3

PUZZLE / 349

9	2	6	4	1	5	7	8	3
1	8	5	7	3	6	2	4	9
7	4	3	8	2	9	1	5	6
5	9	2	3	7	8	4	6	1
4	3	8	1	6	2	9	7	5
6	1	7	5	9	4	3	2	8
3	6	1	2	8	7	5	9	4
8	7	4	9	5	1	6	3	2
2	5	9	6	4	3	8	1	7

PUZZLE / 350

2	1	6	5	8	9	3	4	7
4	3	8	2	7	6	9	5	1
7	9	5	1	3	4	6	8	2
1	7	3	9	5	8	4	2	6
8	5	4	7	6	2	1	9	3
9	6	2	4	1	3	8	7	5
6	8	9	3	2	5	7	1	4
3	2	1	8	4	7	5	6	9
5	4	7	6	9	1	2	3	8

PUZZLE / 351

2	9	7	6	8	5	3	1	4
8	1	5	3	7	4	2	9	6
3	4	6	9	1	2	8	5	7
9	6	3	7	5	8	4	2	1
5	8	4	1	2	3	6	7	9
1	7	2	4	9	6	5	8	3
7	3	8	5	4	9	1	6	2
4	2	1	8	6	7	9	3	5
6	5	9	2	3	1	7	4	8

PUZZLE / 352

6	7	5	1	3	4	9	2	8
3	1	9	2	8	6	4	5	7
2	8	4	5	7	9	3	1	6
1	6	8	3	2	7	5	9	4
9	5	3	6	4	8	1	7	2
7	4	2	9	1	5	6	8	3
4	3	7	8	5	1	2	6	9
5	2	6	7	9	3	8	4	1
8	9	1	4	6	2	7	3	5

PUZZLE / 353

1	4	9	3	2	5	8	7	6
6	7	3	8	9	1	2	5	4
2	5	8	4	7	6	3	9	1
8	9	4	6	1	2	5	3	7
5	3	2	9	4	7	1	6	8
7	1	6	5	8	3	9	4	2
4	8	7	2	5	9	6	1	3
3	2	5	1	6	4	7	8	9
9	6	1	7	3	8	4	2	5

PUZZLE / 354

4	7	1	9	5	8	2	3	6
9	8	3	2	1	6	7	5	4
5	6	2	4	3	7	8	1	9
7	4	8	6	9	5	1	2	3
3	5	6	8	2	1	9	4	7
1	2	9	7	4	3	5	6	8
6	9	4	5	7	2	3	8	1
8	3	5	1	6	9	4	7	2
2	1	7	3	8	4	6	9	5

PUZZLE / 355

9	5	8	2	3	4	7	6	1
4	7	2	9	6	1	8	3	5
3	1	6	8	5	7	4	9	2
5	9	1	7	2	3	6	8	4
7	8	4	6	9	5	2	1	3
2	6	3	4	1	8	9	5	7
6	2	5	3	4	9	1	7	8
1	4	7	5	8	6	3	2	9
8	3	9	1	7	2	5	4	6

PUZZLE / 356

1	9	7	6	5	2	4	8	3
8	4	5	9	3	1	7	6	2
3	6	2	8	4	7	1	9	5
2	5	9	1	7	3	6	4	8
6	8	3	4	2	9	5	1	7
4	7	1	5	8	6	3	2	9
7	2	6	3	9	4	8	5	1
9	1	8	7	6	5	2	3	4
5	3	4	2	1	8	9	7	6

PUZZLE / 357

9	2	8	7	1	3	4	5	6
4	5	7	6	2	9	8	3	1
3	6	1	4	8	5	9	2	7
6	8	5	2	3	4	1	7	9
7	4	2	9	5	1	6	8	3
1	9	3	8	7	6	2	4	5
5	3	6	1	4	8	7	9	2
8	7	9	3	6	2	5	1	4
2	1	4	5	9	7	3	6	8

PUZZLE / 358

8	3	9	2	7	6	4	1	5
1	7	5	9	4	8	6	2	3
6	4	2	1	5	3	9	8	7
2	9	4	7	8	5	3	6	1
5	1	6	3	2	9	8	7	4
7	8	3	4	6	1	2	5	9
4	6	7	5	3	2	1	9	8
9	5	8	6	1	4	7	3	2
3	2	1	8	9	7	5	4	6

PUZZLE / 359

1	6	5	8	4	7	3	9	2
2	9	8	6	3	5	1	4	7
7	4	3	9	1	2	8	6	5
9	7	1	5	8	6	2	3	4
5	3	2	4	9	1	6	7	8
6	8	4	2	7	3	9	5	1
8	5	7	1	6	9	4	2	3
3	1	6	7	2	4	5	8	9
4	2	9	3	5	8	7	1	6

PUZZLE / 360

3	1	2	8	6	7	5	9	4
4	6	9	3	2	5	7	8	1
7	5	8	1	9	4	3	2	6
9	2	4	7	8	6	1	3	5
5	7	1	2	4	3	8	6	9
8	3	6	9	5	1	2	4	7
6	4	3	5	7	8	9	1	2
1	9	5	6	3	2	4	7	8
2	8	7	4	1	9	6	5	3

PUZZLE / 361

9	3	6	5	8	1	4	7	2
5	8	1	7	2	4	6	9	3
4	7	2	6	9	3	8	5	1
7	2	8	3	5	9	1	6	4
1	5	4	2	7	6	9	3	8
6	9	3	1	4	8	5	2	7
2	1	5	8	6	7	3	4	9
8	6	9	4	3	2	7	1	5
3	4	7	9	1	5	2	8	6

PUZZLE / 362

8	1	5	7	4	9	3	6	2
3	9	2	6	1	8	7	4	5
7	6	4	3	5	2	8	9	1
5	8	1	9	3	4	6	2	7
4	3	6	1	2	7	5	8	9
2	7	9	8	6	5	1	3	4
1	2	7	4	8	3	9	5	6
6	5	3	2	9	1	4	7	8
9	4	8	5	7	6	2	1	3

PUZZLE / 363

1	5	9	6	7	3	4	8	2
2	8	3	4	5	1	7	9	6
7	4	6	9	8	2	5	3	1
9	1	4	3	2	7	6	5	8
6	3	2	8	4	5	9	1	7
5	7	8	1	6	9	3	2	4
3	9	7	2	1	4	8	6	5
8	2	5	7	3	6	1	4	9
4	6	1	5	9	8	2	7	3

PUZZLE / 364

7	5	4	2	6	3	9	8	1
6	3	8	9	1	4	5	2	7
2	1	9	7	5	8	3	4	6
8	9	6	4	7	1	2	5	3
5	7	3	8	2	6	4	1	9
1	4	2	3	9	5	6	7	8
9	8	1	5	3	2	7	6	4
4	2	7	6	8	9	1	3	5
3	6	5	1	4	7	8	9	2

PUZZLE / 365

3	6	7	8	2	4	9	1	5
8	5	1	7	9	6	2	4	3
2	4	9	5	3	1	7	6	8
9	2	6	3	4	7	5	8	1
1	3	8	9	6	5	4	2	7
5	7	4	1	8	2	3	9	6
7	8	2	4	1	3	6	5	9
6	1	3	2	5	9	8	7	4
4	9	5	6	7	8	1	3	2

PUZZLE / 366

2	4	8	3	5	7	1	9	6
5	6	7	2	1	9	4	3	8
9	1	3	4	8	6	5	7	2
6	8	5	1	9	4	3	2	7
1	2	9	7	3	5	6	8	4
7	3	4	8	6	2	9	5	1
8	5	2	9	4	1	7	6	3
4	7	6	5	2	3	8	1	9
3	9	1	6	7	8	2	4	5

PUZZLE / 367

9	8	3	5	1	4	6	2	7
1	5	7	2	6	3	9	4	8
6	2	4	8	7	9	3	1	5
5	4	9	6	3	7	2	8	1
3	6	8	1	4	2	7	5	9
7	1	2	9	8	5	4	6	3
8	7	5	4	9	6	1	3	2
2	9	6	3	5	1	8	7	4
4	3	1	7	2	8	5	9	6

PUZZLE / 368

7	5	9	4	1	8	2	6	3
2	6	1	5	9	3	8	4	7
3	8	4	2	6	7	5	1	9
1	3	6	7	8	9	4	5	2
4	2	8	3	5	6	7	9	1
9	7	5	1	2	4	3	8	6
6	9	7	8	3	5	1	2	4
8	1	3	9	4	2	6	7	5
5	4	2	6	7	1	9	3	8

PUZZLE / 369

4	3	8	6	9	5	1	7	2
9	6	7	1	8	2	3	5	4
1	2	5	7	3	4	9	8	6
7	1	2	9	5	3	6	4	8
3	8	9	2	4	6	5	1	7
6	5	4	8	7	1	2	9	3
8	9	6	5	2	7	4	3	1
5	4	1	3	6	8	7	2	9
2	7	3	4	1	9	8	6	5

PUZZLE / 370

6	4	5	1	8	9	7	2	3
7	9	1	3	5	2	4	6	8
2	3	8	4	7	6	1	5	9
8	5	3	7	6	4	2	9	1
1	2	4	8	9	3	5	7	6
9	6	7	5	2	1	8	3	4
3	8	2	9	1	5	6	4	7
5	7	9	6	4	8	3	1	2
4	1	6	2	3	7	9	8	5

PUZZLE / 371

2	5	8	1	3	4	7	6	9
7	3	1	9	6	5	8	4	2
4	9	6	2	7	8	3	5	1
5	1	9	6	2	3	4	8	7
6	4	2	8	5	7	1	9	3
8	7	3	4	1	9	5	2	6
9	2	4	7	8	1	6	3	5
1	8	5	3	9	6	2	7	4
3	6	7	5	4	2	9	1	8

PUZZLE / 372

9	7	6	8	4	3	5	1	2
2	3	1	7	5	6	8	9	4
4	8	5	2	9	1	7	6	3
6	9	7	4	2	8	3	5	1
8	2	4	1	3	5	6	7	9
5	1	3	9	6	7	2	4	8
7	4	2	5	8	9	1	3	6
3	5	9	6	1	2	4	8	7
1	6	8	3	7	4	9	2	5

PUZZLE / 373

6	4	1	2	7	8	5	9	3
3	9	7	6	1	5	2	8	4
2	5	8	3	9	4	6	7	1
8	6	9	1	2	3	7	4	5
7	3	2	4	5	6	8	1	9
5	1	4	7	8	9	3	2	6
9	7	6	8	3	1	4	5	2
1	8	3	5	4	2	9	6	7
4	2	5	9	6	7	1	3	8

PUZZLE / 374

7	9	3	4	8	6	5	1	2
6	2	4	1	9	5	7	8	3
8	1	5	7	2	3	4	6	9
2	5	6	9	4	8	3	7	1
9	3	8	5	1	7	6	2	4
4	7	1	3	6	2	8	9	5
5	8	2	6	3	9	1	4	7
1	6	7	2	5	4	9	3	8
3	4	9	8	7	1	2	5	6

PUZZLE / 375

1	2	6	3	9	8	7	4	5
7	5	9	4	6	2	8	3	1
4	3	8	5	7	1	6	2	9
9	1	5	2	8	3	4	6	7
2	8	7	9	4	6	5	1	3
6	4	3	1	5	7	9	8	2
3	7	4	8	2	9	1	5	6
5	6	1	7	3	4	2	9	8
8	9	2	6	1	5	3	7	4

PUZZLE / 376

6	4	1	7	9	3	2	5	8
9	3	8	6	5	2	7	4	1
7	2	5	4	1	8	6	9	3
1	6	2	5	3	4	9	8	7
8	5	7	9	2	1	3	6	4
3	9	4	8	6	7	1	2	5
2	8	9	1	7	5	4	3	6
5	7	6	3	4	9	8	1	2
4	1	3	2	8	6	5	7	9

PUZZLE / 377

8	9	3	2	6	7	4	5	1
7	2	5	4	1	3	8	9	6
1	4	6	8	5	9	2	7	3
9	8	1	6	2	5	7	3	4
4	6	7	3	9	1	5	2	8
5	3	2	7	8	4	1	6	9
2	5	9	1	3	8	6	4	7
6	1	4	9	7	2	3	8	5
3	7	8	5	4	6	9	1	2

PUZZLE / 378

5	8	6	3	2	4	1	9	7
2	9	1	8	5	7	6	4	3
4	7	3	9	6	1	8	5	2
8	2	4	5	9	6	3	7	1
3	5	9	7	1	2	4	8	6
6	1	7	4	3	8	9	2	5
9	3	2	6	4	5	7	1	8
7	6	5	1	8	9	2	3	4
1	4	8	2	7	3	5	6	9

PUZZLE / 379

7	4	5	1	6	2	9	3	8
3	1	9	4	8	7	5	2	6
2	6	8	3	9	5	1	7	4
4	9	1	8	2	3	7	6	5
6	2	7	9	5	4	3	8	1
5	8	3	6	7	1	2	4	9
8	3	6	2	1	9	4	5	7
9	5	4	7	3	8	6	1	2
1	7	2	5	4	6	8	9	3

PUZZLE / 380

5	2	1	3	6	7	9	8	4
9	6	4	2	8	1	7	5	3
8	3	7	5	9	4	2	1	6
4	7	5	6	2	8	1	3	9
6	9	3	1	7	5	8	4	2
2	1	8	4	3	9	6	7	5
1	8	6	9	4	3	5	2	7
7	4	2	8	5	6	3	9	1
3	5	9	7	1	2	4	6	8

PUZZLE / 381

3	1	4	7	8	2	9	6	5
5	9	8	6	1	3	2	7	4
7	2	6	5	9	4	1	3	8
9	5	7	8	3	1	6	4	2
1	8	2	4	6	5	7	9	3
4	6	3	9	2	7	8	5	1
8	4	5	1	7	6	3	2	9
2	7	1	3	4	9	5	8	6
6	3	9	2	5	8	4	1	7

PUZZLE / 382

7	2	3	6	5	8	1	4	9
5	6	9	1	2	4	8	7	3
1	4	8	7	3	9	5	6	2
2	5	1	9	4	3	6	8	7
3	9	6	8	7	5	2	1	4
4	8	7	2	1	6	9	3	5
9	1	2	3	8	7	4	5	6
8	3	4	5	6	2	7	9	1
6	7	5	4	9	1	3	2	8

PUZZLE / 383

3	1	8	4	7	9	5	2	6
5	2	7	1	3	6	9	8	4
9	6	4	8	2	5	7	3	1
4	3	6	2	9	8	1	7	5
8	5	1	7	6	4	3	9	2
7	9	2	5	1	3	6	4	8
2	8	3	9	5	1	4	6	7
6	7	5	3	4	2	8	1	9
1	4	9	6	8	7	2	5	3

PUZZLE / 384

4	9	8	6	5	1	3	7	2
5	2	6	7	9	3	4	1	8
1	7	3	4	8	2	6	9	5
2	8	9	5	3	4	1	6	7
3	4	1	2	7	6	8	5	9
6	5	7	9	1	8	2	4	3
7	6	4	8	2	5	9	3	1
8	3	5	1	6	9	7	2	4
9	1	2	3	4	7	5	8	6

PUZZLE / 385

8	1	3	6	4	5	2	9	7
9	4	6	7	2	8	3	1	5
5	2	7	1	9	3	8	4	6
3	7	4	2	5	1	6	8	9
6	9	8	3	7	4	1	5	2
1	5	2	8	6	9	4	7	3
4	8	9	5	3	2	7	6	1
2	6	1	9	8	7	5	3	4
7	3	5	4	1	6	9	2	8

PUZZLE / 386

5	3	4	6	7	1	9	2	8
7	8	9	2	4	5	6	3	1
6	1	2	3	8	9	4	7	5
2	6	3	5	9	7	1	8	4
8	4	7	1	3	6	5	9	2
9	5	1	4	2	8	7	6	3
4	9	6	8	5	3	2	1	7
1	2	8	7	6	4	3	5	9
3	7	5	9	1	2	8	4	6

PUZZLE / 387

6	2	7	3	8	1	5	9	4
1	4	8	5	9	2	6	3	7
9	5	3	4	6	7	2	1	8
2	3	9	7	1	5	4	8	6
5	8	4	6	2	3	1	7	9
7	6	1	9	4	8	3	2	5
4	1	5	2	7	9	8	6	3
3	9	2	8	5	6	7	4	1
8	7	6	1	3	4	9	5	2

PUZZLE / 388

7	5	4	6	8	9	1	3	2
8	6	2	1	4	3	5	7	9
3	1	9	7	2	5	8	4	6
5	9	1	4	3	8	6	2	7
4	7	6	2	9	1	3	8	5
2	3	8	5	6	7	9	1	4
6	4	3	9	1	2	7	5	8
1	2	7	8	5	6	4	9	3
9	8	5	3	7	4	2	6	1

PUZZLE / 389

4	7	5	3	2	6	8	9	1
1	8	2	5	7	9	4	3	6
6	3	9	8	1	4	5	7	2
7	9	6	2	8	3	1	4	5
5	2	4	7	6	1	3	8	9
8	1	3	9	4	5	6	2	7
9	5	7	1	3	8	2	6	4
2	6	8	4	5	7	9	1	3
3	4	1	6	9	2	7	5	8

PUZZLE / 390

6	8	4	2	9	1	7	5	3
2	3	9	5	7	8	6	1	4
1	7	5	4	6	3	2	8	9
3	5	1	8	4	6	9	7	2
4	9	2	7	1	5	3	6	8
8	6	7	9	3	2	1	4	5
5	1	3	6	8	9	4	2	7
9	4	8	1	2	7	5	3	6
7	2	6	3	5	4	8	9	1

PUZZLE / 391

1	3	5	2	4	8	9	6	7
8	6	4	9	7	3	1	5	2
2	9	7	1	5	6	4	8	3
7	4	1	8	9	5	3	2	6
3	8	9	6	1	2	7	4	5
5	2	6	7	3	4	8	9	1
9	1	2	5	8	7	6	3	4
4	5	8	3	6	1	2	7	9
6	7	3	4	2	9	5	1	8

PUZZLE / 392

3	6	8	5	1	9	2	7	4
4	1	9	2	8	7	6	3	5
2	7	5	4	6	3	9	1	8
1	8	2	3	4	6	5	9	7
5	4	7	9	2	1	8	6	3
9	3	6	7	5	8	1	4	2
6	2	1	8	7	4	3	5	9
8	9	4	6	3	5	7	2	1
7	5	3	1	9	2	4	8	6

PUZZLE / 393

6	9	3	2	1	4	5	8	7
8	4	1	9	5	7	6	2	3
2	5	7	6	8	3	9	4	1
5	8	2	4	3	1	7	6	9
1	6	9	7	2	5	4	3	8
3	7	4	8	6	9	2	1	5
7	1	6	3	9	2	8	5	4
4	3	8	5	7	6	1	9	2
9	2	5	1	4	8	3	7	6

PUZZLE / 394

3	9	7	8	4	6	5	2	1
8	6	1	5	2	7	9	4	3
2	4	5	1	3	9	6	7	8
5	3	8	9	1	4	7	6	2
1	7	9	6	8	2	4	3	5
4	2	6	3	7	5	1	8	9
6	1	2	4	9	3	8	5	7
9	5	3	7	6	8	2	1	4
7	8	4	2	5	1	3	9	6

PUZZLE / 395

7	8	3	4	5	6	1	2	9
4	2	5	9	8	1	7	6	3
6	1	9	7	3	2	8	5	4
2	5	6	1	4	9	3	7	8
3	7	1	5	2	8	4	9	6
9	4	8	3	6	7	2	1	5
8	9	4	2	7	5	6	3	1
1	3	7	6	9	4	5	8	2
5	6	2	8	1	3	9	4	7

PUZZLE / 396

9	2	8	6	4	1	5	3	7
1	3	6	8	7	5	9	2	4
7	4	5	3	2	9	1	8	6
4	8	9	5	1	6	3	7	2
3	5	7	4	8	2	6	1	9
2	6	1	9	3	7	4	5	8
6	1	4	7	5	8	2	9	3
8	9	2	1	6	3	7	4	5
5	7	3	2	9	4	8	6	1

PUZZLE / 397

4	7	9	8	2	3	5	6	1
3	8	1	9	5	6	4	7	2
2	5	6	1	4	7	8	3	9
7	9	2	3	8	4	1	5	6
8	1	5	6	7	2	9	4	3
6	4	3	5	9	1	2	8	7
9	6	4	2	3	8	7	1	5
5	3	8	7	1	9	6	2	4
1	2	7	4	6	5	3	9	8

PUZZLE / 398

8	1	6	5	4	9	7	2	3
3	2	9	6	8	7	1	5	4
7	5	4	1	3	2	9	6	8
4	3	5	9	1	6	8	7	2
9	6	2	8	7	5	3	4	1
1	8	7	4	2	3	6	9	5
2	4	8	7	6	1	5	3	9
5	7	1	3	9	4	2	8	6
6	9	3	2	5	8	4	1	7

PUZZLE / 399

3	9	8	1	4	5	7	2	6
7	4	2	9	3	6	5	1	8
6	5	1	7	8	2	9	3	4
4	1	6	5	7	8	2	9	3
9	7	3	2	1	4	8	6	5
2	8	5	3	6	9	1	4	7
1	2	7	4	5	3	6	8	9
5	6	4	8	9	1	3	7	2
8	3	9	6	2	7	4	5	1

PUZZLE / 400

5	4	8	6	7	1	3	2	9
2	9	1	4	5	3	6	8	7
3	6	7	9	8	2	5	4	1
8	1	2	5	3	6	9	7	4
4	7	5	1	9	8	2	3	6
6	3	9	7	2	4	8	1	5
7	2	6	3	4	9	1	5	8
1	5	3	8	6	7	4	9	2
9	8	4	2	1	5	7	6	3

PUZZLE / 401

9	2	4	1	5	8	6	3	7
1	6	3	2	9	7	8	5	4
7	5	8	6	4	3	2	1	9
6	4	5	8	1	9	3	7	2
8	1	9	7	3	2	4	6	5
3	7	2	4	6	5	1	9	8
4	9	6	5	8	1	7	2	3
2	3	1	9	7	4	5	8	6
5	8	7	3	2	6	9	4	1

PUZZLE / 402

1	2	8	6	5	4	9	7	3
3	6	5	9	1	7	8	4	2
7	4	9	8	2	3	5	6	1
6	8	3	1	7	2	4	5	9
2	9	4	5	6	8	1	3	7
5	7	1	4	3	9	6	2	8
8	5	7	2	9	6	3	1	4
4	1	2	3	8	5	7	9	6
9	3	6	7	4	1	2	8	5

PUZZLE / 403

8	6	2	5	9	3	4	7	1
3	7	4	8	2	1	6	5	9
1	9	5	4	6	7	2	8	3
5	8	7	9	4	2	1	3	6
9	4	3	1	5	6	7	2	8
2	1	6	7	3	8	5	9	4
4	3	8	2	1	5	9	6	7
7	5	1	6	8	9	3	4	2
6	2	9	3	7	4	8	1	5

PUZZLE / 404

7	8	9	6	5	4	2	3	1
4	2	1	3	7	8	9	6	5
3	5	6	1	2	9	7	4	8
6	1	5	9	8	3	4	2	7
2	7	4	5	6	1	8	9	3
8	9	3	7	4	2	1	5	6
5	4	2	8	3	7	6	1	9
9	6	7	4	1	5	3	8	2
1	3	8	2	9	6	5	7	4

PUZZLE / 405

4	9	1	3	6	5	7	8	2
8	2	3	7	1	9	5	4	6
6	5	7	4	8	2	9	1	3
7	8	4	5	3	6	2	9	1
9	3	5	2	4	1	6	7	8
1	6	2	8	9	7	3	5	4
3	4	6	9	7	8	1	2	5
5	1	9	6	2	4	8	3	7
2	7	8	1	5	3	4	6	9

PUZZLE / 406

1	8	4	3	2	7	5	9	6
9	2	6	1	4	5	8	7	3
5	7	3	6	8	9	2	1	4
7	6	2	4	9	3	1	5	8
3	4	9	8	5	1	6	2	7
8	5	1	2	7	6	3	4	9
6	9	8	7	1	2	4	3	5
2	3	5	9	6	4	7	8	1
4	1	7	5	3	8	9	6	2

PUZZLE / 407

8	7	2	3	9	4	5	1	6
6	1	3	7	8	5	2	4	9
9	4	5	6	2	1	8	3	7
2	3	6	8	5	9	1	7	4
1	5	7	4	3	6	9	8	2
4	8	9	2	1	7	3	6	5
7	2	1	9	6	3	4	5	8
3	6	8	5	4	2	7	9	1
5	9	4	1	7	8	6	2	3

PUZZLE / 408

2	3	9	1	5	7	4	8	6
8	5	6	3	9	4	2	1	7
1	7	4	6	8	2	3	9	5
6	2	5	9	7	3	1	4	8
3	1	8	2	4	5	7	6	9
4	9	7	8	1	6	5	3	2
5	4	1	7	6	9	8	2	3
9	8	3	5	2	1	6	7	4
7	6	2	4	3	8	9	5	1

PUZZLE / 409

5	6	9	2	1	3	4	7	8
3	7	4	5	8	9	6	2	1
1	8	2	4	6	7	9	5	3
9	1	7	3	5	6	2	8	4
8	2	6	9	4	1	5	3	7
4	3	5	8	7	2	1	9	6
7	4	3	1	9	5	8	6	2
2	9	8	6	3	4	7	1	5
6	5	1	7	2	8	3	4	9

PUZZLE / 410

1	5	8	4	7	3	6	9	2
3	9	6	2	8	1	5	7	4
2	7	4	5	9	6	1	8	3
6	4	2	7	3	8	9	5	1
8	1	7	9	5	2	3	4	6
9	3	5	6	1	4	8	2	7
7	8	3	1	4	9	2	6	5
5	6	9	3	2	7	4	1	8
4	2	1	8	6	5	7	3	9

PUZZLE / 411

6	3	5	8	9	1	4	2	7
8	7	1	4	6	2	3	9	5
2	9	4	7	3	5	6	8	1
4	8	7	9	1	3	2	5	6
3	1	2	6	5	4	9	7	8
9	5	6	2	8	7	1	3	4
1	4	8	5	2	9	7	6	3
5	2	3	1	7	6	8	4	9
7	6	9	3	4	8	5	1	2

PUZZLE / 412

8	3	5	4	9	6	2	7	1
1	7	6	8	5	2	3	4	9
2	9	4	7	1	3	5	8	6
4	6	3	2	7	1	9	5	8
7	1	2	9	8	5	4	6	3
5	8	9	3	6	4	7	1	2
3	2	7	1	4	8	6	9	5
9	5	1	6	2	7	8	3	4
6	4	8	5	3	9	1	2	7

PUZZLE / 413

2	7	9	5	6	4	8	1	3
4	1	5	8	3	7	9	6	2
6	8	3	2	1	9	7	4	5
5	6	4	3	7	8	1	2	9
8	2	1	9	4	5	6	3	7
3	9	7	6	2	1	4	5	8
7	3	8	4	5	6	2	9	1
9	4	2	1	8	3	5	7	6
1	5	6	7	9	2	3	8	4

PUZZLE / 414

1	2	7	6	5	8	4	9	3
3	5	4	2	7	9	1	6	8
8	9	6	3	4	1	5	7	2
6	3	9	1	8	2	7	4	5
7	1	2	4	9	5	8	3	6
5	4	8	7	6	3	9	2	1
2	8	3	9	1	4	6	5	7
4	6	5	8	2	7	3	1	9
9	7	1	5	3	6	2	8	4

PUZZLE / 415

5	4	7	8	1	6	2	3	9
2	8	6	3	5	9	7	1	4
3	1	9	7	4	2	5	6	8
4	7	3	9	2	8	6	5	1
9	6	8	5	7	1	3	4	2
1	5	2	4	6	3	9	8	7
8	2	5	1	3	7	4	9	6
6	9	4	2	8	5	1	7	3
7	3	1	6	9	4	8	2	5

PUZZLE / 416

6	2	8	5	1	9	7	3	4
7	1	3	4	2	8	6	5	9
4	5	9	3	6	7	8	2	1
5	6	7	1	8	4	2	9	3
2	3	4	7	9	6	1	8	5
9	8	1	2	5	3	4	7	6
3	4	2	6	7	5	9	1	8
8	7	5	9	4	1	3	6	2
1	9	6	8	3	2	5	4	7

PUZZLE / 417

3	6	8	1	2	5	9	7	4
2	5	7	9	6	4	3	1	8
1	4	9	7	8	3	5	6	2
9	8	3	2	1	6	7	4	5
6	7	5	4	3	8	2	9	1
4	2	1	5	7	9	8	3	6
5	9	2	3	4	1	6	8	7
8	3	4	6	5	7	1	2	9
7	1	6	8	9	2	4	5	3

PUZZLE / 418

7	8	2	1	5	3	9	4	6
3	4	6	8	9	7	5	2	1
9	1	5	2	6	4	7	8	3
8	6	7	3	4	1	2	5	9
2	5	3	9	7	8	6	1	4
4	9	1	6	2	5	3	7	8
1	2	4	5	3	9	8	6	7
5	3	8	7	1	6	4	9	2
6	7	9	4	8	2	1	3	5

PUZZLE / 419

4	7	2	9	8	3	6	1	5
6	5	9	2	1	7	3	4	8
1	8	3	6	5	4	7	2	9
7	2	5	4	3	6	9	8	1
8	3	1	5	2	9	4	7	6
9	6	4	8	7	1	5	3	2
5	1	7	3	9	8	2	6	4
3	9	6	1	4	2	8	5	7
2	4	8	7	6	5	1	9	3

PUZZLE / 420

3	2	5	9	4	1	6	8	7
8	6	1	2	7	3	9	5	4
9	4	7	5	6	8	1	3	2
2	9	8	6	5	4	7	1	3
6	1	4	3	8	7	5	2	9
7	5	3	1	9	2	8	4	6
4	8	2	7	1	9	3	6	5
1	7	6	4	3	5	2	9	8
5	3	9	8	2	6	4	7	1

PUZZLE / 421

4	1	3	9	2	5	8	7	6
5	9	7	8	6	4	2	1	3
6	8	2	1	3	7	9	5	4
2	7	4	6	1	8	3	9	5
1	3	6	5	9	2	7	4	8
8	5	9	7	4	3	6	2	1
9	2	8	4	5	6	1	3	7
7	4	1	3	8	9	5	6	2
3	6	5	2	7	1	4	8	9

PUZZLE / 422

4	2	3	1	9	6	7	8	5
1	5	8	4	7	3	2	6	9
7	9	6	5	8	2	4	3	1
8	4	9	6	1	5	3	2	7
5	6	2	7	3	4	1	9	8
3	7	1	8	2	9	5	4	6
6	1	4	3	5	8	9	7	2
9	3	5	2	6	7	8	1	4
2	8	7	9	4	1	6	5	3

PUZZLE / 423

1	8	5	6	3	7	4	2	9
6	9	4	5	2	8	7	1	3
3	7	2	1	9	4	5	6	8
8	5	1	7	6	9	2	3	4
4	2	6	3	8	1	9	5	7
7	3	9	4	5	2	6	8	1
5	4	3	8	7	6	1	9	2
2	6	7	9	1	3	8	4	5
9	1	8	2	4	5	3	7	6

PUZZLE / 424

5	2	7	8	9	1	6	3	4
8	3	6	5	4	2	9	7	1
4	9	1	7	6	3	2	5	8
1	4	3	9	2	7	8	6	5
2	6	5	3	8	4	7	1	9
7	8	9	6	1	5	4	2	3
6	7	4	1	5	9	3	8	2
3	5	2	4	7	8	1	9	6
9	1	8	2	3	6	5	4	7

PUZZLE / 425

3	8	9	7	2	1	4	6	5
5	7	6	3	9	4	1	8	2
2	1	4	5	6	8	7	9	3
9	5	2	4	3	6	8	7	1
6	4	8	1	7	2	3	5	9
7	3	1	8	5	9	6	2	4
8	9	3	2	4	7	5	1	6
1	6	5	9	8	3	2	4	7
4	2	7	6	1	5	9	3	8

PUZZLE / 426

8	7	5	1	3	6	2	4	9
6	2	9	7	4	5	1	8	3
1	3	4	2	8	9	7	5	6
5	4	8	6	1	3	9	2	7
9	6	2	4	7	8	5	3	1
7	1	3	5	9	2	4	6	8
2	5	7	3	6	1	8	9	4
4	8	6	9	5	7	3	1	2
3	9	1	8	2	4	6	7	5

PUZZLE / 427

9	7	8	1	6	3	2	5	4
2	3	1	5	7	4	9	8	6
4	6	5	9	2	8	7	3	1
7	8	2	4	5	1	3	6	9
5	1	9	7	3	6	4	2	8
3	4	6	8	9	2	5	1	7
1	2	4	3	8	9	6	7	5
8	5	3	6	4	7	1	9	2
6	9	7	2	1	5	8	4	3

PUZZLE / 428

3	2	6	4	9	5	1	8	7
1	7	4	2	8	6	9	5	3
9	8	5	3	7	1	6	4	2
8	9	1	5	3	2	4	7	6
2	4	7	1	6	8	5	3	9
5	6	3	9	4	7	8	2	1
6	3	9	7	5	4	2	1	8
7	5	2	8	1	9	3	6	4
4	1	8	6	2	3	7	9	5

PUZZLE / 429

1	5	4	6	9	3	8	7	2
6	2	7	5	8	4	1	9	3
8	9	3	7	2	1	5	6	4
9	6	2	4	1	7	3	5	8
3	1	8	2	5	9	6	4	7
4	7	5	8	3	6	9	2	1
2	4	1	9	6	8	7	3	5
7	3	9	1	4	5	2	8	6
5	8	6	3	7	2	4	1	9

PUZZLE / **430**

3	7	5	8	4	2	6	9	1
9	1	4	5	6	3	8	7	2
8	6	2	1	9	7	3	5	4
2	3	9	6	5	1	7	4	8
4	8	1	2	7	9	5	3	6
6	5	7	3	8	4	2	1	9
5	4	6	7	1	8	9	2	3
7	9	3	4	2	6	1	8	5
1	2	8	9	3	5	4	6	7

PUZZLE / **431**

3	4	2	9	1	6	8	7	5
1	7	5	8	2	4	3	9	6
6	8	9	3	7	5	1	2	4
7	9	4	6	8	3	2	5	1
2	3	6	1	5	7	4	8	9
5	1	8	2	4	9	7	6	3
4	2	3	5	6	8	9	1	7
8	6	7	4	9	1	5	3	2
9	5	1	7	3	2	6	4	8

PUZZLE / **432**

9	6	5	1	7	3	4	2	8
8	4	3	2	6	5	7	9	1
2	7	1	4	8	9	6	5	3
1	5	8	9	2	6	3	4	7
6	9	4	3	1	7	2	8	5
7	3	2	8	5	4	9	1	6
3	1	7	5	4	2	8	6	9
5	2	6	7	9	8	1	3	4
4	8	9	6	3	1	5	7	2

PUZZLE / **433**

9	4	3	8	5	6	2	1	7
5	2	7	4	3	1	6	8	9
1	8	6	7	2	9	3	5	4
7	5	9	1	4	2	8	6	3
4	3	2	5	6	8	7	9	1
6	1	8	3	9	7	4	2	5
3	7	1	2	8	5	9	4	6
8	9	4	6	1	3	5	7	2
2	6	5	9	7	4	1	3	8

PUZZLE / **434**

1	6	7	3	4	9	2	5	8
5	2	8	7	6	1	4	9	3
9	4	3	2	8	5	1	6	7
2	9	6	4	3	7	8	1	5
4	8	5	1	9	2	3	7	6
3	7	1	8	5	6	9	4	2
8	5	9	6	1	3	7	2	4
6	3	2	9	7	4	5	8	1
7	1	4	5	2	8	6	3	9

PUZZLE / **435**

5	6	2	9	4	3	1	8	7
3	4	9	8	1	7	2	6	5
7	8	1	5	6	2	3	9	4
6	2	8	4	3	5	7	1	9
4	7	5	1	9	8	6	3	2
9	1	3	7	2	6	4	5	8
1	5	4	6	7	9	8	2	3
8	3	6	2	5	4	9	7	1
2	9	7	3	8	1	5	4	6

PUZZLE / **436**

3	1	8	5	9	6	4	2	7
9	2	7	4	1	3	8	5	6
5	6	4	2	8	7	1	3	9
6	8	3	9	5	2	7	4	1
4	5	9	8	7	1	3	6	2
1	7	2	6	3	4	9	8	5
7	9	5	3	2	8	6	1	4
8	4	1	7	6	5	2	9	3
2	3	6	1	4	9	5	7	8

PUZZLE / **437**

9	8	1	5	2	3	6	4	7
4	6	2	9	1	7	3	8	5
3	5	7	8	6	4	9	2	1
5	4	3	6	9	8	7	1	2
1	2	6	7	4	5	8	9	3
7	9	8	2	3	1	4	5	6
8	1	9	3	7	2	5	6	4
6	3	4	1	5	9	2	7	8
2	7	5	4	8	6	1	3	9

PUZZLE / **438**

1	2	5	3	9	7	8	6	4
9	8	3	4	6	1	5	2	7
7	6	4	8	5	2	3	9	1
8	3	2	7	1	4	9	5	6
5	9	7	6	2	3	1	4	8
4	1	6	5	8	9	2	7	3
2	7	9	1	4	8	6	3	5
6	4	8	9	3	5	7	1	2
3	5	1	2	7	6	4	8	9

PUZZLE / **439**

3	1	6	5	4	8	2	9	7
8	4	5	7	2	9	1	6	3
2	7	9	1	6	3	8	4	5
6	3	4	8	5	7	9	1	2
9	2	1	6	3	4	7	5	8
5	8	7	9	1	2	6	3	4
1	9	3	2	8	5	4	7	6
4	6	8	3	7	1	5	2	9
7	5	2	4	9	6	3	8	1

PUZZLE / **440**

2	8	6	5	1	4	9	7	3
7	3	4	9	2	6	1	8	5
1	9	5	8	7	3	6	4	2
5	1	8	4	3	7	2	9	6
4	2	3	6	8	9	7	5	1
9	6	7	2	5	1	8	3	4
8	7	2	3	6	5	4	1	9
3	4	1	7	9	2	5	6	8
6	5	9	1	4	8	3	2	7

PUZZLE / **441**

9	1	6	4	5	3	7	8	2
2	4	7	1	8	6	3	5	9
5	8	3	9	7	2	1	4	6
3	2	8	6	1	5	9	7	4
6	9	5	7	4	8	2	1	3
4	7	1	3	2	9	8	6	5
7	3	2	5	6	1	4	9	8
8	5	4	2	9	7	6	3	1
1	6	9	8	3	4	5	2	7

PUZZLE / **442**

5	2	3	8	7	9	1	6	4
1	8	4	2	6	3	9	5	7
6	7	9	1	5	4	8	3	2
3	5	6	9	1	7	2	4	8
4	1	7	6	2	8	3	9	5
2	9	8	3	4	5	7	1	6
8	3	2	4	9	6	5	7	1
9	4	5	7	8	1	6	2	3
7	6	1	5	3	2	4	8	9

PUZZLE / **443**

8	2	7	6	5	3	4	9	1
4	5	3	9	7	1	6	8	2
6	9	1	2	8	4	3	5	7
7	6	2	5	3	9	1	4	8
3	4	8	1	6	7	9	2	5
9	1	5	4	2	8	7	6	3
1	7	9	8	4	5	2	3	6
5	3	6	7	9	2	8	1	4
2	8	4	3	1	6	5	7	9

PUZZLE / **444**

8	6	3	4	2	5	9	1	7
5	9	7	1	8	6	3	2	4
2	1	4	7	9	3	6	5	8
4	8	6	2	5	9	1	7	3
3	5	1	6	4	7	8	9	2
7	2	9	8	3	1	4	6	5
6	4	8	5	1	2	7	3	9
1	3	2	9	7	8	5	4	6
9	7	5	3	6	4	2	8	1

PUZZLE / **445**

2	9	3	1	7	5	4	6	8
4	8	7	3	9	6	1	2	5
5	1	6	4	2	8	3	9	7
8	5	9	2	6	4	7	1	3
6	7	2	5	1	3	8	4	9
1	3	4	9	8	7	2	5	6
9	4	8	7	5	2	6	3	1
7	2	1	6	3	9	5	8	4
3	6	5	8	4	1	9	7	2

PUZZLE / **446**

9	1	5	3	6	2	4	7	8
2	8	4	5	7	1	3	6	9
7	6	3	9	4	8	2	1	5
5	2	7	4	3	9	1	8	6
6	3	1	8	5	7	9	2	4
8	4	9	2	1	6	5	3	7
4	5	6	1	8	3	7	9	2
1	7	2	6	9	5	8	4	3
3	9	8	7	2	4	6	5	1

PUZZLE / **447**

5	1	2	3	9	8	4	6	7
7	3	6	1	5	4	9	8	2
8	9	4	7	6	2	5	1	3
3	6	7	9	8	1	2	4	5
2	4	8	5	7	6	3	9	1
9	5	1	2	4	3	6	7	8
1	7	5	6	3	9	8	2	4
4	2	9	8	1	5	7	3	6
6	8	3	4	2	7	1	5	9

PUZZLE / **448**

1	7	3	6	2	5	9	8	4
4	6	2	1	8	9	3	5	7
5	9	8	4	7	3	2	6	1
9	8	7	2	3	6	1	4	5
3	4	6	7	5	1	8	2	9
2	5	1	8	9	4	6	7	3
7	2	5	3	1	8	4	9	6
8	3	4	9	6	7	5	1	2
6	1	9	5	4	2	7	3	8

PUZZLE / **449**

3	5	2	7	1	8	4	9	6
7	4	6	3	2	9	5	1	8
1	8	9	5	6	4	3	2	7
6	9	8	1	3	7	2	4	5
4	1	7	9	5	2	8	6	3
5	2	3	8	4	6	1	7	9
8	7	5	4	9	1	6	3	2
2	3	1	6	7	5	9	8	4
9	6	4	2	8	3	7	5	1

PUZZLE / **450**

6	7	2	3	1	8	4	5	9
5	1	9	6	4	2	7	3	8
4	3	8	9	7	5	6	1	2
8	6	3	2	9	4	5	7	1
9	4	1	5	3	7	2	8	6
2	5	7	8	6	1	9	4	3
1	2	6	7	5	3	8	9	4
7	9	4	1	8	6	3	2	5
3	8	5	4	2	9	1	6	7

PUZZLE / **451**

9	4	8	6	2	3	5	1	7
2	7	5	1	8	4	9	6	3
1	6	3	5	7	9	2	8	4
6	5	9	2	1	7	3	4	8
3	1	7	9	4	8	6	2	5
8	2	4	3	6	5	1	7	9
5	8	6	4	3	2	7	9	1
7	9	1	8	5	6	4	3	2
4	3	2	7	9	1	8	5	6

PUZZLE / **452**

3	1	6	5	4	7	2	8	9
7	2	4	8	9	6	5	1	3
8	5	9	1	2	3	7	4	6
6	4	1	2	7	8	3	9	5
2	3	8	6	5	9	4	7	1
5	9	7	3	1	4	8	6	2
1	7	2	4	6	5	9	3	8
4	8	5	9	3	1	6	2	7
9	6	3	7	8	2	1	5	4

PUZZLE / **453**

2	6	4	5	7	8	9	3	1
3	9	5	6	1	2	7	8	4
7	1	8	4	9	3	6	5	2
8	5	3	1	2	9	4	7	6
9	7	6	8	3	4	1	2	5
1	4	2	7	5	6	3	9	8
6	3	9	2	4	5	8	1	7
5	8	7	9	6	1	2	4	3
4	2	1	3	8	7	5	6	9

PUZZLE / **454**

3	2	7	4	1	6	5	9	8
4	8	6	3	9	5	1	2	7
5	1	9	7	2	8	6	3	4
8	9	3	2	6	1	4	7	5
2	4	5	8	7	9	3	6	1
6	7	1	5	3	4	9	8	2
1	3	2	6	4	7	8	5	9
7	5	4	9	8	3	2	1	6
9	6	8	1	5	2	7	4	3

PUZZLE / **455**

6	5	7	1	2	8	4	3	9
3	8	1	4	6	9	5	7	2
4	9	2	5	7	3	1	8	6
9	1	3	6	5	7	2	4	8
7	6	4	8	1	2	3	9	5
5	2	8	9	3	4	7	6	1
1	3	6	7	9	5	8	2	4
8	7	5	2	4	6	9	1	3
2	4	9	3	8	1	6	5	7

PUZZLE / **456**

1	2	3	7	9	6	5	4	8
5	7	9	4	1	8	2	3	6
8	4	6	5	3	2	7	9	1
2	3	1	6	5	9	4	8	7
6	9	7	1	8	4	3	2	5
4	8	5	3	2	7	6	1	9
9	5	8	2	6	3	1	7	4
7	6	2	9	4	1	8	5	3
3	1	4	8	7	5	9	6	2

PUZZLE / **457**

3	8	9	5	4	7	6	2	1
2	6	4	1	8	9	3	7	5
7	5	1	6	2	3	9	4	8
8	1	6	7	9	2	4	5	3
4	3	5	8	6	1	7	9	2
9	7	2	4	3	5	1	8	6
6	2	3	9	7	8	5	1	4
1	4	7	2	5	6	8	3	9
5	9	8	3	1	4	2	6	7

PUZZLE / **458**

2	4	9	5	1	6	3	7	8
1	7	8	4	3	2	5	6	9
5	6	3	8	7	9	2	1	4
3	5	1	9	6	7	4	8	2
9	8	7	1	2	4	6	5	3
4	2	6	3	5	8	1	9	7
8	3	2	6	9	1	7	4	5
7	1	4	2	8	5	9	3	6
6	9	5	7	4	3	8	2	1

PUZZLE / **459**

8	9	5	4	6	3	7	1	2
4	7	1	5	9	2	6	8	3
2	6	3	8	1	7	9	5	4
1	2	7	6	3	4	5	9	8
5	4	9	7	2	8	3	6	1
6	3	8	9	5	1	2	4	7
7	8	6	2	4	5	1	3	9
3	5	4	1	7	9	8	2	6
9	1	2	3	8	6	4	7	5

PUZZLE / **460**

2	8	5	6	1	7	9	3	4
6	1	7	9	3	4	2	5	8
4	3	9	2	8	5	7	6	1
1	2	4	8	7	3	5	9	6
5	6	3	1	9	2	8	4	7
9	7	8	5	4	6	3	1	2
8	5	6	4	2	9	1	7	3
7	4	1	3	5	8	6	2	9
3	9	2	7	6	1	4	8	5

PUZZLE / **461**

3	5	8	2	4	6	7	9	1
7	4	9	8	3	1	6	2	5
2	1	6	5	9	7	3	8	4
6	3	5	9	7	4	2	1	8
8	7	2	1	5	3	9	4	6
1	9	4	6	2	8	5	7	3
4	6	7	3	8	9	1	5	2
5	8	1	7	6	2	4	3	9
9	2	3	4	1	5	8	6	7

PUZZLE / **462**

5	1	6	4	7	8	9	2	3
7	2	4	6	9	3	1	5	8
3	8	9	1	2	5	4	7	6
9	6	2	5	1	7	8	3	4
4	3	5	9	8	6	7	1	2
8	7	1	2	3	4	6	9	5
6	9	3	8	5	1	2	4	7
1	5	8	7	4	2	3	6	9
2	4	7	3	6	9	5	8	1

PUZZLE / **463**

5	2	1	9	8	7	6	3	4
9	6	4	5	2	3	7	8	1
7	8	3	4	1	6	9	2	5
3	4	5	8	9	1	2	7	6
2	7	6	3	4	5	1	9	8
1	9	8	6	7	2	5	4	3
4	1	7	2	6	8	3	5	9
6	5	9	7	3	4	8	1	2
8	3	2	1	5	9	4	6	7

PUZZLE / **464**

5	1	2	3	4	8	9	6	7
7	4	3	5	6	9	1	2	8
8	9	6	7	2	1	5	3	4
1	6	4	8	5	2	3	7	9
2	7	5	4	9	3	6	8	1
9	3	8	6	1	7	2	4	5
6	8	7	9	3	5	4	1	2
4	2	9	1	8	6	7	5	3
3	5	1	2	7	4	8	9	6

PUZZLE / **465**

5	7	4	9	1	2	8	3	6
6	2	3	8	5	7	4	9	1
1	8	9	4	6	3	2	7	5
4	9	7	2	8	6	1	5	3
8	3	5	1	4	9	6	2	7
2	6	1	3	7	5	9	8	4
7	5	8	6	2	4	3	1	9
9	1	6	5	3	8	7	4	2
3	4	2	7	9	1	5	6	8

PUZZLE / **466**

3	9	4	5	1	7	6	2	8
5	1	2	6	8	9	3	4	7
6	8	7	4	3	2	9	1	5
9	2	8	7	6	5	4	3	1
1	6	5	3	4	8	2	7	9
7	4	3	9	2	1	8	5	6
8	3	1	2	7	6	5	9	4
4	5	6	1	9	3	7	8	2
2	7	9	8	5	4	1	6	3

PUZZLE / **467**

2	1	8	3	6	7	5	9	4
3	4	5	2	1	9	7	6	8
9	7	6	5	8	4	2	1	3
8	2	1	6	4	3	9	5	7
4	6	3	9	7	5	8	2	1
5	9	7	8	2	1	4	3	6
7	8	2	1	5	6	3	4	9
6	3	4	7	9	2	1	8	5
1	5	9	4	3	8	6	7	2

PUZZLE / **468**

1	3	6	8	2	9	7	4	5
2	7	5	1	3	4	9	8	6
9	4	8	6	7	5	3	1	2
4	8	2	3	1	6	5	7	9
5	6	1	4	9	7	2	3	8
7	9	3	5	8	2	4	6	1
3	2	4	9	6	8	1	5	7
8	5	7	2	4	1	6	9	3
6	1	9	7	5	3	8	2	4

PUZZLE / **469**

4	2	3	8	7	1	5	6	9
7	5	9	6	3	2	8	4	1
6	8	1	4	9	5	3	7	2
2	7	8	3	1	9	6	5	4
5	1	4	2	6	7	9	8	3
9	3	6	5	8	4	2	1	7
1	6	7	9	2	8	4	3	5
3	4	2	1	5	6	7	9	8
8	9	5	7	4	3	1	2	6

PUZZLE / **470**

8	6	5	3	4	2	7	1	9
1	9	4	5	7	8	3	2	6
7	2	3	1	9	6	8	4	5
2	5	7	8	1	4	6	9	3
6	1	9	7	3	5	2	8	4
4	3	8	6	2	9	1	5	7
9	7	2	4	8	3	5	6	1
3	4	6	2	5	1	9	7	8
5	8	1	9	6	7	4	3	2

PUZZLE / **471**

9	7	8	4	6	3	2	5	1
4	3	6	2	5	1	9	8	7
1	2	5	9	7	8	4	6	3
7	1	3	8	4	2	6	9	5
8	6	2	5	3	9	7	1	4
5	4	9	7	1	6	8	3	2
6	9	1	3	2	4	5	7	8
2	8	7	1	9	5	3	4	6
3	5	4	6	8	7	1	2	9

PUZZLE / **472**

1	9	6	8	3	4	2	7	5
2	8	7	6	9	5	3	1	4
5	3	4	1	7	2	8	6	9
6	2	9	3	5	8	7	4	1
8	1	5	2	4	7	6	9	3
7	4	3	9	6	1	5	8	2
3	6	1	5	8	9	4	2	7
4	5	2	7	1	6	9	3	8
9	7	8	4	2	3	1	5	6

PUZZLE / **473**

9	8	7	2	1	3	6	4	5
1	5	4	9	7	6	8	2	3
2	6	3	5	4	8	9	1	7
4	3	6	7	2	5	1	8	9
5	9	2	4	8	1	3	7	6
7	1	8	3	6	9	2	5	4
8	2	5	6	3	7	4	9	1
3	7	1	8	9	4	5	6	2
6	4	9	1	5	2	7	3	8

PUZZLE / **474**

6	9	4	3	7	5	1	8	2
5	3	2	9	1	8	6	7	4
8	1	7	6	4	2	9	3	5
9	7	8	5	6	4	3	2	1
4	5	6	2	3	1	8	9	7
1	2	3	8	9	7	5	4	6
3	6	1	4	2	9	7	5	8
2	8	9	7	5	6	4	1	3
7	4	5	1	8	3	2	6	9

PUZZLE / **475**

8	4	9	6	3	2	7	1	5
5	1	2	8	9	7	6	3	4
6	3	7	1	4	5	2	8	9
2	9	8	5	1	6	3	4	7
4	6	5	3	7	9	1	2	8
1	7	3	2	8	4	5	9	6
9	8	1	7	5	3	4	6	2
7	2	4	9	6	1	8	5	3
3	5	6	4	2	8	9	7	1

PUZZLE / **476**

4	2	7	1	6	9	3	5	8
9	1	3	5	8	2	7	6	4
6	8	5	3	7	4	2	9	1
5	4	8	2	9	6	1	7	3
3	6	1	7	4	5	8	2	9
2	7	9	8	1	3	6	4	5
8	9	2	4	3	7	5	1	6
7	3	6	9	5	1	4	8	2
1	5	4	6	2	8	9	3	7

PUZZLE / **477**

8	6	5	4	7	1	9	2	3
1	4	3	9	6	2	5	7	8
9	7	2	3	8	5	6	1	4
7	8	1	2	9	4	3	5	6
6	2	4	7	5	3	1	8	9
5	3	9	6	1	8	2	4	7
4	1	8	5	3	6	7	9	2
2	9	6	1	4	7	8	3	5
3	5	7	8	2	9	4	6	1

PUZZLE / **478**

7	6	3	5	8	4	2	9	1
9	4	2	3	6	1	7	5	8
8	1	5	2	9	7	4	6	3
2	8	6	7	3	9	1	4	5
1	5	7	4	2	8	6	3	9
3	9	4	1	5	6	8	2	7
5	7	9	6	1	2	3	8	4
6	3	1	8	4	5	9	7	2
4	2	8	9	7	3	5	1	6

PUZZLE / **479**

1	8	3	5	7	4	9	6	2
7	4	9	2	1	6	3	8	5
5	2	6	9	3	8	4	1	7
2	6	1	8	4	5	7	3	9
8	7	4	1	9	3	2	5	6
3	9	5	7	6	2	8	4	1
9	5	8	4	2	1	6	7	3
6	1	7	3	8	9	5	2	4
4	3	2	6	5	7	1	9	8

PUZZLE / **480**

7	5	1	6	8	2	3	9	4
9	2	6	1	3	4	8	7	5
4	3	8	7	9	5	6	2	1
6	1	3	4	7	8	2	5	9
8	7	4	2	5	9	1	6	3
2	9	5	3	6	1	4	8	7
1	6	7	5	2	3	9	4	8
5	4	9	8	1	6	7	3	2
3	8	2	9	4	7	5	1	6

PUZZLE / **481**

6	3	7	1	8	4	5	2	9
9	8	1	2	3	5	6	7	4
2	4	5	6	9	7	3	8	1
1	7	8	4	5	3	9	6	2
5	9	2	8	6	1	4	3	7
4	6	3	9	7	2	1	5	8
7	5	9	3	1	8	2	4	6
8	2	6	5	4	9	7	1	3
3	1	4	7	2	6	8	9	5

PUZZLE / **482**

3	7	6	2	4	8	9	5	1
8	2	5	9	1	6	3	4	7
4	9	1	3	7	5	2	8	6
9	5	3	1	8	2	7	6	4
7	8	2	6	3	4	5	1	9
1	6	4	7	5	9	8	3	2
2	4	8	5	6	7	1	9	3
5	3	7	4	9	1	6	2	8
6	1	9	8	2	3	4	7	5

PUZZLE / **483**

6	8	5	1	4	7	3	2	9
7	3	2	9	5	6	1	8	4
4	9	1	2	3	8	7	6	5
5	2	4	6	1	9	8	3	7
8	7	9	4	2	3	5	1	6
3	1	6	8	7	5	4	9	2
1	6	8	5	9	4	2	7	3
9	5	3	7	8	2	6	4	1
2	4	7	3	6	1	9	5	8

PUZZLE / **484**

4	3	1	8	9	7	2	5	6
8	9	6	5	2	4	1	7	3
2	7	5	3	6	1	4	8	9
6	4	2	1	7	5	3	9	8
9	5	3	4	8	2	7	6	1
7	1	8	6	3	9	5	2	4
1	6	7	9	5	3	8	4	2
3	2	9	7	4	8	6	1	5
5	8	4	2	1	6	9	3	7

PUZZLE / **485**

6	7	8	1	5	3	9	2	4
5	4	2	8	9	7	1	3	6
9	3	1	6	2	4	7	5	8
7	1	9	5	8	2	4	6	3
2	8	3	9	4	6	5	1	7
4	6	5	7	3	1	8	9	2
1	5	7	2	6	8	3	4	9
3	9	6	4	7	5	2	8	1
8	2	4	3	1	9	6	7	5

PUZZLE / **486**

8	3	1	4	2	9	5	7	6
6	2	7	3	5	1	9	4	8
4	5	9	6	7	8	3	1	2
1	8	4	9	3	6	2	5	7
9	7	5	2	1	4	8	6	3
2	6	3	5	8	7	1	9	4
7	9	8	1	6	3	4	2	5
5	1	6	8	4	2	7	3	9
3	4	2	7	9	5	6	8	1

PUZZLE / **487**

3	7	1	2	6	8	9	5	4
8	4	2	1	9	5	6	3	7
5	6	9	3	4	7	2	8	1
2	5	6	8	3	1	4	7	9
9	1	7	6	5	4	3	2	8
4	3	8	9	7	2	5	1	6
6	2	4	7	1	3	8	9	5
1	8	5	4	2	9	7	6	3
7	9	3	5	8	6	1	4	2

PUZZLE / **488**

9	3	8	2	5	6	7	4	1
5	6	4	1	8	7	2	9	3
1	7	2	3	4	9	8	5	6
6	8	1	9	3	4	5	7	2
2	4	9	6	7	5	1	3	8
3	5	7	8	2	1	9	6	4
8	1	5	7	6	3	4	2	9
4	9	6	5	1	2	3	8	7
7	2	3	4	9	8	6	1	5

PUZZLE / **489**

8	7	9	2	6	1	3	4	5
4	5	1	9	3	8	7	2	6
6	2	3	5	4	7	9	8	1
3	8	6	7	2	5	4	1	9
1	4	5	8	9	3	6	7	2
7	9	2	6	1	4	5	3	8
5	3	8	1	7	6	2	9	4
9	6	4	3	8	2	1	5	7
2	1	7	4	5	9	8	6	3

PUZZLE / 490

3	7	2	8	6	5	4	1	9
4	9	1	2	3	7	6	8	5
5	6	8	4	1	9	7	2	3
2	1	7	9	8	3	5	4	6
6	3	4	7	5	1	2	9	8
9	8	5	6	4	2	3	7	1
7	5	9	1	2	6	8	3	4
1	4	6	3	7	8	9	5	2
8	2	3	5	9	4	1	6	7

PUZZLE / 491

3	5	1	8	6	9	7	2	4
8	7	2	1	3	4	6	5	9
9	4	6	2	7	5	3	1	8
7	1	8	6	4	2	5	9	3
2	3	4	9	5	7	1	8	6
6	9	5	3	8	1	2	4	7
5	6	9	7	2	8	4	3	1
1	2	3	4	9	6	8	7	5
4	8	7	5	1	3	9	6	2

PUZZLE / 492

2	6	8	7	5	1	4	9	3
9	7	3	4	6	2	5	1	8
4	1	5	8	3	9	7	6	2
3	9	7	1	4	6	8	2	5
1	2	4	9	8	5	6	3	7
5	8	6	2	7	3	9	4	1
6	4	2	5	1	7	3	8	9
7	3	9	6	2	8	1	5	4
8	5	1	3	9	4	2	7	6

PUZZLE / 493

3	7	5	4	9	1	2	6	8
2	8	1	6	7	5	4	3	9
9	4	6	8	2	3	7	5	1
6	5	3	1	8	7	9	2	4
7	2	9	3	5	4	8	1	6
4	1	8	9	6	2	5	7	3
1	9	2	7	4	6	3	8	5
5	3	4	2	1	8	6	9	7
8	6	7	5	3	9	1	4	2

PUZZLE / 494

1	4	6	9	7	5	3	8	2
7	9	8	2	3	4	1	5	6
5	2	3	1	8	6	7	4	9
4	3	1	5	2	9	6	7	8
8	7	5	4	6	3	9	2	1
9	6	2	8	1	7	5	3	4
3	8	4	6	5	1	2	9	7
2	1	7	3	9	8	4	6	5
6	5	9	7	4	2	8	1	3

PUZZLE / 495

5	8	7	2	6	9	3	1	4
9	3	1	8	7	4	2	6	5
2	4	6	1	3	5	7	9	8
3	5	4	9	8	7	6	2	1
7	1	2	6	5	3	4	8	9
6	9	8	4	2	1	5	7	3
8	7	9	3	4	2	1	5	6
1	2	3	5	9	6	8	4	7
4	6	5	7	1	8	9	3	2

PUZZLE / 496

6	9	3	4	2	8	7	5	1
1	2	4	9	5	7	3	8	6
8	7	5	3	6	1	2	4	9
5	1	8	7	4	3	9	6	2
7	6	9	2	1	5	4	3	8
3	4	2	8	9	6	5	1	7
4	3	1	6	7	2	8	9	5
9	5	7	1	8	4	6	2	3
2	8	6	5	3	9	1	7	4

PUZZLE / 497

3	9	8	5	1	2	4	6	7
7	4	1	8	9	6	2	3	5
6	2	5	4	3	7	8	1	9
8	3	2	6	7	4	5	9	1
9	6	7	1	5	8	3	2	4
5	1	4	9	2	3	6	7	8
4	7	9	2	6	5	1	8	3
1	8	6	3	4	9	7	5	2
2	5	3	7	8	1	9	4	6

PUZZLE / 498

4	1	2	5	8	9	7	6	3
5	7	3	6	4	2	1	8	9
6	9	8	1	7	3	2	4	5
3	4	9	8	1	6	5	2	7
7	8	1	4	2	5	9	3	6
2	5	6	9	3	7	8	1	4
8	6	4	7	9	1	3	5	2
1	3	7	2	5	4	6	9	8
9	2	5	3	6	8	4	7	1

PUZZLE / 499

2	4	1	3	6	9	7	8	5
3	7	6	1	5	8	9	4	2
5	9	8	7	4	2	3	6	1
1	5	7	9	3	4	6	2	8
4	8	2	6	7	5	1	9	3
9	6	3	2	8	1	5	7	4
8	1	4	5	9	6	2	3	7
6	3	5	4	2	7	8	1	9
7	2	9	8	1	3	4	5	6

PUZZLE / 500

7	1	4	2	9	8	6	5	3
6	9	2	3	4	5	1	7	8
8	5	3	6	7	1	2	4	9
1	8	7	5	6	3	9	2	4
4	2	9	8	1	7	3	6	5
5	3	6	9	2	4	7	8	1
9	6	5	1	8	2	4	3	7
2	4	8	7	3	9	5	1	6
3	7	1	4	5	6	8	9	2

PUZZLE / 501

4	7	2	8	6	1	5	3	9
1	3	6	9	5	4	7	2	8
8	9	5	7	3	2	1	4	6
9	6	1	2	4	8	3	7	5
3	2	8	5	9	7	6	1	4
7	5	4	6	1	3	8	9	2
5	4	9	3	7	6	2	8	1
6	8	3	1	2	9	4	5	7
2	1	7	4	8	5	9	6	3

PUZZLE / 502

3	7	8	9	5	6	4	1	2
2	5	6	8	4	1	9	7	3
9	4	1	7	3	2	5	6	8
6	1	7	5	2	8	3	9	4
5	9	4	3	1	7	8	2	6
8	2	3	4	6	9	1	5	7
4	3	2	1	7	5	6	8	9
1	6	9	2	8	4	7	3	5
7	8	5	6	9	3	2	4	1

PUZZLE / 503

5	3	8	6	1	4	7	2	9
1	6	9	8	2	7	3	4	5
7	2	4	5	9	3	8	6	1
9	1	5	3	8	6	4	7	2
3	8	7	2	4	9	5	1	6
2	4	6	1	7	5	9	8	3
4	5	2	9	6	8	1	3	7
8	9	1	7	3	2	6	5	4
6	7	3	4	5	1	2	9	8

PUZZLE / 504

8	1	7	5	6	3	2	4	9
2	3	5	4	9	7	8	1	6
4	6	9	2	8	1	3	5	7
6	5	2	3	1	9	4	7	8
1	7	8	6	5	4	9	3	2
9	4	3	8	7	2	5	6	1
5	2	1	7	4	8	6	9	3
3	9	4	1	2	6	7	8	5
7	8	6	9	3	5	1	2	4

PUZZLE / 505

7	8	6	9	5	1	3	2	4
5	3	4	8	6	2	7	1	9
2	1	9	4	3	7	6	5	8
8	9	2	5	4	6	1	7	3
1	7	5	3	2	8	4	9	6
6	4	3	7	1	9	5	8	2
3	2	7	6	8	5	9	4	1
4	5	8	1	9	3	2	6	7
9	6	1	2	7	4	8	3	5

PUZZLE / 506

3	4	2	5	9	6	7	1	8
6	8	5	2	1	7	4	9	3
1	7	9	8	4	3	2	6	5
8	6	4	9	2	5	3	7	1
5	3	1	7	8	4	9	2	6
2	9	7	6	3	1	5	8	4
4	2	3	1	7	8	6	5	9
9	5	8	4	6	2	1	3	7
7	1	6	3	5	9	8	4	2

PUZZLE / 507

8	9	3	6	4	7	1	2	5
1	4	5	2	8	9	6	3	7
6	2	7	3	5	1	9	4	8
3	7	6	1	9	4	8	5	2
9	5	4	8	7	2	3	6	1
2	8	1	5	3	6	7	9	4
5	3	9	4	1	8	2	7	6
4	6	8	7	2	3	5	1	9
7	1	2	9	6	5	4	8	3

PUZZLE / 508

8	9	7	2	1	6	3	5	4
3	5	6	4	9	8	2	1	7
2	1	4	5	7	3	6	9	8
4	6	9	3	8	1	5	7	2
5	8	1	9	2	7	4	3	6
7	3	2	6	5	4	9	8	1
9	4	8	7	6	5	1	2	3
6	7	5	1	3	2	8	4	9
1	2	3	8	4	9	7	6	5

PUZZLE / 509

4	1	9	3	8	7	6	5	2
6	5	7	4	2	1	9	8	3
8	2	3	6	9	5	1	7	4
7	4	1	5	6	2	3	9	8
3	9	2	1	7	8	4	6	5
5	8	6	9	3	4	2	1	7
9	6	8	2	5	3	7	4	1
1	3	5	7	4	9	8	2	6
2	7	4	8	1	6	5	3	9

PUZZLE / 510

1	9	3	5	8	4	2	7	6
5	2	7	6	9	1	3	4	8
4	6	8	3	2	7	1	5	9
7	3	4	2	5	6	9	8	1
6	8	9	1	4	3	5	2	7
2	1	5	9	7	8	6	3	4
8	5	2	4	1	9	7	6	3
9	7	6	8	3	2	4	1	5
3	4	1	7	6	5	8	9	2

PUZZLE / 511

4	7	9	5	3	2	1	6	8
5	1	8	7	6	9	4	3	2
2	6	3	1	4	8	5	9	7
1	3	5	9	8	7	2	4	6
7	8	2	6	5	4	3	1	9
6	9	4	3	2	1	7	8	5
8	4	1	2	9	5	6	7	3
9	5	6	4	7	3	8	2	1
3	2	7	8	1	6	9	5	4

PUZZLE / 512

4	6	2	3	9	8	1	7	5
5	3	7	1	4	2	9	6	8
9	8	1	6	5	7	2	4	3
3	1	9	5	6	4	8	2	7
7	2	5	8	3	9	6	1	4
6	4	8	2	7	1	5	3	9
1	9	4	7	2	5	3	8	6
2	5	6	4	8	3	7	9	1
8	7	3	9	1	6	4	5	2

PUZZLE / 513

2	9	3	8	5	4	7	1	6
1	6	4	3	2	7	9	5	8
5	8	7	6	9	1	4	3	2
6	2	1	5	7	3	8	4	9
9	4	5	2	6	8	1	7	3
7	3	8	1	4	9	6	2	5
3	5	9	7	1	6	2	8	4
8	1	6	4	3	2	5	9	7
4	7	2	9	8	5	3	6	1

PUZZLE / 514

4	7	6	5	9	8	2	1	3
5	8	1	3	4	2	9	7	6
2	3	9	6	1	7	5	4	8
8	9	4	1	2	3	6	5	7
7	2	3	4	5	6	8	9	1
6	1	5	7	8	9	4	3	2
9	4	7	8	6	1	3	2	5
3	5	8	2	7	4	1	6	9
1	6	2	9	3	5	7	8	4

PUZZLE / 515

8	4	7	3	1	9	2	5	6
5	9	1	6	4	2	7	3	8
2	6	3	7	8	5	4	1	9
7	5	2	8	9	6	3	4	1
6	1	8	4	2	3	9	7	5
4	3	9	5	7	1	6	8	2
3	8	6	2	5	4	1	9	7
1	2	5	9	3	7	8	6	4
9	7	4	1	6	8	5	2	3

PUZZLE / 516

4	1	7	2	8	3	6	5	9
8	9	6	5	4	1	2	3	7
2	3	5	7	6	9	4	8	1
6	7	2	9	3	4	5	1	8
9	5	1	6	2	8	3	7	4
3	8	4	1	5	7	9	2	6
5	4	8	3	7	6	1	9	2
1	6	3	8	9	2	7	4	5
7	2	9	4	1	5	8	6	3

PUZZLE / 517

8	3	4	5	7	2	6	9	1
9	7	2	1	3	6	5	8	4
6	5	1	4	8	9	2	3	7
1	2	5	9	4	7	3	6	8
7	4	8	3	6	5	9	1	2
3	6	9	8	2	1	7	4	5
5	9	3	2	1	4	8	7	6
2	1	7	6	9	8	4	5	3
4	8	6	7	5	3	1	2	9

PUZZLE / 518

6	4	1	2	3	9	8	5	7
7	8	9	4	1	5	3	6	2
5	3	2	6	7	8	1	4	9
8	5	3	7	9	4	6	2	1
4	2	6	1	5	3	7	9	8
1	9	7	8	6	2	4	3	5
2	6	5	3	8	7	9	1	4
9	1	8	5	4	6	2	7	3
3	7	4	9	2	1	5	8	6

PUZZLE / 519

7	8	5	1	4	3	6	9	2
4	3	6	2	7	9	1	8	5
9	1	2	5	8	6	3	4	7
3	4	8	7	6	5	2	1	9
1	6	9	8	3	2	7	5	4
5	2	7	4	9	1	8	3	6
6	7	4	3	5	8	9	2	1
2	9	3	6	1	4	5	7	8
8	5	1	9	2	7	4	6	3

PUZZLE / 520

5	1	3	7	4	2	8	6	9
4	8	9	5	1	6	2	3	7
6	2	7	9	3	8	4	1	5
1	4	5	2	9	7	6	8	3
9	3	6	8	5	1	7	4	2
8	7	2	4	6	3	5	9	1
2	6	1	3	7	4	9	5	8
7	9	4	1	8	5	3	2	6
3	5	8	6	2	9	1	7	4

PUZZLE / 521

8	2	9	7	5	6	4	3	1
4	5	7	3	2	1	9	6	8
3	1	6	9	4	8	5	2	7
5	7	1	4	3	2	6	8	9
2	6	4	8	9	5	1	7	3
9	3	8	1	6	7	2	5	4
1	9	2	6	7	3	8	4	5
6	8	3	5	1	4	7	9	2
7	4	5	2	8	9	3	1	6

PUZZLE / 522

8	5	1	7	3	4	2	6	9
2	4	7	1	9	6	5	3	8
9	3	6	5	8	2	4	1	7
4	2	8	3	5	9	1	7	6
3	1	9	2	6	7	8	5	4
6	7	5	4	1	8	3	9	2
5	6	2	9	4	1	7	8	3
1	9	4	8	7	3	6	2	5
7	8	3	6	2	5	9	4	1

PUZZLE / 523

1	6	7	2	5	9	3	4	8
3	5	8	1	6	4	7	2	9
2	9	4	3	8	7	5	1	6
8	2	3	5	7	1	9	6	4
5	4	6	9	2	8	1	3	7
7	1	9	4	3	6	8	5	2
6	8	1	7	4	3	2	9	5
4	3	5	8	9	2	6	7	1
9	7	2	6	1	5	4	8	3

PUZZLE / 524

6	5	4	2	3	7	9	1	8
9	1	3	8	6	5	2	7	4
7	8	2	9	4	1	5	3	6
2	3	1	7	5	6	4	8	9
8	4	9	3	1	2	6	5	7
5	7	6	4	8	9	1	2	3
1	9	5	6	7	3	8	4	2
3	6	8	5	2	4	7	9	1
4	2	7	1	9	8	3	6	5

PUZZLE / 525

2	5	3	7	1	9	6	4	8
1	7	6	8	4	2	5	3	9
8	4	9	6	3	5	1	2	7
5	6	4	1	9	7	3	8	2
7	2	8	4	6	3	9	5	1
9	3	1	5	2	8	4	7	6
6	8	7	3	5	1	2	9	4
3	1	2	9	8	4	7	6	5
4	9	5	2	7	6	8	1	3

PUZZLE / 526

3	4	1	6	9	5	7	2	8
5	6	8	2	3	7	4	1	9
7	9	2	8	4	1	6	3	5
4	8	3	5	7	6	1	9	2
2	1	6	9	8	4	3	5	7
9	7	5	3	1	2	8	4	6
1	3	9	7	5	8	2	6	4
6	5	7	4	2	3	9	8	1
8	2	4	1	6	9	5	7	3

PUZZLE / 527

5	1	8	6	9	2	4	3	7
3	7	9	4	1	5	8	6	2
4	6	2	7	8	3	1	9	5
7	8	1	9	4	6	5	2	3
6	4	5	2	3	1	9	7	8
2	9	3	8	5	7	6	1	4
9	5	6	3	2	4	7	8	1
1	3	7	5	6	8	2	4	9
8	2	4	1	7	9	3	5	6

PUZZLE / 528

8	5	1	6	4	2	9	7	3
3	2	6	1	9	7	5	8	4
9	7	4	8	5	3	1	2	6
1	8	5	7	3	4	2	6	9
7	3	2	9	6	5	4	1	8
6	4	9	2	8	1	3	5	7
5	9	7	3	1	6	8	4	2
4	6	8	5	2	9	7	3	1
2	1	3	4	7	8	6	9	5

PUZZLE / 529

6	3	7	1	8	4	2	9	5
9	8	5	3	2	7	6	4	1
4	1	2	6	9	5	8	7	3
3	7	4	8	1	2	9	5	6
1	5	9	4	7	6	3	2	8
8	2	6	9	5	3	7	1	4
5	6	1	7	3	9	4	8	2
7	4	8	2	6	1	5	3	9
2	9	3	5	4	8	1	6	7

PUZZLE / 530

4	3	1	8	2	9	5	6	7
5	9	2	7	3	6	4	1	8
7	8	6	1	5	4	2	3	9
3	6	4	2	9	7	1	8	5
9	1	7	3	8	5	6	4	2
8	2	5	4	6	1	7	9	3
6	4	3	5	7	8	9	2	1
1	5	8	9	4	2	3	7	6
2	7	9	6	1	3	8	5	4

PUZZLE / 531

7	3	8	2	5	1	4	6	9
9	1	6	7	8	4	3	5	2
4	5	2	3	9	6	8	1	7
6	8	9	1	7	5	2	4	3
5	4	3	6	2	8	7	9	1
1	2	7	9	4	3	5	8	6
2	6	5	8	3	9	1	7	4
8	7	1	4	6	2	9	3	5
3	9	4	5	1	7	6	2	8

PUZZLE / 532

4	2	6	8	1	3	7	9	5
9	5	3	7	6	4	2	8	1
7	1	8	2	9	5	4	6	3
5	8	7	4	3	9	6	1	2
2	6	4	1	7	8	5	3	9
3	9	1	5	2	6	8	7	4
6	4	9	3	8	2	1	5	7
1	3	5	6	4	7	9	2	8
8	7	2	9	5	1	3	4	6

PUZZLE / 533

9	5	7	3	6	4	1	2	8
8	3	4	2	9	1	6	7	5
6	1	2	8	7	5	3	9	4
1	7	9	4	8	2	5	6	3
2	6	8	5	3	9	4	1	7
5	4	3	7	1	6	2	8	9
4	8	5	1	2	7	9	3	6
7	2	6	9	5	3	8	4	1
3	9	1	6	4	8	7	5	2

PUZZLE / 534

8	7	9	2	3	5	6	1	4
5	3	2	1	6	4	9	8	7
1	6	4	9	7	8	2	3	5
9	1	3	4	8	2	7	5	6
2	8	6	3	5	7	1	4	9
4	5	7	6	1	9	3	2	8
6	2	5	7	4	1	8	9	3
3	4	1	8	9	6	5	7	2
7	9	8	5	2	3	4	6	1

PUZZLE / 535

2	1	5	4	3	6	8	7	9
7	3	4	9	8	2	5	1	6
6	9	8	1	5	7	4	3	2
9	5	2	8	1	4	3	6	7
1	4	7	3	6	5	9	2	8
8	6	3	2	7	9	1	4	5
3	7	9	6	4	8	2	5	1
4	2	6	5	9	1	7	8	3
5	8	1	7	2	3	6	9	4

PUZZLE / 536

3	9	2	6	8	4	1	5	7
4	7	6	5	9	1	2	8	3
1	8	5	2	3	7	4	9	6
8	1	4	7	6	3	9	2	5
9	2	3	4	5	8	7	6	1
5	6	7	1	2	9	3	4	8
2	4	1	8	7	5	6	3	9
6	3	8	9	1	2	5	7	4
7	5	9	3	4	6	8	1	2

PUZZLE / 537

1	4	8	7	3	9	2	5	6
5	6	2	8	4	1	7	9	3
9	7	3	5	2	6	4	1	8
3	2	5	4	6	7	1	8	9
4	1	7	9	5	8	3	6	2
8	9	6	3	1	2	5	7	4
6	3	4	1	9	5	8	2	7
2	8	1	6	7	4	9	3	5
7	5	9	2	8	3	6	4	1

PUZZLE / 538

9	2	5	1	6	8	7	3	4
8	1	3	9	7	4	6	5	2
6	7	4	5	2	3	9	8	1
4	9	2	6	8	7	5	1	3
3	5	7	2	9	1	4	6	8
1	6	8	4	3	5	2	7	9
5	8	1	7	4	9	3	2	6
2	3	9	8	5	6	1	4	7
7	4	6	3	1	2	8	9	5

PUZZLE / 539

7	9	4	8	6	5	3	2	1
8	3	5	1	2	7	9	6	4
1	2	6	4	3	9	7	8	5
4	8	2	3	9	1	5	7	6
6	5	3	7	8	2	1	4	9
9	1	7	6	5	4	8	3	2
5	7	1	2	4	3	6	9	8
2	6	9	5	7	8	4	1	3
3	4	8	9	1	6	2	5	7

PUZZLE / 540

9	3	5	7	8	1	6	2	4
7	2	6	5	4	3	9	1	8
8	4	1	2	9	6	5	3	7
1	6	2	4	7	8	3	9	5
5	8	7	1	3	9	2	4	6
3	9	4	6	2	5	8	7	1
2	1	8	9	5	4	7	6	3
4	5	9	3	6	7	1	8	2
6	7	3	8	1	2	4	5	9

PUZZLE / 541

1	8	4	2	3	6	5	9	7
5	3	2	7	8	9	1	6	4
9	7	6	5	4	1	8	3	2
8	6	5	1	9	4	2	7	3
7	2	3	8	6	5	4	1	9
4	1	9	3	7	2	6	8	5
3	4	7	6	2	8	9	5	1
6	9	1	4	5	3	7	2	8
2	5	8	9	1	7	3	4	6

PUZZLE / 542

1	7	4	9	3	6	5	8	2
6	8	2	5	7	1	9	3	4
5	9	3	8	2	4	1	7	6
9	3	5	7	8	2	6	4	1
2	1	8	6	4	5	3	9	7
7	4	6	1	9	3	2	5	8
3	6	1	4	5	8	7	2	9
8	5	9	2	6	7	4	1	3
4	2	7	3	1	9	8	6	5

PUZZLE / 543

8	9	1	4	3	6	2	7	5
5	2	6	1	9	7	8	3	4
7	3	4	2	8	5	6	9	1
1	5	2	3	7	8	4	6	9
3	6	7	9	1	4	5	2	8
4	8	9	6	5	2	3	1	7
9	4	5	7	2	3	1	8	6
6	1	3	8	4	9	7	5	2
2	7	8	5	6	1	9	4	3

PUZZLE / 544

5	3	9	4	7	6	8	2	1
6	1	8	3	9	2	7	4	5
2	7	4	5	1	8	6	3	9
4	5	1	9	6	3	2	8	7
9	2	7	1	8	4	5	6	3
8	6	3	7	2	5	9	1	4
1	9	6	8	3	7	4	5	2
3	4	2	6	5	9	1	7	8
7	8	5	2	4	1	3	9	6

PUZZLE / 545

9	1	8	2	7	3	6	4	5
6	7	2	5	1	4	3	8	9
5	4	3	6	8	9	1	7	2
2	6	9	7	5	1	8	3	4
1	5	4	3	6	8	9	2	7
3	8	7	9	4	2	5	6	1
4	2	6	8	9	5	7	1	3
8	3	5	1	2	7	4	9	6
7	9	1	4	3	6	2	5	8

PUZZLE / 546

6	2	5	4	8	1	3	9	7
3	7	8	2	9	6	4	1	5
4	9	1	7	5	3	6	8	2
2	3	7	9	6	8	5	4	1
1	6	9	5	2	4	7	3	8
8	5	4	3	1	7	2	6	9
5	8	2	6	3	9	1	7	4
7	1	3	8	4	5	9	2	6
9	4	6	1	7	2	8	5	3

PUZZLE / 547

2	3	1	9	5	6	8	4	7
9	7	8	2	4	3	5	6	1
4	5	6	7	8	1	2	9	3
3	2	7	4	1	9	6	5	8
6	8	5	3	2	7	9	1	4
1	9	4	8	6	5	7	3	2
8	6	2	5	3	4	1	7	9
7	1	3	6	9	8	4	2	5
5	4	9	1	7	2	3	8	6

PUZZLE / 548

9	3	8	5	2	7	1	6	4
2	6	1	3	4	9	5	7	8
4	7	5	6	1	8	2	9	3
1	8	2	4	7	3	9	5	6
3	5	4	2	9	6	7	8	1
7	9	6	1	8	5	4	3	2
8	1	3	7	5	2	6	4	9
6	4	7	9	3	1	8	2	5
5	2	9	8	6	4	3	1	7

PUZZLE / 549

6	8	2	4	1	9	3	5	7
5	4	1	2	3	7	6	8	9
3	9	7	6	5	8	4	1	2
1	3	6	8	2	5	9	7	4
8	2	5	7	9	4	1	6	3
4	7	9	3	6	1	5	2	8
2	6	8	1	4	3	7	9	5
9	1	4	5	7	2	8	3	6
7	5	3	9	8	6	2	4	1

PUZZLE / 550

9	5	7	6	3	4	1	8	2
6	2	1	9	5	8	4	7	3
4	3	8	2	1	7	9	6	5
1	9	6	7	8	3	5	2	4
3	7	4	1	2	5	6	9	8
2	8	5	4	9	6	3	1	7
5	1	3	8	7	9	2	4	6
8	6	2	3	4	1	7	5	9
7	4	9	5	6	2	8	3	1

PUZZLE / 551

1	8	9	3	6	5	4	7	2
6	7	2	4	1	9	8	3	5
3	5	4	7	2	8	1	9	6
2	4	8	6	5	7	3	1	9
5	6	7	1	9	3	2	4	8
9	3	1	2	8	4	5	6	7
4	9	3	5	7	2	6	8	1
8	1	5	9	3	6	7	2	4
7	2	6	8	4	1	9	5	3

PUZZLE / 552

1	6	8	2	7	5	4	9	3
2	5	7	3	9	4	1	6	8
9	3	4	1	8	6	2	5	7
5	9	1	6	4	7	8	3	2
4	2	3	8	5	1	9	7	6
7	8	6	9	3	2	5	1	4
8	1	5	4	6	3	7	2	9
3	4	2	7	1	9	6	8	5
6	7	9	5	2	8	3	4	1

PUZZLE / 553

8	4	9	3	7	6	2	1	5
7	2	5	9	1	8	4	3	6
1	3	6	4	5	2	8	7	9
3	6	2	8	4	9	1	5	7
9	1	4	5	2	7	6	8	3
5	8	7	1	6	3	9	4	2
6	7	1	2	8	5	3	9	4
2	9	8	7	3	4	5	6	1
4	5	3	6	9	1	7	2	8

PUZZLE / 554

8	1	5	2	9	3	6	4	7
9	4	7	1	6	8	2	5	3
2	6	3	5	4	7	8	1	9
4	8	9	7	1	5	3	6	2
3	2	6	9	8	4	1	7	5
5	7	1	6	3	2	4	9	8
7	9	4	8	2	6	5	3	1
1	3	8	4	5	9	7	2	6
6	5	2	3	7	1	9	8	4

PUZZLE / 555

4	3	9	1	7	6	5	2	8
5	6	2	9	4	8	1	7	3
1	7	8	2	5	3	6	9	4
2	8	5	4	6	1	7	3	9
3	9	6	7	8	5	4	1	2
7	1	4	3	2	9	8	6	5
8	5	7	6	9	2	3	4	1
9	4	3	8	1	7	2	5	6
6	2	1	5	3	4	9	8	7

PUZZLE / 556

8	1	9	5	2	7	6	3	4
4	6	7	8	3	1	2	5	9
2	5	3	9	4	6	7	1	8
7	8	6	2	5	9	3	4	1
1	9	4	6	7	3	5	8	2
5	3	2	1	8	4	9	7	6
9	2	5	7	1	8	4	6	3
3	7	1	4	6	2	8	9	5
6	4	8	3	9	5	1	2	7

PUZZLE / 557

9	5	8	1	7	6	2	4	3
6	4	2	5	8	3	9	7	1
7	3	1	4	2	9	8	6	5
1	2	5	9	6	7	3	8	4
8	6	4	2	3	1	5	9	7
3	9	7	8	5	4	1	2	6
4	7	9	3	1	2	6	5	8
5	1	6	7	9	8	4	3	2
2	8	3	6	4	5	7	1	9

PUZZLE / 558

4	8	1	7	6	3	5	2	9
2	6	3	9	4	5	1	7	8
9	5	7	2	8	1	6	4	3
1	2	8	5	9	6	7	3	4
5	7	9	3	1	4	8	6	2
6	3	4	8	2	7	9	1	5
3	9	2	1	7	8	4	5	6
8	1	6	4	5	2	3	9	7
7	4	5	6	3	9	2	8	1

PUZZLE / 559

9	8	2	7	4	5	1	3	6
5	4	7	1	3	6	9	8	2
1	3	6	2	8	9	4	5	7
2	1	5	4	6	3	8	7	9
4	7	9	5	2	8	3	6	1
3	6	8	9	7	1	2	4	5
6	9	1	3	5	4	7	2	8
7	5	3	8	1	2	6	9	4
8	2	4	6	9	7	5	1	3

PUZZLE / 560

2	5	4	6	3	8	9	1	7
6	9	7	5	1	4	2	3	8
3	8	1	7	2	9	4	6	5
4	6	5	8	9	7	1	2	3
7	2	3	1	5	6	8	9	4
8	1	9	2	4	3	5	7	6
5	7	6	9	8	1	3	4	2
1	4	2	3	7	5	6	8	9
9	3	8	4	6	2	7	5	1

PUZZLE / 561

7	8	6	3	2	1	9	5	4
5	4	9	6	7	8	3	1	2
1	2	3	9	5	4	7	8	6
6	3	1	4	8	2	5	7	9
4	9	2	7	3	5	8	6	1
8	5	7	1	9	6	2	4	3
9	7	4	8	6	3	1	2	5
2	6	8	5	1	9	4	3	7
3	1	5	2	4	7	6	9	8

PUZZLE / 562

7	1	2	3	9	6	5	8	4
5	8	9	2	7	4	3	1	6
6	4	3	5	8	1	7	2	9
3	2	4	7	6	9	1	5	8
1	5	8	4	2	3	9	6	7
9	6	7	1	5	8	2	4	3
8	7	5	6	3	2	4	9	1
4	3	6	9	1	5	8	7	2
2	9	1	8	4	7	6	3	5

PUZZLE / 563

8	9	5	1	3	7	4	2	6
4	1	6	5	9	2	7	3	8
3	2	7	4	8	6	9	5	1
2	7	3	6	4	9	8	1	5
5	4	1	7	2	8	6	9	3
6	8	9	3	5	1	2	7	4
7	6	4	9	1	3	5	8	2
1	5	8	2	7	4	3	6	9
9	3	2	8	6	5	1	4	7

PUZZLE / 564

7	9	4	6	3	8	5	1	2
6	5	1	2	7	9	4	3	8
2	8	3	5	4	1	6	7	9
8	2	6	3	9	4	7	5	1
5	1	7	8	2	6	9	4	3
4	3	9	7	1	5	8	2	6
1	6	2	4	8	7	3	9	5
9	7	8	1	5	3	2	6	4
3	4	5	9	6	2	1	8	7

PUZZLE / 565

9	2	5	8	4	7	1	3	6
8	6	3	1	5	9	2	7	4
7	1	4	6	3	2	5	9	8
6	3	9	5	7	4	8	1	2
5	8	1	2	6	3	7	4	9
4	7	2	9	1	8	3	6	5
3	5	7	4	8	6	9	2	1
2	4	8	3	9	1	6	5	7
1	9	6	7	2	5	4	8	3

PUZZLE / 566

4	8	6	3	1	2	7	5	9
1	7	2	9	8	5	6	3	4
3	9	5	6	4	7	8	1	2
6	1	9	7	3	4	2	8	5
2	4	3	8	5	1	9	7	6
7	5	8	2	6	9	1	4	3
8	6	1	5	2	3	4	9	7
9	3	4	1	7	6	5	2	8
5	2	7	4	9	8	3	6	1

PUZZLE / 567

5	9	3	4	1	6	7	2	8
8	2	4	3	9	7	6	1	5
6	7	1	2	8	5	3	4	9
7	3	9	5	6	2	4	8	1
1	8	2	9	3	4	5	7	6
4	6	5	1	7	8	9	3	2
3	4	8	6	5	1	2	9	7
9	5	7	8	2	3	1	6	4
2	1	6	7	4	9	8	5	3

PUZZLE / 568

2	6	1	7	4	9	5	3	8
7	4	3	1	5	8	6	9	2
9	8	5	2	6	3	7	1	4
6	9	7	3	1	2	4	8	5
5	2	4	9	8	6	1	7	3
1	3	8	5	7	4	9	2	6
3	5	2	6	9	7	8	4	1
8	7	6	4	3	1	2	5	9
4	1	9	8	2	5	3	6	7

PUZZLE / 569

6	4	5	1	7	3	2	9	8
9	1	8	5	6	2	4	3	7
3	7	2	4	9	8	6	1	5
4	8	1	3	5	7	9	6	2
2	5	6	8	4	9	1	7	3
7	9	3	2	1	6	5	8	4
8	2	9	6	3	4	7	5	1
5	6	4	7	8	1	3	2	9
1	3	7	9	2	5	8	4	6

PUZZLE / 570

7	2	1	8	6	9	5	4	3
9	8	5	3	1	4	6	2	7
6	3	4	7	5	2	8	1	9
4	9	2	6	8	3	1	7	5
8	5	7	9	2	1	4	3	6
3	1	6	5	4	7	9	8	2
2	6	9	1	7	8	3	5	4
1	7	3	4	9	5	2	6	8
5	4	8	2	3	6	7	9	1

PUZZLE / 571

6	1	3	9	2	5	7	4	8
2	4	7	3	8	1	9	6	5
8	9	5	7	4	6	2	1	3
1	8	9	2	3	7	4	5	6
4	5	2	6	1	9	8	3	7
3	7	6	8	5	4	1	9	2
5	6	1	4	7	2	3	8	9
9	2	8	1	6	3	5	7	4
7	3	4	5	9	8	6	2	1

PUZZLE / 572

6	4	9	5	3	1	8	2	7
8	5	3	6	7	2	1	9	4
1	7	2	9	4	8	3	6	5
7	9	4	1	2	3	5	8	6
3	8	1	4	5	6	9	7	2
5	2	6	7	8	9	4	3	1
2	1	8	3	6	4	7	5	9
9	3	7	2	1	5	6	4	8
4	6	5	8	9	7	2	1	3

PUZZLE / 573

4	3	7	5	2	8	6	1	9
8	9	1	7	6	3	4	5	2
5	6	2	9	1	4	7	3	8
1	4	3	8	5	6	2	9	7
2	8	6	1	7	9	5	4	3
9	7	5	3	4	2	1	8	6
6	1	9	2	3	5	8	7	4
7	2	8	4	9	1	3	6	5
3	5	4	6	8	7	9	2	1

PUZZLE / 574

4	8	7	6	5	3	2	1	9
2	5	3	1	7	9	8	4	6
9	1	6	8	4	2	5	7	3
7	3	8	9	1	4	6	5	2
1	2	4	5	8	6	9	3	7
5	6	9	3	2	7	1	8	4
3	7	1	2	9	5	4	6	8
8	4	2	7	6	1	3	9	5
6	9	5	4	3	8	7	2	1

PUZZLE / 575

9	7	1	2	8	4	6	5	3
2	6	8	5	9	3	7	1	4
3	5	4	7	1	6	2	9	8
8	1	6	4	7	9	5	3	2
4	9	5	3	2	1	8	6	7
7	3	2	8	6	5	1	4	9
5	2	3	1	4	7	9	8	6
1	8	9	6	3	2	4	7	5
6	4	7	9	5	8	3	2	1

PUZZLE / 576

8	4	1	5	2	7	3	6	9
6	2	9	4	3	1	8	5	7
3	7	5	9	6	8	2	1	4
9	6	8	2	7	4	1	3	5
4	5	7	1	8	3	6	9	2
2	1	3	6	9	5	7	4	8
1	3	2	7	4	9	5	8	6
7	8	4	3	5	6	9	2	1
5	9	6	8	1	2	4	7	3

PUZZLE / 577

3	4	8	7	5	1	2	9	6
1	6	5	4	2	9	8	3	7
2	7	9	8	6	3	5	1	4
8	3	1	6	7	4	9	5	2
7	2	4	9	1	5	6	8	3
9	5	6	3	8	2	4	7	1
6	9	2	5	3	7	1	4	8
5	1	7	2	4	8	3	6	9
4	8	3	1	9	6	7	2	5

PUZZLE / 578

5	3	1	7	6	8	4	2	9
2	4	8	1	3	9	7	5	6
9	7	6	4	5	2	3	8	1
4	5	3	2	9	1	6	7	8
1	6	2	3	8	7	9	4	5
8	9	7	6	4	5	2	1	3
7	1	5	9	2	3	8	6	4
3	8	4	5	7	6	1	9	2
6	2	9	8	1	4	5	3	7

PUZZLE / 579

6	3	5	2	7	1	8	4	9
1	9	2	5	4	8	6	3	7
8	7	4	3	9	6	2	1	5
9	1	8	7	6	3	5	2	4
7	2	3	8	5	4	9	6	1
5	4	6	1	2	9	7	8	3
2	8	9	4	1	7	3	5	6
4	5	7	6	3	2	1	9	8
3	6	1	9	8	5	4	7	2

PUZZLE / 580

6	2	3	8	5	9	4	7	1
9	7	4	3	2	1	6	5	8
5	8	1	6	4	7	2	9	3
4	3	6	7	9	8	1	2	5
7	1	8	5	3	2	9	6	4
2	5	9	4	1	6	3	8	7
1	6	7	2	8	4	5	3	9
3	4	2	9	7	5	8	1	6
8	9	5	1	6	3	7	4	2

PUZZLE / 581

9	7	4	3	2	8	5	6	1
8	1	6	5	9	4	2	7	3
3	2	5	6	7	1	9	8	4
7	3	8	9	6	2	1	4	5
6	4	2	1	8	5	3	9	7
1	5	9	7	4	3	6	2	8
4	6	1	8	5	9	7	3	2
5	8	7	2	3	6	4	1	9
2	9	3	4	1	7	8	5	6

PUZZLE / 582

1	6	4	7	8	3	5	2	9
3	5	2	6	9	1	8	7	4
8	9	7	2	5	4	3	1	6
6	3	9	8	1	2	7	4	5
4	1	5	9	3	7	2	6	8
2	7	8	5	4	6	9	3	1
5	4	6	3	2	8	1	9	7
7	8	3	1	6	9	4	5	2
9	2	1	4	7	5	6	8	3

PUZZLE / 583

7	8	9	4	3	2	1	5	6
2	4	1	6	5	7	3	9	8
5	3	6	9	1	8	2	4	7
6	7	2	8	9	5	4	3	1
3	1	5	2	4	6	7	8	9
8	9	4	3	7	1	6	2	5
1	5	3	7	8	4	9	6	2
4	2	8	1	6	9	5	7	3
9	6	7	5	2	3	8	1	4

PUZZLE / 584

4	2	5	1	8	3	7	6	9
1	6	7	5	9	4	8	2	3
8	3	9	7	6	2	5	4	1
3	7	8	4	1	6	9	5	2
5	4	2	9	3	8	1	7	6
6	9	1	2	5	7	3	8	4
9	5	6	8	2	1	4	3	7
2	1	4	3	7	5	6	9	8
7	8	3	6	4	9	2	1	5

PUZZLE / 585

4	7	5	6	8	9	2	1	3
1	6	9	3	2	5	7	8	4
8	3	2	7	4	1	5	9	6
9	5	1	2	7	4	6	3	8
6	8	7	9	5	3	1	4	2
3	2	4	8	1	6	9	5	7
5	4	3	1	6	2	8	7	9
2	9	8	5	3	7	4	6	1
7	1	6	4	9	8	3	2	5

PUZZLE / 586

1	4	8	6	7	5	3	9	2
6	2	7	9	3	4	1	8	5
9	5	3	1	2	8	6	7	4
5	8	2	3	4	6	7	1	9
7	3	9	5	8	1	4	2	6
4	6	1	2	9	7	5	3	8
8	1	6	7	5	2	9	4	3
3	7	4	8	6	9	2	5	1
2	9	5	4	1	3	8	6	7

PUZZLE / 587

4	6	3	7	1	9	2	8	5
8	2	7	6	4	5	3	9	1
1	5	9	8	2	3	6	4	7
7	4	1	5	9	6	8	2	3
2	9	8	4	3	1	5	7	6
6	3	5	2	7	8	9	1	4
9	7	6	3	8	4	1	5	2
3	8	4	1	5	2	7	6	9
5	1	2	9	6	7	4	3	8

PUZZLE / 588

9	4	6	2	3	5	8	1	7
5	3	2	7	8	1	6	4	9
1	7	8	6	4	9	3	2	5
2	9	3	4	1	7	5	8	6
6	1	7	5	9	8	2	3	4
8	5	4	3	2	6	9	7	1
4	8	5	9	7	2	1	6	3
7	2	9	1	6	3	4	5	8
3	6	1	8	5	4	7	9	2

PUZZLE / 589

1	6	5	8	4	7	3	9	2
4	2	9	3	6	1	5	8	7
8	7	3	5	2	9	6	1	4
5	4	2	7	8	3	9	6	1
3	8	6	1	9	4	7	2	5
9	1	7	6	5	2	8	4	3
2	3	4	9	7	8	1	5	6
7	5	8	2	1	6	4	3	9
6	9	1	4	3	5	2	7	8

PUZZLE / 590

4	2	9	5	7	1	8	3	6
1	7	5	6	3	8	2	4	9
3	6	8	9	4	2	7	1	5
2	1	7	8	9	3	5	6	4
5	9	4	7	2	6	3	8	1
8	3	6	4	1	5	9	2	7
7	5	3	2	6	4	1	9	8
9	4	1	3	8	7	6	5	2
6	8	2	1	5	9	4	7	3

PUZZLE / 591

5	8	3	1	7	9	4	6	2
6	1	4	2	5	8	9	7	3
2	7	9	3	4	6	5	8	1
4	9	7	6	1	3	2	5	8
8	5	1	9	2	4	6	3	7
3	6	2	7	8	5	1	9	4
9	2	5	4	3	7	8	1	6
1	3	6	8	9	2	7	4	5
7	4	8	5	6	1	3	2	9

PUZZLE / 592

2	9	5	3	6	1	4	7	8
6	7	3	4	8	9	1	5	2
4	1	8	5	7	2	9	6	3
9	3	6	7	2	8	5	1	4
8	5	1	6	4	3	7	2	9
7	2	4	9	1	5	8	3	6
5	8	7	2	3	4	6	9	1
3	4	9	1	5	6	2	8	7
1	6	2	8	9	7	3	4	5

PUZZLE / 593

5	2	6	9	8	1	4	3	7
9	8	7	3	6	4	5	2	1
3	1	4	5	2	7	8	6	9
2	6	1	4	9	8	7	5	3
8	4	5	2	7	3	9	1	6
7	9	3	1	5	6	2	8	4
6	3	8	7	4	2	1	9	5
4	5	2	6	1	9	3	7	8
1	7	9	8	3	5	6	4	2

PUZZLE / 594

1	6	7	9	5	2	3	8	4
8	5	3	4	1	6	2	7	9
9	4	2	7	3	8	6	5	1
5	1	9	3	6	7	8	4	2
3	7	4	2	8	9	1	6	5
6	2	8	1	4	5	7	9	3
4	8	6	5	2	3	9	1	7
7	3	1	8	9	4	5	2	6
2	9	5	6	7	1	4	3	8

PUZZLE / **595**

9	8	4	5	6	1	3	7	2
6	2	1	9	7	3	4	5	8
7	3	5	8	2	4	1	9	6
2	4	7	6	5	9	8	1	3
5	1	3	2	4	8	9	6	7
8	9	6	1	3	7	5	2	4
1	7	8	3	9	2	6	4	5
4	5	9	7	8	6	2	3	1
3	6	2	4	1	5	7	8	9

PUZZLE / **596**

5	4	9	8	2	6	7	1	3
8	1	7	4	5	3	9	2	6
6	2	3	7	1	9	4	5	8
1	9	6	5	4	7	3	8	2
3	7	8	1	9	2	6	4	5
2	5	4	3	6	8	1	9	7
7	3	2	9	8	1	5	6	4
9	8	5	6	3	4	2	7	1
4	6	1	2	7	5	8	3	9

PUZZLE / **597**

7	2	3	8	5	6	4	1	9
4	6	1	2	9	3	5	7	8
9	5	8	7	1	4	6	3	2
6	1	5	9	8	2	3	4	7
2	4	9	3	7	5	8	6	1
8	3	7	4	6	1	9	2	5
1	9	4	6	2	8	7	5	3
3	8	2	5	4	7	1	9	6
5	7	6	1	3	9	2	8	4

PUZZLE / **598**

8	9	7	6	4	1	3	5	2
4	1	5	9	3	2	8	6	7
2	6	3	7	8	5	1	4	9
9	8	1	4	5	6	2	7	3
7	5	2	3	1	9	4	8	6
3	4	6	2	7	8	5	9	1
6	3	4	5	2	7	9	1	8
5	7	8	1	9	3	6	2	4
1	2	9	8	6	4	7	3	5

PUZZLE / **599**

6	9	4	2	3	8	5	7	1
1	5	2	7	9	6	3	8	4
7	3	8	4	5	1	6	2	9
4	1	5	8	7	3	2	9	6
2	6	9	1	4	5	8	3	7
8	7	3	6	2	9	1	4	5
9	4	1	5	8	2	7	6	3
5	2	7	3	6	4	9	1	8
3	8	6	9	1	7	4	5	2

PUZZLE / **600**

9	1	5	7	3	8	4	2	6
2	3	4	9	5	6	8	7	1
8	6	7	2	1	4	5	9	3
7	2	8	1	6	9	3	4	5
5	9	1	4	2	3	7	6	8
3	4	6	5	8	7	2	1	9
4	7	3	8	9	1	6	5	2
6	5	9	3	4	2	1	8	7
1	8	2	6	7	5	9	3	4

PUZZLE / **601**

9	6	8	5	3	7	2	4	1
7	1	2	9	8	4	5	3	6
4	5	3	1	6	2	9	8	7
3	9	5	2	4	6	7	1	8
2	4	7	8	5	1	6	9	3
1	8	6	7	9	3	4	2	5
6	3	1	4	7	9	8	5	2
5	7	4	3	2	8	1	6	9
8	2	9	6	1	5	3	7	4

PUZZLE / **602**

5	3	1	8	7	4	6	2	9
6	7	2	3	9	5	4	8	1
8	9	4	2	1	6	3	7	5
7	2	9	6	5	8	1	4	3
3	1	6	4	2	9	8	5	7
4	8	5	1	3	7	2	9	6
1	5	3	7	8	2	9	6	4
9	4	8	5	6	1	7	3	2
2	6	7	9	4	3	5	1	8

PUZZLE / **603**

9	4	7	5	6	1	8	2	3
1	2	8	3	9	7	6	4	5
5	3	6	8	4	2	1	7	9
7	9	5	1	2	3	4	6	8
8	1	2	4	5	6	3	9	7
4	6	3	7	8	9	2	5	1
2	5	4	9	1	8	7	3	6
3	8	9	6	7	4	5	1	2
6	7	1	2	3	5	9	8	4

PUZZLE / **604**

4	6	5	8	7	3	1	2	9
1	8	3	9	5	2	6	4	7
9	7	2	6	1	4	5	8	3
5	9	6	2	8	1	3	7	4
2	4	7	3	6	5	8	9	1
8	3	1	4	9	7	2	6	5
6	5	8	1	4	9	7	3	2
7	2	4	5	3	8	9	1	6
3	1	9	7	2	6	4	5	8

PUZZLE / **605**

5	1	9	2	3	6	8	7	4
2	7	8	9	1	4	3	6	5
3	6	4	8	5	7	9	2	1
4	5	6	7	8	9	2	1	3
1	2	3	6	4	5	7	8	9
8	9	7	1	2	3	4	5	6
9	8	1	3	6	2	5	4	7
7	4	2	5	9	1	6	3	8
6	3	5	4	7	8	1	9	2

PUZZLE / **606**

5	7	9	6	8	1	4	2	3
3	1	8	4	7	2	6	5	9
6	4	2	5	3	9	8	1	7
8	9	5	3	4	6	2	7	1
4	3	7	2	1	8	9	6	5
2	6	1	7	9	5	3	4	8
9	8	4	1	6	7	5	3	2
1	2	3	9	5	4	7	8	6
7	5	6	8	2	3	1	9	4

PUZZLE / **607**

1	4	7	2	3	9	5	8	6
8	2	9	6	5	1	7	4	3
5	3	6	4	8	7	2	9	1
4	8	2	3	1	5	6	7	9
3	6	5	7	9	2	8	1	4
9	7	1	8	6	4	3	5	2
7	9	8	1	2	3	4	6	5
6	1	3	5	4	8	9	2	7
2	5	4	9	7	6	1	3	8

PUZZLE / **608**

7	3	9	5	6	8	4	1	2
8	1	2	9	4	7	5	3	6
4	5	6	3	1	2	7	8	9
9	7	5	2	8	1	6	4	3
1	8	4	7	3	6	2	9	5
2	6	3	4	5	9	1	7	8
6	9	1	8	7	5	3	2	4
3	2	7	6	9	4	8	5	1
5	4	8	1	2	3	9	6	7

PUZZLE / **609**

7	4	5	3	6	8	1	9	2
6	9	8	1	2	7	4	5	3
2	3	1	4	9	5	8	7	6
4	7	6	2	3	9	5	8	1
8	1	2	7	5	4	6	3	9
9	5	3	8	1	6	2	4	7
1	8	9	5	7	2	3	6	4
5	2	7	6	4	3	9	1	8
3	6	4	9	8	1	7	2	5

PUZZLE / **610**

4	5	2	3	8	1	6	7	9
1	3	6	7	9	5	2	4	8
7	9	8	4	6	2	1	3	5
5	7	1	2	4	3	8	9	6
8	2	4	9	1	6	7	5	3
3	6	9	5	7	8	4	1	2
2	4	7	6	3	9	5	8	1
9	1	5	8	2	4	3	6	7
6	8	3	1	5	7	9	2	4

PUZZLE / **611**

9	7	5	4	6	2	1	3	8
8	1	3	7	9	5	2	6	4
4	6	2	1	3	8	7	9	5
7	9	1	2	8	3	5	4	6
6	5	4	9	7	1	8	2	3
3	2	8	6	5	4	9	7	1
1	3	6	5	2	9	4	8	7
5	8	9	3	4	7	6	1	2
2	4	7	8	1	6	3	5	9

PUZZLE / **612**

6	2	3	7	8	5	4	9	1
4	8	1	3	9	6	2	7	5
7	5	9	4	1	2	3	8	6
3	6	2	8	7	9	5	1	4
9	7	5	1	2	4	8	6	3
8	1	4	5	6	3	7	2	9
5	9	7	6	3	8	1	4	2
1	4	6	2	5	7	9	3	8
2	3	8	9	4	1	6	5	7

PUZZLE / **613**

7	5	6	8	1	4	3	9	2
4	2	3	5	7	9	1	6	8
9	1	8	3	2	6	7	4	5
8	6	7	9	3	2	4	5	1
2	9	1	4	6	5	8	7	3
5	3	4	7	8	1	6	2	9
3	7	2	6	9	8	5	1	4
1	8	5	2	4	7	9	3	6
6	4	9	1	5	3	2	8	7

PUZZLE / **614**

6	9	2	3	8	7	1	4	5
8	5	4	1	9	2	7	6	3
1	3	7	5	6	4	9	2	8
5	6	9	2	7	1	3	8	4
4	7	1	8	5	3	2	9	6
2	8	3	9	4	6	5	1	7
9	4	8	7	1	5	6	3	2
7	2	6	4	3	9	8	5	1
3	1	5	6	2	8	4	7	9

PUZZLE / **615**

7	1	5	3	9	8	2	4	6
4	8	2	5	1	6	9	7	3
6	3	9	7	4	2	5	1	8
5	2	1	9	7	3	6	8	4
3	6	8	4	2	5	1	9	7
9	4	7	6	8	1	3	5	2
1	5	6	8	3	4	7	2	9
8	9	3	2	5	7	4	6	1
2	7	4	1	6	9	8	3	5

PUZZLE / **616**

9	1	4	6	8	7	2	5	3
6	5	8	3	4	2	1	9	7
3	7	2	5	9	1	4	6	8
2	9	5	1	7	8	6	3	4
4	6	7	9	5	3	8	2	1
1	8	3	2	6	4	9	7	5
5	2	1	4	3	6	7	8	9
8	4	9	7	2	5	3	1	6
7	3	6	8	1	9	5	4	2

PUZZLE / **617**

1	9	7	8	3	5	6	2	4
5	3	4	6	2	1	7	8	9
2	6	8	9	7	4	1	5	3
4	8	3	5	6	9	2	1	7
6	5	2	1	4	7	9	3	8
9	7	1	2	8	3	5	4	6
8	4	5	7	9	2	3	6	1
7	1	6	3	5	8	4	9	2
3	2	9	4	1	6	8	7	5

PUZZLE / **618**

5	6	4	8	1	2	3	7	9
7	1	3	4	5	9	2	6	8
9	2	8	7	6	3	1	5	4
4	8	7	1	9	5	6	2	3
1	5	2	3	4	6	8	9	7
3	9	6	2	8	7	5	4	1
6	3	5	9	7	1	4	8	2
2	4	9	6	3	8	7	1	5
8	7	1	5	2	4	9	3	6

PUZZLE / **619**

5	8	6	3	9	1	7	2	4
9	1	2	4	8	7	3	5	6
7	3	4	2	6	5	8	9	1
6	4	9	8	5	3	1	7	2
3	2	5	7	1	9	6	4	8
1	7	8	6	4	2	9	3	5
2	5	1	9	7	8	4	6	3
8	6	7	5	3	4	2	1	9
4	9	3	1	2	6	5	8	7

PUZZLE / **620**

6	8	7	2	4	5	9	3	1
9	5	4	6	1	3	8	2	7
1	3	2	9	8	7	5	4	6
8	2	1	7	3	6	4	9	5
4	9	3	1	5	8	7	6	2
5	7	6	4	2	9	1	8	3
3	4	5	8	7	2	6	1	9
7	6	8	3	9	1	2	5	4
2	1	9	5	6	4	3	7	8

PUZZLE / **621**

6	9	4	3	8	5	7	1	2
8	2	1	4	7	6	3	5	9
5	7	3	1	2	9	6	8	4
1	5	9	7	4	2	8	3	6
2	8	6	9	1	3	5	4	7
3	4	7	6	5	8	2	9	1
7	6	5	8	9	1	4	2	3
9	3	2	5	6	4	1	7	8
4	1	8	2	3	7	9	6	5

PUZZLE / **622**

6	9	4	3	1	7	5	8	2
1	3	8	2	5	6	9	7	4
5	7	2	8	9	4	3	6	1
8	5	7	6	4	2	1	9	3
2	6	9	7	3	1	4	5	8
3	4	1	9	8	5	6	2	7
7	1	5	4	2	9	8	3	6
9	2	3	1	6	8	7	4	5
4	8	6	5	7	3	2	1	9

PUZZLE / **623**

9	1	5	3	7	4	6	2	8
4	8	7	6	2	5	1	9	3
3	6	2	8	1	9	7	5	4
5	2	1	7	8	6	4	3	9
7	4	3	1	9	2	5	8	6
6	9	8	4	5	3	2	7	1
2	3	4	9	6	7	8	1	5
8	7	9	5	4	1	3	6	2
1	5	6	2	3	8	9	4	7

PUZZLE / **624**

5	4	1	2	9	6	7	8	3
6	8	9	7	5	3	4	1	2
7	2	3	8	1	4	6	9	5
3	1	6	9	7	2	8	5	4
2	5	7	3	4	8	1	6	9
4	9	8	5	6	1	2	3	7
9	7	2	1	8	5	3	4	6
8	3	4	6	2	9	5	7	1
1	6	5	4	3	7	9	2	8

PUZZLE / 625

7	6	1	3	8	9	4	2	5
3	8	2	4	6	5	7	9	1
4	5	9	7	1	2	8	6	3
5	9	8	2	7	1	3	4	6
1	7	3	5	4	6	9	8	2
6	2	4	8	9	3	5	1	7
8	4	5	6	2	7	1	3	9
2	1	7	9	3	8	6	5	4
9	3	6	1	5	4	2	7	8

PUZZLE / 626

9	2	1	5	6	4	7	3	8
5	3	6	8	2	7	9	4	1
4	7	8	1	3	9	5	2	6
1	4	3	2	9	8	6	5	7
8	5	9	6	7	3	2	1	4
2	6	7	4	1	5	3	8	9
6	1	4	9	5	2	8	7	3
7	9	5	3	8	1	4	6	2
3	8	2	7	4	6	1	9	5

PUZZLE / 627

7	9	1	2	8	5	4	3	6
4	5	8	9	6	3	1	2	7
6	3	2	7	4	1	8	9	5
9	1	6	8	5	2	3	7	4
8	4	7	3	9	6	5	1	2
3	2	5	4	1	7	6	8	9
5	7	3	1	2	4	9	6	8
2	8	4	6	3	9	7	5	1
1	6	9	5	7	8	2	4	3

PUZZLE / 628

5	1	7	3	6	4	2	8	9
3	9	6	8	2	5	7	1	4
8	2	4	7	1	9	6	3	5
9	7	1	5	3	2	4	6	8
6	3	2	4	9	8	1	5	7
4	8	5	1	7	6	3	9	2
2	4	9	6	5	3	8	7	1
1	6	8	9	4	7	5	2	3
7	5	3	2	8	1	9	4	6

PUZZLE / 629

1	6	7	3	4	9	8	2	5
8	3	2	5	6	1	7	9	4
9	4	5	8	7	2	6	3	1
5	9	8	7	2	3	4	1	6
6	2	1	4	9	5	3	7	8
3	7	4	6	1	8	9	5	2
4	5	3	1	8	7	2	6	9
7	8	9	2	5	6	1	4	3
2	1	6	9	3	4	5	8	7

PUZZLE / 630

8	7	6	9	1	2	3	4	5
2	3	9	4	5	8	1	7	6
1	4	5	6	3	7	9	2	8
9	6	7	2	4	5	8	3	1
4	5	1	8	6	3	7	9	2
3	8	2	7	9	1	5	6	4
5	1	4	3	7	6	2	8	9
6	2	3	5	8	9	4	1	7
7	9	8	1	2	4	6	5	3

PUZZLE / 631

7	4	2	9	6	5	3	8	1
5	9	3	1	2	8	4	6	7
8	6	1	4	7	3	5	2	9
2	1	5	8	9	4	6	7	3
4	7	6	3	5	2	1	9	8
3	8	9	6	1	7	2	5	4
1	2	8	7	3	6	9	4	5
6	3	4	5	8	9	7	1	2
9	5	7	2	4	1	8	3	6

PUZZLE / 632

4	9	3	2	1	8	5	7	6
5	8	7	6	3	9	4	2	1
6	1	2	5	4	7	8	3	9
7	2	6	9	5	4	3	1	8
9	4	5	3	8	1	7	6	2
8	3	1	7	2	6	9	5	4
3	5	8	1	9	2	6	4	7
2	6	4	8	7	5	1	9	3
1	7	9	4	6	3	2	8	5

PUZZLE / 633

5	2	8	3	4	1	6	7	9
6	9	3	2	7	5	1	4	8
7	4	1	8	9	6	2	5	3
8	7	5	6	2	4	3	9	1
3	6	2	7	1	9	4	8	5
4	1	9	5	8	3	7	2	6
9	8	6	4	3	2	5	1	7
2	3	7	1	5	8	9	6	4
1	5	4	9	6	7	8	3	2

PUZZLE / 634

3	4	6	9	2	8	5	7	1
9	5	8	7	4	1	3	2	6
7	1	2	3	6	5	8	9	4
1	3	4	5	7	9	6	8	2
2	6	5	4	8	3	9	1	7
8	7	9	2	1	6	4	5	3
5	2	1	8	3	4	7	6	9
4	8	7	6	9	2	1	3	5
6	9	3	1	5	7	2	4	8

PUZZLE / 635

2	1	6	4	8	5	9	7	3
7	5	9	2	6	3	8	4	1
3	4	8	1	9	7	5	6	2
4	9	3	8	1	6	7	2	5
6	8	7	5	4	2	3	1	9
5	2	1	3	7	9	4	8	6
8	3	4	6	5	1	2	9	7
9	6	2	7	3	8	1	5	4
1	7	5	9	2	4	6	3	8

PUZZLE / 636

8	3	1	2	4	7	6	5	9
6	5	4	8	9	3	1	7	2
2	9	7	5	1	6	4	8	3
4	7	6	1	3	9	8	2	5
9	8	5	6	7	2	3	1	4
1	2	3	4	8	5	9	6	7
3	6	9	7	2	8	5	4	1
5	1	2	3	6	4	7	9	8
7	4	8	9	5	1	2	3	6

PUZZLE / 637

5	8	2	4	7	6	3	9	1
1	9	4	3	2	8	7	5	6
7	6	3	1	9	5	8	4	2
6	7	5	9	3	1	4	2	8
4	1	9	8	6	2	5	3	7
2	3	8	5	4	7	1	6	9
8	2	1	6	5	4	9	7	3
9	4	7	2	1	3	6	8	5
3	5	6	7	8	9	2	1	4

PUZZLE / 638

8	7	4	1	6	3	2	5	9
1	3	9	7	5	2	4	6	8
2	5	6	4	8	9	1	7	3
3	9	8	6	1	7	5	4	2
4	1	7	8	2	5	9	3	6
6	2	5	3	9	4	7	8	1
9	4	3	2	7	8	6	1	5
7	6	2	5	3	1	8	9	4
5	8	1	9	4	6	3	2	7

PUZZLE / 639

9	1	4	7	6	2	5	8	3
6	3	7	5	9	8	4	1	2
8	2	5	3	1	4	7	6	9
1	7	9	8	3	6	2	4	5
3	5	6	2	4	9	1	7	8
4	8	2	1	7	5	9	3	6
2	4	1	9	8	3	6	5	7
5	6	3	4	2	7	8	9	1
7	9	8	6	5	1	3	2	4

PUZZLE / 640

2	3	6	4	9	5	1	7	8
1	9	8	6	2	7	4	3	5
4	5	7	1	3	8	6	9	2
3	4	5	2	6	9	8	1	7
8	7	1	3	5	4	2	6	9
6	2	9	8	7	1	3	5	4
7	8	2	9	1	6	5	4	3
9	1	3	5	4	2	7	8	6
5	6	4	7	8	3	9	2	1

PUZZLE / 641

5	4	8	9	7	3	1	6	2
1	9	2	8	5	6	4	3	7
6	3	7	1	4	2	8	9	5
7	2	4	6	1	9	3	5	8
9	8	6	3	2	5	7	1	4
3	1	5	7	8	4	9	2	6
8	5	3	2	9	7	6	4	1
4	6	1	5	3	8	2	7	9
2	7	9	4	6	1	5	8	3

PUZZLE / 642

7	9	8	4	5	1	2	3	6
2	3	1	6	8	7	5	4	9
4	5	6	9	2	3	1	7	8
8	7	3	2	6	5	9	1	4
5	1	9	3	4	8	6	2	7
6	2	4	7	1	9	8	5	3
3	8	7	5	9	2	4	6	1
9	6	5	1	7	4	3	8	2
1	4	2	8	3	6	7	9	5

PUZZLE / 643

9	5	3	4	7	8	1	6	2
1	6	8	5	2	3	9	7	4
4	7	2	6	1	9	3	5	8
3	4	7	1	8	5	6	2	9
2	8	1	7	9	6	5	4	3
6	9	5	2	3	4	8	1	7
5	2	9	8	4	1	7	3	6
7	3	6	9	5	2	4	8	1
8	1	4	3	6	7	2	9	5

PUZZLE / 644

5	6	2	4	7	3	8	1	9
1	7	4	8	6	9	5	2	3
3	8	9	5	2	1	4	6	7
7	3	5	2	1	4	6	9	8
9	2	8	6	3	7	1	4	5
4	1	6	9	5	8	3	7	2
6	5	1	7	8	2	9	3	4
8	4	7	3	9	6	2	5	1
2	9	3	1	4	5	7	8	6

PUZZLE / 645

7	6	9	3	8	1	5	2	4
5	1	3	4	2	7	8	9	6
4	2	8	9	5	6	1	7	3
1	5	2	6	4	3	9	8	7
6	8	7	1	9	5	3	4	2
3	9	4	8	7	2	6	1	5
8	3	5	7	1	4	2	6	9
9	4	6	2	3	8	7	5	1
2	7	1	5	6	9	4	3	8

PUZZLE / 646

4	2	7	3	9	8	5	6	1
8	3	6	4	5	1	2	7	9
1	9	5	7	2	6	3	8	4
2	7	4	9	8	5	6	1	3
5	8	3	6	1	7	9	4	2
9	6	1	2	4	3	8	5	7
6	5	2	1	7	9	4	3	8
3	1	9	8	6	4	7	2	5
7	4	8	5	3	2	1	9	6

PUZZLE / 647

2	9	5	8	7	6	4	1	3
6	8	1	3	5	4	2	9	7
7	3	4	9	2	1	8	5	6
3	5	2	1	4	7	6	8	9
8	1	7	6	9	3	5	4	2
4	6	9	2	8	5	7	3	1
9	7	3	5	6	8	1	2	4
1	4	8	7	3	2	9	6	5
5	2	6	4	1	9	3	7	8

PUZZLE / 648

5	6	9	1	7	2	8	3	4
4	1	8	5	9	3	6	2	7
2	3	7	8	4	6	5	1	9
8	9	4	7	6	1	3	5	2
7	2	1	3	5	8	9	4	6
6	5	3	4	2	9	7	8	1
3	7	5	9	1	4	2	6	8
9	4	6	2	8	5	1	7	3
1	8	2	6	3	7	4	9	5

PUZZLE / 649

8	9	3	1	2	5	6	4	7
7	5	2	6	8	4	3	9	1
1	6	4	3	9	7	2	8	5
3	8	6	5	4	1	9	7	2
4	2	7	9	6	3	1	5	8
9	1	5	8	7	2	4	3	6
6	3	9	7	1	8	5	2	4
2	7	1	4	5	9	8	6	3
5	4	8	2	3	6	7	1	9

PUZZLE / 650

9	4	3	2	5	7	8	6	1
1	5	7	4	6	8	3	9	2
6	2	8	9	3	1	5	7	4
3	9	5	6	7	4	2	1	8
7	8	6	3	1	2	9	4	5
2	1	4	8	9	5	6	3	7
4	7	9	5	8	6	1	2	3
8	3	1	7	2	9	4	5	6
5	6	2	1	4	3	7	8	9

PUZZLE / 651

7	3	9	2	8	4	1	5	6
1	8	5	9	3	6	7	4	2
2	4	6	7	5	1	8	3	9
6	1	8	4	7	3	9	2	5
5	2	3	1	9	8	6	7	4
4	9	7	6	2	5	3	8	1
3	6	1	8	4	2	5	9	7
9	5	2	3	6	7	4	1	8
8	7	4	5	1	9	2	6	3

PUZZLE / 652

4	1	6	3	9	5	7	2	8
9	8	7	2	4	6	3	1	5
3	5	2	7	8	1	6	9	4
8	9	4	1	2	3	5	7	6
5	7	1	4	6	8	9	3	2
6	2	3	5	7	9	8	4	1
1	3	9	6	5	4	2	8	7
7	6	8	9	1	2	4	5	3
2	4	5	8	3	7	1	6	9

PUZZLE / 653

1	3	6	4	8	2	5	9	7
4	7	8	1	9	5	2	6	3
2	9	5	6	7	3	4	8	1
7	8	3	5	6	1	9	4	2
6	2	1	9	4	8	7	3	5
9	5	4	3	2	7	6	1	8
8	6	7	2	1	4	3	5	9
3	1	9	7	5	6	8	2	4
5	4	2	8	3	9	1	7	6

PUZZLE / 654

1	2	8	9	6	3	7	5	4
3	6	5	7	1	4	9	2	8
7	9	4	8	5	2	1	6	3
5	1	3	4	9	6	8	7	2
9	8	6	2	7	5	4	3	1
4	7	2	3	8	1	5	9	6
2	5	9	1	3	8	6	4	7
8	4	7	6	2	9	3	1	5
6	3	1	5	4	7	2	8	9

PUZZLE / 655

8	6	1	3	7	4	2	5	9
3	9	5	8	6	2	7	1	4
7	2	4	1	9	5	8	6	3
6	5	3	9	1	8	4	7	2
4	1	2	5	3	7	9	8	6
9	7	8	2	4	6	5	3	1
2	8	9	6	5	1	3	4	7
1	3	7	4	8	9	6	2	5
5	4	6	7	2	3	1	9	8

PUZZLE / 656

2	8	6	3	7	5	4	1	9
3	7	1	4	2	9	5	8	6
5	4	9	8	6	1	7	2	3
9	1	5	6	3	8	2	7	4
4	6	7	1	5	2	9	3	8
8	3	2	7	9	4	6	5	1
7	5	3	9	1	6	8	4	2
6	2	4	5	8	3	1	9	7
1	9	8	2	4	7	3	6	5

PUZZLE / 657

4	3	9	1	2	7	8	5	6
6	8	2	3	4	5	7	1	9
7	5	1	9	8	6	4	3	2
2	1	7	6	5	4	3	9	8
8	9	5	7	1	3	2	6	4
3	6	4	2	9	8	5	7	1
1	4	8	5	3	9	6	2	7
5	2	6	8	7	1	9	4	3
9	7	3	4	6	2	1	8	5

PUZZLE / 658

1	5	2	9	8	4	6	7	3
7	9	3	5	2	6	4	1	8
6	8	4	1	7	3	5	9	2
9	3	8	2	5	7	1	6	4
5	1	6	3	4	9	8	2	7
2	4	7	8	6	1	3	5	9
3	6	9	4	1	2	7	8	5
8	2	1	7	3	5	9	4	6
4	7	5	6	9	8	2	3	1

PUZZLE / 659

2	1	4	7	3	9	6	5	8
7	8	9	6	5	1	2	3	4
5	3	6	8	2	4	1	7	9
8	7	3	4	1	6	9	2	5
4	6	5	3	9	2	7	8	1
1	9	2	5	8	7	3	4	6
3	5	7	1	6	8	4	9	2
6	2	8	9	4	3	5	1	7
9	4	1	2	7	5	8	6	3

PUZZLE / 660

4	9	1	8	6	5	2	7	3
2	3	8	4	7	1	9	5	6
5	7	6	9	2	3	8	4	1
1	5	2	7	8	6	4	3	9
3	4	7	1	5	9	6	8	2
6	8	9	3	4	2	5	1	7
9	2	4	5	3	7	1	6	8
7	1	5	6	9	8	3	2	4
8	6	3	2	1	4	7	9	5

PUZZLE / 661

9	1	6	5	8	4	7	3	2
5	2	4	3	9	7	1	8	6
7	3	8	1	2	6	9	5	4
4	5	9	7	1	2	3	6	8
1	6	7	4	3	8	2	9	5
3	8	2	6	5	9	4	7	1
8	9	1	2	7	5	6	4	3
6	7	3	8	4	1	5	2	9
2	4	5	9	6	3	8	1	7

PUZZLE / 662

6	4	9	1	7	3	2	5	8
5	2	1	8	6	4	3	9	7
7	3	8	2	9	5	4	6	1
4	1	3	5	8	7	9	2	6
2	7	5	6	3	9	1	8	4
9	8	6	4	1	2	7	3	5
3	6	4	7	2	8	5	1	9
1	9	7	3	5	6	8	4	2
8	5	2	9	4	1	6	7	3

PUZZLE / 663

3	5	8	7	6	2	4	9	1
7	4	2	9	1	3	6	5	8
9	6	1	4	8	5	7	2	3
4	8	7	3	2	9	5	1	6
6	9	5	1	4	7	3	8	2
1	2	3	8	5	6	9	7	4
5	1	4	6	7	8	2	3	9
2	3	6	5	9	1	8	4	7
8	7	9	2	3	4	1	6	5

PUZZLE / 664

9	1	2	3	8	6	7	4	5
3	8	5	7	4	9	1	6	2
6	7	4	1	5	2	8	9	3
2	9	1	5	7	4	3	8	6
8	4	6	2	1	3	5	7	9
5	3	7	9	6	8	2	1	4
7	2	9	6	3	1	4	5	8
1	6	8	4	2	5	9	3	7
4	5	3	8	9	7	6	2	1

PUZZLE / 665

7	1	9	6	4	8	3	2	5
8	6	5	1	2	3	4	7	9
2	3	4	9	7	5	8	6	1
4	7	3	8	9	1	2	5	6
1	2	8	4	5	6	7	9	3
9	5	6	2	3	7	1	4	8
3	9	2	5	1	4	6	8	7
6	4	1	7	8	9	5	3	2
5	8	7	3	6	2	9	1	4

PUZZLE / 666

3	5	7	4	1	9	8	2	6
8	4	1	3	6	2	5	7	9
6	9	2	8	5	7	1	4	3
7	1	4	9	3	8	6	5	2
2	6	5	1	7	4	9	3	8
9	3	8	6	2	5	7	1	4
4	7	3	5	8	6	2	9	1
1	2	6	7	9	3	4	8	5
5	8	9	2	4	1	3	6	7

PUZZLE / 667

5	1	2	9	4	7	6	8	3
3	9	8	6	1	2	4	7	5
6	4	7	5	8	3	2	9	1
9	3	5	8	2	6	7	1	4
1	2	4	7	5	9	3	6	8
8	7	6	4	3	1	9	5	2
7	8	3	2	6	5	1	4	9
4	6	1	3	9	8	5	2	7
2	5	9	1	7	4	8	3	6

PUZZLE / 668

5	9	8	6	3	2	4	7	1
3	6	2	1	7	4	8	5	9
4	7	1	8	9	5	6	2	3
7	2	3	5	8	6	9	1	4
8	5	4	7	1	9	2	3	6
9	1	6	4	2	3	7	8	5
1	4	9	2	5	7	3	6	8
6	8	7	3	4	1	5	9	2
2	3	5	9	6	8	1	4	7

PUZZLE / 669

9	6	5	7	1	2	8	4	3
4	2	8	6	3	9	7	1	5
1	3	7	5	4	8	9	6	2
2	4	1	8	5	3	6	9	7
3	7	6	4	9	1	2	5	8
8	5	9	2	7	6	1	3	4
6	1	4	3	2	7	5	8	9
5	8	2	9	6	4	3	7	1
7	9	3	1	8	5	4	2	6

PUZZLE / 670

3	5	2	6	4	7	8	9	1
9	7	1	8	5	3	4	2	6
8	6	4	2	1	9	5	3	7
4	1	3	5	9	8	6	7	2
5	2	9	4	7	6	1	8	3
6	8	7	3	2	1	9	4	5
2	9	6	7	8	5	3	1	4
1	4	5	9	3	2	7	6	8
7	3	8	1	6	4	2	5	9

PUZZLE / 671

4	2	3	8	9	7	5	1	6
1	6	5	4	3	2	9	7	8
7	9	8	5	6	1	2	3	4
2	4	6	7	1	9	3	8	5
3	7	9	2	5	8	4	6	1
8	5	1	6	4	3	7	9	2
9	3	2	1	8	4	6	5	7
6	8	4	3	7	5	1	2	9
5	1	7	9	2	6	8	4	3

PUZZLE / 672

1	7	5	2	4	9	3	8	6
4	9	3	6	8	1	2	5	7
2	6	8	7	5	3	4	9	1
9	5	7	8	3	2	6	1	4
6	8	2	4	1	7	9	3	5
3	1	4	5	9	6	8	7	2
5	4	1	3	6	8	7	2	9
8	2	9	1	7	4	5	6	3
7	3	6	9	2	5	1	4	8

PUZZLE / 673

8	6	5	7	9	1	4	3	2
9	7	2	3	8	4	5	6	1
3	4	1	5	6	2	9	7	8
1	5	9	2	4	7	6	8	3
2	8	4	6	3	5	7	1	9
6	3	7	9	1	8	2	4	5
4	1	6	8	2	9	3	5	7
7	2	8	4	5	3	1	9	6
5	9	3	1	7	6	8	2	4

PUZZLE / 674

7	5	3	2	1	4	8	9	6
1	4	9	5	6	8	7	3	2
8	6	2	9	7	3	5	1	4
5	1	6	3	4	2	9	8	7
9	3	4	7	8	1	2	6	5
2	8	7	6	9	5	1	4	3
6	9	5	1	3	7	4	2	8
3	2	8	4	5	9	6	7	1
4	7	1	8	2	6	3	5	9

PUZZLE / 675

4	9	3	6	7	5	8	1	2
8	2	6	1	3	4	5	9	7
1	7	5	9	8	2	6	3	4
5	6	2	4	1	9	3	7	8
3	4	1	7	5	8	2	6	9
9	8	7	3	2	6	1	4	5
7	3	8	5	4	1	9	2	6
2	1	9	8	6	7	4	5	3
6	5	4	2	9	3	7	8	1

PUZZLE / 676

8	3	9	6	2	1	4	7	5
7	5	1	3	9	4	2	6	8
4	2	6	7	5	8	9	1	3
9	6	4	2	3	5	1	8	7
2	7	3	8	1	6	5	4	9
5	1	8	4	7	9	6	3	2
6	4	7	9	8	2	3	5	1
1	8	2	5	6	3	7	9	4
3	9	5	1	4	7	8	2	6

PUZZLE / 677

5	4	8	2	3	1	9	7	6
3	6	2	9	7	8	1	5	4
9	1	7	4	6	5	2	8	3
6	8	5	3	4	2	7	9	1
2	9	3	6	1	7	5	4	8
1	7	4	8	5	9	3	6	2
4	2	9	5	8	3	6	1	7
8	5	1	7	2	6	4	3	9
7	3	6	1	9	4	8	2	5

PUZZLE / 678

9	7	8	2	3	5	4	6	1
6	1	3	4	7	9	8	2	5
5	4	2	1	6	8	9	7	3
8	3	6	7	4	2	1	5	9
1	9	4	3	5	6	7	8	2
7	2	5	9	8	1	3	4	6
3	8	1	5	2	4	6	9	7
2	6	9	8	1	7	5	3	4
4	5	7	6	9	3	2	1	8

PUZZLE / 679

2	5	4	1	6	7	3	8	9
9	6	3	8	2	4	1	7	5
1	8	7	5	9	3	6	4	2
6	4	5	3	7	1	2	9	8
7	9	8	2	5	6	4	3	1
3	2	1	9	4	8	7	5	6
8	3	6	4	1	5	9	2	7
4	7	9	6	8	2	5	1	3
5	1	2	7	3	9	8	6	4

PUZZLE / 680

5	3	8	9	7	4	2	6	1
2	4	1	8	3	6	9	7	5
9	7	6	5	1	2	8	4	3
8	5	7	1	4	9	6	3	2
3	9	4	6	2	8	5	1	7
1	6	2	7	5	3	4	8	9
7	2	9	4	6	1	3	5	8
6	1	3	2	8	5	7	9	4
4	8	5	3	9	7	1	2	6

PUZZLE / 681

5	6	7	8	9	2	4	3	1
3	8	1	6	4	5	2	7	9
9	2	4	1	7	3	6	8	5
1	4	6	3	5	9	8	2	7
7	9	2	4	8	6	5	1	3
8	5	3	2	1	7	9	6	4
4	3	5	7	6	8	1	9	2
2	1	8	9	3	4	7	5	6
6	7	9	5	2	1	3	4	8

PUZZLE / 682

6	1	2	8	7	4	5	3	9
3	7	8	6	9	5	2	4	1
9	5	4	1	2	3	6	7	8
2	4	3	9	1	8	7	6	5
7	8	1	4	5	6	3	9	2
5	6	9	2	3	7	8	1	4
1	3	5	7	8	9	4	2	6
8	2	6	3	4	1	9	5	7
4	9	7	5	6	2	1	8	3

PUZZLE / 683

6	7	3	1	5	2	4	9	8
4	8	1	9	6	7	5	3	2
5	2	9	8	4	3	1	7	6
8	9	4	7	2	6	3	1	5
3	6	2	4	1	5	7	8	9
1	5	7	3	8	9	2	6	4
7	4	8	2	9	1	6	5	3
2	3	6	5	7	8	9	4	1
9	1	5	6	3	4	8	2	7

PUZZLE / 684

8	5	2	4	6	1	9	3	7
1	4	9	5	7	3	8	2	6
6	7	3	2	8	9	4	5	1
5	2	7	9	3	8	1	6	4
3	8	6	1	4	2	7	9	5
4	9	1	7	5	6	3	8	2
2	6	8	3	1	4	5	7	9
9	1	5	8	2	7	6	4	3
7	3	4	6	9	5	2	1	8

PUZZLE / **685**

2	6	5	3	9	7	1	8	4
7	1	8	4	6	2	3	9	5
3	9	4	1	5	8	6	2	7
6	7	1	2	3	9	5	4	8
4	2	3	5	8	6	7	1	9
5	8	9	7	1	4	2	6	3
8	3	7	9	2	1	4	5	6
9	5	2	6	4	3	8	7	1
1	4	6	8	7	5	9	3	2

PUZZLE / **686**

5	1	8	6	7	9	4	3	2
6	2	4	3	8	5	9	7	1
7	3	9	4	1	2	5	8	6
8	6	2	7	9	4	1	5	3
3	4	5	1	2	8	7	6	9
1	9	7	5	3	6	2	4	8
9	8	3	2	4	7	6	1	5
2	7	6	8	5	1	3	9	4
4	5	1	9	6	3	8	2	7

PUZZLE / **687**

6	4	3	2	5	7	8	1	9
8	2	5	9	3	1	4	7	6
1	9	7	8	4	6	2	5	3
9	3	6	1	8	2	5	4	7
4	8	2	5	7	3	6	9	1
5	7	1	6	9	4	3	2	8
7	1	8	4	6	5	9	3	2
2	5	9	3	1	8	7	6	4
3	6	4	7	2	9	1	8	5

PUZZLE / **688**

4	7	1	8	5	3	6	2	9
3	9	5	2	6	4	1	8	7
8	2	6	9	1	7	4	3	5
7	6	9	4	8	2	5	1	3
5	8	2	1	3	9	7	6	4
1	3	4	5	7	6	8	9	2
6	4	7	3	2	8	9	5	1
2	5	8	7	9	1	3	4	6
9	1	3	6	4	5	2	7	8

PUZZLE / **689**

3	6	2	1	8	4	5	9	7
1	8	5	7	9	6	4	2	3
4	9	7	3	2	5	8	6	1
8	3	9	5	4	2	1	7	6
6	5	4	9	7	1	3	8	2
2	7	1	6	3	8	9	4	5
9	2	6	4	5	3	7	1	8
7	1	3	8	6	9	2	5	4
5	4	8	2	1	7	6	3	9

PUZZLE / **690**

7	4	5	9	6	8	2	3	1
1	8	3	4	2	7	9	6	5
6	2	9	1	5	3	4	8	7
4	7	8	3	9	5	1	2	6
5	3	6	2	7	1	8	9	4
9	1	2	8	4	6	5	7	3
2	5	7	6	1	9	3	4	8
3	6	4	5	8	2	7	1	9
8	9	1	7	3	4	6	5	2

PUZZLE / **691**

1	5	7	2	3	4	6	8	9
9	3	2	5	6	8	1	7	4
4	6	8	9	7	1	3	5	2
2	1	5	7	4	9	8	6	3
8	4	6	3	1	2	7	9	5
7	9	3	8	5	6	4	2	1
6	2	9	1	8	3	5	4	7
3	7	4	6	2	5	9	1	8
5	8	1	4	9	7	2	3	6

PUZZLE / **692**

8	5	2	6	4	7	3	1	9
3	1	4	9	8	5	6	7	2
7	9	6	3	2	1	8	5	4
5	6	8	7	3	4	2	9	1
2	4	1	8	6	9	5	3	7
9	3	7	1	5	2	4	6	8
1	8	5	4	7	3	9	2	6
4	7	3	2	9	6	1	8	5
6	2	9	5	1	8	7	4	3

PUZZLE / **693**

4	5	9	7	6	2	8	1	3
6	1	8	3	9	4	5	2	7
2	3	7	5	1	8	6	9	4
5	8	6	1	4	7	2	3	9
1	2	3	6	8	9	4	7	5
7	9	4	2	3	5	1	8	6
3	7	2	8	5	6	9	4	1
9	6	1	4	2	3	7	5	8
8	4	5	9	7	1	3	6	2

PUZZLE / **694**

5	3	8	1	2	6	9	4	7
9	6	7	8	4	5	1	3	2
4	1	2	7	3	9	6	5	8
7	5	9	2	8	4	3	1	6
2	8	1	6	9	3	5	7	4
3	4	6	5	7	1	8	2	9
1	7	5	4	6	8	2	9	3
8	9	4	3	1	2	7	6	5
6	2	3	9	5	7	4	8	1

PUZZLE / **695**

4	9	2	8	5	7	1	3	6
6	7	8	2	1	3	9	4	5
5	3	1	6	9	4	7	2	8
8	5	9	4	2	1	6	7	3
3	1	4	5	7	6	2	8	9
2	6	7	3	8	9	5	1	4
7	8	3	1	6	5	4	9	2
9	2	5	7	4	8	3	6	1
1	4	6	9	3	2	8	5	7

PUZZLE / **696**

7	4	8	6	1	2	3	9	5
3	5	6	4	7	9	2	1	8
1	9	2	5	3	8	6	7	4
9	8	4	2	6	7	5	3	1
5	3	7	8	4	1	9	6	2
6	2	1	3	9	5	8	4	7
8	6	3	7	2	4	1	5	9
4	1	5	9	8	6	7	2	3
2	7	9	1	5	3	4	8	6

PUZZLE / **697**

9	2	1	6	3	7	5	4	8
5	8	7	1	4	2	3	9	6
6	3	4	5	9	8	7	2	1
2	5	3	4	8	1	9	6	7
4	9	8	7	5	6	2	1	3
1	7	6	9	2	3	4	8	5
3	1	2	8	7	4	6	5	9
7	6	9	2	1	5	8	3	4
8	4	5	3	6	9	1	7	2

PUZZLE / **698**

3	4	7	8	5	1	2	6	9
8	6	9	2	7	3	5	4	1
2	5	1	4	9	6	3	7	8
9	1	6	7	3	2	4	8	5
4	3	8	9	6	5	7	1	2
5	7	2	1	8	4	9	3	6
6	2	4	5	1	7	8	9	3
1	9	5	3	4	8	6	2	7
7	8	3	6	2	9	1	5	4

PUZZLE / **699**

9	4	5	2	1	7	8	3	6
8	3	1	4	9	6	7	5	2
7	6	2	5	3	8	4	9	1
5	9	6	1	4	3	2	7	8
1	7	8	6	2	5	3	4	9
3	2	4	7	8	9	1	6	5
2	5	9	3	7	1	6	8	4
4	8	3	9	6	2	5	1	7
6	1	7	8	5	4	9	2	3

PUZZLE / **700**

5	1	9	4	8	6	7	3	2
2	8	4	5	3	7	1	9	6
6	7	3	1	2	9	5	8	4
1	3	5	6	4	2	8	7	9
9	2	8	3	7	5	4	6	1
4	6	7	9	1	8	3	2	5
3	5	2	8	6	4	9	1	7
8	4	6	7	9	1	2	5	3
7	9	1	2	5	3	6	4	8

PUZZLE / **701**

3	1	7	9	5	2	6	8	4
4	6	9	8	1	7	2	5	3
8	5	2	6	3	4	7	1	9
6	7	8	2	4	1	9	3	5
9	3	1	5	7	6	8	4	2
5	2	4	3	9	8	1	6	7
7	4	6	1	2	3	5	9	8
2	8	5	4	6	9	3	7	1
1	9	3	7	8	5	4	2	6

PUZZLE / **702**

9	1	3	4	7	5	6	2	8
5	8	4	3	2	6	7	9	1
7	6	2	8	9	1	5	3	4
6	7	8	9	5	3	4	1	2
2	4	9	1	6	7	8	5	3
1	3	5	2	8	4	9	6	7
8	2	6	7	1	9	3	4	5
3	9	7	5	4	2	1	8	6
4	5	1	6	3	8	2	7	9

PUZZLE / **703**

7	6	1	2	3	8	9	4	5
5	3	8	7	4	9	2	1	6
9	2	4	5	6	1	7	3	8
1	5	9	8	2	3	4	6	7
3	8	7	4	9	6	5	2	1
6	4	2	1	7	5	8	9	3
2	7	5	3	1	4	6	8	9
8	9	3	6	5	2	1	7	4
4	1	6	9	8	7	3	5	2

PUZZLE / **704**

7	1	3	8	4	5	6	2	9
5	6	2	3	9	1	8	4	7
9	8	4	6	7	2	1	5	3
6	4	9	2	1	7	5	3	8
3	7	8	4	5	6	9	1	2
2	5	1	9	3	8	7	6	4
1	2	5	7	8	3	4	9	6
4	3	7	1	6	9	2	8	5
8	9	6	5	2	4	3	7	1

PUZZLE / **705**

7	4	2	3	1	9	8	6	5
8	1	3	6	2	5	9	7	4
6	9	5	7	4	8	2	3	1
4	3	7	1	9	2	6	5	8
5	6	1	4	8	3	7	9	2
9	2	8	5	6	7	4	1	3
2	7	6	8	5	1	3	4	9
1	8	4	9	3	6	5	2	7
3	5	9	2	7	4	1	8	6

PUZZLE / **706**

2	1	5	6	7	3	4	8	9
6	9	4	5	2	8	7	3	1
8	7	3	9	4	1	2	6	5
5	4	9	1	3	2	8	7	6
7	3	2	8	5	6	1	9	4
1	8	6	4	9	7	3	5	2
9	6	7	3	1	4	5	2	8
3	5	1	2	8	9	6	4	7
4	2	8	7	6	5	9	1	3

PUZZLE / **707**

6	3	4	7	9	1	8	2	5
9	2	5	3	4	8	6	7	1
8	1	7	2	5	6	4	9	3
3	4	2	1	7	5	9	8	6
5	8	9	6	2	4	1	3	7
1	7	6	9	8	3	2	5	4
2	6	1	8	3	7	5	4	9
7	5	8	4	1	9	3	6	2
4	9	3	5	6	2	7	1	8

PUZZLE / **708**

5	9	4	8	3	7	2	1	6
2	3	1	4	6	9	7	8	5
8	7	6	2	5	1	3	9	4
4	1	9	3	7	5	8	6	2
7	8	3	9	2	6	4	5	1
6	2	5	1	8	4	9	7	3
3	5	7	6	4	8	1	2	9
1	4	8	5	9	2	6	3	7
9	6	2	7	1	3	5	4	8

PUZZLE / 709

7	6	9	1	2	5	3	8	4
1	8	3	6	4	7	5	2	9
4	2	5	8	9	3	1	6	7
2	7	1	3	6	9	8	4	5
5	9	6	7	8	4	2	1	3
8	3	4	5	1	2	7	9	6
6	5	8	4	3	1	9	7	2
9	1	7	2	5	6	4	3	8
3	4	2	9	7	8	6	5	1

PUZZLE / 710

1	8	2	4	6	5	7	9	3
6	5	9	8	3	7	4	1	2
4	7	3	1	9	2	6	5	8
2	3	6	7	5	4	1	8	9
7	4	5	9	8	1	3	2	6
8	9	1	6	2	3	5	4	7
9	2	7	5	1	6	8	3	4
3	1	4	2	7	8	9	6	5
5	6	8	3	4	9	2	7	1

PUZZLE / 711

8	4	3	5	1	7	2	9	6
7	2	6	4	8	9	1	3	5
5	1	9	3	2	6	7	4	8
4	9	1	8	3	2	6	5	7
3	6	5	1	7	4	9	8	2
2	8	7	6	9	5	4	1	3
1	5	4	7	6	8	3	2	9
9	7	8	2	4	3	5	6	1
6	3	2	9	5	1	8	7	4

PUZZLE / 712

7	8	3	9	2	4	5	1	6
6	1	2	3	5	8	7	9	4
9	4	5	6	7	1	8	3	2
4	7	8	1	9	6	3	2	5
5	2	9	7	4	3	1	6	8
1	3	6	2	8	5	9	4	7
2	6	7	5	3	9	4	8	1
8	9	1	4	6	7	2	5	3
3	5	4	8	1	2	6	7	9

PUZZLE / 713

6	5	2	4	8	3	7	1	9
7	1	9	5	2	6	4	8	3
4	3	8	1	9	7	6	5	2
5	7	4	8	1	2	3	9	6
9	2	1	3	6	5	8	7	4
3	8	6	7	4	9	1	2	5
1	4	3	2	5	8	9	6	7
8	6	5	9	7	4	2	3	1
2	9	7	6	3	1	5	4	8

PUZZLE / 714

5	2	6	1	9	4	3	7	8
4	3	8	5	6	7	9	2	1
7	1	9	8	2	3	5	4	6
1	4	7	6	3	5	8	9	2
3	6	2	9	7	8	4	1	5
8	9	5	2	4	1	6	3	7
6	5	4	3	1	2	7	8	9
9	7	1	4	8	6	2	5	3
2	8	3	7	5	9	1	6	4

PUZZLE / 715

4	8	5	9	7	2	1	3	6
9	3	1	4	6	5	7	2	8
6	2	7	3	1	8	5	4	9
1	7	9	8	4	6	2	5	3
5	4	2	7	9	3	6	8	1
3	6	8	2	5	1	4	9	7
7	9	3	6	2	4	8	1	5
2	1	6	5	8	9	3	7	4
8	5	4	1	3	7	9	6	2

PUZZLE / 716

7	1	8	6	4	5	3	2	9
4	5	2	3	7	9	6	8	1
6	9	3	1	2	8	5	7	4
9	2	5	4	6	1	8	3	7
8	6	1	5	3	7	4	9	2
3	4	7	9	8	2	1	5	6
5	8	6	2	9	4	7	1	3
1	3	9	7	5	6	2	4	8
2	7	4	8	1	3	9	6	5

PUZZLE / 717

1	9	7	8	2	6	3	5	4
4	8	5	3	7	9	1	2	6
3	6	2	1	4	5	8	7	9
7	1	4	2	9	8	6	3	5
9	3	8	6	5	1	2	4	7
2	5	6	4	3	7	9	8	1
6	4	9	5	8	3	7	1	2
5	7	3	9	1	2	4	6	8
8	2	1	7	6	4	5	9	3

PUZZLE / 718

7	1	8	3	4	9	6	2	5
6	3	9	5	1	2	8	4	7
2	5	4	6	7	8	3	9	1
4	7	6	8	5	3	9	1	2
1	9	3	7	2	4	5	6	8
5	8	2	9	6	1	7	3	4
3	4	7	1	9	5	2	8	6
8	2	5	4	3	6	1	7	9
9	6	1	2	8	7	4	5	3

PUZZLE / 719

8	2	9	1	6	4	7	5	3
4	3	6	2	5	7	9	8	1
5	7	1	8	9	3	2	4	6
2	5	7	9	1	8	3	6	4
3	1	4	7	2	6	5	9	8
6	9	8	4	3	5	1	7	2
9	4	2	6	7	1	8	3	5
1	8	3	5	4	9	6	2	7
7	6	5	3	8	2	4	1	9

PUZZLE / 720

8	3	7	5	9	1	2	6	4
9	1	2	6	7	4	5	3	8
6	4	5	3	2	8	7	1	9
2	8	6	7	4	3	1	9	5
1	9	3	2	5	6	8	4	7
7	5	4	1	8	9	3	2	6
3	6	9	8	1	7	4	5	2
5	7	1	4	6	2	9	8	3
4	2	8	9	3	5	6	7	1

PUZZLE / 721

9	1	2	5	3	7	6	4	8
4	7	8	2	9	6	1	5	3
3	5	6	4	1	8	9	2	7
1	6	3	8	4	5	7	9	2
7	8	9	6	2	1	5	3	4
5	2	4	9	7	3	8	1	6
2	3	7	1	8	9	4	6	5
6	4	1	7	5	2	3	8	9
8	9	5	3	6	4	2	7	1

PUZZLE / 722

9	2	3	7	6	5	1	4	8
4	6	1	2	8	3	5	7	9
8	5	7	9	1	4	2	6	3
2	9	8	6	7	1	3	5	4
7	3	4	8	5	9	6	1	2
5	1	6	3	4	2	9	8	7
3	4	5	1	9	7	8	2	6
1	8	2	4	3	6	7	9	5
6	7	9	5	2	8	4	3	1

PUZZLE / 723

1	7	4	2	9	3	8	5	6
2	8	3	4	6	5	9	7	1
5	9	6	1	7	8	2	4	3
9	2	7	8	5	6	3	1	4
4	5	1	7	3	2	6	8	9
3	6	8	9	4	1	7	2	5
8	4	2	6	1	9	5	3	7
6	1	5	3	2	7	4	9	8
7	3	9	5	8	4	1	6	2

PUZZLE / 724

9	5	7	4	6	1	2	3	8
4	3	1	2	9	8	6	7	5
2	6	8	5	3	7	9	4	1
8	7	3	1	4	6	5	9	2
5	1	2	3	7	9	4	8	6
6	4	9	8	2	5	7	1	3
3	2	6	7	8	4	1	5	9
7	9	5	6	1	3	8	2	4
1	8	4	9	5	2	3	6	7

PUZZLE / 725

1	6	8	2	7	9	3	4	5
7	5	9	3	1	4	8	2	6
3	2	4	6	8	5	1	9	7
4	9	3	7	5	8	6	1	2
5	1	7	9	6	2	4	3	8
6	8	2	4	3	1	7	5	9
2	3	1	8	9	7	5	6	4
8	4	6	5	2	3	9	7	1
9	7	5	1	4	6	2	8	3

PUZZLE / 726

4	6	5	3	2	8	1	9	7
1	2	3	7	9	5	8	4	6
7	9	8	6	1	4	5	3	2
2	4	7	5	6	9	3	8	1
8	3	6	2	4	1	9	7	5
5	1	9	8	7	3	6	2	4
6	7	1	9	3	2	4	5	8
3	8	2	4	5	6	7	1	9
9	5	4	1	8	7	2	6	3

PUZZLE / 727

9	5	7	6	1	2	4	3	8
4	1	2	9	8	3	6	7	5
3	6	8	7	5	4	9	1	2
1	4	6	2	3	8	5	9	7
7	3	9	5	6	1	8	2	4
8	2	5	4	9	7	3	6	1
6	8	4	1	2	9	7	5	3
2	9	3	8	7	5	1	4	6
5	7	1	3	4	6	2	8	9

PUZZLE / 728

2	1	4	5	7	6	9	8	3
8	3	7	9	4	2	6	1	5
6	9	5	8	3	1	7	4	2
9	2	3	4	1	8	5	6	7
5	8	6	2	9	7	4	3	1
4	7	1	3	6	5	2	9	8
1	4	9	7	5	3	8	2	6
3	5	2	6	8	4	1	7	9
7	6	8	1	2	9	3	5	4

PUZZLE / 729

4	5	7	2	3	6	1	9	8
2	9	8	1	7	4	6	3	5
3	1	6	9	8	5	4	7	2
7	3	5	4	6	9	2	8	1
8	2	4	7	5	1	3	6	9
1	6	9	3	2	8	7	5	4
6	7	1	5	9	2	8	4	3
5	4	3	8	1	7	9	2	6
9	8	2	6	4	3	5	1	7

PUZZLE / 730

9	6	4	3	1	5	8	7	2
1	3	8	4	7	2	6	9	5
7	5	2	6	9	8	3	4	1
8	9	3	7	5	4	1	2	6
4	1	5	9	2	6	7	3	8
6	2	7	1	8	3	4	5	9
2	8	6	5	4	7	9	1	3
3	7	1	2	6	9	5	8	4
5	4	9	8	3	1	2	6	7

PUZZLE / 731

8	7	9	6	2	3	1	5	4
2	6	3	4	5	1	7	9	8
4	1	5	9	7	8	6	2	3
3	2	7	8	4	6	9	1	5
6	8	4	1	9	5	3	7	2
9	5	1	2	3	7	8	4	6
7	4	8	3	1	2	5	6	9
1	3	2	5	6	9	4	8	7
5	9	6	7	8	4	2	3	1

PUZZLE / 732

2	6	1	8	7	3	9	5	4
4	8	9	2	5	6	1	3	7
5	7	3	4	9	1	6	8	2
7	5	6	3	8	4	2	1	9
9	4	2	7	1	5	8	6	3
3	1	8	9	6	2	4	7	5
1	2	7	5	4	8	3	9	6
6	3	5	1	2	9	7	4	8
8	9	4	6	3	7	5	2	1

PUZZLE / 733

3	4	8	9	1	5	2	7	6
2	6	1	4	3	7	9	5	8
9	5	7	2	8	6	1	3	4
8	7	2	6	4	1	3	9	5
4	1	9	8	5	3	6	2	7
6	3	5	7	2	9	4	8	1
7	8	4	3	6	2	5	1	9
5	2	6	1	9	8	7	4	3
1	9	3	5	7	4	8	6	2

PUZZLE / 734

9	1	7	2	5	6	4	8	3
4	5	2	3	8	1	7	6	9
6	8	3	7	9	4	5	1	2
2	4	6	1	3	5	8	9	7
8	3	1	9	7	2	6	4	5
7	9	5	6	4	8	3	2	1
3	6	8	5	1	9	2	7	4
1	7	4	8	2	3	9	5	6
5	2	9	4	6	7	1	3	8

PUZZLE / 735

7	8	1	3	4	6	9	5	2
5	9	6	2	1	7	4	3	8
3	4	2	9	8	5	7	1	6
1	5	8	7	9	4	6	2	3
2	3	9	5	6	1	8	7	4
6	7	4	8	2	3	1	9	5
9	1	5	4	3	8	2	6	7
8	6	7	1	5	2	3	4	9
4	2	3	6	7	9	5	8	1

PUZZLE / 736

3	6	1	2	5	4	9	7	8
2	5	9	6	7	8	1	3	4
4	7	8	9	3	1	6	5	2
8	3	5	1	2	9	7	4	6
7	2	6	4	8	5	3	9	1
9	1	4	3	6	7	8	2	5
6	4	2	8	9	3	5	1	7
1	9	7	5	4	6	2	8	3
5	8	3	7	1	2	4	6	9

PUZZLE / 737

1	2	8	7	3	5	4	6	9
4	7	5	9	1	6	8	3	2
9	6	3	2	8	4	1	7	5
2	4	6	5	9	3	7	8	1
5	8	1	4	2	7	6	9	3
3	9	7	1	6	8	5	2	4
6	5	4	3	7	2	9	1	8
8	3	9	6	5	1	2	4	7
7	1	2	8	4	9	3	5	6

PUZZLE / 738

1	9	4	2	7	6	8	5	3
7	2	5	1	3	8	4	9	6
6	8	3	4	5	9	7	1	2
5	3	9	6	4	1	2	8	7
4	6	8	5	2	7	1	3	9
2	1	7	8	9	3	5	6	4
9	7	2	3	8	5	6	4	1
8	4	6	9	1	2	3	7	5
3	5	1	7	6	4	9	2	8

PUZZLE / 739

6	4	2	1	9	7	5	3	8
9	1	3	4	8	5	6	2	7
7	8	5	6	3	2	4	1	9
8	5	9	2	6	4	3	7	1
3	7	1	9	5	8	2	6	4
2	6	4	3	7	1	8	9	5
1	9	6	5	4	3	7	8	2
4	2	7	8	1	6	9	5	3
5	3	8	7	2	9	1	4	6

PUZZLE / 740

9	3	4	7	2	5	6	8	1
7	2	5	8	1	6	9	4	3
1	6	8	9	3	4	2	7	5
8	5	6	2	4	3	7	1	9
2	4	7	1	9	8	3	5	6
3	1	9	6	5	7	4	2	8
4	8	3	5	7	9	1	6	2
6	7	1	3	8	2	5	9	4
5	9	2	4	6	1	8	3	7

PUZZLE / 741

3	4	1	7	9	5	8	2	6
9	8	5	6	2	4	3	7	1
7	6	2	3	1	8	9	4	5
5	7	9	8	6	3	4	1	2
8	3	6	2	4	1	7	5	9
1	2	4	5	7	9	6	8	3
2	5	8	4	3	6	1	9	7
6	1	7	9	8	2	5	3	4
4	9	3	1	5	7	2	6	8

PUZZLE / 742

6	2	8	3	1	9	5	7	4
1	9	7	5	6	4	2	3	8
4	5	3	8	2	7	6	1	9
7	1	6	9	8	2	3	4	5
3	4	5	1	7	6	9	8	2
9	8	2	4	5	3	7	6	1
2	3	9	6	4	8	1	5	7
8	7	1	2	3	5	4	9	6
5	6	4	7	9	1	8	2	3

PUZZLE / 743

1	5	7	2	8	4	9	6	3
8	9	3	6	5	1	7	2	4
2	6	4	7	3	9	1	5	8
9	2	6	4	7	5	3	8	1
4	3	8	1	9	2	6	7	5
5	7	1	3	6	8	4	9	2
6	1	5	8	4	7	2	3	9
7	4	9	5	2	3	8	1	6
3	8	2	9	1	6	5	4	7

PUZZLE / 744

7	5	3	2	1	8	9	6	4
6	2	9	7	5	4	8	3	1
4	8	1	6	9	3	5	7	2
8	7	4	3	6	2	1	5	9
2	9	5	1	4	7	6	8	3
3	1	6	9	8	5	2	4	7
9	4	2	5	3	6	7	1	8
5	3	7	8	2	1	4	9	6
1	6	8	4	7	9	3	2	5

PUZZLE / 745

6	4	7	1	8	9	5	2	3
2	5	9	6	3	4	1	8	7
1	8	3	5	7	2	6	9	4
3	1	8	4	9	5	2	7	6
9	6	5	3	2	7	4	1	8
4	7	2	8	1	6	9	3	5
5	2	1	7	6	8	3	4	9
7	3	6	9	4	1	8	5	2
8	9	4	2	5	3	7	6	1

PUZZLE / 746

8	6	1	3	9	5	4	2	7
3	7	5	8	4	2	9	1	6
9	4	2	1	7	6	5	3	8
7	2	9	4	8	3	6	5	1
6	5	3	9	2	1	8	7	4
4	1	8	5	6	7	3	9	2
5	8	7	6	1	9	2	4	3
1	3	6	2	5	4	7	8	9
2	9	4	7	3	8	1	6	5

PUZZLE / 747

2	5	6	4	9	3	7	1	8
7	8	4	1	2	6	3	5	9
3	9	1	5	7	8	6	2	4
5	2	7	8	3	1	4	9	6
9	6	3	2	4	7	5	8	1
4	1	8	9	6	5	2	3	7
8	7	9	6	5	2	1	4	3
1	3	5	7	8	4	9	6	2
6	4	2	3	1	9	8	7	5

PUZZLE / 748

5	9	6	8	3	4	2	7	1
8	7	2	9	1	6	4	5	3
1	4	3	7	5	2	9	6	8
9	2	1	5	6	8	3	4	7
6	3	5	4	7	1	8	2	9
4	8	7	3	2	9	6	1	5
2	5	9	6	8	7	1	3	4
3	6	4	1	9	5	7	8	2
7	1	8	2	4	3	5	9	6

PUZZLE / 749

4	3	8	5	9	7	6	1	2
9	2	1	4	6	3	8	7	5
5	7	6	1	8	2	4	9	3
7	8	9	2	5	4	1	3	6
1	4	5	3	7	6	9	2	8
3	6	2	9	1	8	7	5	4
6	5	7	8	3	9	2	4	1
8	1	4	7	2	5	3	6	9
2	9	3	6	4	1	5	8	7

PUZZLE / 750

3	2	5	9	8	7	6	4	1
8	6	9	1	4	3	7	2	5
7	4	1	5	2	6	3	8	9
6	1	8	7	9	4	2	5	3
2	9	4	3	5	8	1	6	7
5	7	3	6	1	2	8	9	4
4	3	7	8	6	5	9	1	2
1	8	2	4	7	9	5	3	6
9	5	6	2	3	1	4	7	8

PUZZLE / 751

8	5	4	6	1	7	3	2	9
6	3	1	9	8	2	5	4	7
2	9	7	4	5	3	6	1	8
1	4	8	7	2	6	9	5	3
3	7	9	1	4	5	2	8	6
5	6	2	8	3	9	1	7	4
4	2	5	3	6	8	7	9	1
7	1	6	5	9	4	8	3	2
9	8	3	2	7	1	4	6	5

PUZZLE / 752

7	5	4	6	3	2	8	1	9
2	9	1	7	5	8	6	3	4
3	8	6	4	9	1	7	5	2
5	6	2	9	4	3	1	7	8
4	7	3	1	8	5	9	2	6
9	1	8	2	7	6	5	4	3
6	4	9	3	1	7	2	8	5
8	2	7	5	6	4	3	9	1
1	3	5	8	2	9	4	6	7

PUZZLE / 753

6	4	7	2	1	9	8	5	3
9	3	2	6	8	5	4	1	7
1	5	8	7	3	4	6	2	9
7	9	5	3	6	1	2	4	8
3	1	6	4	2	8	9	7	5
2	8	4	5	9	7	3	6	1
4	7	3	9	5	6	1	8	2
8	6	9	1	7	2	5	3	4
5	2	1	8	4	3	7	9	6

PUZZLE / 754

4	7	6	3	2	9	1	8	5
3	1	8	7	6	5	4	9	2
9	5	2	4	8	1	6	7	3
5	9	1	6	3	2	7	4	8
8	2	4	9	5	7	3	1	6
7	6	3	1	4	8	2	5	9
2	4	9	5	7	3	8	6	1
1	8	7	2	9	6	5	3	4
6	3	5	8	1	4	9	2	7

PUZZLE / 755

8	1	9	3	2	7	6	4	5
5	4	3	6	1	8	7	9	2
7	6	2	9	5	4	3	8	1
1	8	7	5	4	6	9	2	3
4	2	5	7	9	3	8	1	6
3	9	6	1	8	2	4	5	7
9	3	8	2	6	5	1	7	4
2	7	4	8	3	1	5	6	9
6	5	1	4	7	9	2	3	8

PUZZLE / 756

5	9	6	1	3	4	8	2	7
1	4	2	7	9	8	3	5	6
7	3	8	2	6	5	9	4	1
4	6	7	9	8	2	1	3	5
8	5	9	3	1	6	2	7	4
3	2	1	5	4	7	6	8	9
2	1	3	4	7	9	5	6	8
6	7	5	8	2	1	4	9	3
9	8	4	6	5	3	7	1	2

PUZZLE / 757

6	2	5	4	8	3	7	1	9
4	3	1	9	7	6	2	8	5
7	8	9	5	2	1	3	4	6
1	6	7	2	3	8	5	9	4
5	9	2	6	4	7	1	3	8
3	4	8	1	5	9	6	7	2
9	7	3	8	6	2	4	5	1
8	5	6	3	1	4	9	2	7
2	1	4	7	9	5	8	6	3

PUZZLE / 758

7	8	6	1	2	3	9	5	4
5	3	1	8	9	4	7	6	2
2	4	9	5	6	7	8	3	1
8	9	7	6	3	1	2	4	5
6	2	3	4	5	9	1	7	8
1	5	4	2	7	8	3	9	6
4	7	8	9	1	6	5	2	3
9	6	2	3	8	5	4	1	7
3	1	5	7	4	2	6	8	9

PUZZLE / 759

6	5	7	2	8	9	1	3	4
3	1	2	4	5	7	6	8	9
9	8	4	1	6	3	2	5	7
2	7	5	8	1	4	9	6	3
4	6	1	9	3	5	7	2	8
8	3	9	7	2	6	4	1	5
7	2	3	5	4	1	8	9	6
5	4	8	6	9	2	3	7	1
1	9	6	3	7	8	5	4	2

PUZZLE / 760

4	9	1	3	7	8	5	6	2
3	5	8	1	6	2	9	7	4
7	6	2	5	9	4	3	1	8
9	1	4	6	3	7	8	2	5
5	8	6	2	4	9	1	3	7
2	3	7	8	1	5	4	9	6
8	4	9	7	2	3	6	5	1
6	7	5	9	8	1	2	4	3
1	2	3	4	5	6	7	8	9

PUZZLE / 761

3	5	2	6	4	1	8	9	7
9	4	6	7	8	3	2	1	5
8	7	1	2	5	9	3	6	4
6	2	7	8	3	5	1	4	9
5	8	9	4	1	7	6	2	3
1	3	4	9	2	6	7	5	8
7	6	5	1	9	8	4	3	2
2	1	3	5	7	4	9	8	6
4	9	8	3	6	2	5	7	1

PUZZLE / 762

8	5	4	6	9	3	7	1	2
1	6	9	7	2	8	5	4	3
7	3	2	1	4	5	8	9	6
4	9	1	3	5	2	6	7	8
6	8	3	9	7	1	4	2	5
2	7	5	8	6	4	9	3	1
9	1	8	5	3	7	2	6	4
3	2	6	4	8	9	1	5	7
5	4	7	2	1	6	3	8	9

PUZZLE / 763

3	4	7	5	9	6	2	1	8
9	1	6	4	2	8	7	3	5
8	2	5	7	1	3	4	9	6
5	8	2	1	7	9	3	6	4
1	6	4	2	3	5	8	7	9
7	9	3	8	6	4	1	5	2
6	7	9	3	4	2	5	8	1
2	5	1	9	8	7	6	4	3
4	3	8	6	5	1	9	2	7

PUZZLE / 764

5	7	1	3	8	6	9	4	2
8	2	9	4	7	1	3	6	5
4	6	3	5	9	2	1	8	7
3	1	5	8	6	4	2	7	9
2	9	4	1	3	7	6	5	8
7	8	6	9	2	5	4	1	3
9	3	7	6	1	8	5	2	4
6	5	8	2	4	3	7	9	1
1	4	2	7	5	9	8	3	6

PUZZLE / 765

7	4	8	9	5	1	6	3	2
1	9	3	4	2	6	8	7	5
6	2	5	7	8	3	9	1	4
5	1	9	6	7	2	3	4	8
4	7	6	8	3	9	2	5	1
3	8	2	1	4	5	7	6	9
8	3	7	5	9	4	1	2	6
2	6	4	3	1	8	5	9	7
9	5	1	2	6	7	4	8	3

PUZZLE / 766

6	3	1	8	5	2	7	4	9
7	2	9	6	1	4	5	8	3
8	5	4	3	7	9	2	1	6
9	7	5	1	4	8	3	6	2
1	4	6	2	9	3	8	5	7
3	8	2	7	6	5	1	9	4
2	1	3	9	8	6	4	7	5
5	6	8	4	2	7	9	3	1
4	9	7	5	3	1	6	2	8

PUZZLE / 767

4	2	6	5	7	8	9	1	3
1	7	9	6	2	3	5	4	8
5	3	8	4	1	9	6	7	2
3	9	1	7	5	2	4	8	6
2	6	7	8	3	4	1	9	5
8	5	4	1	9	6	3	2	7
9	4	3	2	6	7	8	5	1
6	1	2	9	8	5	7	3	4
7	8	5	3	4	1	2	6	9

PUZZLE / 768

1	8	9	2	7	4	5	6	3
5	6	4	1	9	3	7	2	8
2	7	3	6	5	8	4	9	1
4	5	7	8	1	6	9	3	2
6	3	8	9	2	5	1	4	7
9	1	2	3	4	7	8	5	6
7	4	6	5	8	2	3	1	9
8	2	1	4	3	9	6	7	5
3	9	5	7	6	1	2	8	4

PUZZLE / 769

8	2	6	4	7	1	9	3	5
1	9	3	6	2	5	8	4	7
5	4	7	9	8	3	1	2	6
9	7	4	2	1	6	3	5	8
2	1	5	8	3	4	7	6	9
3	6	8	7	5	9	2	1	4
7	8	1	5	4	2	6	9	3
6	5	2	3	9	8	4	7	1
4	3	9	1	6	7	5	8	2

PUZZLE / 770

1	7	3	8	5	9	4	6	2
5	4	2	7	3	6	1	9	8
6	9	8	1	2	4	3	5	7
3	8	4	5	7	2	9	1	6
2	6	9	4	1	3	8	7	5
7	5	1	9	6	8	2	4	3
4	2	6	3	9	5	7	8	1
9	3	7	6	8	1	5	2	4
8	1	5	2	4	7	6	3	9

PUZZLE / 771

9	4	1	8	3	6	7	2	5
8	3	2	5	7	9	1	4	6
5	6	7	1	4	2	8	9	3
2	1	9	3	6	7	5	8	4
3	7	5	4	2	8	9	6	1
6	8	4	9	5	1	2	3	7
1	5	8	6	9	4	3	7	2
4	2	3	7	8	5	6	1	9
7	9	6	2	1	3	4	5	8

PUZZLE / 772

7	1	5	4	9	2	3	6	8
4	8	2	3	5	6	9	7	1
6	9	3	8	7	1	4	5	2
1	2	6	9	3	7	8	4	5
3	5	7	1	4	8	2	9	6
9	4	8	6	2	5	7	1	3
5	7	9	2	6	3	1	8	4
2	6	1	7	8	4	5	3	9
8	3	4	5	1	9	6	2	7

PUZZLE / 773

3	7	1	9	8	4	6	5	2
8	2	6	5	3	7	9	1	4
5	9	4	6	1	2	8	3	7
4	1	9	3	6	8	2	7	5
6	5	2	4	7	1	3	9	8
7	8	3	2	5	9	4	6	1
2	4	5	7	9	3	1	8	6
9	6	8	1	4	5	7	2	3
1	3	7	8	2	6	5	4	9

PUZZLE / 774

2	4	5	3	7	8	1	9	6
9	6	7	1	2	4	8	3	5
1	3	8	6	9	5	2	4	7
7	9	1	4	6	2	5	8	3
8	2	4	5	3	9	6	7	1
6	5	3	7	8	1	9	2	4
3	7	9	8	1	6	4	5	2
4	8	6	2	5	3	7	1	9
5	1	2	9	4	7	3	6	8

PUZZLE / 775

5	1	6	3	8	4	9	2	7
3	4	2	7	9	6	1	8	5
8	9	7	5	2	1	3	4	6
1	5	9	2	4	7	8	6	3
4	2	8	6	5	3	7	1	9
6	7	3	8	1	9	2	5	4
9	6	5	1	7	2	4	3	8
2	8	4	9	3	5	6	7	1
7	3	1	4	6	8	5	9	2

PUZZLE / 776

5	3	7	1	9	2	4	8	6
9	4	2	5	8	6	1	7	3
1	6	8	3	7	4	5	9	2
3	9	5	7	1	8	6	2	4
6	7	1	2	4	5	9	3	8
2	8	4	9	6	3	7	1	5
4	1	6	8	3	7	2	5	9
8	2	9	4	5	1	3	6	7
7	5	3	6	2	9	8	4	1

PUZZLE / 777

6	7	8	1	4	9	2	3	5
2	1	3	6	5	8	4	9	7
4	9	5	3	2	7	8	1	6
3	5	4	2	9	6	7	8	1
7	6	9	5	8	1	3	2	4
8	2	1	4	7	3	5	6	9
5	8	2	9	1	4	6	7	3
1	4	6	7	3	2	9	5	8
9	3	7	8	6	5	1	4	2

PUZZLE / 778

4	6	2	7	3	5	8	1	9
9	7	8	4	1	6	3	2	5
3	1	5	9	8	2	7	4	6
2	3	9	1	6	8	4	5	7
5	4	1	2	9	7	6	3	8
6	8	7	3	5	4	1	9	2
7	2	3	6	4	9	5	8	1
8	9	4	5	7	1	2	6	3
1	5	6	8	2	3	9	7	4

PUZZLE / 779

6	1	8	5	2	3	4	9	7
7	3	4	8	1	9	5	6	2
2	9	5	6	7	4	1	3	8
5	8	9	2	3	7	6	4	1
1	2	3	4	5	6	7	8	9
4	6	7	9	8	1	3	2	5
8	5	6	1	4	2	9	7	3
3	4	2	7	9	5	8	1	6
9	7	1	3	6	8	2	5	4

PUZZLE / 780

5	7	3	8	2	9	1	6	4
4	2	6	5	7	1	3	9	8
8	1	9	4	3	6	5	7	2
3	9	8	6	1	7	4	2	5
7	4	1	2	9	5	8	3	6
2	6	5	3	8	4	9	1	7
6	3	7	9	5	8	2	4	1
1	8	2	7	4	3	6	5	9
9	5	4	1	6	2	7	8	3

PUZZLE / 781

5	8	3	1	4	6	7	9	2
4	1	6	2	9	7	3	5	8
2	9	7	8	5	3	4	1	6
6	7	2	3	1	9	8	4	5
9	4	5	7	2	8	6	3	1
1	3	8	4	6	5	9	2	7
7	5	1	9	8	4	2	6	3
3	6	9	5	7	2	1	8	4
8	2	4	6	3	1	5	7	9

PUZZLE / 782

7	1	5	2	6	3	4	8	9
6	8	3	4	9	1	7	5	2
2	4	9	5	8	7	3	1	6
1	3	8	6	5	9	2	4	7
4	2	6	3	7	8	1	9	5
5	9	7	1	4	2	8	6	3
8	5	2	7	1	6	9	3	4
3	6	1	9	2	4	5	7	8
9	7	4	8	3	5	6	2	1

PUZZLE / 783

6	4	3	8	7	5	2	1	9
8	2	1	6	4	9	7	3	5
7	5	9	3	1	2	4	6	8
2	6	7	1	3	8	5	9	4
9	1	8	4	5	6	3	2	7
4	3	5	9	2	7	6	8	1
1	7	2	5	8	3	9	4	6
5	9	4	2	6	1	8	7	3
3	8	6	7	9	4	1	5	2

PUZZLE / **784**

6	7	2	3	4	5	9	1	8
1	4	9	7	8	2	5	6	3
8	3	5	1	6	9	2	4	7
2	1	3	5	7	8	4	9	6
9	8	6	4	2	1	7	3	5
4	5	7	6	9	3	1	8	2
5	2	1	8	3	4	6	7	9
3	6	4	9	5	7	8	2	1
7	9	8	2	1	6	3	5	4

PUZZLE / **785**

6	2	5	3	8	7	1	9	4
4	9	8	6	5	1	7	2	3
3	1	7	4	2	9	5	8	6
5	4	3	9	1	2	8	6	7
7	6	1	8	3	5	9	4	2
9	8	2	7	6	4	3	1	5
1	3	9	5	4	6	2	7	8
8	7	6	2	9	3	4	5	1
2	5	4	1	7	8	6	3	9

PUZZLE / **786**

7	4	8	6	3	2	1	9	5
9	1	2	7	8	5	4	3	6
3	5	6	9	1	4	8	2	7
4	3	9	2	7	1	6	5	8
6	7	5	8	4	3	9	1	2
2	8	1	5	6	9	3	7	4
5	6	7	3	9	8	2	4	1
8	9	4	1	2	7	5	6	3
1	2	3	4	5	6	7	8	9

PUZZLE / **787**

4	8	3	9	7	2	5	1	6
1	9	5	8	3	6	2	7	4
7	6	2	5	4	1	8	3	9
8	3	7	6	2	5	9	4	1
9	5	4	7	1	8	6	2	3
6	2	1	4	9	3	7	5	8
2	4	8	3	5	9	1	6	7
5	7	6	1	8	4	3	9	2
3	1	9	2	6	7	4	8	5

PUZZLE / **788**

6	9	4	7	1	2	3	8	5
1	2	8	5	3	9	7	4	6
7	5	3	4	6	8	9	1	2
5	1	9	8	7	6	2	3	4
3	4	7	1	2	5	8	6	9
2	8	6	9	4	3	1	5	7
9	6	1	2	8	4	5	7	3
4	7	2	3	5	1	6	9	8
8	3	5	6	9	7	4	2	1

PUZZLE / **789**

5	6	8	1	4	9	3	2	7
4	3	7	5	2	8	6	1	9
1	9	2	6	7	3	4	5	8
2	7	4	9	6	5	1	8	3
3	5	9	7	8	1	2	4	6
8	1	6	2	3	4	9	7	5
6	8	3	4	5	2	7	9	1
7	2	1	8	9	6	5	3	4
9	4	5	3	1	7	8	6	2

PUZZLE / **790**

6	1	7	5	4	9	3	2	8
5	9	2	6	3	8	1	4	7
8	4	3	2	1	7	6	5	9
9	3	5	4	7	2	8	6	1
4	7	1	8	6	3	2	9	5
2	8	6	1	9	5	4	7	3
1	6	9	3	5	4	7	8	2
3	5	8	7	2	6	9	1	4
7	2	4	9	8	1	5	3	6

PUZZLE / **791**

9	3	6	2	8	1	4	7	5
4	8	5	3	9	7	6	1	2
1	2	7	4	5	6	9	3	8
5	7	1	9	4	2	8	6	3
3	6	2	5	7	8	1	4	9
8	9	4	1	6	3	5	2	7
2	4	3	8	1	9	7	5	6
6	1	9	7	3	5	2	8	4
7	5	8	6	2	4	3	9	1

PUZZLE / **792**

9	3	8	2	6	1	5	4	7
7	4	1	5	9	3	6	8	2
5	6	2	4	8	7	3	9	1
2	7	4	8	1	6	9	3	5
6	1	5	9	3	2	4	7	8
8	9	3	7	5	4	1	2	6
4	8	6	3	7	5	2	1	9
3	5	9	1	2	8	7	6	4
1	2	7	6	4	9	8	5	3

PUZZLE / **793**

5	2	9	7	8	6	1	4	3
1	3	8	4	2	9	5	6	7
6	7	4	1	3	5	9	2	8
8	4	5	3	9	7	2	1	6
7	6	1	2	4	8	3	9	5
2	9	3	5	6	1	8	7	4
3	5	2	6	1	4	7	8	9
4	8	7	9	5	2	6	3	1
9	1	6	8	7	3	4	5	2

PUZZLE / **794**

5	4	7	6	3	1	9	8	2
9	6	8	7	5	2	1	3	4
2	3	1	4	8	9	5	6	7
4	1	3	9	6	8	2	7	5
8	2	5	3	1	7	6	4	9
7	9	6	2	4	5	3	1	8
1	8	4	5	9	3	7	2	6
3	7	9	8	2	6	4	5	1
6	5	2	1	7	4	8	9	3

PUZZLE / **795**

7	6	1	9	2	4	3	8	5
9	3	4	1	8	5	6	7	2
8	2	5	7	6	3	4	1	9
5	7	2	6	3	8	1	9	4
1	9	8	5	4	7	2	3	6
3	4	6	2	1	9	7	5	8
2	8	3	4	5	1	9	6	7
4	5	7	3	9	6	8	2	1
6	1	9	8	7	2	5	4	3

PUZZLE / **796**

2	3	7	6	1	4	8	5	9
4	9	5	2	7	8	3	6	1
8	6	1	9	5	3	2	4	7
7	2	9	3	8	5	6	1	4
1	5	8	4	6	9	7	2	3
3	4	6	1	2	7	5	9	8
9	8	3	5	4	6	1	7	2
5	1	4	7	3	2	9	8	6
6	7	2	8	9	1	4	3	5

PUZZLE / **797**

8	6	7	1	3	5	4	9	2
4	5	1	6	2	9	8	7	3
3	9	2	8	7	4	1	5	6
2	8	9	4	5	7	6	3	1
5	1	3	9	6	2	7	4	8
7	4	6	3	8	1	5	2	9
9	7	5	2	1	6	3	8	4
6	3	4	7	9	8	2	1	5
1	2	8	5	4	3	9	6	7

PUZZLE / **798**

4	2	9	5	8	1	3	7	6
5	6	3	4	9	7	2	1	8
7	1	8	2	3	6	5	9	4
3	5	6	8	7	2	9	4	1
8	7	4	1	5	9	6	3	2
2	9	1	3	6	4	7	8	5
9	4	2	7	1	5	8	6	3
1	3	7	6	2	8	4	5	9
6	8	5	9	4	3	1	2	7

PUZZLE / 799

8	6	3	7	1	9	2	5	4
7	5	4	2	3	8	6	1	9
1	9	2	6	4	5	3	7	8
2	4	9	1	7	3	8	6	5
3	7	8	9	5	6	4	2	1
5	1	6	8	2	4	7	9	3
4	8	7	5	9	2	1	3	6
9	3	1	4	6	7	5	8	2
6	2	5	3	8	1	9	4	7

PUZZLE / 800

1	9	4	2	3	6	7	8	5
7	6	8	9	5	1	3	2	4
3	2	5	4	8	7	9	1	6
9	7	2	6	1	4	8	5	3
5	4	3	8	7	9	1	6	2
8	1	6	5	2	3	4	7	9
6	5	1	3	9	8	2	4	7
2	8	9	7	4	5	6	3	1
4	3	7	1	6	2	5	9	8

PUZZLE / 801

1	6	4	5	3	9	2	7	8
3	2	5	4	7	8	6	9	1
9	8	7	1	6	2	3	4	5
5	7	1	9	2	6	4	8	3
4	9	2	8	5	3	7	1	6
8	3	6	7	4	1	9	5	2
6	5	9	2	8	4	1	3	7
2	4	8	3	1	7	5	6	9
7	1	3	6	9	5	8	2	4

PUZZLE / 802

9	2	7	4	3	8	1	6	5
5	1	4	2	7	6	9	3	8
6	8	3	9	5	1	4	7	2
2	5	1	8	6	9	7	4	3
7	3	6	5	1	4	2	8	9
4	9	8	3	2	7	5	1	6
3	7	5	6	4	2	8	9	1
8	4	2	1	9	3	6	5	7
1	6	9	7	8	5	3	2	4

PUZZLE / 803

1	2	5	7	8	3	9	4	6
3	4	8	2	9	6	7	1	5
9	7	6	5	4	1	2	8	3
4	9	7	6	5	8	3	2	1
6	5	1	3	2	9	4	7	8
2	8	3	4	1	7	5	6	9
5	1	2	8	3	4	6	9	7
7	3	9	1	6	2	8	5	4
8	6	4	9	7	5	1	3	2

PUZZLE / 804

7	9	6	5	8	2	3	1	4
3	2	4	7	9	1	6	5	8
5	1	8	6	3	4	7	9	2
9	6	7	2	1	8	4	3	5
2	3	5	9	4	7	1	8	6
8	4	1	3	5	6	9	2	7
4	8	2	1	6	9	5	7	3
6	5	9	8	7	3	2	4	1
1	7	3	4	2	5	8	6	9

PUZZLE / 805

8	2	1	5	6	3	7	4	9
6	4	3	1	9	7	2	5	8
9	5	7	4	8	2	3	1	6
2	8	4	9	7	6	5	3	1
1	9	6	3	5	4	8	2	7
3	7	5	2	1	8	6	9	4
7	1	9	8	3	5	4	6	2
4	3	8	6	2	9	1	7	5
5	6	2	7	4	1	9	8	3

PUZZLE / 806

9	7	8	2	3	5	6	1	4
1	2	4	9	6	7	3	8	5
3	6	5	1	4	8	2	9	7
5	3	7	4	9	2	8	6	1
2	8	9	5	1	6	7	4	3
6	4	1	8	7	3	9	5	2
4	1	2	3	8	9	5	7	6
7	9	3	6	5	4	1	2	8
8	5	6	7	2	1	4	3	9

PUZZLE / 807

4	5	8	1	9	2	6	3	7
9	3	2	6	7	4	8	1	5
1	6	7	3	5	8	4	9	2
5	4	3	8	6	7	9	2	1
2	7	9	4	3	1	5	6	8
6	8	1	5	2	9	7	4	3
7	2	6	9	8	3	1	5	4
8	9	4	2	1	5	3	7	6
3	1	5	7	4	6	2	8	9

PUZZLE / 808

2	3	6	4	8	5	1	9	7
4	1	9	2	7	3	8	6	5
7	8	5	1	6	9	2	4	3
5	6	2	8	1	7	4	3	9
9	4	8	5	3	2	7	1	6
3	7	1	9	4	6	5	2	8
1	5	7	6	9	4	3	8	2
8	9	3	7	2	1	6	5	4
6	2	4	3	5	8	9	7	1

PUZZLE / 809

7	1	5	8	2	6	9	4	3
8	3	9	4	1	5	2	6	7
6	4	2	7	9	3	1	5	8
4	8	6	1	7	2	5	3	9
3	2	7	9	5	8	4	1	6
5	9	1	3	6	4	8	7	2
1	6	8	2	4	7	3	9	5
9	5	3	6	8	1	7	2	4
2	7	4	5	3	9	6	8	1

PUZZLE / 810

8	3	9	7	5	6	4	2	1
7	5	4	2	1	8	9	6	3
1	2	6	3	4	9	8	5	7
6	4	2	8	3	7	1	9	5
9	1	8	6	2	5	3	7	4
3	7	5	1	9	4	6	8	2
4	9	7	5	6	1	2	3	8
2	8	1	9	7	3	5	4	6
5	6	3	4	8	2	7	1	9

PUZZLE / 811

2	3	8	1	7	6	9	4	5
1	5	9	4	2	3	7	8	6
7	4	6	9	5	8	3	2	1
6	7	3	2	8	1	4	5	9
9	1	4	5	3	7	8	6	2
8	2	5	6	9	4	1	7	3
3	8	2	7	6	9	5	1	4
5	9	1	8	4	2	6	3	7
4	6	7	3	1	5	2	9	8

PUZZLE / 812

8	4	6	3	7	1	9	5	2
1	3	2	5	8	9	7	6	4
9	5	7	2	6	4	3	8	1
3	2	1	4	5	6	8	9	7
4	6	9	8	3	7	2	1	5
7	8	5	1	9	2	6	4	3
2	9	4	6	1	3	5	7	8
6	1	8	7	2	5	4	3	9
5	7	3	9	4	8	1	2	6

PUZZLE / 813

3	1	4	9	5	2	7	8	6
7	8	2	4	3	6	9	5	1
5	6	9	1	8	7	4	2	3
4	7	8	2	1	5	6	3	9
1	5	3	7	6	9	2	4	8
9	2	6	8	4	3	5	1	7
8	3	7	6	2	4	1	9	5
6	4	1	5	9	8	3	7	2
2	9	5	3	7	1	8	6	4

PUZZLE / **814**

1	2	6	5	3	9	7	4	8
7	4	9	2	1	8	3	5	6
8	3	5	4	6	7	9	2	1
2	9	1	6	8	3	4	7	5
6	7	3	9	4	5	8	1	2
5	8	4	1	7	2	6	3	9
3	5	7	8	2	6	1	9	4
4	6	2	7	9	1	5	8	3
9	1	8	3	5	4	2	6	7

PUZZLE / **815**

4	6	2	8	5	7	3	9	1
1	9	7	2	3	4	5	8	6
8	5	3	9	6	1	7	4	2
6	8	5	7	4	9	1	2	3
2	3	4	5	1	6	8	7	9
7	1	9	3	8	2	4	6	5
9	4	8	1	2	3	6	5	7
5	2	1	6	7	8	9	3	4
3	7	6	4	9	5	2	1	8

PUZZLE / **816**

6	1	8	3	9	4	5	2	7
2	4	9	5	7	6	8	1	3
3	5	7	1	8	2	4	6	9
8	7	5	4	1	3	2	9	6
9	2	3	7	6	8	1	5	4
4	6	1	9	2	5	3	7	8
5	8	2	6	4	9	7	3	1
7	3	6	8	5	1	9	4	2
1	9	4	2	3	7	6	8	5

PUZZLE / **817**

5	6	2	8	3	7	9	4	1
9	8	7	6	1	4	2	3	5
1	4	3	5	9	2	7	6	8
3	7	9	2	6	5	1	8	4
8	2	4	3	7	1	6	5	9
6	1	5	9	4	8	3	2	7
7	5	8	1	2	3	4	9	6
2	9	1	4	5	6	8	7	3
4	3	6	7	8	9	5	1	2

PUZZLE / **818**

3	4	9	2	5	6	7	8	1
1	8	5	7	4	9	2	3	6
2	7	6	3	8	1	5	9	4
6	1	2	4	9	3	8	7	5
8	9	7	1	6	5	3	4	2
4	5	3	8	7	2	1	6	9
9	6	1	5	3	7	4	2	8
7	2	8	6	1	4	9	5	3
5	3	4	9	2	8	6	1	7

PUZZLE / **819**

4	3	7	9	8	6	5	1	2
6	2	8	1	5	7	9	4	3
1	5	9	3	4	2	6	7	8
9	6	4	8	1	3	7	2	5
3	8	2	6	7	5	4	9	1
5	7	1	2	9	4	8	3	6
2	1	5	7	6	9	3	8	4
7	4	3	5	2	8	1	6	9
8	9	6	4	3	1	2	5	7

PUZZLE / **820**

7	1	6	9	8	2	3	4	5
4	5	9	7	3	6	8	1	2
8	3	2	4	1	5	7	6	9
5	4	3	2	6	9	1	8	7
9	6	8	1	5	7	2	3	4
1	2	7	3	4	8	9	5	6
2	8	4	6	9	1	5	7	3
6	9	5	8	7	3	4	2	1
3	7	1	5	2	4	6	9	8

PUZZLE / **821**

8	4	2	3	9	7	1	5	6
1	9	5	8	2	6	3	7	4
6	3	7	1	4	5	2	8	9
2	5	4	6	3	8	7	9	1
7	6	9	5	1	2	4	3	8
3	1	8	4	7	9	6	2	5
9	7	1	2	8	4	5	6	3
4	8	6	7	5	3	9	1	2
5	2	3	9	6	1	8	4	7

PUZZLE / **822**

5	7	4	9	2	3	8	6	1
6	1	2	4	8	7	3	5	9
8	3	9	6	5	1	2	7	4
2	5	3	1	4	6	7	9	8
7	4	8	5	9	2	1	3	6
1	9	6	7	3	8	4	2	5
4	6	1	3	7	5	9	8	2
3	8	5	2	1	9	6	4	7
9	2	7	8	6	4	5	1	3

PUZZLE / **823**

2	7	9	8	5	3	1	4	6
6	8	4	7	1	2	9	3	5
3	1	5	4	9	6	2	7	8
8	9	1	3	6	5	7	2	4
5	4	2	9	8	7	6	1	3
7	3	6	1	2	4	8	5	9
1	5	7	6	4	8	3	9	2
4	6	3	2	7	9	5	8	1
9	2	8	5	3	1	4	6	7

PUZZLE / **824**

8	4	7	2	6	3	1	5	9
1	6	3	9	8	5	7	2	4
2	5	9	7	4	1	6	3	8
9	3	6	5	7	8	2	4	1
5	2	4	3	1	6	8	9	7
7	1	8	4	9	2	5	6	3
3	7	1	6	2	4	9	8	5
4	8	2	1	5	9	3	7	6
6	9	5	8	3	7	4	1	2

PUZZLE / **825**

3	2	7	1	4	8	9	5	6
4	8	5	2	9	6	3	1	7
1	6	9	7	3	5	2	8	4
7	4	6	3	8	2	1	9	5
9	5	2	6	7	1	4	3	8
8	1	3	4	5	9	7	6	2
2	9	1	5	6	4	8	7	3
5	7	4	8	1	3	6	2	9
6	3	8	9	2	7	5	4	1

PUZZLE / **826**

2	9	4	7	1	3	8	5	6
8	7	3	2	5	6	1	9	4
1	5	6	4	8	9	7	3	2
9	4	1	8	2	7	3	6	5
6	8	5	1	3	4	2	7	9
7	3	2	6	9	5	4	1	8
5	2	7	9	4	1	6	8	3
3	1	8	5	6	2	9	4	7
4	6	9	3	7	8	5	2	1

PUZZLE / **827**

3	2	9	4	1	8	7	6	5
4	5	8	7	6	3	1	2	9
7	1	6	9	5	2	3	8	4
8	7	5	2	4	9	6	3	1
6	9	1	5	3	7	8	4	2
2	4	3	1	8	6	9	5	7
1	6	2	3	7	5	4	9	8
5	8	7	6	9	4	2	1	3
9	3	4	8	2	1	5	7	6

PUZZLE / **828**

9	5	6	7	8	2	3	4	1
4	1	2	9	3	5	7	8	6
3	7	8	4	6	1	9	5	2
2	6	3	8	5	9	1	7	4
1	4	5	3	2	7	8	6	9
8	9	7	6	1	4	2	3	5
5	8	1	2	4	3	6	9	7
7	3	4	1	9	6	5	2	8
6	2	9	5	7	8	4	1	3

PUZZLE / 829

1	2	9	6	8	4	3	7	5
4	3	5	7	9	2	1	6	8
6	8	7	3	1	5	4	2	9
3	7	2	1	4	8	9	5	6
5	9	6	2	3	7	8	4	1
8	1	4	5	6	9	2	3	7
9	5	1	4	7	3	6	8	2
7	6	3	8	2	1	5	9	4
2	4	8	9	5	6	7	1	3

PUZZLE / 830

8	4	9	7	6	3	5	1	2
6	3	1	5	2	8	7	9	4
7	2	5	1	4	9	8	6	3
1	6	4	9	8	5	3	2	7
9	8	3	2	1	7	6	4	5
5	7	2	4	3	6	1	8	9
3	5	8	6	9	4	2	7	1
4	1	7	8	5	2	9	3	6
2	9	6	3	7	1	4	5	8

PUZZLE / 831

2	8	5	9	1	7	6	3	4
9	6	7	8	3	4	1	2	5
1	4	3	6	5	2	9	8	7
3	5	1	2	6	8	7	4	9
8	7	2	4	9	5	3	6	1
6	9	4	3	7	1	8	5	2
4	2	9	7	8	3	5	1	6
5	3	6	1	2	9	4	7	8
7	1	8	5	4	6	2	9	3

PUZZLE / 832

1	4	5	7	8	2	3	6	9
6	2	8	9	3	1	7	5	4
9	7	3	4	5	6	1	2	8
4	8	1	5	2	7	6	9	3
5	3	7	6	9	8	2	4	1
2	6	9	1	4	3	8	7	5
7	9	6	3	1	5	4	8	2
3	5	2	8	6	4	9	1	7
8	1	4	2	7	9	5	3	6

PUZZLE / 833

7	3	9	2	5	6	8	1	4
6	1	4	7	3	8	9	5	2
8	2	5	4	1	9	7	6	3
9	8	6	3	2	5	1	4	7
5	4	2	8	7	1	3	9	6
3	7	1	6	9	4	5	2	8
4	9	3	5	8	2	6	7	1
1	6	7	9	4	3	2	8	5
2	5	8	1	6	7	4	3	9

PUZZLE / 834

4	9	8	2	1	6	5	7	3
6	2	1	7	3	5	4	9	8
5	3	7	8	9	4	1	2	6
7	1	6	5	4	3	9	8	2
9	8	3	1	6	2	7	5	4
2	4	5	9	8	7	6	3	1
3	7	4	6	2	9	8	1	5
8	5	2	4	7	1	3	6	9
1	6	9	3	5	8	2	4	7

PUZZLE / 835

6	9	4	2	7	1	3	5	8
5	3	7	9	6	8	4	1	2
2	8	1	5	4	3	9	6	7
7	5	2	1	8	9	6	4	3
8	6	9	4	3	5	2	7	1
4	1	3	7	2	6	5	8	9
1	7	5	3	9	4	8	2	6
9	4	8	6	1	2	7	3	5
3	2	6	8	5	7	1	9	4

PUZZLE / 836

7	3	4	6	1	8	5	9	2
9	8	2	7	5	4	1	6	3
5	1	6	2	3	9	7	4	8
4	9	3	1	6	7	2	8	5
2	6	5	9	8	3	4	7	1
8	7	1	5	4	2	9	3	6
3	5	8	4	9	1	6	2	7
6	2	9	8	7	5	3	1	4
1	4	7	3	2	6	8	5	9

PUZZLE / 837

9	2	4	3	7	5	1	6	8
1	6	3	2	4	8	5	9	7
5	7	8	6	9	1	4	3	2
3	5	2	4	6	9	7	8	1
4	8	6	5	1	7	9	2	3
7	1	9	8	3	2	6	5	4
6	3	5	7	8	4	2	1	9
8	4	1	9	2	6	3	7	5
2	9	7	1	5	3	8	4	6

PUZZLE / 838

6	9	7	2	5	1	4	3	8
3	5	1	6	8	4	9	2	7
8	4	2	3	7	9	5	1	6
1	6	8	5	9	2	7	4	3
9	2	4	7	6	3	1	8	5
5	7	3	4	1	8	2	6	9
4	1	5	8	3	7	6	9	2
7	8	9	1	2	6	3	5	4
2	3	6	9	4	5	8	7	1

PUZZLE / 839

9	5	2	8	6	3	4	1	7
1	3	6	7	2	4	8	5	9
4	7	8	1	9	5	6	2	3
3	1	5	6	4	7	9	8	2
2	9	4	5	8	1	7	3	6
8	6	7	9	3	2	5	4	1
5	4	1	2	7	6	3	9	8
6	2	9	3	5	8	1	7	4
7	8	3	4	1	9	2	6	5

PUZZLE / 840

2	9	1	4	3	8	5	7	6
6	7	3	9	2	5	8	4	1
8	5	4	7	6	1	3	9	2
7	2	8	3	4	9	6	1	5
1	4	6	8	5	2	9	3	7
9	3	5	6	1	7	2	8	4
3	6	9	2	7	4	1	5	8
5	8	7	1	9	6	4	2	3
4	1	2	5	8	3	7	6	9

PUZZLE / 841

4	2	7	6	9	8	3	5	1
8	5	1	3	2	4	6	9	7
3	9	6	5	1	7	8	4	2
1	3	9	4	7	2	5	6	8
2	6	8	9	5	1	4	7	3
5	7	4	8	6	3	1	2	9
7	1	3	2	4	5	9	8	6
6	4	2	1	8	9	7	3	5
9	8	5	7	3	6	2	1	4

PUZZLE / 842

8	3	6	4	1	2	5	7	9
4	5	9	7	3	6	1	2	8
2	1	7	5	8	9	6	4	3
7	2	4	9	6	5	3	8	1
6	8	5	1	7	3	2	9	4
1	9	3	8	2	4	7	5	6
5	6	8	2	9	1	4	3	7
9	4	1	3	5	7	8	6	2
3	7	2	6	4	8	9	1	5

PUZZLE / 843

1	4	7	9	3	8	2	6	5
3	8	9	2	6	5	4	1	7
2	5	6	7	4	1	9	3	8
7	6	8	4	1	3	5	9	2
5	2	3	8	9	6	7	4	1
4	9	1	5	7	2	6	8	3
8	3	4	6	5	7	1	2	9
9	7	2	1	8	4	3	5	6
6	1	5	3	2	9	8	7	4

PUZZLE / **844**

5	6	1	8	9	7	3	2	4
8	2	7	4	1	3	5	6	9
9	4	3	6	2	5	7	8	1
4	5	2	3	6	1	8	9	7
7	8	6	2	5	9	1	4	3
1	3	9	7	4	8	2	5	6
6	9	8	1	7	2	4	3	5
2	1	4	5	3	6	9	7	8
3	7	5	9	8	4	6	1	2

PUZZLE / **845**

4	2	9	8	5	1	3	6	7
1	3	8	7	2	6	4	5	9
7	6	5	9	4	3	2	8	1
2	7	4	3	6	8	1	9	5
3	8	1	2	9	5	6	7	4
9	5	6	1	7	4	8	2	3
6	9	2	4	3	7	5	1	8
8	4	7	5	1	2	9	3	6
5	1	3	6	8	9	7	4	2

PUZZLE / **846**

3	5	7	6	1	4	2	9	8
8	2	6	9	5	3	4	1	7
9	1	4	8	2	7	6	5	3
4	8	9	1	7	5	3	6	2
5	6	2	3	4	9	7	8	1
7	3	1	2	6	8	9	4	5
2	4	3	5	9	1	8	7	6
1	9	8	7	3	6	5	2	4
6	7	5	4	8	2	1	3	9

PUZZLE / **847**

1	9	4	5	8	6	7	3	2
3	7	8	9	4	2	6	1	5
2	5	6	1	3	7	4	8	9
5	1	9	3	6	8	2	4	7
6	4	3	2	7	5	8	9	1
8	2	7	4	1	9	3	5	6
4	3	5	6	2	1	9	7	8
7	6	1	8	9	3	5	2	4
9	8	2	7	5	4	1	6	3

PUZZLE / **848**

4	7	6	8	3	9	1	5	2
8	5	9	1	6	2	3	4	7
1	3	2	7	5	4	9	6	8
3	1	5	2	9	7	4	8	6
2	9	7	6	4	8	5	3	1
6	4	8	3	1	5	2	7	9
9	2	4	5	8	6	7	1	3
5	8	1	9	7	3	6	2	4
7	6	3	4	2	1	8	9	5

PUZZLE / **849**

6	8	4	9	5	1	2	3	7
5	7	9	8	3	2	4	1	6
1	2	3	7	6	4	5	8	9
7	6	5	4	9	3	1	2	8
4	9	2	6	1	8	3	7	5
8	3	1	2	7	5	9	6	4
9	4	7	1	2	6	8	5	3
2	5	6	3	8	9	7	4	1
3	1	8	5	4	7	6	9	2

PUZZLE / **850**

8	2	9	3	5	1	4	6	7
1	3	6	9	4	7	5	8	2
7	4	5	6	2	8	3	1	9
9	5	7	2	6	3	8	4	1
4	8	3	7	1	9	6	2	5
6	1	2	5	8	4	7	9	3
2	9	4	8	3	5	1	7	6
5	6	8	1	7	2	9	3	4
3	7	1	4	9	6	2	5	8

PUZZLE / **851**

4	6	3	1	8	7	5	9	2
8	5	2	3	4	9	1	6	7
1	9	7	2	5	6	3	8	4
2	3	5	4	6	1	9	7	8
6	8	9	7	3	2	4	1	5
7	1	4	8	9	5	6	2	3
9	2	1	5	7	4	8	3	6
5	7	8	6	1	3	2	4	9
3	4	6	9	2	8	7	5	1

PUZZLE / **852**

2	8	9	7	1	4	5	6	3
3	7	5	2	9	6	4	8	1
1	6	4	8	5	3	7	9	2
8	9	7	5	6	1	2	3	4
6	5	3	4	2	9	1	7	8
4	2	1	3	7	8	9	5	6
9	4	2	6	8	7	3	1	5
7	3	6	1	4	5	8	2	9
5	1	8	9	3	2	6	4	7

PUZZLE / **853**

2	6	9	7	4	1	8	3	5
7	1	5	8	9	3	4	2	6
4	3	8	2	6	5	7	1	9
6	9	1	5	2	8	3	7	4
8	5	2	3	7	4	9	6	1
3	4	7	9	1	6	2	5	8
1	2	6	4	8	7	5	9	3
5	7	4	1	3	9	6	8	2
9	8	3	6	5	2	1	4	7

PUZZLE / **854**

1	7	5	3	4	8	2	6	9
8	2	3	9	6	1	7	4	5
6	4	9	7	2	5	3	1	8
3	9	6	5	1	7	4	8	2
5	8	4	2	3	6	1	9	7
7	1	2	4	8	9	5	3	6
2	3	8	6	5	4	9	7	1
9	5	1	8	7	3	6	2	4
4	6	7	1	9	2	8	5	3

PUZZLE / **855**

6	1	4	9	7	3	2	8	5
7	8	3	2	5	4	1	6	9
9	2	5	1	8	6	3	7	4
5	9	6	3	4	2	8	1	7
8	3	2	7	1	9	4	5	6
4	7	1	8	6	5	9	2	3
1	6	8	4	9	7	5	3	2
2	4	7	5	3	1	6	9	8
3	5	9	6	2	8	7	4	1

PUZZLE / **856**

3	2	8	9	5	4	1	6	7
1	7	5	8	3	6	2	4	9
4	9	6	2	7	1	3	5	8
5	1	4	6	9	8	7	2	3
8	6	7	3	2	5	9	1	4
9	3	2	4	1	7	5	8	6
2	4	1	7	6	9	8	3	5
6	5	9	1	8	3	4	7	2
7	8	3	5	4	2	6	9	1

PUZZLE / **857**

1	3	9	8	4	2	7	5	6
2	5	8	9	7	6	1	4	3
6	7	4	3	5	1	9	2	8
5	6	2	1	9	4	3	8	7
7	8	1	2	3	5	6	9	4
4	9	3	6	8	7	5	1	2
9	4	5	7	2	3	8	6	1
3	2	6	5	1	8	4	7	9
8	1	7	4	6	9	2	3	5

PUZZLE / **858**

8	3	6	2	1	4	7	5	9
2	9	1	8	5	7	6	4	3
5	7	4	6	9	3	8	2	1
7	2	3	9	8	5	4	1	6
9	6	8	4	3	1	2	7	5
4	1	5	7	6	2	3	9	8
3	4	9	5	2	6	1	8	7
6	8	7	1	4	9	5	3	2
1	5	2	3	7	8	9	6	4

PUZZLE / **859**

6	2	8	1	3	9	4	7	5
7	3	5	4	2	6	1	8	9
9	4	1	5	8	7	3	6	2
3	5	4	8	6	1	9	2	7
8	7	2	9	4	5	6	1	3
1	6	9	2	7	3	5	4	8
5	1	6	7	9	8	2	3	4
4	9	7	3	1	2	8	5	6
2	8	3	6	5	4	7	9	1

PUZZLE / **860**

4	5	1	8	3	7	9	2	6
8	3	7	6	2	9	5	4	1
2	9	6	5	1	4	3	8	7
1	7	5	2	4	8	6	3	9
6	8	2	9	5	3	7	1	4
3	4	9	7	6	1	8	5	2
7	6	4	3	8	2	1	9	5
9	1	3	4	7	5	2	6	8
5	2	8	1	9	6	4	7	3

PUZZLE / **861**

7	9	3	4	8	1	6	2	5
1	6	2	3	9	5	8	4	7
5	4	8	2	7	6	1	9	3
2	5	6	7	4	8	9	3	1
3	1	4	5	6	9	7	8	2
8	7	9	1	3	2	5	6	4
9	3	1	6	5	4	2	7	8
4	8	5	9	2	7	3	1	6
6	2	7	8	1	3	4	5	9

PUZZLE / **862**

2	3	7	4	5	8	1	6	9
6	4	5	1	9	3	7	8	2
1	8	9	2	6	7	5	4	3
9	5	4	8	3	2	6	7	1
8	6	2	7	1	5	9	3	4
3	7	1	6	4	9	2	5	8
4	2	8	5	7	1	3	9	6
7	9	6	3	2	4	8	1	5
5	1	3	9	8	6	4	2	7

PUZZLE / **863**

7	1	6	4	2	5	8	3	9
2	8	5	9	7	3	6	1	4
4	3	9	1	8	6	2	5	7
1	4	2	8	5	9	7	6	3
9	7	8	3	6	2	5	4	1
6	5	3	7	4	1	9	8	2
3	6	1	2	9	8	4	7	5
8	2	7	5	1	4	3	9	6
5	9	4	6	3	7	1	2	8

PUZZLE / **864**

5	3	6	9	2	8	1	4	7
4	7	2	3	5	1	8	6	9
9	8	1	4	6	7	2	5	3
7	5	3	2	9	6	4	8	1
1	4	9	8	3	5	7	2	6
2	6	8	1	7	4	3	9	5
8	9	4	6	1	3	5	7	2
3	2	5	7	4	9	6	1	8
6	1	7	5	8	2	9	3	4

PUZZLE / **865**

7	6	8	9	4	2	3	5	1
5	4	2	3	8	1	9	6	7
9	3	1	7	6	5	4	2	8
6	9	3	1	5	4	8	7	2
2	1	5	8	7	9	6	3	4
4	8	7	6	2	3	1	9	5
3	7	6	2	1	8	5	4	9
8	5	9	4	3	7	2	1	6
1	2	4	5	9	6	7	8	3

PUZZLE / **866**

5	4	7	9	2	3	1	6	8
3	6	8	4	5	1	2	9	7
9	1	2	8	6	7	4	3	5
6	7	5	2	8	9	3	4	1
2	8	9	3	1	4	5	7	6
1	3	4	5	7	6	9	8	2
7	5	3	1	9	8	6	2	4
8	9	1	6	4	2	7	5	3
4	2	6	7	3	5	8	1	9

PUZZLE / **867**

9	1	8	6	2	4	7	3	5
4	5	7	3	8	1	9	6	2
2	6	3	5	9	7	4	1	8
3	8	2	7	5	6	1	4	9
5	4	6	8	1	9	3	2	7
7	9	1	2	4	3	5	8	6
8	7	5	4	3	2	6	9	1
1	2	4	9	6	5	8	7	3
6	3	9	1	7	8	2	5	4

PUZZLE / **868**

2	4	8	9	6	1	5	7	3
5	6	9	7	3	8	2	1	4
1	3	7	5	2	4	8	9	6
9	1	4	6	5	2	7	3	8
6	2	3	8	9	7	4	5	1
7	8	5	1	4	3	6	2	9
4	9	1	2	7	6	3	8	5
8	7	6	3	1	5	9	4	2
3	5	2	4	8	9	1	6	7

PUZZLE / **869**

2	3	7	9	4	1	6	8	5
1	5	4	3	6	8	2	7	9
8	6	9	2	7	5	1	3	4
3	7	6	1	2	9	4	5	8
9	4	2	8	5	6	3	1	7
5	1	8	7	3	4	9	2	6
4	8	1	5	9	3	7	6	2
7	9	3	6	8	2	5	4	1
6	2	5	4	1	7	8	9	3

PUZZLE / **870**

6	7	5	3	2	9	8	4	1
3	4	1	5	6	8	7	2	9
2	8	9	7	1	4	5	6	3
9	1	7	8	4	6	3	5	2
8	6	2	9	3	5	1	7	4
4	5	3	1	7	2	9	8	6
1	3	6	4	5	7	2	9	8
5	2	8	6	9	3	4	1	7
7	9	4	2	8	1	6	3	5

PUZZLE / **871**

1	5	7	6	4	8	9	2	3
4	3	9	2	1	5	6	8	7
8	6	2	7	3	9	5	4	1
6	7	4	3	9	1	8	5	2
3	1	5	4	8	2	7	9	6
2	9	8	5	7	6	3	1	4
9	8	6	1	2	7	4	3	5
7	2	3	8	5	4	1	6	9
5	4	1	9	6	3	2	7	8

PUZZLE / **872**

6	3	7	9	4	2	1	8	5
5	9	4	3	8	1	2	7	6
8	2	1	5	6	7	9	3	4
1	8	3	2	5	6	7	4	9
9	4	6	7	1	8	5	2	3
7	5	2	4	3	9	6	1	8
3	7	5	1	9	4	8	6	2
4	1	8	6	2	5	3	9	7
2	6	9	8	7	3	4	5	1

PUZZLE / **873**

1	4	8	2	6	7	5	9	3
6	7	9	1	3	5	8	4	2
2	5	3	8	4	9	6	1	7
7	2	1	9	8	6	4	3	5
3	8	6	5	7	4	1	2	9
5	9	4	3	2	1	7	6	8
8	6	2	7	1	3	9	5	4
9	1	7	4	5	2	3	8	6
4	3	5	6	9	8	2	7	1

PUZZLE / 874

6	7	4	2	3	9	1	5	8
8	2	5	4	7	1	3	6	9
3	9	1	8	5	6	7	2	4
9	5	3	7	6	8	4	1	2
2	4	6	5	1	3	8	9	7
1	8	7	9	4	2	6	3	5
4	1	9	6	2	7	5	8	3
7	6	2	3	8	5	9	4	1
5	3	8	1	9	4	2	7	6

PUZZLE / 875

1	7	5	8	6	2	4	3	9
2	9	3	4	7	5	1	6	8
6	8	4	9	1	3	2	5	7
4	3	7	2	5	1	9	8	6
9	1	8	3	4	6	7	2	5
5	2	6	7	8	9	3	1	4
7	4	1	5	2	8	6	9	3
8	6	9	1	3	7	5	4	2
3	5	2	6	9	4	8	7	1

PUZZLE / 876

5	1	7	8	6	3	2	9	4
9	6	3	7	2	4	8	5	1
2	8	4	1	9	5	3	7	6
3	2	6	4	8	9	5	1	7
4	5	8	3	1	7	6	2	9
7	9	1	2	5	6	4	3	8
6	4	9	5	7	2	1	8	3
8	7	5	6	3	1	9	4	2
1	3	2	9	4	8	7	6	5

PUZZLE / 877

6	2	8	4	7	5	1	9	3
4	7	9	3	1	8	6	5	2
3	1	5	9	2	6	4	7	8
5	9	7	6	3	1	2	8	4
2	4	3	8	5	9	7	6	1
1	8	6	7	4	2	5	3	9
8	5	4	1	9	7	3	2	6
9	3	2	5	6	4	8	1	7
7	6	1	2	8	3	9	4	5

PUZZLE / 878

2	1	9	6	5	8	7	4	3
7	3	4	2	9	1	6	8	5
8	5	6	3	4	7	1	9	2
5	2	8	1	6	4	9	3	7
6	4	1	7	3	9	2	5	8
9	7	3	5	8	2	4	6	1
4	9	2	8	7	3	5	1	6
3	6	7	9	1	5	8	2	4
1	8	5	4	2	6	3	7	9

PUZZLE / 879

7	4	5	9	3	8	1	2	6
1	9	6	5	4	2	8	7	3
3	2	8	7	1	6	4	5	9
2	5	3	1	8	7	9	6	4
9	6	7	3	2	4	5	1	8
8	1	4	6	5	9	7	3	2
5	7	2	4	9	3	6	8	1
4	3	1	8	6	5	2	9	7
6	8	9	2	7	1	3	4	5

PUZZLE / 880

2	1	9	3	8	6	4	7	5
5	4	6	7	2	1	8	9	3
3	7	8	9	5	4	1	2	6
7	8	1	6	3	2	5	4	9
6	3	2	4	9	5	7	8	1
9	5	4	1	7	8	3	6	2
4	6	3	8	1	9	2	5	7
1	9	5	2	4	7	6	3	8
8	2	7	5	6	3	9	1	4

PUZZLE / 881

8	9	6	5	4	3	2	1	7
4	7	3	2	6	1	5	8	9
1	2	5	9	8	7	6	3	4
9	5	1	3	7	4	8	2	6
6	3	7	8	5	2	9	4	1
2	4	8	6	1	9	3	7	5
7	8	9	1	3	5	4	6	2
3	1	2	4	9	6	7	5	8
5	6	4	7	2	8	1	9	3

PUZZLE / 882

2	3	7	6	1	9	8	4	5
1	8	9	5	4	3	2	7	6
6	5	4	7	2	8	3	9	1
5	2	8	4	3	1	7	6	9
9	4	1	2	6	7	5	8	3
3	7	6	9	8	5	1	2	4
8	9	2	1	5	6	4	3	7
4	6	5	3	7	2	9	1	8
7	1	3	8	9	4	6	5	2

PUZZLE / 883

5	7	9	6	2	3	1	8	4
6	8	2	1	5	4	9	3	7
4	3	1	7	9	8	2	5	6
9	6	7	5	3	1	4	2	8
2	4	5	8	7	9	3	6	1
3	1	8	2	4	6	5	7	9
8	5	6	4	1	2	7	9	3
7	9	4	3	8	5	6	1	2
1	2	3	9	6	7	8	4	5

PUZZLE / 884

2	1	6	5	4	3	7	8	9
5	9	3	7	8	2	6	4	1
8	4	7	1	6	9	3	5	2
3	7	9	8	2	4	1	6	5
4	2	8	6	1	5	9	3	7
6	5	1	3	9	7	8	2	4
7	6	2	4	3	1	5	9	8
9	3	5	2	7	8	4	1	6
1	8	4	9	5	6	2	7	3

PUZZLE / 885

9	5	6	7	3	8	1	2	4
3	1	2	6	4	9	7	8	5
8	7	4	5	2	1	3	6	9
4	3	1	9	7	6	8	5	2
7	2	8	4	5	3	9	1	6
5	6	9	8	1	2	4	7	3
1	8	3	2	6	4	5	9	7
6	4	5	1	9	7	2	3	8
2	9	7	3	8	5	6	4	1

PUZZLE / 886

2	5	4	9	8	1	3	7	6
6	1	9	7	3	5	4	8	2
3	7	8	4	2	6	9	1	5
1	8	6	2	7	9	5	3	4
4	9	5	8	1	3	6	2	7
7	2	3	5	6	4	8	9	1
8	3	2	6	4	7	1	5	9
5	6	7	1	9	8	2	4	3
9	4	1	3	5	2	7	6	8

PUZZLE / 887

6	2	5	7	8	4	9	3	1
7	4	9	5	3	1	2	8	6
3	1	8	2	9	6	4	5	7
5	3	2	8	6	9	7	1	4
4	7	6	3	1	5	8	2	9
8	9	1	4	7	2	5	6	3
1	6	4	9	2	8	3	7	5
2	5	7	6	4	3	1	9	8
9	8	3	1	5	7	6	4	2

PUZZLE / 888

SOLUTIONS EXTRA HARD

1	3	8	9	5	6	4	2	7
9	4	6	2	3	7	8	5	1
7	5	2	1	4	8	9	3	6
4	8	5	3	7	2	6	1	9
2	6	7	5	1	9	3	8	4
3	9	1	6	8	4	5	7	2
5	2	3	4	9	1	7	6	8
6	7	4	8	2	5	1	9	3
8	1	9	7	6	3	2	4	5

PUZZLE / 889

5	1	7	6	4	3	2	9	8
3	8	2	7	9	5	4	6	1
6	9	4	1	8	2	7	3	5
1	2	6	4	3	8	9	5	7
8	4	9	5	7	6	1	2	3
7	5	3	9	2	1	6	8	4
2	7	5	8	6	4	3	1	9
4	6	8	3	1	9	5	7	2
9	3	1	2	5	7	8	4	6

PUZZLE / 890

4	1	2	3	5	9	8	6	7
9	7	8	6	2	4	3	5	1
5	6	3	1	7	8	2	4	9
3	8	1	5	6	2	7	9	4
7	4	6	9	3	1	5	8	2
2	5	9	4	8	7	6	1	3
8	3	4	7	9	6	1	2	5
6	9	5	2	1	3	4	7	8
1	2	7	8	4	5	9	3	6

PUZZLE / 891

4	9	1	3	2	5	6	7	8
5	7	2	4	8	6	9	3	1
8	6	3	7	1	9	5	4	2
2	8	4	6	7	3	1	5	9
1	5	7	2	9	4	8	6	3
6	3	9	8	5	1	4	2	7
3	4	8	1	6	2	7	9	5
7	2	5	9	4	8	3	1	6
9	1	6	5	3	7	2	8	4

PUZZLE / 892

4	6	9	7	1	2	3	8	5
2	7	5	4	3	8	6	9	1
1	3	8	9	5	6	2	4	7
7	5	2	1	9	3	8	6	4
9	8	1	6	4	7	5	2	3
3	4	6	8	2	5	7	1	9
6	2	4	3	7	9	1	5	8
5	9	7	2	8	1	4	3	6
8	1	3	5	6	4	9	7	2

PUZZLE / 893

7	1	2	4	6	5	3	8	9
5	9	3	1	8	7	2	6	4
4	6	8	3	9	2	5	7	1
1	4	5	8	3	6	7	9	2
9	8	6	7	2	4	1	3	5
3	2	7	9	5	1	6	4	8
2	3	4	5	7	8	9	1	6
6	7	1	2	4	9	8	5	3
8	5	9	6	1	3	4	2	7

PUZZLE / 894

7	5	9	3	2	6	8	4	1
1	4	3	8	7	5	6	9	2
2	8	6	9	4	1	3	7	5
3	1	8	4	6	2	7	5	9
6	7	5	1	9	8	4	2	3
4	9	2	5	3	7	1	8	6
5	2	4	6	8	3	9	1	7
9	3	1	7	5	4	2	6	8
8	6	7	2	1	9	5	3	4

PUZZLE / 895

6	3	5	9	7	4	8	2	1
2	1	7	6	3	8	9	5	4
4	8	9	5	2	1	3	6	7
1	7	6	4	9	2	5	3	8
5	2	4	7	8	3	1	9	6
8	9	3	1	6	5	7	4	2
7	6	1	3	4	9	2	8	5
9	5	8	2	1	6	4	7	3
3	4	2	8	5	7	6	1	9

PUZZLE / 896

9	8	2	4	5	3	1	7	6
1	4	5	7	8	6	9	2	3
7	3	6	2	1	9	8	4	5
5	7	8	1	6	4	2	3	9
3	2	1	5	9	7	4	6	8
6	9	4	8	3	2	7	5	1
4	1	3	6	2	8	5	9	7
8	6	7	9	4	5	3	1	2
2	5	9	3	7	1	6	8	4

PUZZLE / 897

8	6	5	3	4	2	1	9	7
3	2	4	9	7	1	5	8	6
1	9	7	8	5	6	2	4	3
4	7	2	5	6	9	8	3	1
6	3	8	2	1	7	4	5	9
5	1	9	4	8	3	6	7	2
9	8	3	6	2	5	7	1	4
2	5	1	7	3	4	9	6	8
7	4	6	1	9	8	3	2	5

PUZZLE / 898

6	9	2	7	3	8	4	5	1
8	4	3	6	1	5	2	9	7
1	5	7	4	2	9	3	6	8
7	3	1	5	8	6	9	4	2
5	6	4	9	7	2	8	1	3
9	2	8	3	4	1	6	7	5
2	7	5	8	6	4	1	3	9
3	1	6	2	9	7	5	8	4
4	8	9	1	5	3	7	2	6

PUZZLE / 899

1	3	5	9	4	7	2	6	8
7	8	2	1	6	5	9	3	4
6	9	4	8	2	3	1	7	5
4	2	7	5	3	6	8	1	9
8	6	9	2	1	4	7	5	3
5	1	3	7	8	9	6	4	2
9	5	6	4	7	2	3	8	1
2	7	8	3	5	1	4	9	6
3	4	1	6	9	8	5	2	7

PUZZLE / 900

7	9	8	1	4	2	5	6	3
6	5	4	8	9	3	1	2	7
3	2	1	5	7	6	4	8	9
9	4	7	3	6	5	8	1	2
2	8	3	4	1	9	7	5	6
1	6	5	7	2	8	3	9	4
4	1	9	6	5	7	2	3	8
5	3	6	2	8	4	9	7	1
8	7	2	9	3	1	6	4	5

PUZZLE / 901

6	7	1	4	2	5	3	8	9
3	8	5	6	9	1	2	7	4
9	4	2	3	7	8	6	5	1
7	6	8	9	3	4	1	2	5
2	5	9	7	1	6	4	3	8
4	1	3	5	8	2	7	9	6
8	3	6	2	4	9	5	1	7
5	9	7	1	6	3	8	4	2
1	2	4	8	5	7	9	6	3

PUZZLE / 902

5	3	2	6	7	1	4	9	8
6	8	9	4	5	3	7	2	1
7	4	1	2	9	8	3	6	5
4	1	5	7	2	6	9	8	3
3	2	6	9	8	5	1	7	4
9	7	8	1	3	4	6	5	2
2	6	4	5	1	9	8	3	7
1	5	3	8	6	7	2	4	9
8	9	7	3	4	2	5	1	6

PUZZLE / 903

3	4	7	8	5	2	6	9	1
1	9	5	6	7	3	4	8	2
8	2	6	1	4	9	7	5	3
4	6	9	3	2	1	8	7	5
7	3	1	9	8	5	2	6	4
2	5	8	7	6	4	1	3	9
9	7	3	4	1	8	5	2	6
6	1	2	5	9	7	3	4	8
5	8	4	2	3	6	9	1	7

PUZZLE / **904**

8	3	5	4	1	9	7	6	2
7	4	1	5	6	2	8	3	9
9	2	6	3	8	7	1	5	4
5	7	4	2	9	8	3	1	6
2	1	9	6	7	3	4	8	5
3	6	8	1	4	5	2	9	7
6	9	7	8	3	4	5	2	1
4	5	3	9	2	1	6	7	8
1	8	2	7	5	6	9	4	3

PUZZLE / **905**

2	8	7	4	3	5	1	9	6
4	6	3	8	9	1	7	2	5
5	1	9	7	2	6	8	4	3
9	4	2	1	6	7	5	3	8
8	7	6	9	5	3	4	1	2
1	3	5	2	8	4	9	6	7
3	5	8	6	4	9	2	7	1
7	2	4	3	1	8	6	5	9
6	9	1	5	7	2	3	8	4

PUZZLE / **906**

7	6	9	4	1	3	5	2	8
8	2	5	6	9	7	1	3	4
3	1	4	5	2	8	7	9	6
1	5	7	8	6	2	3	4	9
9	4	6	3	7	5	2	8	1
2	3	8	1	4	9	6	7	5
6	9	2	7	8	1	4	5	3
4	7	3	9	5	6	8	1	2
5	8	1	2	3	4	9	6	7

PUZZLE / **907**

6	1	3	2	5	4	7	9	8
2	7	8	1	3	9	5	6	4
5	4	9	7	8	6	3	2	1
7	2	4	9	1	3	6	8	5
8	6	1	5	2	7	9	4	3
9	3	5	6	4	8	2	1	7
3	5	2	4	6	1	8	7	9
4	9	6	8	7	5	1	3	2
1	8	7	3	9	2	4	5	6

PUZZLE / **908**

4	2	9	8	1	7	6	3	5
6	3	8	2	5	9	1	7	4
1	5	7	3	6	4	8	2	9
5	4	6	7	2	8	9	1	3
8	7	3	6	9	1	5	4	2
9	1	2	4	3	5	7	8	6
2	9	4	1	7	6	3	5	8
3	6	1	5	8	2	4	9	7
7	8	5	9	4	3	2	6	1

PUZZLE / **909**

8	6	2	7	4	5	9	3	1
3	5	9	8	1	6	4	7	2
4	1	7	3	9	2	6	5	8
6	8	1	9	3	7	2	4	5
5	2	3	4	6	1	8	9	7
9	7	4	5	2	8	3	1	6
2	9	6	1	7	4	5	8	3
1	3	5	2	8	9	7	6	4
7	4	8	6	5	3	1	2	9

PUZZLE / **910**

5	3	8	2	4	7	9	6	1
4	2	1	5	9	6	8	3	7
9	6	7	1	8	3	2	4	5
3	5	6	9	1	4	7	2	8
8	1	4	7	3	2	5	9	6
2	7	9	6	5	8	3	1	4
6	8	2	4	7	9	1	5	3
7	4	5	3	2	1	6	8	9
1	9	3	8	6	5	4	7	2

PUZZLE / **911**

4	8	6	1	3	7	9	5	2
5	7	3	6	9	2	8	1	4
1	2	9	5	4	8	3	6	7
8	5	7	3	2	6	4	9	1
9	6	1	7	8	4	2	3	5
2	3	4	9	1	5	6	7	8
7	1	2	4	6	9	5	8	3
6	4	5	8	7	3	1	2	9
3	9	8	2	5	1	7	4	6

PUZZLE / **912**

8	7	4	3	6	1	5	2	9
2	3	6	8	9	5	7	4	1
1	9	5	2	4	7	8	6	3
5	4	9	7	1	6	2	3	8
6	8	3	4	5	2	1	9	7
7	1	2	9	3	8	6	5	4
3	6	7	1	2	9	4	8	5
4	5	8	6	7	3	9	1	2
9	2	1	5	8	4	3	7	6

PUZZLE / 913

3	5	4	1	9	2	6	8	7
2	1	7	4	6	8	3	5	9
8	6	9	5	3	7	4	2	1
6	8	1	7	2	4	9	3	5
9	3	2	6	1	5	7	4	8
4	7	5	3	8	9	2	1	6
1	4	3	9	5	6	8	7	2
5	9	8	2	7	3	1	6	4
7	2	6	8	4	1	5	9	3

PUZZLE / 914

9	1	6	7	4	3	2	5	8
8	7	4	5	1	2	6	9	3
2	5	3	9	6	8	4	1	7
7	4	5	2	8	9	3	6	1
6	2	8	1	3	7	5	4	9
3	9	1	4	5	6	8	7	2
1	8	7	6	2	4	9	3	5
5	6	2	3	9	1	7	8	4
4	3	9	8	7	5	1	2	6

PUZZLE / 915

2	4	6	5	3	1	7	9	8
5	7	9	4	8	2	1	3	6
1	8	3	9	7	6	5	4	2
8	1	7	3	2	9	6	5	4
6	9	2	8	5	4	3	1	7
3	5	4	1	6	7	2	8	9
4	6	1	2	9	3	8	7	5
7	3	8	6	4	5	9	2	1
9	2	5	7	1	8	4	6	3

PUZZLE / 916

8	5	6	7	3	4	9	2	1
7	1	2	5	9	8	4	3	6
9	3	4	6	2	1	8	7	5
2	8	3	1	5	6	7	9	4
1	9	7	8	4	2	6	5	3
4	6	5	9	7	3	2	1	8
6	2	8	3	1	7	5	4	9
5	7	1	4	6	9	3	8	2
3	4	9	2	8	5	1	6	7

PUZZLE / 917

1	4	2	3	8	9	7	5	6
6	8	7	5	4	1	3	9	2
9	5	3	2	7	6	1	8	4
3	7	9	4	6	5	8	2	1
2	6	8	7	1	3	9	4	5
5	1	4	8	9	2	6	3	7
7	9	5	1	2	8	4	6	3
8	2	1	6	3	4	5	7	9
4	3	6	9	5	7	2	1	8

PUZZLE / 918

8	2	5	7	9	3	4	6	1
4	6	3	5	1	8	7	9	2
7	9	1	4	2	6	8	5	3
3	1	8	6	7	2	9	4	5
5	4	6	3	8	9	1	2	7
9	7	2	1	4	5	3	8	6
6	5	4	8	3	7	2	1	9
2	8	7	9	6	1	5	3	4
1	3	9	2	5	4	6	7	8

PUZZLE / 919

3	1	6	2	8	5	9	7	4
2	7	4	3	9	1	6	5	8
5	8	9	6	4	7	1	2	3
8	2	3	5	7	6	4	1	9
7	9	1	8	2	4	3	6	5
4	6	5	9	1	3	2	8	7
1	5	8	4	6	9	7	3	2
9	3	7	1	5	2	8	4	6
6	4	2	7	3	8	5	9	1

PUZZLE / 920

7	6	8	5	3	1	2	4	9
4	1	9	6	2	7	5	3	8
2	5	3	4	8	9	6	1	7
1	8	5	3	7	4	9	6	2
9	3	2	1	5	6	7	8	4
6	4	7	8	9	2	1	5	3
5	9	4	2	1	3	8	7	6
3	2	1	7	6	8	4	9	5
8	7	6	9	4	5	3	2	1

PUZZLE / 921

7	8	6	9	2	1	4	3	5
4	5	1	3	7	6	8	9	2
3	2	9	8	5	4	7	1	6
2	4	8	1	6	5	9	7	3
1	9	7	2	4	3	5	6	8
6	3	5	7	9	8	1	2	4
5	1	4	6	3	7	2	8	9
9	7	3	4	8	2	6	5	1
8	6	2	5	1	9	3	4	7

PUZZLE / 922

4	5	1	8	9	7	2	6	3
2	3	8	6	4	5	1	9	7
6	9	7	3	1	2	5	4	8
1	7	3	4	8	9	6	5	2
8	6	5	2	3	1	9	7	4
9	2	4	7	5	6	8	3	1
7	4	9	5	2	8	3	1	6
3	1	2	9	6	4	7	8	5
5	8	6	1	7	3	4	2	9

PUZZLE / 923

4	6	8	3	1	2	7	5	9
1	3	9	7	8	5	2	4	6
7	2	5	9	4	6	3	1	8
5	9	2	4	7	3	6	8	1
6	7	3	1	5	8	4	9	2
8	4	1	2	6	9	5	3	7
3	1	4	8	2	7	9	6	5
2	8	6	5	9	4	1	7	3
9	5	7	6	3	1	8	2	4

PUZZLE / 924

3	1	8	6	5	2	9	7	4
5	2	7	3	9	4	6	1	8
4	9	6	7	1	8	2	5	3
1	5	2	8	3	7	4	6	9
8	6	9	2	4	1	5	3	7
7	4	3	9	6	5	8	2	1
9	8	1	5	2	3	7	4	6
2	7	4	1	8	6	3	9	5
6	3	5	4	7	9	1	8	2

PUZZLE / 925

3	8	7	2	5	1	4	9	6
5	9	4	6	8	7	3	1	2
2	6	1	4	9	3	5	7	8
1	3	2	5	4	8	7	6	9
7	5	9	1	2	6	8	4	3
6	4	8	3	7	9	1	2	5
4	7	6	8	3	2	9	5	1
9	2	3	7	1	5	6	8	4
8	1	5	9	6	4	2	3	7

PUZZLE / 926

5	1	2	7	6	8	3	4	9
4	7	9	3	2	5	8	6	1
6	3	8	4	1	9	5	7	2
7	4	5	2	8	3	9	1	6
9	2	6	5	7	1	4	3	8
1	8	3	6	9	4	2	5	7
3	9	7	1	5	2	6	8	4
2	5	1	8	4	6	7	9	3
8	6	4	9	3	7	1	2	5

PUZZLE / 927

6	1	8	7	3	5	9	2	4
3	9	5	2	4	8	6	7	1
2	4	7	6	9	1	3	8	5
8	7	1	5	6	4	2	3	9
5	3	2	1	7	9	4	6	8
9	6	4	3	8	2	5	1	7
1	2	3	9	5	7	8	4	6
4	5	6	8	1	3	7	9	2
7	8	9	4	2	6	1	5	3

PUZZLE / 928

5	7	6	1	4	8	3	9	2
9	3	8	5	6	2	1	7	4
2	4	1	3	9	7	6	8	5
7	8	5	6	2	1	9	4	3
4	1	3	9	8	5	2	6	7
6	2	9	4	7	3	8	5	1
1	9	7	8	3	4	5	2	6
3	6	4	2	5	9	7	1	8
8	5	2	7	1	6	4	3	9

PUZZLE / 929

6	1	2	8	7	5	3	4	9
3	8	4	6	9	1	2	7	5
9	7	5	3	2	4	1	8	6
7	6	9	2	4	8	5	3	1
4	5	1	7	6	3	9	2	8
8	2	3	1	5	9	4	6	7
2	3	7	9	1	6	8	5	4
1	4	6	5	8	2	7	9	3
5	9	8	4	3	7	6	1	2

PUZZLE / 930

7	5	6	8	3	4	2	9	1
8	1	9	7	2	5	4	6	3
4	3	2	6	1	9	5	8	7
6	7	8	4	9	2	3	1	5
2	9	5	1	8	3	7	4	6
3	4	1	5	6	7	8	2	9
9	8	7	2	5	1	6	3	4
5	6	3	9	4	8	1	7	2
1	2	4	3	7	6	9	5	8

PUZZLE / 931

4	2	6	8	5	1	9	3	7
7	3	1	4	9	6	8	2	5
8	9	5	2	3	7	4	6	1
3	7	2	5	6	9	1	8	4
1	4	9	7	8	3	6	5	2
6	5	8	1	2	4	3	7	9
5	6	3	9	1	2	7	4	8
2	1	7	3	4	8	5	9	6
9	8	4	6	7	5	2	1	3

PUZZLE / 932

8	1	7	2	5	3	9	4	6
6	9	5	8	4	1	3	7	2
2	3	4	6	9	7	1	5	8
7	4	2	9	1	6	8	3	5
5	8	3	4	7	2	6	9	1
1	6	9	5	3	8	4	2	7
9	7	8	1	2	4	5	6	3
3	5	1	7	6	9	2	8	4
4	2	6	3	8	5	7	1	9

PUZZLE / 933

3	2	8	4	6	1	7	5	9
5	4	7	3	9	8	1	2	6
1	6	9	7	5	2	4	3	8
8	7	1	6	3	9	2	4	5
6	5	2	1	8	4	3	9	7
9	3	4	5	2	7	8	6	1
7	1	5	2	4	6	9	8	3
4	8	3	9	1	5	6	7	2
2	9	6	8	7	3	5	1	4

PUZZLE / 934

3	2	8	4	6	9	5	7	1
1	6	5	7	2	3	4	8	9
4	7	9	8	1	5	6	2	3
8	9	3	5	7	2	1	4	6
6	5	2	1	3	4	8	9	7
7	1	4	6	9	8	2	3	5
5	3	1	2	4	7	9	6	8
2	8	7	9	5	6	3	1	4
9	4	6	3	8	1	7	5	2

PUZZLE / 935

3	2	6	7	4	9	8	1	5
1	7	4	6	8	5	3	9	2
9	5	8	2	3	1	6	7	4
6	3	2	5	7	4	1	8	9
5	9	7	3	1	8	2	4	6
8	4	1	9	2	6	7	5	3
4	8	9	1	6	3	5	2	7
2	6	5	8	9	7	4	3	1
7	1	3	4	5	2	9	6	8

PUZZLE / 936

1	5	8	9	3	4	7	6	2
9	4	7	6	2	5	3	1	8
3	6	2	7	8	1	5	9	4
4	3	1	5	6	7	2	8	9
8	9	5	2	1	3	6	4	7
7	2	6	4	9	8	1	5	3
2	1	3	8	5	9	4	7	6
5	7	9	3	4	6	8	2	1
6	8	4	1	7	2	9	3	5

PUZZLE / 937

1	4	2	3	9	5	7	8	6
7	5	6	8	2	1	4	9	3
3	9	8	6	7	4	2	5	1
9	1	4	5	8	7	3	6	2
6	2	5	9	4	3	1	7	8
8	3	7	1	6	2	9	4	5
4	8	3	7	1	6	5	2	9
2	6	1	4	5	9	8	3	7
5	7	9	2	3	8	6	1	4

PUZZLE / 938

5	1	8	7	9	2	3	6	4
9	6	2	3	4	5	1	7	8
3	7	4	6	8	1	2	9	5
2	4	6	8	5	9	7	1	3
7	8	9	1	2	3	4	5	6
1	3	5	4	6	7	8	2	9
4	9	1	5	7	8	6	3	2
8	5	7	2	3	6	9	4	1
6	2	3	9	1	4	5	8	7

PUZZLE / 939

9	1	5	3	6	2	8	7	4
4	7	2	5	9	8	1	3	6
3	6	8	7	1	4	2	5	9
5	9	1	4	3	6	7	2	8
8	4	3	2	7	1	9	6	5
7	2	6	9	8	5	3	4	1
1	8	4	6	2	7	5	9	3
6	3	7	1	5	9	4	8	2
2	5	9	8	4	3	6	1	7

PUZZLE / 940

8	3	2	7	5	6	4	9	1
6	4	5	1	3	9	7	2	8
7	1	9	4	2	8	5	6	3
9	2	3	5	6	4	8	1	7
1	8	4	9	7	3	2	5	6
5	6	7	2	8	1	3	4	9
3	5	8	6	1	2	9	7	4
2	9	6	3	4	7	1	8	5
4	7	1	8	9	5	6	3	2

PUZZLE / 941

1	8	2	7	4	5	3	9	6
4	3	9	1	6	8	7	2	5
5	6	7	3	2	9	1	8	4
9	2	4	6	5	3	8	7	1
7	1	3	9	8	4	5	6	2
8	5	6	2	1	7	4	3	9
3	9	1	5	7	6	2	4	8
2	7	8	4	9	1	6	5	3
6	4	5	8	3	2	9	1	7

PUZZLE / 942

2	1	6	5	8	9	7	4	3
3	4	9	1	7	6	5	8	2
8	5	7	3	4	2	1	6	9
4	6	8	9	5	3	2	7	1
1	7	3	2	6	8	4	9	5
9	2	5	4	1	7	8	3	6
5	8	4	6	3	1	9	2	7
7	3	2	8	9	5	6	1	4
6	9	1	7	2	4	3	5	8

PUZZLE / 943

8	7	4	5	1	9	2	3	6
5	9	2	6	8	3	1	7	4
6	3	1	2	7	4	5	8	9
7	4	5	8	9	1	3	6	2
3	2	8	7	5	6	4	9	1
9	1	6	3	4	2	8	5	7
2	8	7	4	6	5	9	1	3
1	5	3	9	2	7	6	4	8
4	6	9	1	3	8	7	2	5

PUZZLE / 944

6	8	7	3	2	1	4	5	9
3	2	9	5	4	6	7	1	8
4	1	5	9	7	8	6	2	3
7	3	8	1	9	4	2	6	5
1	6	4	2	3	5	9	8	7
5	9	2	6	8	7	1	3	4
8	7	6	4	1	3	5	9	2
2	4	1	8	5	9	3	7	6
9	5	3	7	6	2	8	4	1

PUZZLE / 945

6	3	7	8	2	4	5	1	9
5	1	2	6	9	3	8	7	4
8	9	4	1	7	5	6	3	2
7	4	8	9	3	2	1	5	6
3	2	1	7	5	6	9	4	8
9	5	6	4	8	1	7	2	3
1	8	3	2	6	7	4	9	5
4	6	5	3	1	9	2	8	7
2	7	9	5	4	8	3	6	1

PUZZLE / 946

3	7	6	9	4	2	8	1	5
1	5	4	6	3	8	9	7	2
9	8	2	1	7	5	6	4	3
6	1	5	4	8	9	2	3	7
4	3	7	5	2	6	1	8	9
2	9	8	7	1	3	5	6	4
8	2	1	3	5	4	7	9	6
7	4	9	2	6	1	3	5	8
5	6	3	8	9	7	4	2	1

PUZZLE / 947

2	1	5	3	4	7	9	8	6
9	4	8	1	2	6	3	5	7
6	3	7	5	9	8	2	1	4
8	5	2	7	3	4	6	9	1
7	6	1	9	8	5	4	3	2
4	9	3	6	1	2	5	7	8
1	7	6	4	5	9	8	2	3
5	2	4	8	7	3	1	6	9
3	8	9	2	6	1	7	4	5

PUZZLE / 948

2	7	9	1	4	5	6	8	3
1	6	4	3	7	8	2	9	5
3	8	5	6	2	9	4	1	7
6	5	2	4	8	1	7	3	9
8	4	3	7	9	2	5	6	1
7	9	1	5	3	6	8	2	4
4	2	7	9	6	3	1	5	8
5	3	6	8	1	4	9	7	2
9	1	8	2	5	7	3	4	6

PUZZLE / 949

4	2	9	1	8	6	5	7	3
6	1	8	3	7	5	4	9	2
7	3	5	2	4	9	6	8	1
9	5	7	6	1	4	3	2	8
3	6	1	8	9	2	7	5	4
8	4	2	5	3	7	1	6	9
5	9	6	4	2	1	8	3	7
2	8	4	7	6	3	9	1	5
1	7	3	9	5	8	2	4	6

PUZZLE / 950

6	2	1	8	3	9	5	4	7
3	9	4	5	7	6	8	1	2
5	7	8	4	1	2	3	9	6
9	1	2	6	8	3	7	5	4
4	3	7	1	2	5	9	6	8
8	5	6	9	4	7	2	3	1
2	6	5	7	9	1	4	8	3
1	4	3	2	5	8	6	7	9
7	8	9	3	6	4	1	2	5

PUZZLE / 951

6	7	5	9	3	4	2	1	8
1	8	4	2	6	7	9	5	3
9	2	3	5	8	1	7	4	6
3	1	8	7	2	6	4	9	5
2	4	7	8	9	5	3	6	1
5	9	6	1	4	3	8	2	7
4	6	1	3	7	9	5	8	2
7	5	2	4	1	8	6	3	9
8	3	9	6	5	2	1	7	4

PUZZLE / 952

3	6	7	9	2	4	8	5	1
4	5	8	6	3	1	9	2	7
2	1	9	7	8	5	6	3	4
1	7	4	3	9	2	5	8	6
5	8	2	1	7	6	3	4	9
6	9	3	5	4	8	7	1	2
7	2	1	8	5	9	4	6	3
9	4	5	2	6	3	1	7	8
8	3	6	4	1	7	2	9	5

PUZZLE / 953

8	2	6	9	7	1	3	4	5
5	4	7	2	3	8	6	1	9
1	3	9	6	4	5	2	7	8
9	5	4	1	2	3	8	6	7
7	8	2	4	5	6	9	3	1
3	6	1	7	8	9	4	5	2
2	1	8	3	6	7	5	9	4
4	7	3	5	9	2	1	8	6
6	9	5	8	1	4	7	2	3

PUZZLE / 954

1	4	3	8	6	9	5	7	2
9	5	6	2	4	7	3	8	1
2	7	8	1	5	3	9	6	4
7	3	5	6	2	1	4	9	8
8	6	2	9	3	4	7	1	5
4	9	1	5	7	8	2	3	6
3	2	4	7	8	6	1	5	9
6	1	7	4	9	5	8	2	3
5	8	9	3	1	2	6	4	7

PUZZLE / 955

4	9	5	2	3	6	8	1	7
8	7	6	1	4	9	5	3	2
2	1	3	5	8	7	6	4	9
7	4	8	9	6	2	3	5	1
6	2	1	8	5	3	7	9	4
3	5	9	4	7	1	2	8	6
9	6	4	3	2	5	1	7	8
1	3	7	6	9	8	4	2	5
5	8	2	7	1	4	9	6	3

PUZZLE / 956

4	6	7	5	1	8	2	9	3
9	5	2	3	7	6	4	8	1
8	1	3	2	4	9	6	5	7
7	4	1	9	6	5	8	3	2
3	8	5	1	2	4	9	7	6
2	9	6	8	3	7	1	4	5
5	7	9	6	8	1	3	2	4
6	2	8	4	5	3	7	1	9
1	3	4	7	9	2	5	6	8

PUZZLE / 957

7	8	4	5	3	2	6	1	9
1	6	3	8	9	4	2	5	7
9	5	2	1	7	6	8	3	4
5	3	1	2	4	7	9	8	6
2	4	9	6	5	8	3	7	1
8	7	6	3	1	9	4	2	5
6	1	5	9	2	3	7	4	8
3	9	7	4	8	5	1	6	2
4	2	8	7	6	1	5	9	3

PUZZLE / 958

9	1	5	2	3	8	6	7	4
8	6	7	9	1	4	2	3	5
4	3	2	6	7	5	9	1	8
5	2	8	1	4	3	7	9	6
1	9	3	7	8	6	5	4	2
6	7	4	5	9	2	1	8	3
7	8	6	3	2	9	4	5	1
3	5	9	4	6	1	8	2	7
2	4	1	8	5	7	3	6	9

PUZZLE / 959

8	4	5	7	2	9	1	6	3
7	6	1	5	8	3	9	2	4
3	9	2	4	1	6	8	7	5
2	8	6	1	3	5	4	9	7
1	7	4	6	9	8	3	5	2
9	5	3	2	4	7	6	1	8
6	1	7	3	5	4	2	8	9
5	3	8	9	6	2	7	4	1
4	2	9	8	7	1	5	3	6

PUZZLE / 960

1	2	8	3	5	6	9	4	7
4	5	9	7	8	2	1	3	6
7	6	3	4	1	9	8	2	5
6	1	4	8	2	7	3	5	9
3	7	2	9	6	5	4	8	1
8	9	5	1	4	3	7	6	2
5	4	7	2	3	1	6	9	8
9	8	6	5	7	4	2	1	3
2	3	1	6	9	8	5	7	4

PUZZLE / 961

4	8	5	9	7	1	3	6	2
9	2	1	6	3	8	7	4	5
7	3	6	2	5	4	9	8	1
5	9	7	4	1	3	8	2	6
2	1	4	8	9	6	5	3	7
3	6	8	7	2	5	1	9	4
8	7	9	1	4	2	6	5	3
6	5	2	3	8	7	4	1	9
1	4	3	5	6	9	2	7	8

PUZZLE / 962

5	9	6	4	2	1	7	3	8
4	1	3	7	9	8	5	2	6
7	8	2	3	5	6	9	4	1
9	7	1	5	6	3	4	8	2
2	6	4	9	8	7	1	5	3
8	3	5	2	1	4	6	9	7
6	5	7	8	4	2	3	1	9
3	4	8	1	7	9	2	6	5
1	2	9	6	3	5	8	7	4

PUZZLE / 963

3	9	8	6	5	1	4	7	2
4	7	1	3	9	2	6	5	8
2	6	5	8	4	7	9	3	1
7	5	3	4	2	9	1	8	6
1	4	6	5	7	8	3	2	9
8	2	9	1	3	6	7	4	5
6	1	2	7	8	3	5	9	4
9	3	4	2	1	5	8	6	7
5	8	7	9	6	4	2	1	3

PUZZLE / 964

2	6	7	4	5	1	3	8	9
3	8	9	7	6	2	5	1	4
5	1	4	8	9	3	6	7	2
4	9	8	6	7	5	2	3	1
7	2	3	9	1	4	8	6	5
1	5	6	3	2	8	4	9	7
8	7	5	2	3	9	1	4	6
6	3	2	1	4	7	9	5	8
9	4	1	5	8	6	7	2	3

PUZZLE / 965

3	6	5	2	7	8	9	1	4
8	2	7	4	9	1	6	3	5
1	4	9	5	6	3	7	8	2
6	7	2	1	4	5	8	9	3
9	8	3	6	2	7	5	4	1
4	5	1	3	8	9	2	6	7
7	3	8	9	1	2	4	5	6
5	9	6	7	3	4	1	2	8
2	1	4	8	5	6	3	7	9

PUZZLE / 966

5	2	9	4	7	3	6	1	8
6	7	1	5	2	8	9	4	3
4	3	8	6	9	1	5	7	2
1	9	5	3	8	7	4	2	6
8	6	3	1	4	2	7	5	9
7	4	2	9	5	6	3	8	1
9	8	7	2	6	5	1	3	4
3	5	4	8	1	9	2	6	7
2	1	6	7	3	4	8	9	5

PUZZLE / 967

4	2	9	6	8	5	3	7	1
8	5	1	7	3	2	9	6	4
7	3	6	1	4	9	2	5	8
1	4	3	8	9	6	7	2	5
6	7	2	5	1	3	8	4	9
9	8	5	2	7	4	6	1	3
2	1	8	9	5	7	4	3	6
5	6	4	3	2	8	1	9	7
3	9	7	4	6	1	5	8	2

PUZZLE / 968

7	6	2	1	8	4	9	5	3
9	8	3	5	2	7	4	1	6
4	5	1	9	3	6	2	8	7
3	1	6	2	7	8	5	4	9
5	4	8	6	9	1	7	3	2
2	7	9	4	5	3	8	6	1
6	3	5	7	4	9	1	2	8
1	9	4	8	6	2	3	7	5
8	2	7	3	1	5	6	9	4

PUZZLE / 969

2	8	1	6	7	5	9	3	4
7	4	6	9	8	3	2	1	5
9	3	5	4	2	1	8	7	6
8	7	4	5	3	6	1	9	2
1	5	3	2	9	4	6	8	7
6	2	9	7	1	8	5	4	3
5	1	8	3	6	7	4	2	9
4	9	7	8	5	2	3	6	1
3	6	2	1	4	9	7	5	8

PUZZLE / 970

5	1	8	9	6	3	7	4	2
9	6	2	8	7	4	3	1	5
3	7	4	2	1	5	6	8	9
7	9	3	6	5	1	4	2	8
2	4	5	3	9	8	1	7	6
1	8	6	4	2	7	9	5	3
4	2	1	5	3	9	8	6	7
6	3	7	1	8	2	5	9	4
8	5	9	7	4	6	2	3	1

PUZZLE / 971

4	7	1	9	6	2	5	3	8
9	6	5	8	3	4	1	7	2
2	3	8	1	7	5	4	6	9
5	9	7	2	1	6	3	8	4
6	8	2	4	9	3	7	1	5
1	4	3	7	5	8	9	2	6
7	2	9	6	4	1	8	5	3
3	1	6	5	8	9	2	4	7
8	5	4	3	2	7	6	9	1

PUZZLE / 972

9	1	4	8	5	7	3	6	2
3	6	2	1	9	4	5	7	8
5	7	8	3	6	2	9	1	4
7	2	3	9	4	1	6	8	5
8	5	6	7	2	3	1	4	9
1	4	9	6	8	5	7	2	3
2	9	7	4	3	6	8	5	1
6	3	5	2	1	8	4	9	7
4	8	1	5	7	9	2	3	6

PUZZLE / 973

1	2	4	9	8	3	6	5	7
7	9	6	2	5	4	3	1	8
8	3	5	7	6	1	9	2	4
5	4	8	1	3	9	2	7	6
2	7	1	8	4	6	5	9	3
3	6	9	5	2	7	4	8	1
4	8	7	6	9	2	1	3	5
9	5	3	4	1	8	7	6	2
6	1	2	3	7	5	8	4	9

PUZZLE / 974

2	4	8	1	9	3	7	5	6
3	5	9	7	6	2	8	1	4
1	7	6	5	4	8	3	2	9
4	6	2	9	7	1	5	3	8
5	1	3	8	2	4	9	6	7
9	8	7	3	5	6	2	4	1
6	9	4	2	8	5	1	7	3
8	2	1	4	3	7	6	9	5
7	3	5	6	1	9	4	8	2

PUZZLE / 975

6	4	3	1	8	9	2	7	5
1	2	8	4	7	5	6	3	9
9	7	5	3	6	2	1	4	8
8	5	4	6	9	1	3	2	7
7	3	1	2	5	8	9	6	4
2	9	6	7	4	3	5	8	1
5	6	9	8	2	4	7	1	3
3	8	7	9	1	6	4	5	2
4	1	2	5	3	7	8	9	6

PUZZLE / 976

2	9	8	4	7	1	3	6	5
4	1	3	5	8	6	2	7	9
7	5	6	9	3	2	4	8	1
3	8	7	1	2	5	6	9	4
6	2	5	3	9	4	8	1	7
1	4	9	7	6	8	5	3	2
8	6	1	2	4	7	9	5	3
5	3	2	8	1	9	7	4	6
9	7	4	6	5	3	1	2	8

PUZZLE / 977

1	6	2	8	3	9	4	7	5
9	3	8	5	7	4	1	2	6
4	5	7	1	6	2	8	9	3
3	8	6	2	1	7	5	4	9
5	9	1	3	4	8	7	6	2
7	2	4	9	5	6	3	1	8
2	4	9	7	8	5	6	3	1
6	1	5	4	9	3	2	8	7
8	7	3	6	2	1	9	5	4

PUZZLE / 978

1	9	6	5	4	2	7	8	3
2	3	7	8	9	6	5	4	1
4	8	5	3	7	1	2	6	9
9	1	2	4	8	5	3	7	6
7	6	8	9	2	3	4	1	5
3	5	4	6	1	7	8	9	2
5	7	9	1	3	8	6	2	4
8	4	3	2	6	9	1	5	7
6	2	1	7	5	4	9	3	8

PUZZLE / 979

3	1	9	8	6	7	4	2	5
2	5	7	3	9	4	6	8	1
8	4	6	2	1	5	3	7	9
9	2	4	1	7	8	5	3	6
6	8	5	4	3	2	1	9	7
7	3	1	9	5	6	2	4	8
4	7	8	5	2	1	9	6	3
1	9	2	6	8	3	7	5	4
5	6	3	7	4	9	8	1	2

PUZZLE / 980

8	7	1	4	3	9	5	6	2
9	4	6	8	2	5	1	7	3
3	5	2	6	7	1	9	8	4
4	1	3	9	8	6	2	5	7
6	9	7	2	5	3	4	1	8
5	2	8	7	1	4	6	3	9
2	6	5	3	9	8	7	4	1
7	3	4	1	6	2	8	9	5
1	8	9	5	4	7	3	2	6

PUZZLE / 981

7	3	4	8	9	5	2	6	1
2	5	6	1	7	3	8	9	4
1	8	9	2	4	6	7	3	5
9	6	2	3	5	8	1	4	7
3	4	8	6	1	7	5	2	9
5	7	1	9	2	4	6	8	3
6	9	5	7	3	2	4	1	8
4	2	3	5	8	1	9	7	6
8	1	7	4	6	9	3	5	2

PUZZLE / 982

9	5	6	8	2	3	1	7	4
3	8	7	1	5	4	9	2	6
4	1	2	9	7	6	5	3	8
6	4	3	5	9	2	8	1	7
5	7	9	4	1	8	3	6	2
8	2	1	6	3	7	4	5	9
1	6	5	2	4	9	7	8	3
2	3	4	7	8	5	6	9	1
7	9	8	3	6	1	2	4	5

PUZZLE / 983

9	5	6	4	8	2	7	1	3
4	3	8	7	1	5	9	2	6
7	1	2	3	9	6	5	4	8
8	9	7	5	3	4	2	6	1
2	4	5	8	6	1	3	7	9
3	6	1	2	7	9	8	5	4
5	2	3	1	4	8	6	9	7
6	7	4	9	2	3	1	8	5
1	8	9	6	5	7	4	3	2

PUZZLE / 984

4	5	3	2	6	9	7	8	1
7	2	9	1	8	4	6	5	3
6	1	8	7	3	5	2	9	4
9	4	5	6	1	2	3	7	8
1	3	7	4	5	8	9	6	2
8	6	2	9	7	3	1	4	5
3	7	1	8	4	6	5	2	9
5	9	4	3	2	7	8	1	6
2	8	6	5	9	1	4	3	7

PUZZLE / 985

3	4	8	9	6	5	2	1	7
5	9	6	2	7	1	4	3	8
1	2	7	8	3	4	5	9	6
2	8	5	3	9	6	1	7	4
4	7	1	5	2	8	9	6	3
9	6	3	4	1	7	8	5	2
6	5	4	1	8	3	7	2	9
7	1	9	6	4	2	3	8	5
8	3	2	7	5	9	6	4	1

PUZZLE / 986

3	2	9	6	5	7	1	4	8
8	7	6	4	1	3	2	5	9
1	4	5	8	2	9	6	3	7
9	1	4	3	6	2	8	7	5
5	6	7	1	9	8	4	2	3
2	8	3	7	4	5	9	6	1
6	5	8	2	3	1	7	9	4
4	3	1	9	7	6	5	8	2
7	9	2	5	8	4	3	1	6

PUZZLE / 987

2	5	3	4	9	1	8	6	7
7	6	4	5	8	3	1	9	2
8	9	1	2	6	7	4	3	5
9	8	5	6	1	4	2	7	3
1	2	7	9	3	8	5	4	6
4	3	6	7	5	2	9	1	8
5	1	9	3	2	6	7	8	4
3	7	2	8	4	9	6	5	1
6	4	8	1	7	5	3	2	9

PUZZLE / 988

5	1	6	3	8	2	7	4	9
8	7	4	9	1	5	6	2	3
9	3	2	4	7	6	5	8	1
4	5	8	2	6	9	3	1	7
6	2	1	7	5	3	8	9	4
3	9	7	8	4	1	2	6	5
1	8	3	5	2	4	9	7	6
2	4	5	6	9	7	1	3	8
7	6	9	1	3	8	4	5	2

PUZZLE / 989

8	7	9	4	3	5	1	2	6
6	2	3	1	7	9	4	8	5
5	1	4	2	6	8	9	3	7
3	5	1	6	8	7	2	4	9
2	9	6	3	5	4	8	7	1
4	8	7	9	1	2	6	5	3
9	4	5	7	2	6	3	1	8
7	3	2	8	9	1	5	6	4
1	6	8	5	4	3	7	9	2

PUZZLE / 990

4	9	7	8	6	3	1	5	2
3	8	1	7	5	2	6	9	4
6	2	5	1	9	4	7	8	3
2	1	8	4	3	9	5	7	6
9	7	3	6	8	5	4	2	1
5	6	4	2	7	1	8	3	9
1	5	6	9	2	7	3	4	8
8	3	2	5	4	6	9	1	7
7	4	9	3	1	8	2	6	5

PUZZLE / 991

2	5	4	8	1	3	6	9	7
3	1	9	7	6	2	4	8	5
8	7	6	4	9	5	3	2	1
7	9	3	1	2	8	5	6	4
4	6	2	3	5	7	8	1	9
5	8	1	6	4	9	2	7	3
9	2	8	5	3	1	7	4	6
6	3	7	9	8	4	1	5	2
1	4	5	2	7	6	9	3	8

PUZZLE / 992

8	6	1	5	7	2	9	3	4
7	2	9	3	8	4	6	1	5
3	5	4	1	6	9	8	7	2
4	9	2	8	5	3	1	6	7
5	1	3	6	9	7	4	2	8
6	8	7	4	2	1	5	9	3
1	3	6	7	4	8	2	5	9
2	4	5	9	3	6	7	8	1
9	7	8	2	1	5	3	4	6

PUZZLE / 993

8	6	9	7	4	3	1	5	2
1	2	5	6	8	9	7	4	3
3	4	7	1	5	2	8	9	6
4	5	1	9	2	6	3	8	7
2	9	8	3	7	4	6	1	5
6	7	3	8	1	5	4	2	9
5	1	4	2	6	7	9	3	8
9	8	6	5	3	1	2	7	4
7	3	2	4	9	8	5	6	1

PUZZLE / 994

4	6	3	9	5	8	7	2	1
5	9	8	1	2	7	6	3	4
1	7	2	4	3	6	8	5	9
9	1	7	5	4	3	2	6	8
3	5	4	8	6	2	1	9	7
2	8	6	7	1	9	3	4	5
6	4	5	3	7	1	9	8	2
7	2	9	6	8	5	4	1	3
8	3	1	2	9	4	5	7	6

PUZZLE / 995

1	6	8	7	3	4	5	2	9
3	5	2	1	8	9	4	7	6
7	4	9	5	6	2	1	3	8
8	3	6	9	2	5	7	1	4
9	7	4	6	1	3	8	5	2
5	2	1	4	7	8	9	6	3
2	1	7	8	4	6	3	9	5
4	9	3	2	5	7	6	8	1
6	8	5	3	9	1	2	4	7

PUZZLE / 996

5	9	7	3	8	6	2	4	1
6	4	8	2	5	1	7	9	3
3	1	2	4	9	7	5	8	6
8	6	3	7	4	5	1	2	9
9	2	4	6	1	3	8	5	7
1	7	5	8	2	9	6	3	4
4	8	1	9	7	2	3	6	5
2	5	6	1	3	4	9	7	8
7	3	9	5	6	8	4	1	2

PUZZLE / 997

6	7	3	5	9	1	2	8	4
2	5	9	4	7	8	1	6	3
1	8	4	3	2	6	5	7	9
9	6	2	7	4	3	8	1	5
3	1	8	6	5	2	9	4	7
5	4	7	1	8	9	3	2	6
8	2	5	9	6	4	7	3	1
7	3	6	8	1	5	4	9	2
4	9	1	2	3	7	6	5	8

PUZZLE / 998

4	6	7	3	9	1	5	8	2
8	5	9	6	2	7	4	1	3
3	2	1	8	5	4	9	6	7
5	4	3	7	6	9	8	2	1
6	9	8	2	1	3	7	4	5
1	7	2	5	4	8	3	9	6
2	1	4	9	7	5	6	3	8
7	8	6	4	3	2	1	5	9
9	3	5	1	8	6	2	7	4

PUZZLE / 999

3	1	4	8	5	7	9	2	6
7	9	5	2	6	1	8	3	4
2	6	8	9	3	4	1	5	7
8	4	9	3	7	2	5	6	1
5	7	3	6	1	8	4	9	2
6	2	1	5	4	9	7	8	3
1	3	2	7	8	5	6	4	9
4	8	6	1	9	3	2	7	5
9	5	7	4	2	6	3	1	8

PUZZLE / 1000

6	5	9	2	7	8	4	1	3
4	1	3	9	6	5	7	2	8
2	8	7	4	1	3	5	6	9
5	3	1	7	4	6	8	9	2
8	9	4	3	2	1	6	7	5
7	6	2	8	5	9	1	3	4
9	4	8	1	3	7	2	5	6
3	7	5	6	8	2	9	4	1
1	2	6	5	9	4	3	8	7

PUZZLE / 1001

2	5	6	7	8	3	1	4	9
3	7	9	6	1	4	5	2	8
1	4	8	9	2	5	3	7	6
7	6	3	4	9	1	2	8	5
5	9	1	2	6	8	4	3	7
4	8	2	3	5	7	6	9	1
8	2	7	1	3	6	9	5	4
6	3	5	8	4	9	7	1	2
9	1	4	5	7	2	8	6	3

PUZZLE / 1002

2	8	6	4	5	3	1	7	9
5	1	3	8	7	9	4	2	6
7	4	9	1	6	2	8	3	5
4	6	2	5	3	1	9	8	7
1	9	8	6	2	7	5	4	3
3	5	7	9	4	8	6	1	2
8	7	1	2	9	6	3	5	4
9	2	4	3	1	5	7	6	8
6	3	5	7	8	4	2	9	1

PUZZLE / 1003

2	6	8	4	5	3	1	9	7
4	1	7	6	9	2	8	3	5
3	9	5	1	7	8	2	4	6
1	5	4	7	2	6	3	8	9
9	7	2	8	3	5	4	6	1
6	8	3	9	4	1	7	5	2
7	3	9	2	6	4	5	1	8
8	4	6	5	1	7	9	2	3
5	2	1	3	8	9	6	7	4

PUZZLE / 1004

4	3	8	1	7	5	9	2	6
2	7	1	9	6	4	8	3	5
6	9	5	3	8	2	4	7	1
5	8	4	7	3	9	1	6	2
1	2	3	4	5	6	7	8	9
7	6	9	2	1	8	3	5	4
3	4	6	5	9	7	2	1	8
9	5	7	8	2	1	6	4	3
8	1	2	6	4	3	5	9	7

PUZZLE / 1005

8	5	2	6	7	4	9	1	3
4	1	3	9	2	5	8	7	6
6	9	7	8	3	1	4	2	5
7	3	6	2	4	9	1	5	8
5	2	4	1	8	7	6	3	9
1	8	9	5	6	3	2	4	7
2	6	5	3	1	8	7	9	4
9	4	1	7	5	6	3	8	2
3	7	8	4	9	2	5	6	1

PUZZLE / 1006

4	1	9	6	8	3	7	2	5
3	5	2	4	1	7	9	8	6
8	6	7	5	9	2	1	3	4
6	4	5	3	7	8	2	9	1
9	3	8	1	2	6	4	5	7
2	7	1	9	5	4	3	6	8
1	9	4	8	3	5	6	7	2
5	2	3	7	6	1	8	4	9
7	8	6	2	4	9	5	1	3

PUZZLE / 1007

7	4	2	5	1	6	8	9	3
6	5	3	7	9	8	1	2	4
1	9	8	3	4	2	7	5	6
3	6	9	1	8	5	2	4	7
5	7	4	6	2	9	3	1	8
2	8	1	4	3	7	9	6	5
9	2	5	8	7	4	6	3	1
4	3	7	9	6	1	5	8	2
8	1	6	2	5	3	4	7	9

PUZZLE / 1008

4	5	1	2	3	7	6	9	8
6	7	8	9	5	1	3	4	2
3	2	9	6	8	4	1	7	5
1	4	6	8	9	2	7	5	3
8	3	7	5	1	6	4	2	9
5	9	2	7	4	3	8	6	1
2	8	3	4	6	9	5	1	7
9	1	4	3	7	5	2	8	6
7	6	5	1	2	8	9	3	4

PUZZLE / 1009

2	6	8	3	5	9	1	7	4
5	4	9	6	1	7	8	2	3
7	3	1	2	4	8	5	6	9
8	1	5	4	3	2	7	9	6
3	2	6	9	7	1	4	5	8
9	7	4	5	8	6	2	3	1
6	8	2	7	9	4	3	1	5
1	9	3	8	2	5	6	4	7
4	5	7	1	6	3	9	8	2

PUZZLE / 1010

5	6	2	7	9	3	4	1	8
4	1	9	6	2	8	7	5	3
3	8	7	4	1	5	2	9	6
9	4	3	8	5	6	1	2	7
6	2	5	3	7	1	9	8	4
8	7	1	9	4	2	6	3	5
1	5	6	2	8	4	3	7	9
7	3	8	1	6	9	5	4	2
2	9	4	5	3	7	8	6	1

PUZZLE / 1011

1	3	4	7	6	8	9	5	2
9	7	2	5	1	3	8	4	6
8	6	5	2	9	4	3	7	1
5	8	6	1	7	2	4	9	3
4	2	7	9	3	6	1	8	5
3	1	9	4	8	5	6	2	7
6	9	3	8	2	7	5	1	4
7	5	1	3	4	9	2	6	8
2	4	8	6	5	1	7	3	9

PUZZLE / 1012

6	9	7	1	4	3	5	8	2
4	5	2	9	7	8	6	1	3
8	3	1	2	6	5	9	4	7
3	6	8	4	9	2	7	5	1
7	2	9	5	3	1	8	6	4
1	4	5	7	8	6	2	3	9
9	8	4	6	1	7	3	2	5
2	1	6	3	5	9	4	7	8
5	7	3	8	2	4	1	9	6

PUZZLE / 1013

3	1	8	5	6	7	4	9	2
5	6	4	1	9	2	3	7	8
2	7	9	8	4	3	6	5	1
9	2	7	4	1	8	5	3	6
8	4	1	3	5	6	9	2	7
6	5	3	2	7	9	1	8	4
1	3	2	6	8	5	7	4	9
7	8	6	9	3	4	2	1	5
4	9	5	7	2	1	8	6	3

PUZZLE / 1014

About the Authors

Based in Tokyo, Nikoli was founded in 1980 and published the first puzzle magazine in Japan. Since then, Nikoli has been publishing its own puzzle magazine and books, as well as supplying original puzzles to many newspapers and other weekly and monthly publications throughout Japan and the world. Nikoli's editors have created more than 300 types of logic puzzles, and their founder, Maki Kaji (also known as "the godfather of Sudoku"), is credited with giving Sudoku its name. Many of Nikoli's puzzles are handcrafted, which makes the company admired by puzzle makers and solvers around the world.